SURVIVING PRIVILEGE

R. Raven

Copyright © *R. Raven*, 2025

All Rights Reserved

This book is subject to the condition that no part of this book is to be reproduced, transmitted in any form or means; electronic or mechanical, stored in a retrieval system, photocopied, recorded, scanned, or otherwise. Any of these actions require the proper written permission of the author.

AUTHOR'S NOTE

This book is an account of my childhood and subsequent adulthood, as I experienced it. Others who were present may have experienced it differently. But this is my story.

All names, including mine, have been changed to protect the identities.

Table of Contents

Chapter 1 Telling My Story 1

Chapter 2 Naples (ages 5-10) 10

Chapter 3 Life in Naples 16

Chapter 4 Milan (ages 9-11) 29

Chapter 5 Boarding School 36

Chapter 6 Food & Shopping 49

Chapter 7 First Kisses and Boyfriends 59

Chapter 8 Mean Girls 63

Chapter 9 The Wank 74

Chapter 10 Family Holidays 89

Chapter 11 Hockey 94

Chapter 12 Pneumonia 98

Chapter 13 Boarding School Continued 106

Chapter 14 Tom – Madrid 122

Chapter 15 University 127

Chapter 16 Barcelona 133

Chapter 17 Working Out 140

Chapter 18 New York 143

Chapter 19 Medical 156

Chapter 20 Therapy 160

Chapter 21 Dickhead & Baby Number One 165

Chapter 22 The Wedding 194

Chapter 23 Child Number Two 203

Chapter 24 Time For A Change 221

Chapter 25 More Therapy.. 242

Chapter 26 Dad.. 253

Chapter 27 Baby Number Three 288

Chapter 28 Me 293

Chapter 29 Mother 310

Chapter 30 Mark 343

Chapter 31 Suicide.. 363

Chapter 32 Divorce & Nastiness 374

Chapter 33 The Will 448

Chapter 34 Death... 456

Chapter 35 The Funeral... 516

Chapter 36 The Executor of the Estate........................... 537

Chapter 37 Dreams and Nightmares............................... 562

Chapter 38 No Win No Fee 567

Chapter 39 Jeffrey... 572

Chapter 40 More Boarding School.................................. 583

Chapter 41 Dickhead and Mum, Revisited 598

Chapter 42 Narcissistic Personality Disorder & more....... 618

Epilogue 633

Useful Contacts And Books 636

Prologue

This is my autobiography from as far back as I can remember. Many of the memories recounted here are just snapshots of the events that occurred and nothing else – hence why certain parts of this book may read like bullet points or factual statements.

My father worked for an international bank. As he rose through the ranks – and as his job description, title, and pay grade changed – we found ourselves moving country every four years or so.

As an international staff member, my father's salary also covered the rent of our homes and the costs of boarding school fees. It wasn't a tradition to send children to boarding school within my family; we were the first.

We always lived in large, impressive houses – usually with our own swimming pool or at least access to one. I was nine years old when I first rode in a stretch limo; the big boss sent it over so we could go to his house for dinner.

Let's just say I was used to the fancy things in life, and I was surrounded by people who lived the same kind of lifestyle.

When my uni friends came to visit, they would say things like, "Both our houses could fit in your downstairs, and there would still be space left over."

We never wanted for anything financially. We had nice cars and fancy holidays every year. I never really had to think about money, or the value of money – until recently.

I never knew how much my father earned, but I do know that in the crash of 2008, he lost £4 million and was utterly devastated (who wouldn't be?!).

Despite all these advantages, however, my story illustrates how no amount of family money, material things, or expensive holidays can make a child feel loved or valued. It also tells of how a fancy education, society's perception of riches, and the British 'stiff upper lip' can have a profound lifelong impact on a child – a child who survived, not thrived, in their privilege.

When children are born into a supposed life of privilege, they are conditioned not to complain about it. After all, we've been provided with a 'gift' that others should supposedly envy and covet. We are given all that we could possibly want, thanks to the wealth and position afforded to us.

But we must remain silent and grateful for all these great blessings in our lives.

No matter what.

Chapter 1
Telling My Story

How do you write about your life when it has been such a struggle?

I want to get it all down, but for what purpose? Honestly, I'm not sure.

Therapy has mostly helped me to sort my head of the 'hows,' but I feel there is something more to say – maybe it's the idea that telling my truth will validate it somehow or that my experiences could help someone else who finds themselves in a similar life situation? Or maybe it's just the notion that getting it all down on paper could be cathartic? Who knows? What I do know is that it has been in my head for many, many years that I want to write a book. So here it is.

I put off writing this account of my life for a long time. I kept stopping and starting it, afraid of any potential repercussions from those mentioned in the book, fearing their reactions or responses.

But then I kept seeing this quote:

"You own everything that happened to you. Tell your stories. If people wanted you to write warmly about them, they should have behaved better."

~ Anne Lamott

With this in mind, I started to write. After all, I wanted to tell my story. I *needed* to tell my story.

So, what is privilege?

The *Oxford English Dictionary* describes it as "a special right or advantage that a particular person or group has."

I bet you're reading this and thinking that anyone born into any kind of privilege must be lucky. Surely, they must be content, happy, and absolutely overflowing with confidence and self-esteem. My story shows a different perspective.

We started out like any other regular family.

I was born near London in the 1980's, and we were already pretty lucky as we – me, my mum and dad, and Jeffrey, my older brother by nearly three years – lived in a four-bed detached house with a shared driveway and a medium-sized garden. I had the room furthest away from everyone else.

As I was just five years old when we left the UK, I only have a few memories of our life in England.

Those few memories are not ones of happiness and giggles.

I remember playing in the mud by the front door, making mud pies, creating rose water perfume, and riding my bike around the garden. I did all this alone. My brother and I didn't play together. While there were moments when we'd both play with the neighbours' kids, it was never really just the two of us.

No one really asked or answered questions in my family. Personally, I was the kind of kid who would always ask 'why' about anything and everything. Very rarely did I get a proper explanation. I was an annoyance.

Much to my disappointment – then and throughout my life – we were not a family of 'sharers.'

I have memories of being hit by my brother, getting pushed around, being forced out of his room, him forcing his way into mine, doors slammed in my face, hands being placed around my throat… you get the picture.

There never seemed to be any consequences to these infractions either. Perhaps, at the time, it was just seen as normal sibling rivalry, but it took me many years to realise that other brothers and sisters didn't fight quite like we did.

Jeffrey always acted like he was superior to me; he told me off like he was a grown-up and always acted older than he was. My parents seemed to treat him as a mini adult – even at the age of seven – and so that was how I saw him.

One memory is vivid in my mind, even to this day. We were playing in the shared driveway with the next-door neighbours' kids; we were playing Mummies and Daddies, and I was the baby, so I was lying on a blanket in the middle of the drive while my brother and our friends were standing over by the house.

Mother was getting the car sorted for something, and she got behind the wheel. I saw her look for my brother, and I guess she assumed I was with him. The next thing I knew, she had reversed over me – I was now under the car!

He must have told her what had happened because, before I knew it, she was dragging me out from under the car. We had a few cuddles in the lounge, but after that, it was never discussed or mentioned again, at least not to my memory.

One question, of course, kept cropping up for me after that: why had she not looked for ME?

I tell you this story not to point the finger and say, 'See, she was a negligent mother,' but because this – combined with everything else that came after – clearly illustrates the facts.

On shopping trips, I would often end up holding a stranger's hand; one minute, my mum was there, and the next, she wasn't. It was never her looking for me but always me searching for her, desperately upset that I'd lost her. Looking back, she never seemed to worry about where I was, no matter what the situation. Often, I would need a store clerk to help me search her out, but within minutes of finding her, she'd be gone again. I would look around in a panic, desperately searching out and studying the faces of every woman with short, dark hair.

I did tend to daydream a lot, but I don't think that is a valid reason to constantly leave your child behind.

My daughter has told me that on the few occasions she went out with my mother, she looked up to see she was holding the hand of a stranger – so it wasn't just me, then!

One time, when I was just three or four years old, I woke in the night to find that my parents weren't at home. I searched all over: their bedroom, the kitchen, the lounge… all the lights were off, and it felt like it must have been the middle of the night.

The panic – I thought they had left us!

Thankfully, the mini adult – still just seven years old – took charge. He somehow knew to go next door to ask for help.

Well, as it turned out, our parents were over there! They had left us alone at night, asleep, with no warning and no note. And these were the days before baby monitors. I had been absolutely terrified when I woke up. I remember it so well.

My desperate need to be close to my mother was born of... what? Insecurity? Unmet needs? Whatever it was, it came up a lot when I was being 'left' somewhere. For instance, I would scream and cry most days on being left at playschool and then school. The teacher would have to pry me off her and then hold me up to wave at the window as she left. It would take me a good while to stop crying.

I think this stemmed from my mother simply 'disappearing' when she dropped me off at playschool; I would turn around from playing, and she would just be gone. I never saw her leave, and there was no goodbye, no waving, no warning, nothing. At such a young age, I found this utterly heart-wrenching. It made me very anxious and very clingy.

Both my parents have always told me I was a difficult child, and that they tried being with me, they tried leaving me alone – all sorts, apparently – but I was never happy with their actions. It seems I was just a pain in the arse.

Well... aren't all two, three, and four-year-olds difficult?

In fact, while they're no doubt difficult and incredibly tiring, they can also be lovely, sweet, and so beautiful. I can tell you thousands of positives about my own babies during those sleep-deprived years. But, apparently, I was just awful and difficult.

Once, when I was in my 30s and had kids of my own, I asked my mother, "Do you have nothing good to say about me as a child?"

Her reply – after a long pause – was, "Errrmmm, well... you were very cuddly."

I was a clingy kid, as I've said. I needed affection, reassurance, and unconditional love. As I didn't get any of these, I spent my life searching for them, thinking I was the problem – that my needs were too great and that I was a freak, unlovable. But now I know the truth...

The problem wasn't me. It was them.

How can someone who came from such privilege have had such a hard and traumatic life? When I was around 16, my own mother expressed something similar to me: "How can you be depressed when you have everything you could possibly ever want?"

In my view, the fact that she even asked that question proves I didn't have what I so very much needed – a loving and emotionally nurturing family.

She also said something similar to my ex-husband after our divorce.

Some of my earliest memories are from when I was around three or four years old.

For instance, my mother was seemingly too busy doing housework to pay any attention to me, so I pretended to fall over in the hall and then splashed water on my face to make it seem like I was crying – anything to get her attention.

I came to all sorts of harm, and as a mother now myself, I can't understand how I came to be in those situations. Personally, I always tried my best to ensure that my young ones never suffered such injuries.

For example, the time she was brushing my hair while I played with my Dad's razor – only for me to slice my finger open on the razor blades. Or the time I was left – at three years old – to walk up the stairs alone while they were being recarpeted, and I fell and got a nail in my hand. Or the many times I fell down the stairs in the night after going to the loo, as the door to my bedroom was right next to the stairs – one foot wrong and, instead of my foot hitting my bedroom floor, I would find myself falling through the air, tumbling head over heels down the stairs.

I once told my mother that I had the most lovely memories of the two of us going to the woods, picking bluebells, and then going home, where we ate crackers and watched *Emmerdale Farm*. In response, she looked at me blankly and said, "We only did that once."

There were never any explanations given for why things had to happen. Why we had to move country? Why we had to go to a new school. Why we had to live in a hotel for six months? Why we ended up on a bumpy old bus taking us to a new school while we sat at the back, crying and looking bewildered? Why my eight-year-old brother and I were in the same class at school.

Everything just seemed to simply 'be' – with no explanation and seemingly no reasoning behind it. We just had to get on with it.

I do, however, remember my brother being told more about life than I ever was. I would get, "You won't understand; you're too little. Maybe when you're older."

Yet another way I didn't 'fit' in the family. I was the youngest. I was also the outcast.

It is extremely hard to get a good sense of self, intuition, self-esteem, or confidence when you're constantly being told you're wrong, that you don't know what you're talking about, and that even when you KNOW you're right… no, you're actually wrong. It does an odd thing to one's head.

Even now, at the age of 44, I can't get my head around the fact that there are still people around me who try to gaslight me. To know the facts, to know the truth, but to be told a different version by someone else who is so adamant that they are correct – that their version is right – is mind-boggling. It leaves you confused and speechless, shaking you to your core.

After nine years of therapy – and after finally seeing these people for who and what they truly are – it doesn't shake my confidence or my belief in the truth as it once did, but it still affects me. It still has an unpleasant, long-lasting internal effect.

In fact, I actually feel physically sick after dealing with these people; they leave me weak and nauseated, and the desire to run away is overwhelming. Hence why, in the last few years, I've had so many holidays. The more I had to deal with them, the more I had to get away.

As we got older and I started to answer my brother back more – fighting incessantly with each other – his hatred towards me grew. He felt that I was the 'favourite,' despite the fact that he was always treated with so much more freedom and was given far more allowances than I was. He was treated like an adult, able to do and say more or less as he wished.

Around the age of 14 or 15, he stopped coming home from boarding school for the holidays; he preferred to stay with friends. I think this in itself says a lot. After a recent talk, I attended about ex-boarders, I wonder if it was too hard for him to keep coming back and then leaving again. Or, maybe he just didn't like it at home.

While my mother would come over for half-terms and take me to a hotel or a cottage for a week, he would just come to have dinner or lunch with her – nothing more.

I guess I need to backtrack here a little.

You see, at the age of 11, I was sent to the same boarding school as my brother. I wasn't consulted about it – it was just a given. My fate was sealed the day Jeffrey was sent away; I would be following in his footsteps, whether I liked it or not.

I remember it all so vividly, even now.

In his first two years at this school, my brother was bullied pretty badly. Other than the day we left him there, I never saw my mum cry about having left her son in a different country.

I didn't see her cry the day she left me there, either.

But before we get to that, let's delve into my childhood pre-boarding school…

Chapter 2
Naples (ages 5-10)

I have no memory of how we arrived in Naples, Italy.

I do remember, however, that we lived in a hotel for a few months while a house was found.

There were always meals out with people from my dad's work, and these often went on quite late. During these times, I would amuse myself by taking the dregs from coffee cups, wine glasses, and anything else I could find and then mixing it all up with sugar. As a result, my hand would get a gentle smack, and I would get a disapproving look from my mother; I was misbehaving again.

Really? I was being quiet, and I wasn't running around causing chaos like many of the other kids around us, so what was the issue?

During one of these dinners out, I fell asleep and woke up just before we were leaving, but I pretended to still be asleep; I was only five at the time, and I didn't want to walk back to the hotel.

So, my father carried me over his shoulder and upon arriving back at the hotel room, he laid me on the bed, and both parents started to undress me. I kicked out so violently and suddenly that I caught my mother in the face.

They were both angry with me. I just didn't want to be undressed by them, so I did it myself.

I still puzzle over this reaction of mine – what would make a five-year-old not want to be undressed or seen by her parents?

A lack of trust is all I can come up with.

The school bus would come each morning, and we would sit at the back, sobbing. I hated leaving my mum, and everything was so strange there, in that new place, having to deal with a new school and a new language all at once.

The bus had no suspension, so we would bounce around in the back, getting thrown all over the place as we made our way to school.

The International School of Naples was our destination. I was five, my brother was eight, and we were in the same class – probably because I was the youngest in the school and there was no class for children my age.

During breaks, we would head to the school's tuck shop, where we would eat snacks like chocolate boobies! These were basically chocolate-covered marshmallows on a tiny biscuit, shaped… well… like a boob!

I would also spend my break times collecting fag butts from the playground floor, using the bigger ones as pretend cigarettes. Everyone smoked back then, so I was just emulating most of the adults I knew.

During my time at school, I learnt volleyball, Italian, and the recorder.

As fun as it could be to live in a hotel, I was happy when we finally moved into a house. It was very tall – maybe four or five floors – and the key for the front door was so long it folded in half.

The garden surrounded the house on different levels, with palm trees and shrubs all around. There was also a shed, in which Jeffrey once got 'locked.' In reality, he was just pushing the door instead of pulling, but it caused all kinds of panic for my mother. I have never seen her show such worry or care for me. The lounge was on the second floor, and the kitchen was on the ground. I don't remember much about the bedrooms.

All I can really remember is waking up one morning and getting it into my head that I wanted to open my huge bedroom window. It was when my grandparents were visiting, and I knew that the key to the window was in a pot in the spare room where they were currently sleeping. I sneaked into their room over and over again until I found the correct key. Why it didn't occur to me to take the whole pot, I don't know… but I suppose I was only five years old.

After finally getting the window open, I climbed up on some furniture and stood on the window sill. It opened onto a steep, very high roof – it had quite the view. It was literally a step down onto the roof of the house, probably about a metre squared. One step out, and I would fall to the ground below.

I remember standing there as the sun was coming up, the wind blowing in my hair. I don't know what I was thinking at the time, but it certainly wasn't the usual thoughts and actions of one so young.

Then, suddenly, Nanny appeared beside me, grabbed me around the waist, and pulled me back into the room. She told me off, asked me what the hell I was doing, and then shut the window.

The incident was never mentioned again by anyone.

Within six months of living there, sewage started coming through the kitchen wall, and – before I knew it – we were back living in the hotel.

It was almost like a home for us. We had a two-bedroom suite with a large balcony, and I think my parents had an en suite in their bedroom.

Around this time, the doctor came to treat me for many serious cases of nits. He would wash my hair in vinegar – oh, the sting! – from where I had scratched myself raw. Then, later on, the whole family had to have treatment, which involved powder and a shower cap worn overnight. Dad was not impressed!

I also had worms during this period – again, this occurred countless times – and I was supposed to show Mum my poo to see if I was better.

One time, I had to wander around the hotel to find them as they'd gone down to the restaurant after we'd gone to bed. Once again, Dad did not look impressed. He would get this look on his face – in his eyes – like he resented me. But what exactly did he resent? My presence? My taking up my mother's time and attention?

I wasn't sure, but whatever it was, I felt like such a burden to him. Like my very existence was just one big nuisance.

Had he even wanted children? Had she?

My mother once told me that the only reason they had kids was because it was expected of them; after they married, they kept getting asked when a baby was coming… so they had a baby. She was 24 at the time. Then, once again, they were asked when the second was coming. So, at 27, they had another.

She said that each time, she knew straight away that she was pregnant – as soon as they had 'done it.' She hated each pregnancy because she felt like an alien was growing inside her. She never even tried to make it sound like we were wanted, like *I* was wanted. We were made simply because society expected it.

And then, of course, she was stuck with these children to raise and look after. As was my dad.

Several people have said to me, "She isn't a mother; she is a woman who had children." I feel the same could be said of my Dad.

We were a tie, a bind, a burden.

My father wanted to travel around the world with his career. He wanted to make choices based on his preferences rather than being dictated to by his family.

So, boarding school was obviously on the cards when we each reached the age of 11.

My Mum mentioned several times that, apparently, I should have been grateful they didn't send us aged seven, as others around her had suggested. Her mother advised her not to send us at all.

Email between me and my mother:

"Don't judge us too harshly. When we lived in Naples I was told by the Vice Consul's wife that we were irresponsible not sending you both when aged seven. I cried for a week after that."

She denied that she had 'sent me away.' She denied me the right to talk about it, to query the decision, or to complain about it. So did my Dad.

In this family dynamic, there were several unspoken rules – rules I didn't even know I'd broken until it was too late. It left me feeling wary and constantly on edge.

After all, how can you completely relax if you're never quite sure where you stand and never know what you're allowed – or not allowed – to say or do?

Can you ever really be yourself under such circumstances?

I certainly wasn't; I always held parts of myself back when I was around my so-called family. In fact, the only time in my life when I've ever felt completely free to be myself – to express my true self – has been since I've left all these people behind.

Until recently, my head and my heart have been in a constant battle. My heart 'knew' I deserved better, but my head couldn't understand what I'd done wrong or why I wasn't being treated the way I deserved. I knew I'd done no wrong, but if that were true, then why were people acting as they were? My head was a mess.

What does it do to you when you grow up in such a muddle? Well, I have recently learnt the term for this: cognitive dissonance.
*

> *** COGNITIVE DISSONANCE**
>
> Taken from 'Psychology Today' magazine – May 24, 2021:
>
> "It is very common in emotionally abusive situations and in relationships with narcissists.
>
> The individual who is emotionally abused experiences cognitive dissonance through the strategic, structured manipulation by the narcissist.
>
> The constant state of heightened alertness, uncertainty, confusion, feelings of neglect, and the stark contrast in morals, values, and emotions compared to those around you – coupled with the lack of affection and reassurance – all lead to low self-esteem, diminished confidence, disassociation, and feelings of worthlessness.
>
> It makes you look for love and affection in all the wrong – and potentially dangerous – places.

Chapter 3
Life in Naples

We had by now moved to a lovely house – that didn't have sewage pouring out of the walls – and we were also attending a new school, The British Forces School of Naples. Knowing so many Forces families meant we could use the NAAFI shop on the military base; this was very cool as there was a severe lack of any kind of British food there.

The house was big, with marble and stone floors, two lounges, and a garden surrounding the building. There was also a large, separate 'kids' garden, where we were allowed to do anything we wanted.

So, we climbed the tangerine trees, had orange fights, lit fires, smoked, made dens, and poked at the brambles down the end of the garden. Surprisingly, despite the presence of snakes, we were never cautioned against playing there.

There was also a wasteland over the road from our house that we would dare each other to go in – and that was full of snakes, too.

The 'adult' garden – which surrounded the house – had orange and lemon trees, the latter of which Mum would use to make delicious lemon meringue pies. There was a cat that, every year, would have a litter under one of our trees. Sadly, we weren't allowed to leave food or anything out for her or her babies, as my family were not into animals at all. I have always wanted pets and have a deep love for animals.

The house was lovely, but, being in Italy, it was not designed for poor weather. If we had a bad thunderstorm, for instance, the windows would leak. Water would gush through the non-existent seals and flood the surrounding floor, often pouring down the marble staircase.

Our job on nights such as these was to get out of bed and race around, putting towels and newspapers under the windows and on the floor – anywhere to try to stem the flow.

My father slept through all the commotion every single time.

Often, it was the shrill sound of the house alarm system that woke me on those stormy nights; when the electricity was tripped, it would set off the alarm, and since the control box was in my bedroom, I endured the full force of the noise.

Next door, at the back, there was an abandoned house. As it was so creepy, we devised another game where we would dare each other to go in – we wanted to see who could get the furthest into the grounds before running back, scared.

I was a real tomboy, and I hated anything too girly; the most 'girly' thing I did was play with my Barbie.

This was a big disappointment for my mother, as she had always wanted a girl she could 'dress up.' I, however, refused to wear dresses or anything frilly. On the odd occasion when I was forced into something stiff and flouncy, I would be in a mood the whole time. My hair was cut into the same short, unattractive style as hers; I wasn't allowed to grow my hair long until I was about 10 or 11.

Each night before bed, Dad would have to go on lizard patrol. These little beasties were everywhere, and he would catch them and throw them out of the house. If I woke in the night and saw one in my room, however, I was told to just not look at it.

One night, there was one on the ceiling right above my bed, and I was so worried he would fall on me! Dad was asleep by this point, so Mum just told me to deal with it.

When Dad was away on business trips, it became Jeffrey's job to hunt the lizards. One time, he caught one in a can, put the lid on, and proceeded to shake the can aggressively! I shouted at him to stop. Mum did nothing. The boys at school would often catch these little lizards and pull their tails off. I hated it.

We had gas in the kitchen to fuel the hob, and it was stored in canisters called 'bombolas.' If there was an issue, a little man would come around and hold a naked flame around the bombolas until he found where the leak was coming from!

Once again, I had the room furthest away from everyone else, right at the end of the house. I remember going through a stage of being scared of whatever was under my bed; I was terrified of getting out of bed in case the 'thing' under there grabbed my foot, but I was also scared to be *in* the bed in case he poked a huge, long needle through the mattress and into my body. It was a catch-22. I never told anyone about this.

At age 7 my finger got sliced by a fan, there was blood all over but I dealt with it by myself. I cleaned myself up and bandaged it with cotton wool and cellotape. I still have a scar.

The flush on the loo scared me, too, as it was so loud. I would have the door open, ready to run, and then do a flush-and-dash as fast as I could.

There must have been a reason I didn't tell anyone about any of my fears or concerns.

When I was seven, I asked my best friend, in the disabled toilet at school, if she ever felt like she was in the wrong family. Specifically if her mum wasn't hers. As if perhaps she got switched at the hospital.

She replied, "No, I've never felt like that," dismissing it all very quickly. I, however, felt more of a freak than ever, which almost confirmed my suspicions that *I* was the problem. I was the difficult one – it was me who was the issue, just like my family had always made me feel.

As we lived on a compound that was gated and guarded by dogs, we were allowed to go and explore on our bikes. On one such adventure, I stumbled upon a small building which was hidden amongst the trees. I climbed onto the roof and sat up there. This, I thought, would be a good place to hide. So, I went home and packed a bag: some spare clothes, some cupasoups, some money, and my Snoopy.

My plan was to live on that roof alone. I was about seven or eight years old at the time.

As I went to say goodbye to my mother – leaving my bag hidden outside as I did – she called me 'Sweetheart.' This alone was enough to make me change my mind. Maybe she did love me, after all? This tendency to cling to any small act or word of kindness or affection haunted me throughout my life, to my detriment. It was like breadcrumbs for the starving.

The pool was the main attraction during the summer months – a large communal pool where each household would have an allocated post and sun umbrella. We were both like little fish in the water all day. I excelled at swimming class at school.

A few swimming-related incidents stick out in my mind.

One time, I swam out too far with my mask and snorkel and got into trouble. My mask was filling up, and when I went to empty it, I found I could no longer stand. I panicked and started thrashing about. I remember a blur of colours coming at me – this blur was about six or so men diving in to save me.

I was lifted up, and when I looked to my right, I saw my brother. I leaned down to go to him and realised it was my father who had grabbed me first. When I saw the look of resignation and defeat on his face as he passed me to my brother, I felt guilty. I was confused and scared. I had seen the first familiar face and attached to him; I had not seen who was holding me.

Another incident involved Jeffrey and me arguing with one of the American girls who used to be a friend. The majority of the people who lived in the compound were US Army families, plus a sprinkling of wealthy Italians. I have no idea why the argument started, but she got all up in Jeffrey's face in the pool and started threatening him. Wanting to protect my brother, I lashed out and slapped her across the face! As a result, she demanded that we meet up by the trees later that day to fight it out.

Jeffrey was so angry at me, but I'd just been trying to protect him – I loved him! Thankfully, we never went to the fight meet.

One year – just as the pool was closing at the end of summer – I asked if I could go and have one last swim. My mum wouldn't come with me, and she knew that there'd be no one there to supervise, but she let me go anyway – at just seven or eight years old – to the pool alone. It was covered in pine needles and freezing. Totally alone, I slipped into the water and had a few minutes in there by myself.

As a mother now, it scares me to think what could have happened.

When I was eight, I got whooping cough. I had it badly, and several blood vessels burst in my eye from all the coughing. One day, as I was recovering, I fell out of bed and was shocked to find my mother's jewellery boxes beneath it! I called her up, and we tried to figure out what they were doing there. I swore I hadn't been playing with them. Jeffrey was at the pool with my grandparents, who were visiting, so we couldn't ask him.

On checking her drawers, my mother discovered that most of her jewellery was missing – we had been burgled! We also discovered that Nanny's engagement ring and eternity ring were missing.

She told me to run to the pool to get everyone home, so I wheezed and coughed my way up the hill to get them. On arrival, I threw up phlegm and goop.

There were mulberry prints up the stairs (there was mulberry tree in the driveway that always dropped a lot of fruit), and we deduced that while us girls had been out that morning and while Jeffrey and Grandad had been watching TV In the lounge, a few local boys must had come into the house via the front door, crept past the lounge, and gone upstairs.

The police were called, but, of course, nothing could be done.

It was scary to think that if Jeffrey or Grandad had come out of the lounge, they may have startled the burglars. Who knows what would have happened then?

I believe I was eight or so when my brother first told me I ruined his life – by being born. He was back from boarding school for a holiday, and he just screamed it at me in the hallway. I was shocked. I had so been looking forward to his homecoming; obviously, the feeling was not mutual.

It was around this time that Jeffrey started using his ornamental weapons on me! His favourite was the crossbow. He would sit me down, threaten me so I didn't move, and then he'd actually shoot it at me! Luckily, he missed, but his teddy ended up with a hole in the chest.

He had daggers, the crossbow, and a Samurai sword. Even after telling my mother what he'd done, they weren't taken from him; he merely got told not to use them on me anymore! I could never get my head around why he never got told off properly, why it was always my word against his. Why he always had the upper hand and why they always believed him over me.

During our time in Naples, I had two pretty bad accidents.

One time, I borrowed a friend's bike and was riding it down the steep hill from their house to mine. As I picked up speed, however, I realised – with sheer panic – that the brakes didn't work. The only way I could stop was to crash into the wall of our driveway, putting my arms out to break my fall. Luckily, Mum was doing some gardening and heard the crash.

I don't remember getting much sympathy, and we certainly didn't go to a doctor or the hospital. I was in a makeshift sling for weeks, and any movement I made, and certainly any pressure put on it or any fall (a few of which did happen), resulted in agony.

I believe now that I probably broke my clavicle. This has never been medically proven with X-rays or anything, but after describing the incident and the pain to a therapist who was previously a nurse, we made this educated guess together.

My next accident also included a bike and that same god-awful hill. I have no idea which accident came first, but I do recall that, after one of them, I didn't ride for about a year.

I was speeding down the hill as usual – I could do this cool spin and turn to get onto the drive without braking too much – and these workmen walked past me, saying hello.

As I replied, I turned to look back at them. When I returned my gaze to the front, I realised there was a parked car right in front of me, causing me to turn and fall off my bike. I fell straight on my face and carried on travelling down the hill at speed.

Jeffrey ran off to get Mum, and the next-door neighbour picked me up while I cried.

I remember blood dripping onto my T-shirt.

The neighbour started to apply iodine to my face just as Mum appeared with Jeffrey. Jeffrey said to her, "She was speeding down the hill like hell."

When we got to the house, my mum covered my bed with towels and laid me down; I think I was supposed to rest after the shock of it all. I felt so lonely and in such pain!

When walking to the bathroom – which was a good 15 metres or more – I remember having to hold my head forward and down because of the pain and because I was dripping blood all the way there and back.

The scab, as it formed, went from the bridge of my nose down to my chin; I could only open my mouth enough to allow in a straw. I took a few days, maybe a week, off school. Once again, there were no doctors. I still have a scar above my top lip and a lump at the bridge of my nose.

However, when Jeffrey fractured his arm after tripping at school, he was taken straight to the hospital and got X-rays and a cast.

One day, Jeffrey and one of his school friends decided it would be funny to come into my bedroom while my friend and I were changing for swimming. We must have been about nine years old.

They barged in, stole our clothes, and then just stood there, trying to 'see' us while we screamed at them and told them to "Get out!" We were trying to grab sheets, blankets… anything we could to cover ourselves, but whatever we grabbed, they just took those from us too.

Then, in an act of defiance, I stood on my bed and threw my toy metal gun at them. My plan had been for it to hit my desk, make a loud bang very close to them, and scare them away.

Unfortunately, my aim was off, and the piece of metal hit Jeffrey's friend dead in the middle of his shoulder blades. He cried out in pain, and it was at that point that Mum arrived on the scene.

Obviously, I was the one who got in trouble. I was the one who got reprimanded. And, once again, I was the one who couldn't understand why. They were the aggressors – they had come into my room to spy on us naked – so how was I the one in trouble?!

It was like when Jeffrey would take my prized possession, Snoopy – my love, the teddy I carried everywhere – away from me. He would hang him out of the car window while we sped along the motorway, dangling from his flimsy wool necklace. I would be crying and pleading, and we would both get in trouble for the noise. Or he would steal him and pull his ears, arms or head off. No punishment would be dished out to Jeffrey, but I would get told not to be so silly, not to be so sensitive. That was a common accusation in my house. I was 'too sensitive' and 'overly emotional.'

When I started hitting Jeffrey over the head with Snoopy's thick plastic feet in retaliation, however, the plastic inserts were promptly removed, while I – of course – got told off.

Jeffrey seemed to take such joy in upsetting me, in hurting me. For years, I thought this was just normal sibling behaviour, despite never once seeing any other siblings fight like we did. I gave almost as good as I got, though. One time, I bit his shoulder and left a big bruise on the skin.

He seemed to truly despise me, but even so, I put him on such a high pedestal.

So, when he fell off that pedestal in 2007, it came as a huge shock to me.

When I was nine years old, my school took us on an exchange trip to Germany. We stayed a week with a host family, and then they were to return and stay a week with us.

Bloody hell, it was torture. I sobbed and cried the entire week. My poor host family didn't know what to do with me! My homesickness was so extreme I thought I would actually die from the heartache!

Mum and I would talk on the phone most days, and I would sob as though my heart was breaking. I needed her. I yearned for her and felt I couldn't survive without her. Mum did say she was proud of me, though, as I'd given a lovely thank you letter to the host Mum on my departure. There was disbelief all around, as she thought my Mum had told me to write it – when, in reality, she had no idea I'd done it.

When the girl then came to stay with us, for some reason – which is still unknown to me – I was not very friendly with her. I regret acting that way, and even while I was doing it, I knew I was behaving meanly… I just couldn't help myself.

When Jeffrey was 12 and I was nine, Mum had to go over to the UK for his Confirmation. She would be gone a week but, as I had school, I had to stay. Dad was at work and therefore couldn't look after me. I don't really know why, though, because it was only a week, and he could have just worked during school hours.

When Mum left, I sobbed my heart out.

That first night, Dad and I attended a party at a family friend's house; I spent most of it hiding in the bathroom, crying. The next day, he dropped me off at my teacher's house to spend the week with him and his family. They had three little boys and the wife was my piano teacher.

Once again, I was in tears when Dad left me there.

Fortunately, the teacher and his family were very kind to me. They gave me my own room and respected my independence. It was a calm week, and all went well – apart from the food. I was 'fussy,' so meals like tuna and pea pasta were a nightmare for me. On the weekend before I went home, they had a BBQ, and I was allowed to invite a friend.

It was a really lovely week. I felt like the big sister, helping out with the boys – getting them ready for school, assisting with meal times, and reading them stories at bedtime. I really enjoyed my time with them.

Rather unfairly, later that year – when I was caught bringing cigarettes into school – my teacher threw the line, "We treated you like family!" in my face. I wasn't sure of the connection, but I think it added to the overall mystery I felt when it came to grown-ups.

I would steal my Dad's fags and smoke them out of my bedroom window. Afterwards, I would spray hairspray around to mask the smell. No one ever queried it. I know the house smelled due to my Dad's smoking, but it wasn't a strong smell anywhere other than in the lounge and his study.

I'm not sure where my mother's ability to ask people to look after her children came from. She was also not opposed, once I was at boarding school, to asking people to travel to collect me and have me for the weekend, even though some of them were practically strangers.

Another time that someone else had to be responsible for me was when my Dad had to go to the hospital because of the slipped discs in his back. It was a weekend, and I was due to play the xylophone at the school fair.

My Mum dropped me off at Dad's work friend's house (not someone from school) and had them take me to the fair the next morning. We were late, however, so I missed most of the performance. This resulted in my teacher throwing me evil stares and telling me off afterwards. I tried to explain about my father and why I was late, but he just brushed it aside.

If anyone had asked me what I wanted, it would have been to stay at home or be with my parents!

A few weeks later, when I was doing badly in a lesson, my teacher brought up my Dad and said he knew he was in hospital but that I couldn't let that be an excuse; I had to focus!

Despite all these incidents, however, the years we spent in Naples were the happiest and most carefree of my childhood. I remember fun times playing in the pool, Dad throwing us about in the water, and the sun shining down on us.

But there was also this big hole. I felt it then, and now – as an adult – I can see what it was.

It was a lack of affection. A lack of connection.

A lack of love.

CHAPTER 4
MILAN (AGES 9-11)

Once again, we had to relocate for Dad's job – this time to Milan. It wasn't unexpected, though, or that big of a deal; after all, my time at The British Forces School was coming to an end, as it only went up to age 11.

Looking for houses was tricky, even though the bank always provided a good agent to take us around all the 'suitable' places. With Milan being a city, we couldn't have a huge house with a garden like before, so this time we were looking at apartments. I wanted something quirky and strange.

Thankfully, my parents found us somewhere suitable that had a large balcony, so at least we had some outside space.

I attended the International School of Milan, which was fine – as far as schools went. I had some nice friends, the teachers were OK, and nothing much happened there.

Due to the move, my confidence was low, and as a result, I gave up playing piano and swimming. No one encouraged me to continue with these two things that I'd been so good at and had enjoyed so much in my last school/life.

I did have friends, but at break times, I preferred to sit and read my books; I was an avid reader and would often get lost in the stories. This, of course, was discouraged, and I was forced to go and 'play' instead.

During the Gulf War, I vividly recall the unsettling experience of being barred from the playground for several weeks or even months. The signs on the school bus were ominously blacked out, and no explanations were given other than 'because of the war.' This left me with a mild undercurrent of fear while at school. Were we in danger? Were we going to be bombed? What was going to happen?

Late one night – at around this time – I felt sore down there, so I tried to soothe myself with wet tissues.

Suddenly, my father opened my bedroom door and asked, "Why is your light on?" When he saw what I was doing, he stopped in the doorway and just stared at me.

I froze.

I understood that what I was doing was wrong and shameful somehow – even if I was only doing it to help myself – and, without saying a word, he backed up and closed the door.

This incident was never mentioned by anyone, and I was left feeling dirty.

I never doubted that every problem I faced had to be tackled alone by myself. After all, we weren't exactly a family of talkers.

After I'd been absent from school for an extended period due to glandular fever – and the added complication of anaemia – it was suggested to my mum that she take me back to the UK for the fresh air. Well, that was the idea. In reality, I believe we spent five days in London… so the air wasn't much fresher than Milan!

When I returned to Italy, I went to school and was immediately told I couldn't be there without a doctor's note. So, my Dad's PA collected me from school and took me to his office.

A work friend (who became a lifelong family friend) took me out for a Wendy's, and even though I didn't want it all, she made me finish my meal. Then my father drove me home. Once there, he told me he had to go back to the office but that Mum would be home in a few hours. It all felt very rushed.

I was ten years old, and that was the first time I was left home alone.

When it came to my Dad, work would always come first; it trumped everything and everyone.

At just 10 years old, I was allowed to walk to town alone, even though it involved crossing a fair few busy main roads. And, seeing as though 'town' meant the city of Milan, the Duomo, and all the vast crowds of tourists… in hindsight, it seems rather dangerous.

I was also allowed to walk to the video shop, over 20 minutes away, where I would – with my mother's knowledge – take out 18-rated horror movies. The only person to ever try to stop me was one of the shop clerks. Mum never asked any questions. She never took any interest in what I was doing.

In Milan, I took up smoking properly. I would buy fags from the tobacconists at the entrance to our 'block,' then I'd go around the back of the building and smoke. The cigarettes were slim, white, and pearly-tipped – so fancy.

Then, I decided to take it up a notch; I started to smoke in the bathroom at home. I wanted to be a 'proper grown-up' and smoke while reading, just like Dad. So, I would take two-hour baths, read, have snacks and drinks, and smoke.

The bathroom was outside my parents' bedroom, yet farthest from the lounge. Sometimes, my Mum would knock on the door and ask if I'd gone down the plug hole.

On occasion, I would make a three-course dinner for my parents. I would set up the fancy dining table with a tablecloth, napkins, and candles, and I would serve them like a waiter. I would always eat in the kitchen to give them some alone time, as I figured my being around all the time was not exactly conducive to a healthy marriage.

My efforts were humoured, though often with a dismissive huff and puff from my father.

During these meals, I never heard much chatter (from my position in the kitchen), and they always got up and left the minute the last mouthful had been eaten.

Even though it felt like my efforts were for nothing, I kept trying.

Sometimes, on a weekend, I would use my pocket money to buy my mother some flowers and my father a newspaper, which I'd present to them in the lounge. Getting my Dad to the lounge in the first place, however, was something of a struggle, as I'd get snapped at and puffed at.

This would, of course, leave me feeling rejected, dejected, and stupid for even trying. After giving the gifts and not getting much praise in return, I would retreat to my room and cry.

They both treated my attempts at kindness and affection as mere childish antics rather than sincere gestures. There's that overly sensitive girl again!

It was in this flat that, one day – while my Dad was at work and my Mum was out shopping – Jeffrey, back from boarding school, took great offence to my leaving a can of Coke on the coffee table. He would have been around 14 years old at the time.

He shouted at me to move it, and when I asked why – and when I said that I could leave it there if I liked, and who was he to tell me what to do anyway? – he went to the cutlery drawer and pulled out a big carving knife.

I had never seen his face like that before – his eyes turned black, and he looked so serious and incredibly angry. So, I started to run… and he chased me.

I slammed my bedroom door, locked it with the key, and then hid in my wardrobe. He began to hammer at my bedroom door, saying he was going to break it down. I was utterly terrified. There was no doubt in my mind that if he got to me, he would kill me.

Fortunately, after a while, the banging stopped. I stayed in my wardrobe until my mother got home, and when I told her the story, she laughed!

Many of the nightmares I've had over the years have featured a knife, but it was only in the last year or so that I made the connection.

Before the knife incident – before I started at boarding school with him – my brother was the first person who kissed me. I was 10 years old at the time.

He was on his computer in his bedroom, and we were kind of playing a game where I needed to get his attention. The t-shirt and leggings I was wearing weren't doing the trick, so I made the t-shirt shorter.

'Shorter,' he told me.

This went on until I was strutting into his room with the T-shirt tied in a knot above my boobs. I was developed a fair bit by that age.

The next thing I remember is him standing up, putting his mouth on mine, and then putting his tongue in my mouth.

Not wanting to be rejected and not wanting to cause a fuss, I stood there and did nothing. I mean, attention is attention, right? Good girls don't make a fuss.

Next, he pushed me onto the bed and climbed on top of me. I tried to fidget and move, but he pinned my legs down – with his on either side of mine – while holding my arms above my head.

He kissed me for a few more minutes, and then he simply got up and told me to get out of his room.

Later that day – or maybe it was another day – we were play fighting in the lounge, and when we fell over, he started kissing me again. Mum walked in, and we pulled apart. I explained that we were just playing a game, and her response was, "That's OK; I'm glad you're getting on."

I'm not sure what she saw… was she OK with this incestuous kissing, or had she just not seen it?

I kept this event secret until 2022, when I told my therapist, as well as sharing it with Mark (who I'll introduce you to later in the book). I still feel shame and disgust about the whole thing.

I made the difficult choice to include it in this book to illustrate something: how I learned early on that my body and what it could offer were seen as a means of getting attention and affection.

On top of this, from such a young age, I was conditioned not to have any autonomy, to be unaware of my worth or my right to say no.

I never felt like I was understood. It was like I was a different species entirely.

It was those three vs. me. Never all of us together. Never a whole family unit.

They were the unit; I was the outsider.

Chapter 5
Boarding School

I remember, at the age of 11, putting on my stiff, scratchy uniform at my grandmother's house in the UK and then having to sit in a too-hot car squashed between my brother and several suitcases as we made the two-hour journey to what would become, for the next 7 years, my second home.

For some reason, I wore my horrible blazer for the whole journey, along with the long-sleeved blue shirt and tie. The uniform was so stiff and thick, it was horrible.

On top of everything else, I had started my period that very morning, though I hadn't told anyone. I think I hoped that if I ignored it – just pretended it wasn't happening – then maybe it would go away. I was not comfortable enough to share this information with anyone, anyway. Anything to do with my body felt shameful to me.

I was using some folded-up toilet roll as a pad and was constantly fretting that I would leak. My tummy hurt, and I felt ashamed and embarrassed. The thick winter tights I was wearing made me all sweaty. I was beyond uncomfortable.

Once at the school, there was some kind of assembly for the newcomers and parents, which we had to attend. After that, we had to unload the car and find my dorm. I was sharing with three others in the dorm closest to the houseparents' house.

Mum and Dad started to help me unpack. I had a single wardrobe, a wooden bed with two big drawers underneath, a matching bedside table, a matching desk with shelves, and a little cupboard underneath, which you could lock with a padlock. There was also a corkboard on the wall behind the bed for pinning up pictures or whatever. You were never allowed to stick anything straight on the wall.

My Dad was struggling with putting my duvet cover on; I had, of course, chosen an awkward one with a side opening instead of a regular opening. I pleaded with them that the other cover would be fine, as I felt it was my fault that he was getting so irate. They wanted me to have the one I wanted, however, so they persevered. I felt so guilty and like I had ruined our last moments together.

Once I was mostly unpacked, the dreaded time came for them to leave.

I walked with them up to the quad, where the rental car was parked and where they were to meet with my brother to take him to dinner; he didn't need to be back at school until later.

I had a lump in my throat. My stomach was churning. I could barely breathe. I was, once again, on the outskirts. The three of them doing one thing together, leaving me behind.

I can still remember the exact moment my heart broke. I was standing there, all alone, knowing that my life was never going to be the same again.

I can't even describe the emotion of that moment. Even as I write this now, I can feel my pulse quicken and a semblance of that day return to me. I wanted to beg my Mum to stay. To not leave me. How could I live here, without her?

It is said that for children who attended boarding school, the moment they're left there is either seared into their memory, to be recalled in every fine detail for all time, or they have no recollection of it whatsoever.

I can vividly recall every single detail and every single emotion. I can see myself standing outside the music room steps. I can see the grass and the buildings. I can feel my sorrow and resignation.

After they disappeared from sight and I started walking towards the boarding house, I was overcome with the need to see them again. So, I raced up to the quad to look for their car… but they had already gone.

I repeated this behaviour later in the evening when I was hoping they'd be back to drop Jeffrey off. I didn't catch them that time, either. The pain of building up your hopes, longing to see them – and to share a cuddle – only to have those hopes dashed brings a fresh wave of grief crashing down upon you.

There was nothing homely or warm about the boarding house. It had thin brown carpet tiles and single window panes with rusting metal frames that had cracks between the seals. The walls were a wee yellow, as were the single bedsheets they provided. I can't stand this type of yellow even now, especially on walls.

It was while living in that dorm that I first saw 'Mr Telephone Man.' This was the name I gave to the ghost/shadow I saw every time I left the dorm at night to go to the loo. He would turn to look at me as I crossed the corridor. It was very scary.

A few other girls said they saw something down there, too, but we never discussed it much. I was so scared that I stopped looking down there whenever I left the dorm.

He was still there the following year when I moved down a dorm, and on a few occasions, I was too scared to go to the loo. One time, I laid some t-shirts on the floor , balled another on top of that and then urinated on them; I'd been too scared to go into the hallway, and I'd been desperate for the toilet!

I assume now that it was just a shadow, but with the fear I felt, I wonder if it was more. The boarding house was an old sanitorium, and people must have died there. So, of course, there were rumours it was haunted.

My biggest fear – which terrified me to my soul – was that, while I was away, my parents would die. That I wouldn't be there and that I wouldn't know about it, but also that I would be powerless to help them... and I wouldn't be able to say goodbye. These thoughts literally took my breath away.

I cried solidly for two weeks. During lessons, during prep, during meals... all the time – until, one day, it just stopped. It felt like I had run out of tears. In that moment, I realised how truly alone I was.

Years later, in a therapy session that I invited my mother to, she complained about how I would often phone her, crying – and how distressing that was for her, how it affected her. But not once did she think about how that crying was affecting me. Or why, for that matter, I was crying so desperately and for so long.

Had my tearfulness at the German exchange student's house – or at her leaving for Jeffrey's Confirmation – taught them nothing?

Since the age of five, my report cards all said I was a quiet child who lacked confidence. So, surely, sending me away to fend for myself without any kind of love and affection was not the way to increase my self-esteem or self-confidence!

If I ever said I hated it and wanted to leave, my mum would tell me to find myself another boarding school. It had been drummed into me early on that going to the local American school in whatever country they were living in would be no good for my education, as it would mean I could never go to a UK university as the schooling systems are so different. Then, in therapy, my mum used this against me, saying she had offered for me to go to American school. I could recall one instance when she mentioned it as an option, but I declined because I was worried about my future. It was never mentioned as an option for her to come and live in the UK and look after us like a regular mother.

A few years ago, I asked her about that option, and she said it had never even been a thought.

Email between me and my mother:

"We never considered me staying in the UK."

"If I knew then what I know now, I would have talked to you more about how you were feeling and encouraged you to go to the American school, but was never sure you would have been happy there either, with the education system being so different."

This was a direct lie – she had never talked to me about feelings at all. Even years later, if I brought up any of the past, I would immediately get shut down. I was literally told, "Find yourself another boarding school," on the phone by her when I told her how unhappy I was.

She had a way of making out that things weren't as bad for me – her, us – as it was for others. But, really, I was never allowed to talk about how bad things were, and certainly not after the fact. It was always shut down pretty quickly, and she would close down, too.

As the longer holidays drew to a close, I would start to feel anxious at the prospect of returning to the hellhole. The experience of packing would be wretched, and the shopping for supplies utterly depressing.

I would usually manage to keep myself together when I was around others and then allow myself to fall apart when I was alone in my bed at night. The goodbyes at the airport would often tip me over the edge, though – there would never be any emotion from my parents, but I certainly felt the anguish deep inside. After all, I was being ripped away from the life I wanted to be living and forced to endure a lonely, strict, work-fuelled life in a cold country.

Being an unaccompanied minor in the airport and on the plane did make me feel independent and grown up, but I also felt very lonely. As I got older, I would book a 'smoking' seat and sit and smoke while I read my book and drank my Coke. All so grown up.

For the first year or two, Jeffrey came with me, but then he stopped, and I was all alone.

The people who were charged with looking after us during term time were called houseparents and were 'in loco parentis' – acting in place of the parents.

They were, however, the farthest thing from ideal parents you could imagine. They were strict, ugly, self-righteous, controlling, and just plain mean. He had huge, flaring nostrils. She was taller and wore old, long, dark, flowered skirts. Think curtains. They would patrol the corridors to 'catch' people out. Catch you not being where you should be. Catch you having fun or being silly. Catch you somehow 'misbehaving.'

They had a reputation as being the strictest, meanest houseparents in the school.

Email to Mum 2018:

They were bullies, and they kept us in a constant state of anxiety. They were known throughout the school, even by the other teachers, as being very cruel, mean and strict.

He would roam the halls looking for people to shout at.

If you were out of your desk during prep, even to go to the loo, he would shout at you.

He would listen outside rooms to see if people were chatting.

He shouted at me once for reading a Stephen King book Dad had lent me - told me how awful it was etc, etc.

If you had a hole in your tights, he would call you a slut.

He had people in tears every day.

He would walk in when we were getting changed then when we tried to hide, he would say, 'i have seen it all before'

in evening call over, he would quiz us all on current affairs - he would stand there until you came up with an answer and then mock you if you were wrong. then he would berate us all for having right-wing parents etc, etc.

Usually ended with a girl crying.

at weekends, he would come in while we were watching tv, turn it off and tell us all to get outside and that we weren't allowed back for at least 2 hours, nd he would lock the front door.

At evening prep break, he would stand by the door, and we had to bring him our school shoes, he wouldn't let us out till they were sparkling clean. he would send us back again and again to clean them. Took a while for us to figure out the only way to get them clean enough was to cover them with lip balm - he wanted them that shiny (obviously impossible with just a brush and polish)

when i ran away they took me into their office and had a go at me and then mrs P stood in front of the door so i couldn't leave. i felt very trapped and bullied. it was scary - i was in a room alone with the 2 of them and no one knew i was there. i didn't know what was gonna happen.

when i didn't do the hockey thing (and the reason for that was cos i was anxious and scared and needed someone to be there with me to give me the confidence to go through with it!) he took me in his room and had a big go at me telling me how selfish i was etc etc then sent me to my room and told me not to come out!

if you came down to call over in the morning not 100% dressed you were pulled aside and told off. i came down tying my tie and was told off quite badly. i was lazy etc etc.

you could never relax. never chill.

our life was run by bells.

we had the whole school day - teaching from 9 till 5.30, dinner (i would often burst out cying when i saw what was for dinner cos i was so hungry but it was so nasty) then straight down for prep which was 6.30 till 7.10. 10 min wee break, then 7.20 till 8. 20 minute break. In certain years groups you were allowed up to see the boys at this prep break but like said he would do the spot check on the shoes sometimes, and he would lock the door at 8.25 so if you were late back you would have to ring the bell so he would know and punish you.

then more prep till 9.

anyone who accidentally burnt the toast and set the fire alarm off would be punished. if you were ever in the house during the *day and you 'shouldn't' have been there you were told off. so we had nowhere to feel safe.*

I was told off once for breaking the 6-inch rule (no one was allowed closer than 6 inches to another person) with Jeffery!! he was giving me a very rare cuddle cos i was crying.

There was no softness, no kindness, no gentleness, no humanity.

We were there for him to bully and he spend his time trying to catch us out and make us miserable.

So the other week when we were at Wisley when I said I would send him a bag of dog poo (which obviously I would never actually do) it is because I hate him, they were horrible people and for me to say that I would have hoped you would see that.

But no all you saw was that Raven was being childish and dramatic and mean because you somehow very easliy forget that I am actually a very kind, good person. you see me as a child and so easy to criticise rather than trying to understand why I say and do the things I do.

I am sure there are many, many more things that they did, but i cant think right now.

When i told all this to Kim, she said it was abuse.

The stories of their nastiness are countless…

There were times they would come in after lights out and tell us off for talking, then make us stand in the corridor for ages in the cold and the dark to teach us a lesson. The times they would come in during prep and shout at us – whether we were talking or not – at our desks. And it wasn't just the houseparents. As was often the case, the prefects (sixth formers put in charge of the rest of us) would come in and make us stand outside or give us 'sides' (lines of one sentence written over and over).

The houseparents would stand at the door during morning 'call over' and quiz us on world events; they would single people out, mocking them when they couldn't answer or when they got it wrong. He would wait in the corridor as we traipsed down after the morning bells, trying to catch us out in some form or other – for me, it was usually because my tie wasn't yet done, my shirt was untucked, or I had a hole in my tights. He would dish out punishments and humiliation with glee and a glint in his eye.

He was my worst enemy, yet he was also supposed to be the person I turned to in my time of need while at school. It was one big fucked-up mess.

Only once – in seven years – did my mother call him to stick up for me. I do wonder how that phone call went. I imagine he placated her pretty easily.

He had pulled me aside one morning for my shirt being untucked as I came into the room for morning call-over. That day he must have been in a particularly nasty mood because he berated me viciously. I was very upset and, this time, I did complain to my mother. I had already dealt with six years of his bullying and had had enough. I was starting to see how wrong and unjust his treatment of us all was.

My brother made it clear before I started at 'his' school that I wasn't to ruin his reputation. He would never come and talk to me unless it was to tell me off for some rule he had decided I'd broken – like talking to the wrong person, smoking, or if he had to tell a boy off for liking me.

If he saw I was homesick, he would visibly huff and roll his eyes before comforting me for a minute or two – though that was very rare.

He felt he could control me and tell me what and how to do things. His evident anger, if he didn't get his way, was hard for me to deal with.

For a long while, I was known as 'Jeffrey's sister' rather than as my own person, which was hard to take – especially as his dislike of me was so clear. I still held him on such a high pedestal, though I have no idea why!

Anyway, back to the first few weeks of school.

I had vivid dreams and fantasies of grabbing the knife in the kitchen – a blunt bread knife! – and killing the houseparents, then opening up the locked front door and somehow getting a taxi to take me the two hours to my grandmother's house, where my mother was staying for a week or so before returning to Italy.

Needless to say, none of this ever materialised. I simply carried on going through the motions.

I would wake early, and – as I had no idea what time the morning bells were supposed to go off – I would get dressed before going back to bed, dozing until the first bell. I was terrified of being late, of being left behind by the other girls. I was the only one out of my class in my dorm and my boarding house, so I was left to find my classes on my own.

During the first week, I got lost a few times and ended up wandering around where I thought the classes should be, getting more and more panicked. I had no clue what to do or who to ask about finding the correct place. Luckily, after a few minutes, I'd inevitably be discovered by a sixth former who would help me get to class. I would then walk in, tearful, exhausted, embarrassed, and alone. The only one late, the only one who hadn't been able to find the classroom.

Once again, I was the odd one out.

There is a whole new language at boarding school that you have to learn: prep, exeat, fagging, sides, call over… it was a lot to take in all at once.

I was often teased for sounding too posh, though at home, my mother would tell me off for not speaking properly. Even if I was trying to tell her a story or trying to bare my soul to her (which was rare), she would correct my grammar or – as I got older – chastise me for swearing.

It seemed that I didn't sound right anywhere!

In the first week, I had to buy a hockey stick. I was taken to the tiny school shop, given a stick, and it was written in a book – this would then be put on my end-of-term school bill for my parents to pay.

A few days later, some 'day girls' – who were a few years above me – came running up to me and my friends, saying they had hockey and had lost their stick, and could they borrow mine? I knew these girls were very popular, so of course, I wanted to get on their good side. They were being so friendly and lovely too.

I gave it over, and they said they would return it later.

Well, by the time my hockey lesson came around a few days later, I still had no hockey stick! So, I went to find these girls, but they denied ever borrowing my stick. Naïvely, I found a teacher and explained the situation. The girls swore the stick was theirs.

In the end, it was decided that the only way to figure this out was to look at the shop book to see if it was written in there, considering I'd bought it so recently.

It wasn't, however, in the book! WTF?!

I remember going into the shop in my first week and being given it – it was supposed to have been put in the book!

Now, not only did everyone think I was a liar, but they also thought I was a troublemaker who made up stories and tried to get others in trouble!

Why were these girls doing this? I asked myself. They knew what they had done; they knew the truth! Not only was I hurt and upset, I was confused and angry. Who acts like this?

Those girls became enemies of mine all through my school life.

CHAPTER 6
FOOD & SHOPPING

My eating disorder began at boarding school. At the age of 11, I felt so distraught at being left there, alone, that I couldn't eat. I had spent my life being told I was fussy, so I just put it down to not liking the food – and, to be fair, it was pretty horrendous.

Fried eggs dripping in grease. Blue cups of full-fat milk sitting out and getting warm, all with something black or a hair floating in them. Boring cereals. Lettuce leaves with greenflies and big troughs of ketchup with spoons collecting at the bottom – or, worse yet, no ketchup at all!

Soon, people in my house were tasked with keeping an eye on me and reporting back about what I'd eaten at meals. Then, my house matron started to accompany me to lunch. A motherly crutch, as it were. This just made things worse. I would sit and cry over the meal as she told me I had to eat it as I had taken it.

I just couldn't eat.

As the weeks and years went on, I would often walk into dinner at 17.30, see what the 'menu' was, and walk out again, crying. I was so hungry, but the food was just so repulsive to me.

For weeks at a time, I would only eat an apple a day. I would faint if I ran. When I was 15, I fainted in aerobics class and other than it being commented on, no action was taken. Parents weren't informed, and no follow-up was conducted.

I think the eating issues began because I was just so sad and unhappy. And, being heartbroken, I couldn't eat. I just couldn't stomach it.

It then developed into something much more – a deep disgust of the food, sure, but also, eating was the only thing I had any control over in my life. Everything else was decided and mapped out for me.

It didn't begin as my choice, but then it became out of control. It was controlling me.

The feeling of being hungry, of being empty… it was addictive. It becomes all you can think about. It feels powerful… until you get dizzy and pass out. Then, of course, you feel sick and shit. You start to notice the weakness in your limbs, the effort it takes to breathe fully, and how you can't think straight.

You know that you must eat. You also know that it will only get worse – that you will only feel worse if you don't eat – but that would be giving up. That would be giving up this power.

Also, at that point, the thought of food makes you feel physically sick. Your body gets so used to not eating that it doesn't feel right to eat anything at all.

One day, I was persuaded to go to lunch by a girl in the year above who also had an eating disorder and who, years later, would become so emaciated that you could literally see every bone in her body. She told me to eat.

So, I got myself a slice of white bread, some shredded lettuce, and some Thousand Island sauce that I made myself by mixing ketchup with salad cream. I made it into a sandwich, and I forced it down. It was nice to eat, but as soon as I was halfway through, I felt disgusted with myself. What was I doing? I would get fat, and I was giving up my willpower.

As I raced to the boarding house loos, I knew what I had to do. With my fingers down my throat and tears in my eyes, I threw up my meagre lunch.

This soon became my routine.

Usually, with bulimia, there is the bingeing that comes before the purge. I, however, never binged. I ate very little if anything, yet I still made myself sick.

I enjoyed the punishment. Enjoyed the pain. It was what I deserved. It made me feel real, here, present.

After a while, some blood vessels burst in my eye from all the puking, and it was at that point that Jeffrey took me to the doctor. I don't recall exactly what Jeffrey knew about it all, but I told the male doctor that I wasn't eating because I felt bad for all the starving children in the world. He didn't believe me.

Jeffrey then stayed behind as he had a 'regular' slot with the doctor – therapy, I wonder?

He told me he wasn't confident but that he pretended to be. I couldn't believe that anyone could pretend that well… that convincingly.

There was never any follow-up, care, or questions regarding this situation.

I have struggled with restrictive eating my whole life – only now I can catch it early enough to stop it. I don't want my children to see this or for them to not have me at my best. After all, I can't take care of them or drive them to and from school if I haven't eaten.

I also hate that it is a toxic trait carried through from my past. My battle with my body is such an ingrained behaviour. At this point, it is almost who I am.

I was very impressed with myself recently, though. I bought a gorgeous black dress – stunning – but when I tried it on, all I could see was the fat deposits by my armpits. I took the dress off and arranged to mail it back. Instead of turning inwards and hating myself or choosing not to eat for the next few months in order to 'correct' my body, I just got on with the rest of my day.

What did that mean? Was it OK to kind of accept myself as I now am? Was it OK to not look or try to look 'perfect' all the time? Was I giving up? Was that OK?

I knew that if I carried on fighting myself, I would forever feel as dissatisfied and unhappy as I'd felt my entire life. Something simply had to change.

Maybe I was nearly there?

Back to boarding school. Other than being physically starving, I was also lacking any emotional connection.

On my first day, I latched onto a girl in the year above me, Emma. I saw her in the dorm next to mine and recognised her from the newcomers' assembly. I could tell she was getting angry at me as I was hanging around while her parents were still helping her set up her space. I just couldn't be alone, however, so feeling her resentment seemed far better than walking away.

From that moment on, every opportunity I got, I would be with her. As the weeks went on and, we each made new friends, however, I felt more comfortable being away from her.

The first few years were pretty OK, friends-wise. Things weren't too complicated. I had my boarding friends and my day pupil friends. I also had a best friend, who would invite me over to her house some exeat weekends or just for the day. Those were great days spent in a carefree family home with a Mum and nice food. I even spent a few weekends with families we'd met on holidays, as my Mum would ask if I could go to them.

I was always wary of my friends' fathers, though. I wondered why they were at home and not at work – after all, my Dad was hardly ever at home and always at work.

For the first three weekends, new boarders weren't allowed out on weekends. Supposedly, this was to give us a chance to properly settle in. In reality, it just made the whole place feel like a prison!

Luckily, in Form 1, we had a lovely house tutor – a kindly French lady who would hang out with us during third prep when the other years were still doing homework. She would play games with us and make us special drinks. It was only for 30 minutes, but as there were only three of us, it made me feel taken care of and safe. Unfortunately, this would often make me sadder because it was so fleeting.

The only phone we had access to was a massive yellow payphone attached to the wall in the main corridor, so there was never any privacy or quiet. The younger years were not allowed on it during prep, and it was only allowed to be used for 10 minutes at a time – and only during certain hours. This felt so constricting and made me panic a bit if I went to use the phone and someone was on it.

A few times I got told off by the housemistress for coming back to the boarding house during the day, in tears, to call my mum. There was no compassion or sympathy in that woman.

After the first week, my mum said I could only call her if I stopped crying.

I even had to call her for help with my English homework; I was behind due to moving schools and not following the same UK curriculum as everyone else. The turmoil and anxiety I felt over homework that I couldn't manage and trying to explain it over the phone and have her understand what was required without being able to show her anything was incredibly challenging.

Our homework times – or prep, as it was called – were from 18.30 – 19.10, 19.20- 20.00, and 20.25-21.00. The short break was just so we could go to the loo and get a drink, but during the longer one, we were allowed to watch TV.

Then, from Form 4 onwards, we were allowed out of the house to go up to the boys' boarding houses to socialise – though God help you if you were late back! The housemaster would lock the door dead on 20.25 and wait by the door to catch you out. Then, of course, you weren't allowed out the next night.

Sometimes, he would stand by the door and wouldn't let you out until you'd shined your shoes. No matter how much you cleaned and buffed them, however, they were never good enough. So, you wasted your entire 25-minute break trying to please him with your shiny shoes. As it turned out, they would only be shiny enough once we'd slathered them in Vaseline or Body Shop Kiwi lip balm!

It was as though he delighted in ruining our lives. In making us miserable. In taking away the only things we enjoyed.

So, if you didn't go out for prep break, you would usually watch TV in the common room – though, of course, back in those days, we only had the usual four channels, and there was no pausing or rewinding, etc. The sixth formers controlled the remote, deciding what everyone would watch. Sometimes, they even kicked people out of seats they wanted.

Evening call-over was at 21.00, and we would all have to be present and accounted for. If he could, the housemaster would find a way to humiliate us. Then, we'd be allowed a 'treat.' Most nights, this meant having two biscuits each, but once a week, it was doughnuts, and once a week, it was sticky willies (iced buns). I hated the sticky willies. It was a first-come, first-served affair, with a chaotic pushing and shoving frenzy. If you were fortunate, you got your allowance, but arriving late or failing to fight your way through left you with nothing but crumbs, broken pieces, and unwanted scraps.

I distinctly remember my first-morning chapel. Form 1 went up to the balcony, and I was so anxious and scared that I remember cold sweat running down my spine. That feeling has never left me.

The chapel was quite big, and each year group had their own section that they sat in. This would rotate each year. The balcony was at the back and above the rest of the chapel, and they often put the younger year groups up there – maybe to contain them? I was scared as this was my first day at school and the first time meeting others in my year group. As if being left with strangers wasn't bad enough, now I had to meet more people and start school – and all from a place of not feeling safe.

I struggled not to cry too noisily during the songs and messages, and on that day, I latched onto a day girl who would become a friend of mine for many years: Lucy.

I'm 100% sure my parents told me that if I was unhappy after a term, I could leave. Well, term one ended, and I happily told them I didn't want to go back – only to be told, "No, no – we said a year!"

So, once again, I was left distraught and alone.

Every morning, I would search the little shelf by the front door, hoping I had some post; it was usually there once we returned from breakfast. On the mornings I got something I felt good, loved, and thought of. My mother and grandmother's letters and cards were never long, but at least I'd been thought of.

The house matron was a short, plump, older lady who – although not motherly – did at least create a safe place to hang out during breaks. She took it upon herself to look after me a bit, as I was clearly floundering. She even cut my toenails for me a few times, as I guess I wasn't aware I should be doing it. Mum ended up giving her money each term to buy me fresh fruit, and she ended up being the first person I asked to give me sanitary pads.

She gave me these huge, bulky things that had loops designed for a sanitary belt! Sanitary belts were used from Victorian times up to around 1970. I felt uncomfortable and self-conscious that they could be seen sticking out the back of my skirt as they were so long and huge.

After giving me one or two for a few months, however, she told me I had to start buying my own. So, I went back to using the loo roll. There was no way I was going to go through the shame and embarrassment of buying my own in the tiny village shop, where all the kids bought their break-time snacks.

I don't know where I read it, but I found out that cold water can stop your flow for a short while, so I risked not using any protection while swimming – as, obviously, I couldn't use the toilet paper in the pool.

It took me a whole year to tell my mum; I decided to tell her by writing a letter during one holiday. After folding it up, I stapled it shut and handed it to my brother to deliver to her, all while I remained hidden in my room. In the letter, I said that I didn't want to talk about it but that I just needed some 'things' to use. I felt so embarrassed and ashamed about it all.

We had never really talked about periods or sex. She had given me a pamphlet from a box of tampons (obviously some kind of teaching book) and told me to ask if I had any questions. I think my only question had been about changing a pad. She just said I'd be able to smell it if I'd left it too long (gross).

I never felt comfortable discussing this kind of stuff with her. I didn't like her being too close to me or sitting or lying on my bed. I think her demeanour – along with our broken, surface-level relationship – was the reason for this. Instead of holding hands when we walked around the shops, I would hold her arm; I think touching hands was way too intimate for me.

She actually became angry with me soon after getting my 'period letter' – she was annoyed that I hadn't felt comfortable enough to open up to her!

When I was on holiday from school, she would take me shopping nearly every day, buying me anything and everything. Bags and bags full of clothes. Any book I wanted. I looked at it, and it became mine. There was no looking at price tags, no choosing this or that. I would have armfuls of clothes at each shop's checkout. No wonder I confused money and material things with love for so many years.

I believed she was expressing her love for me – perhaps it was the only way she knew how to show me anything. There have always been lots of silence between us, so I wonder if it was easier to take me shopping than to talk to me? After all, you can't do too much talking in busy shopping crowds, especially when there are so many shops and so little time.

All this buying of stuff led my grandfather to believe I was spoilt; he alluded to it many times over the years.

Mum and I didn't really share anything else, and there are very few people I can shop with now. Shopping used to be my hobby – the rush of finding something pretty, the retail therapy… I loved it.

I don't really enjoy it much these days.

CHAPTER 7
FIRST KISSES AND BOYFRIENDS

At the age of 11, I was incredibly self-aware. I had also developed physically early. When I had my first kiss, I hated it! We hid behind some bushes, and even though I didn't really want to do it, I knew it was expected. I don't remember too much about it because it kind of felt like I blacked out! I wrote him a letter a few days later as I didn't want to do it again, but apparently this really upset him – he even said he wanted to die because he liked me so much. This added to my belief that I had to please others before myself.

Another boyfriend I had was a friend of my brother's – he'd been warned by Jeffrey not to touch me below the shoulders, or there'd be trouble!

After a few months of meeting at breaks and between classes, kissing and giggling, he told me he'd kissed another girl when he went home one weekend. I tried to act like it didn't matter… but of course it did! It was from this experience that I began to realise how people lie, cheat, and can't always be trusted.

From then on, I only stayed with a boy for three weeks or so before dumping them. I'm not sure why I chose three weeks, but it seemed to be around that time that I started to feel uncomfortable with the closeness.

From age 11, I had boys mocking me and constantly commenting on my boobs and lack of bra. Then, once everyone became more familiar with each other, one boy in particular – who would go on to be an issue for me throughout my school career – started grabbing me down below. I was terrified that one day he would feel the pad, giving me yet another issue for me to handle.

One boy in my science class would stand very close behind me (when we were doing practicals and were allowed to move about) and touch my hair. He would stroke it and feel it. It creeped me out, and I didn't quite know how to get him to stop.

When I was in Form 3 , there was another boy a few years above me who chose to set his sights on me and began to wait for me outside my classes – though I have no idea how he knew where I'd be at certain times of the day. He would also wait for me at dinner and sit with me and my friends. I hated it; it felt like I was being stalked. On top of all this, I was so self-conscious about eating with boys that I stopped eating again.

This boy freaked me out way too much, and despite my asking him to stop, he carried on. In the end, I had to get Jeffrey to warn him off; I think it was the only time having a brother was actually useful to me.

For me, the opposite sex seemed to fall into one of two categories: they were either utter arseholes who cheated and messed you around, or they were all over you and obsessed with you. What utter shit! Despite my experiences, however, I was still sure there must be a good one out there somewhere…!

Another thing I started having to endure when I was just 12 years old was a few of the boys deciding it was their right to touch my boobs.

The only other two 'developed' girls in my year had boyfriends, so I guess that made me a prime target. One would grab my arms and hold them behind my back while the other few would feel me up. Everyone would laugh, and – as much as I hated it, and despite how powerless I felt – I would laugh along, too.

Even to this day, I'm not sure why I reacted like that; I think it was a desire to not cause trouble, to not be disliked. Good girls don't complain and make a fuss, right?! People pleasing at its most toxic and destructive.

Around year 5, when I was 14 or 15, however, I did make a fuss.

We had gone on a geography field trip to York for five days, and one night, these boys grabbed me, doing their usual. I got angry, so I – along with a few other girls, who they'd started doing it to as well – went to the female teacher to complain. All the girls at the table had something to say, and they all said they wanted it to stop. Thankfully, she listened to what we said and took us seriously.

Consequently, the female teacher – along with a male teacher – gathered all the boys together and had a word with them. The fallout from this was that, somehow, I was to blame; all the boys and the girls turned against me and only me! They all decided that because I'd laughed every time they did it, I had allowed it – even wanted it – to happen. And now that I'd told on them? I was the bad guy.

For the remainder of the trip, no one talked to me, and I was chucked with many evil stares. Some people even started arguments with me. My supposed best friend at the time, whom I was sharing a room with, turned on me, too. From that day on, our friendship was never the same.

I remember one of the arguments distinctly: a boy from Turkmenistan told me I needed to chill out and get laid!

Sometime later – I can't remember how long, a few months or perhaps even a year – this same boy was out on the sports fields one night when I was out with a few other people. It was dark, and we were all just walking around, smoking, messing about, and generally being teenagers. He grabbed me, stuck his tongue in my mouth, and wouldn't let go. I pushed and pushed, eventually managing to get him off me, but then he grabbed me again as I was walking away and tried to trip me up backwards to put me on my back. I realised at this point that this wasn't a laugh or a joke; I realised I was actually in danger. But there was no way he'd go any further… right?

We were alone at this point, as everyone else had wandered off. I don't think they even knew that he'd appeared. Luckily, I managed to keep my footing and pull away from him, running into the light and back to my friends.

I dread to think what he would have done if I hadn't got away.

Chapter 8
Mean Girls

There were two boys' boarding houses: Westminster and St Margaret's. Jeffrey was in Margaret's, and I was always under the impression that the 'better' boys were in this house.

I often hung out in front of this house, and on the very rare occasion that we were allowed in to watch TV with the boys, it would always be at St Margaret's.

But maybe my opinion was wrong.

On many occasions, when loitering just inside the front door – the furthest we were allowed to go – I would get dragged into the communal showers while the boys were in there. One day, I stumbled across some boys watching porn and looking at porn mags in the common room.

During a coed party in that same common room, one of my brother's friends tried to kiss me and feel me up; he wouldn't stop, and some of the other boys had to step in. Where were the teachers?

A few years later, this same boy would be abused so badly he could hardly walk. I was aghast when I found out he'd had a torch and a chopstick shoved up his rectum. Who had done this? And why?!

When I was 12, I somehow became very friendly with my friend Emma's brother and his best mate. They were both 17, both in Margaret's. We would chat and flirt and say 'hi' when passing each other at school. We'd hang out at prep breaks.

One weekend, when Jim – Emma's brother – was out on exeat, it was just me, my friend, and this 17-year-old boy, Rob, hanging out. We wandered around the school and the fields and ended up finding an abandoned shack deep in the woods.

We hung out in there for ages, smoking, giggling, and flirting, and – somehow – Rob and I ended up kissing.

It must have been a good hour or more of deep, full-on French kissing.

I kind of hoped this would mean we'd become a couple, but when we parted ways, and I asked if I'd see him tomorrow, he said, "Errmmm, no, I don't think so," with a look of shock and disbelief on his face.

Come Monday, Jim was back at school, and he cornered me after breakfast, saying I'd done a terrible thing – that what I had done was really wrong and that I couldn't ever see Rob again.

Shocked and confused, I tried to understand what he meant. Then, he gave me a letter he'd written.

Basically, it said that Rob could get in lots of trouble for what had happened, that it was my fault for kissing him, and that I should have known better. Not only had I lost this potential boyfriend, but I'd also lost two very good friends. I was incredibly upset.

At one point or other, I started going over to Westminster House to see if the boys over there were any nicer. They seemed to have less strict rules about girls going into the common room; so most weekends, I would find myself in there, watching whatever movie they had on.

One day, I ended up sitting next to one of the two German boys who I believe were over for just a year. I didn't fancy him – in fact, I didn't find him attractive at all. Somehow, however, our hands touched, and neither of us moved them. It was nice, not in a sexual way, but rather as just a comforting touch.

The next weekend, the same thing happened again, having engineered it so we were sitting next to each other again. Each time we touched, we became more confident and purposeful. Soon enough, we were almost holding hands.

It was the comfort of human touch, nothing more, but I delighted in it. I longed for the next time we could 'sorta hold hands.' It was the only stable bit of comfort and touch I had.

To say this out loud – that I was holding hands with some random guy simply just to get some human contact, some comfort, some connection, at maybe 13 or 14 years old – is so heart-wrenching.

Being quite a small school of about 500 – and with fewer than half of those students being boarders – it would make sense that many of us ended up 'going out' with each other. After all, there were no 'outside' people we could date; we only had each other.

We were all boy-mad, and it was the main reason for doing anything. But I guess that when you have no other means of affection, attention, or attachment, all your energy goes into attracting the opposite sex in order to get those things we crave and desire so much – not to mention that we were all in our formative years, going through puberty. What else were we to do anyway? It was all schoolwork, sports matches, and nothing else.

On weekends – well, half of Saturday and most of Sunday – we were left to our own devices… which meant smoking, drinking, and, if possible, sex, or at least something close. We were hormonal teenagers, after all!

Vodka was my first drink, hidden in a water bottle to disguise it, and I got drunk in the girls' boarding house hallway! What a giggle! I was around 14 or 15 then, and it happened more and more as the years went on.

I liked drinking because when I was drunk, life was bearable! I actually laughed, though I don't think I laughed much after the first two years. In those first years, things were a bit more carefree in our dorms. We had pillow fights and giggles after lights out.

One weekend, I went home with a friend, and as her parents weren't home, we drank ourselves silly. I threw up on my trousers and my Snoopy teddy, and the next morning, I had to walk down the road in my PJs to call Mum and ask her the best way to wash Snoopy.

I told her we had gotten drunk, and all I got was a tut.

For my brother's 18th birthday party, I dressed as a belly dancer. I took my best friend, who was dressed as a circus ring leader.

We downed a few beers and got in the swing of the dancing. A few of his friends took an interest in me, and I kissed one or two. Seeing this, Jeffrey grabbed me and dragged me away, saying, "You're not getting pregnant at my 18th party!"

One of the boys touched my heart, and I found myself sobbing the next week when all the upper sixth left after their last A level.

Oh, and doing a mock English paper when you're still drunk helps, by the way!

To this day, I still can't smell peach schnapps without feeling sick.

This followed a night in lower sixth where a group of us sat in someone's 'show' (a single or double room rather than a dorm) and just drank and drank.

We ended up climbing out of the window and sitting on this small window ledge above the main entrance to the boarding house. I woke up the next morning feeling so incredibly hungover, but I managed to drag my arse out of bed and go to my classes.

Every now and then, with no warning whatsoever, we would have 'room inspections.' These consisted of Debra, the matron, going through your room – including your wardrobe and all your drawers – to see if it was tidy and if you had any contraband.

It was very invasive, but thankfully, I always kept my space immaculate; I was actually held up as an example of how to keep your space.

Debra was the one who would take us to the dentist, doctor, or any other appointments we needed.

One day, for some reason, I had to go to the podiatrist. I think I had a verruca. Even to this day, I'm still suffering from what happened during that appointment.

The lady shaved away the skin on the sides of my big toes and then proceeded to burn me with acid. It was agony. She did it so deeply and for so long that I have painful scar tissue and sensitive spots on both of my big toes.

Not many teachers threw around praise or kindness (much like at home!), but I did get a kind of backhanded compliment in one area of school. I was good at some sports, and apparently, the reason for my ability to throw and catch in netball and rounders was because I had an older brother. Now... I couldn't quite figure this one out, as we'd never thrown a ball between us even once, but I guess the teacher knew what she was talking about, so maybe the wonderfulness of having a male in the household simply rubbed off on the inferior female?

When I was 15, I discovered that a teacher was lusting after a girl who'd joined us for swimming for the day. I was so mystified by the wrongness of this, especially when he offered to put sun cream on her shoulders!

All males and boys at that school were obsessed with boobs. The attention I got simply for having boobs bigger than most of my year was shocking.

Some of my female friendships went through hardships as boys became more of a 'thing' in their lives. My best friend, Kay, for instance, ended up siding with the abusive little twat who, years previous, had grabbed me repeatedly down below. I simply couldn't figure out what pull he had over her; I thought we were so close.

There was also a girl in my house called Michaela, and at one point, her brother was my brother's best friend. She was a nasty piece of work – befriending you and then betraying your trust just to get a laugh or some attention from the boys. She would hang out with her brother and his friends, but of course, I wasn't allowed to do that, and she used this against me when it came to the popularity stakes.

For some reason, we had to sit next to each other in maths – we were both in the B set – and if I couldn't do the work, she would mock me. If I could do it, she would copy me.

Thankfully, after a year of not being able to keep up, we – plus two others – were moved down a set. Now, I was top of the C set rather than bottom of the B. My maths confidence rose while hers stayed not so great. Finally, I had something better than her.

She was tall and thin with long, blonde hair, blue eyes, and pale skin – everything I wasn't. And, obviously, she was a big hit with the boys. She and her friends were like that posse of mean girls from the movie *Mean Girls*, and I would dread crossing her path around school as she'd always have some kind of cutting remark.

One day, she and her 'girls' decided to take me under their wing and desperate for the bullying to stop, I joined in. Oh, to be part of the popular group, right?

Two days later, I was unceremoniously dropped. It had been a lot of work trying to fit in with them, however, so I wasn't too fussed; I just hoped the nit-picking would end!

It definitely dropped off and then became even less once I started going out with The Wank. More on him later.

In Form 3, you had to join the CCF – Combined Cadet Force. And, once you were in, you HAD to stay for two years.

You had to attend every Monday at lunch and then for the last few lessons of the day. Each session lasted about two hours. You had to get changed into the old, cold, leftover WW2 kit and do a parade on the quad. It was very strict. Practice for the Army!

Then we went and did Army stuff. I was in the Engineers rather than the Infantry, so our job was to learn how to read maps and build things. Engineers were seen as 'less than' the Infantry. Not as hard, not as cool. We were the ones who set things up so they could go in and do their cool thing.

The only time I enjoyed this was when we did shooting, which I was good at. And for me, being good at something at school was a rare occurrence. What I dreaded the most, however, was the twice-a-year Field Day, when we went 'camping' over a weekend and had to do more in-depth Army stuff.

And, when I say camping, there were no tents; we had to put up Bashas. This is literally just a tarpaulin that you fashion to form a shelter.

I never went on a Field Day where it didn't rain. It was horrific.

One year, during our night manoeuvres, it was pitch black, and I ended up running straight into a lake. I was fully drenched and freezing. Then, the next day, I got in trouble as I hadn't known I should have slept in my wet gear in order to dry it out.

It was probably that year that I got a mild case of hypothermia.

Another year, I fell and sliced my hand open. There were these older boys who, while doing a day's exercise, kept sending me back to the bottom of this hill over and over again as they could 'see' me, and I wasn't camouflaged enough due to my hair colour. I was struggling not to faint due to the blood pouring out of my hand.

Next, we had to do some marching, and Michaela and her cronies kept messing about, so we had to keep repeating it. I told her to stop so we could get moving, and oh my goodness, I got it in the ear for speaking up!

In recent years, I've read many books about boarding school and the effects it can have on people. The best and most useful have been *Boarding School Syndrome: The psychological trauma of the 'privileged' child* by Joy Schaverien and *The Making of Them* by Nick Duffell. Alex Renton also made a documentary titled

Boarding Schools: The Secret Shame – Exposure, which was very enlightening.

A podcaster called Piers Cross has also been very helpful in my healing.

I have just listened to an LBC radio show with James O'Brien, in which he spoke of the repressed emotions of those who board. As such young children, we had to be self-reliant and look after ourselves. We were also expected to hold all our emotions in – otherwise, we'd be seen as weak.

These books and shows have helped me gain a better understanding of many of the issues I suffer from and have taught me that I am not alone.

I think the most helpful thing, however, was an in-person event I attended. It was called 'Boarding is not okay', and it was hosted by an ex-boarder called Penny. There were 16 people in attendance – about five of whom were therapists, who were there to gain a better understanding of how ex-boarders think and feel.

This time, I saw that I truly was not alone! There were actual real life people there who had experienced similar things to me and who were still feeling the effects of it 20, 30, even 40-plus years later!

Penny opened my eyes to countless falsehoods, ones I hadn't even realised existed. For instance, the misleading claims found on school websites, the crap parents believe about what goes on there, and the way we were left to our own devices while simultaneously having every aspect of our lives meticulously regulated.

How were we supposed to come out as high-functioning members of society when our self-esteem was in tatters, and we hadn't been given a chance to flourish?

Not to mention all the to and fro between home and school, the different beds we had to sleep in, and – for those of us with parents who moved a lot – the fact that, when we went home, we'd go back to new houses and new bedrooms.

We belonged nowhere and with no one.

Our basic human needs were not being met at boarding school.

Our mealtimes were dictated, and we were called to them by a bell. Many kids, me included, hated the food and often found it inedible.

We had to ask to get a drink or go to the loo. We were not allowed out of our seats during prep – and goodness help you if you tried!

Your sleep was often disturbed from being in a room with so many others.

We never got a moment to ourselves, to be alone, to process our day or our situation.

We had to hide tears after lights out, hide our bodies while we got changed – yet the bloody random 'housemaster' was allowed to walk in whenever! We had absolutely NO privacy during our most formative years!

I didn't get my own door until Form 5 when I was 15 years old.

Those incredibly important developmental years were full of feelings of not being safe, having to hide, having to get permission for everything, not being individual, and receiving zero affection or personal attention. We had no 'rights' and no privilege.

We constantly felt not good enough, we compared ourselves to others, and we didn't have any faith or belief in our judgement or gut instinct – how could we? We had never been allowed to be ourselves, to have our own thoughts or opinions.

We were a collective, a group… never an individual.

Add all of that to my pre-existing feeling of not belonging to my family, and I was double fucked.

When at home with my parents my father would often grumble and complain that I wanted to eat dinner around 6pm. He was used to eating later, what with work and living in Spain. But my body was conditioned to eat early. UK boarding schools will do that to you – so once again I didn't 'fit', I was a nuisance and an inconvenience.

Chapter 9
The Wank

In Form 5, a new boy started in the lower sixth; he was bigger than all the other boys, and there was something mysterious about him.

By now, my brother had left, so this was my first year of being at school without him. I felt free.

I was told that this boy was interested in me, and when I confided in a friend, she expressed her shock that such a boy would be interested in someone like me by asking, incredulously, "Him?!" In that moment, I felt so unworthy and ugly. Over the years, our friendship had gone from being best friends to mere acquaintances. She was the one who'd chosen a boy who had bullied me over our friendship, and she'd been one of the girls who'd turned against me when the grabbing incident came out.

Fast forward a bit, and the boy – The Wank – and I became an item. It was 18 months of abuse – both physical and emotional – including condescension and possessiveness to the point that I lost all my friends. Finally, as if that wasn't enough, he cheated on me.

Like I said, he was big. He was probably close to 6 ft, very broad and muscular, and he wasn't afraid to use it. He would block my path when I tried to get away from him, he'd hold me back if I tried to give as good as I got, he strangled me and left marks, and he threw me to the floor and repeatedly kicked me, leaving bruises all over.

I would try to fight back by kicking him in the balls and trying to headbutt him; if he was holding me back by the arms, these were my only options. Unfortunately, after a few fights, he became wise to my moves. Then, I was powerless against him.

I'm pretty sure he had a few fights with his housemates, too, as one night, he met me at a long prep break with a big red cut over the bridge of his nose. He told me he'd run into a branch, but now, thinking about it, I think he was punched in the face. He was a Margaret's boy.

A week or so later, we were arguing, and – as a way of trying to scare me into doing whatever it was he wanted – he threatened to pull off his very deep scab. He got his finger under the edge and started slowly tugging at it. It was awful.

He was quick to anger, quick to get jealous, and quick to make me feel shite.

It was around this time that I started self-harming. I had a Swiss Army Knife, and I used it on my arms and wrists. Drawing the blade over my skin, I would feel better as I saw the blood bead in a neat line. I didn't go deep, just enough to bleed.

Cutting made me feel in control. It made me feel alive. It gave me relief from all the emotions swirling around inside me – emotions I couldn't name, not that I had anyone to express them to.

Throughout my school years, I'd used this fairly dull Swiss Army Knife to cut my arms. I dread to think what damage I would have inflicted on myself if I'd had proper razor blades – if I'd figured out how to take my leg razor apart to use those blades.

Even today, I cannot have razor blades in my house; I know that, in the depths of despair, I would not be able to stop myself from using them.

One night – after a particularly awful argument about him being off with another girl – I stood in front of him and cut my arm badly, wanting him to see it all. I still have the scar from this one.

The pain and the blood were like a release to me. It calmed me. This was then followed later by the stinging in the bath, which was like a punishment I felt I deserved.

One Christmas, I joined The Wank in Paris, where his family lived. As a treat, we went for 'dinner and a show,' and we dressed up all fancy.

The Wank, however, behaved in his usual way and stormed off from the table.

"Does he act like this with you at school?" his family asked.

I denied it; I wanted to protect him. However, I also hesitated to acknowledge how undeserving I felt of being treated well.

That night, I got horrendously drunk on red wine, embarrassing his parents and making a fool of myself. The following day, they wouldn't talk to me; they could hardly even look at me. Thankfully, I left the next day. I think I was trying to block out my embarrassment at The Wank's behaviour – and my shame at not being able to admit what was happening.

One day, after my period was late and I became scared that I was pregnant, I called my Mum. Naïvely, I was hoping she would support and nurture me over the phone about my false alarm.

How wrong I was!

Instead, an argument ensued, and I hung up.

When I called back, my father answered the phone and told me off for starting "all of this" and causing trouble. He hardly ever spoke to me on the phone, so this was a big deal. I was sort of scared of him; he was an enigma to me. He was just this man in the background who I only saw for a few weeks of the year, and even then, only a few hours a day – if that.

Mum told me she was coming over. It was midterm, and she had never once come over during midterm before… clearly, I was in trouble!

She arrived, watched me play hockey (there's a first time for everything), and then took me to a hotel for the weekend. We could have spoken at dinner, after dinner, in the morning… any time… but instead, she chose to talk to me once we were in bed with the lights out. It was pitch black. She was angry; I was sad, disappointed, and angry. The accusations, shaming, and blaming were all just so cringeworthy.

I told her she was pushing me away.

"I am doing no such thing!" she protested.

I just felt so hurt that she didn't seem to understand where I was coming from. I was 16, we were in love, we were in boarding school… what else did she expect?

I think the conversation ended with her telling me I had to go on the Pill.

Fine! Surely all of that could have been said in the light, in a nice, calm manner, and with proper communication?

A year later, I found out that – at the age of 17 – my brother and his then-girlfriend had got pregnant, and she had had an abortion. I'm pretty sure that would have been useful to know during this exchange, but once again, I was kept in the dark! Literally!

One evening, after arguing with and screaming at The Wank on the school fields, I ran off and headed towards the main road off the school grounds. I then sat on the grassy verge, crying, hurt, and alone.

For a moment, I considered throwing myself off the verge and into the traffic.

But then I thought… what about the innocent person driving?

And… would anyone care?

And… would it hurt?

Spent and exhausted, I eventually went back to the field.

We often argued – always screaming and crying and violent – and I would usually end up hurt. One time, I got a bruised neck from where he'd strangled me and lifted me off the floor. Another time, he grabbed me by the arms, pushed me to the ground, and kicked me. I heard that some people in the village had informed the school that they'd seen him hitting me and being rough – but nothing was ever done about it.

He was no stranger to having lots of friends who were girls. These girls would often tell me how good-looking he was, and I would see him looking at the other girls or going off to chat with them instead of me.

One prep break, I couldn't find him. I'd been in trouble with the housemaster, so I was late up, and I desperately needed to talk with him. People were being shady and evasive about where he was, which convinced me that he was cheating. My instincts were buzzing.

As I walked up the path by the tuck shop, feeling sure that he'd gone for a fag with a girl, I saw them walking slowly back together, looking very cosy. She was not my friend and not someone I trusted. In fact, we'd had many fights over the years, and even now – as I write this – I can feel my heart bubbling up with all the betrayal, secrecy, and lies.

My insecurities and my jealousy went through the roof. I trusted no one, as I still hadn't learnt to trust my gut instinct. These jealous emotions were utterly overwhelming; I wanted to die just so they'd stop.

Surely I was overreacting? No one would actually do all the terrible things I was imagining, right? I think this boy and this time was my first exposure to gaslighting.

On another occasion, I ran away from him and then headbutted a wall over and over. I just wanted the thoughts out of my head.

A paracetamol overdose – which I attempted another time – didn't work either. I downed maybe 30 pills. I hoped it was enough. I threw up on my bedroom floor.

Still alive.

Why couldn't I just end my life?!

At one point, when I was trying to deal with this arsehole during my GCSEs, I decided I'd had enough, and I ran away. I called the cab company that the school always used and asked them to take me to the airport. My flight home wasn't for another two weeks, but I didn't care. I figured I would just wait in the airport – anything was better than staying at school.

For some reason, the cab company called my houseparents while I was sitting in the back of the cab, and the driver was ordered to take me back to school. I pleaded with him, begged him. I even asked him whether, if I paid him cash rather than it going on the school bill, he'd still take me. He said no, sorry.

The housemistress was waiting for me when I got back. She ushered me into the office and then blocked the door by standing in front of it. She was a tall, intimidating woman. She quizzed me and wouldn't let me leave.

Then the housemaster arrived. I was double-teamed.

The two of them badgered me with questions, making me feel bombarded and harassed. They worked as a team to push me further into the room, trapping me there.

I held my bag in front of me like a shield – until she pulled it away. I felt like I had no control over any aspect of my life. No choice in anything. If I exercised choice and made my own decisions, I was punished. No one else knew I was in their office, and I feared what they would do to me.

I cried and said nothing. I felt angry, embarrassed, and totally exasperated.

Eventually, they let me leave. Nothing happened. No one came to help me out, no one came to comfort me, no one understood.

Unfortunately, this caused a change in the way they ordered taxis for the boarders; now, it all had to go through the houseparents. From then on, no child could order their own taxi.

You'll be pleased to know that, despite all this, I passed all 11 GCSEs grade A-C. My fear of failure had been so great that I sobbed and cried before every exam. I had to prove I was worth something. For years later this awful fear of failing would illicit tears and terror at every exam, no matter how small.

On another occasion, I was leaning out of my bedroom window and talking to The Wank, who was on the path below. The housemaster came along and told us off.

Well… I blew up! I slammed the window shut and ran down the stairs so I could catch the housemaster as he was entering the house. I then screamed at him, "Fuck off!"

He told me to come back, but I stormed off to meet my boyfriend.

I thought The Wank would be proud of me for sticking up for myself. After all, I'd suffered six years of abuse from this man, and now I'd finally said what I wanted to say to him.

But no… he had a go at me too.

I was devastated; I'd thought he was on my side. He knew all the crap this man had put me through, knew all the hassle we – and I personally – had experienced because of him, and, finally, I'd said something back.

I'd been trying to protect us! To do my bit for us! To show this idiot, he couldn't tell us when and how to talk! We'd been getting shit from teachers ever since we got together, and, finally, I had said something back.

I just couldn't win!

At his sixth form dinner dance, we had an argument so bad that some passing police took me aside for questioning to see if I was OK. Of course, I lied. I did this not only to protect him but because I didn't believe I deserved any better.

During one nasty argument, with me leaning out my bedroom window and him standing on the path below, I slammed the window shut and then banged it over and over with my hand and wrist. I broke the double glazing, and a shard of glass went into my wrist.

I was shocked. I was in pain. I had to go and tell the house tutor who was on duty, as I'd damaged property and needed help getting the glass out.

Thankfully, I didn't get in any trouble, and the next day the window was replaced. My parents were never informed, and nothing was said about it ever again.

When I went to shower the next morning, and I took the bandage off my wrist, I felt faint and awful. I just about managed to make it back to my room, but I fainted in the doorway.

No one was around when I came to; I just dragged myself over to my bed. I then called out for someone to come in and asked them to go and get the houseparent. I needed a day off school.

When she arrived, I told her I'd fainted.

"You can miss breakfast," she replied, "but you need to get up and go to your lessons."

Once again, there was no care or attention, no nurturing or concern of any kind for the students.

My fears and instincts about The Wank were proved correct in my first week of work experience.

I was working in a hotel kitchen as I wanted to be a chef, but it was awful. It was just a bunch of guys, all talking shite and not making any effort to communicate with me. I was given OK jobs to do, but I was exhausted from not eating and hardly sleeping. I had no food for my breaks and no one to talk to.

My suspicions of men just wanting women for sex were confirmed when, one day, the guys were talking about a holiday one of them had booked. "She'd better not be on the rag when we go, or else I'm cancelling," one declared about his long-term girlfriend. How lovely!

On returning to school, on my second to last day of working in the kitchen, I went looking for The Wank. Immediately, something felt wrong.

Looking back, I can see that my instincts have always been spot-on throughout my whole life; I just never trusted myself enough to listen to them. I was never taught to listen to my body, to do what I knew was right for me.

When I found him, he was in another boy's room and there was a day girl in there too. He was acting weird. He seemed totally uninterested in me and kept looking at the girl, so I left.

I went back to my house, but then I decided that I wasn't going to take such shit and that I wanted the truth of the situation. So, I went back to the boys' house and asked the boy whose room it was what had been happening. He was very vague with me, which set off alarm bells again. The Wank and the girl had disappeared after I'd left.

As it turned out, this girl was known as the school slut; apparently, she gave out blow jobs here, there, and everywhere. I walked around the school for a while and eventually spotted them in the distance, coming out of the bushes from another field. I stupidly hadn't brought my glasses with me, so I couldn't make them out properly, but once they saw me, they turned together and stopped for a bit. I don't know if they hugged or kissed as they were too far away, but then she disappeared back into the bushes, and he stormed angrily towards me.

We had a physical fight. He threw me to the floor, kicked me, and then pushed me around once I got up. I was kicking and punching back, but I was just so small and useless compared to him.

He swore blind that nothing had happened. That they'd just been talking.

I was boiling with rage and hurt, shame and embarrassment.

After a few days, against my better judgement, I forgave him. Or, rather, I missed him so much that I had no choice but to forgive him. After all, I had no one else, and I had this physical need to be with him.

By this point, I had stopped eating completely due to all the stress, and while on my second week of work experience in a primary school, I nearly fainted a few times. The teachers were lovely, but I was so deep inside myself at this point that I spoke to no one and ate nothing on my breaks, aside from the odd chocolate bar. I asked no useful questions, kept falling asleep in the break room, and – if I had more than a few minutes to think – I couldn't help but start crying. I must have come across as a total state.

Once we were back on good terms and things were supposedly going well with The Wank, he dropped a bombshell – he told me the girl had given him a blow job!

Apparently, it had 'just happened,' but it was OK – he said – because he'd stopped it after a few minutes, and he hadn't cum.

I felt so disgusted and so betrayed!

We broke up for a bit after that, but of course, I was so obsessed with him – and I needed the attention and 'love' he gave me – that I got back with him again. I now understand that this is called a trauma bond. *

*TRAUMA BOND

Taken from https://www.healthline.com/health/mental-health/trauma-bonding#fa-qs :

A trauma bond is when a person forms a deep emotional attachment with someone that causes them harm. It often develops from a repeated cycle of abuse and positive reinforcement. When this occurs between partners, this is a trauma-bonded relationship.

What are the signs of trauma bonding?

All people experience trauma differently. However, typical signs of trauma bonding include:

- denial of the other person's fault
- justification of their actions
- increasing isolation from support structures
- increasing dependence on the partner

What are the 7 stages of trauma bonding?

Some people define trauma bonding in seven stages. They are:

- love bombing
- gaining trust and increasing dependency
- criticism and devaluation
- gaslighting
- submission and resignation
- loss of self and value
- emotional dependence.

At school, I felt more and more of an outsider. I knew that other people were aware of the troubles in our relationship; after all, they'd heard the screaming fights and probably knew he'd cheated on me. I took that shame on myself rather than recognising that it was about him and his mistake. I thought it meant I wasn't good enough, that I couldn't keep him, that *I was* the one lacking – that I wasn't pretty enough or good enough for him.

Every now and then, after yet more fighting, we would break up for a few days.

One evening, a girl in my boarding house came flying into the common room, all smiles and giggling, but when she saw me, she stopped dead in her tracks and started acting weirdly. Alarm bells rang in my head; instinctively, I knew what had happened.

Sure enough, a day or two later, I found out that The Wank had kissed her that night. He'd cheated on me again!

I guess you might be thinking that this was a Rachel and Ross from *Friends* type situation – and you would be right – but in my heart, I was cheated on. This time, we were done!

But he wouldn't leave me alone. He waited for me after classes. He shouted at me and kept trying to grab me. He told me he was going to join the Army and that he'd get way more girls that way than I would boys by going to uni. Errr, OK, whatever. I presume he was trying to make me jealous.

Eventually, after shouting at each other outside at lunch one day, the Headmaster came over and said he wanted to see us both in his office later that day. Immediately, I felt nervous. After all, it wasn't a normal thing – especially for me – to be called to see the Head. I decided to use the opportunity to tell my side of events.

While waiting outside his office, The Wank started threatening me. He told me he was going to take the 50p piece in his pocket and shove it down my throat. He told me he had an older girlfriend back home in Paris and that she was so much better than me. The intimidation tactics were obvious and childlike, but I was scared of him. So far, he'd been able to do whatever he wanted to me, and no one had tried to stop him. I had no protection.

Eventually, I went in to talk to the Head on my own. I was open and honest and told him how I wanted to be left alone by this boy. He said he would have teachers and prefects look out for me and keep me safe.

A few days later, The Wank started shouting at me again, and he had to be wrestled to the floor by four other sixth-formers. Seeing how violent it all was, I burst into tears. Now, I was definitely scared of him. I had no idea how far things would or could go.

Around the same time, there was a girl in the year below – a girl who had always seemed to take an interest in me. It was an odd sort of interest, though, involving lots of staring. One Saturday, after school – yes, we did Saturday school until 1.30 pm, and then it was team sports against other schools – she invited me to go to her aunt's house for the weekend. She had wanted her friend to come with her but her permission slip hadn't come through yet.

I was in lower sixth by then, and I couldn't give a shit about things like permission slips , so I just called my grandmother and asked if she was OK for me to go. She, of course, said yes, so I just signed myself out.

The weekend was a disaster.

For one thing, I had to share a bed with her little sister, who snored horribly. Also, the two of us went out on a Saturday night, but, as we were pretty young and were expected back at her aunt's house by 10 pm, we couldn't exactly do much. So, we just wandered around Leicester Square aimlessly. She was head to toe in black leather, so, of course, she got lots of attention. In comparison, I felt invisible and fat.

The next morning, her aunt made me eat this odd omelette cake thing – I cried a little while I ate it, as I told her I didn't like it, but she said I'd taken it, so I must finish it.

It would seem that the main point of the invitation was to pick my brains about the ex-boyfriend. In response, I told her to steer clear; he was trouble. I even told her how he'd hit me.

Evidently, my words had no effect, as a few days later, I saw them together at long prep break! She never talked to me again – she'd just used me for info! Info she'd completely ignored.

Later, I found out that he never bothered turning up for any of his A levels. Thankfully, I never saw him or heard from him again.

CHAPTER 10
FAMILY HOLIDAYS

We had a few holidays in my early years that I remember bits and pieces of. Driving to France. Staying in a caravan. Big flying ants nesting outside our mobile home. Me getting so horrifically sunburnt that I couldn't sleep because anything that touched my tender three or four-year-old sun-reddened skin was agony. A giant blister on my foot from sunburn that spurted a clear liquid all over the car as it popped. Blistered shoulders that were sore for weeks. Being sent to the kids' club even though I howled and cried, saying I wanted to stay with my parents. My Dad, with a fag hanging out his mouth or between his fingers, trying to persuade me to go to these clubs. Me wiggling and getting burnt as I tried to get away.

When I was a bit older, I would make friends during these holidays – and they weren't always kids. When I was six, for instance, I made friends with an older lady. Older than my parents. We would chat by the pool. One day, when my parents and Jeffrey went out for a day trip, they allowed me to stay behind in the resort by myself. Mum asked this lady if I could have lunch with her, but I couldn't find her at lunch, so I just waited for them to get back.

On their return, Jeffrey found me first and told me that Mum and Dad weren't coming back because they didn't love me anymore. I knew it was a joke, but these jokes were common and they fed into my deepest fears.

This lady – Anne – and I would end up writing to each other for years and years, and I even went to visit her on two separate occasions while at boarding school.

The following year, my family and I went to Egypt on a cruise. On this trip, I made friends with a group of three adults who were travelling together – a couple and a single lady. They were American and none of them had children. I was seven and spent most of the excursions with them.

No one found it odd, and it wasn't until I was an adult and told people about this that I realised it was a bit weird. Now, as a mother, I can see that it was very strange. Why was I spending all my time with other adults instead of my own parents?

Another memory I have of our holidays is how my father loved to sunbathe… naked. This meant he would seek out the 'nudie' beach and just hang out there. Mum would also spend a lot of time on the beach with him, going topless.

Understandably, Jeffrey and I didn't want to be surrounded by naked people, so we stayed by the pool. I just found it all very cringe. So much for a family holiday!

So, from a young age, we had to fend for ourselves. Thankfully, we were both strong swimmers, but we had no one looking out for us. If we needed anything, we had to go and search my parents out on this 'special' area of the beach.

"Keep your eyes down" was my mantra.

As I got older, they encouraged me to go topless too, but I was having none of it!

As the years went on, I made friends closer to my own age. Then, at the age of 11, just before starting at boarding school, I was befriended by a staff member at one of the resorts. Another girl and I would hang out with him and we even went to his staff quarters.

Before I left, he told me that when I was 18, he would look me up.

Lo and behold, when I was 18 and in hospital with pneumonia, I got a phone call at the nurses' station – it was him! Somehow, he had tracked me down!

It seems he had called the school and they had told him I was in hospital and which one. I hadn't started at boarding school when we met – I was just about to go – so I'm not sure how he knew who to call. Maybe he googled my name? I have no idea.

I was very vague and standoffish when I was on the phone with him. I told him I had a boyfriend.

That year was the last year I made any friends on holiday. From then on, holidays – much like any other time in my life – were spent alone and lonely.

I would sit and watch the waves and smoke my fags. I would wander aimlessly, watching the other families and children having fun. I was, once again, separate from my family. I simply didn't fit in with them, but then again, I didn't fit anywhere else either.

When I was 15, a friend from school came away with us, and we spent the week sunbathing, getting drunk, and being hungover. My Dad spent most of it being pissed off at me that I wasn't eating enough, embarrassing me in front of my friend, and making me cry.

When we were alone, we had a great time – until, one night, when we got far too drunk!

Some other kids, who had taken offence to our fun over the week, stole our Club Med money (you didn't pay for things with money there, but with a booklet of coloured cards that you bought on arrival, so you didn't have to carry cash around), and my brother was disgusted at us for being drunk. Some boys we'd been hanging around with were pissed off at us too. So, to get away from all this, we went to the nightclub and two staff members started dancing with us.

After a bit, they asked how old we were and quickly backed off. Then, this leery man – who'd been eyeing me all week – came over and wouldn't back off despite my telling him I wasn't interested. The boy who I'd been hanging out with some of the week came over to try to intervene, and things got a bit silly.

Once he'd left, we went and sat in the hall outside the nightclub, and that's when I saw someone walking towards me who looked rather familiar – it was my father! The boy had gone to find him!

He hoisted me up until I was standing and then took us both back to our room.

My parents' room was next door to ours, and as we neared the room, I saw my mother standing in the hallway in her flowery nightie. It took all my effort not to burst out laughing. She thrust some water at me and told me to drink.

The next day, we were banned from drinking for the rest of the holiday! We were also subjected to many evil eyes and disapproving looks from both the parents and the brother. FFS… we were 15, on holiday, and having fun. No one got hurt!

I don't recall any more family holidays after this one, though we did go to Las Vegas with my grandparents and uncle's family one year for some family celebration – a few milestone wedding anniversaries, perhaps?

I can only recall bits and pieces of that trip. Other than a cool helicopter ride over the Grand Canyon with Jeffrey and awkwardly staring in wonder – and not talking – at the huge chasm, there wasn't much to report... other than, once again, feeling a sense of not belonging.

Of being an outsider.

Chapter 11
Hockey

My sport was hockey, and I played goalkeeper. As it turned out, I was pretty damn good at it; at 16, I was asked to play for South East England.

One day, my sports teacher took me and two other girls to tryouts, though I don't think I really knew what was happening. I was sent off to practise with the other goalies, and I did my best. Obviously, I impressed them, as by the end, they had sent all the rest away and had the best goalscorers come over and shoot against me – often eight of them all at the same time.

My teammates didn't get in, but I was asked to return.

I presume that, as I was the only one, my teacher could no longer be bothered to accompany me. Instead, I was told to meet some woman and her kids in the car park; they would take me to the next tryout.

However, my anxiety, coupled with low self-esteem and the absence of anyone to support me, made me hesitant to attend the tryouts alone. So, I took a friend with me, but that pissed off the stranger Mum in the car.

When we arrived at the tryouts and I saw all the different girls doing their thing, I froze. I just got too shy and overwhelmed by it all, so I sat it out with my friend and just waited to be picked up.

This Mum then complained to my teacher that I had brought my friend along, taken up space in the car, and not even participated.

It was unfair. I needed help; I needed support. Instead, I just got in trouble.

I was still offered the place but I turned down the opportunity, as I was also reluctant to give up what little free time I had. Every moment of every day was already dictated for me – now, not just half my weekend would be taken up with commitments, but the entire thing. No thank you. I was also feeling so alone with it all. Maybe if I'd had someone cheering me on, I would have done it.

I was told off for making a decision by myself. For saying no. After being berated by the housemaster I was told to stay in my room, but I immediately slipped out and called home, thinking they would have my back. Wrong!

Dad answered as Mum was out, and I told him what had happened with the tryouts. Just like everyone else, his voice was filled with anger and disappointment. He didn't support my decision or the fact that I had made the choice for myself.

Another lesson learnt – don't make your own decisions that best suit you. Just do what you are told! People please. Put yourself last. No matter what.

In this school, you received a tie for sporting excellence. Half colours and full colours. These were ties I really coveted, and my brother had gotten neither, so it was even more of an achievement when I got my half colours.

In sixth form, I remember crying to my mum as I was worried I wasn't going to get my full colours in that day's assembly. It meant so much to me. So few people earned them that to be awarded this tie was a great thing.

Shockingly, during the assembly, I was the only one called up for full colours for hockey. I felt so proud, especially because I was certain I hadn't achieved it.

I called Mum immediately, afterwards, so excited to share my news and hoping she would be as thrilled as me.

"Oh right," was her reply.

Obviously, it wasn't such an achievement after all. My excitement and pride vanished in an instant.

I was so confused… she knew I'd wanted it, she knew I was scared I wouldn't get it, and she knew how much it meant to me. So why wasn't she pleased?

I don't recall my parents ever telling me they were proud of me – at least, not without me asking first.

This leads to my academic achievements…

My grade cards each term and my reports each year were good. Although I was no scholar, there was never anything below a C, and mostly As and Bs. My parents never commented. No matter if the card was full of As – not even 1As, the best you could get – I still got no remark.

What the fuck did I need to do to get a reaction?

How perfect need I be to get noticed?

I had proved to myself, over the years, that my grades didn't matter. An A or a C got the same reaction from my parents – nothing. This made me develop perfectionistic tendencies.

What had Jeffrey done to get so revered by them? To get a free pass to do whatever he pleased? To crash my mum's car time and again, yet still be allowed to drive it each time it got fixed? To smoke in front of them with no repercussions? To be able to act so free and just be himself?

Why was it so hard for me?

They were always so proud of him.

Texts between Mum and Jeffery:

CHAPTER 12
PNEUMONIA

At the beginning of February 1998, I started to feel pretty ill. I developed a cough and had some breathing troubles. Stupidly, this didn't stop me from sneaking off to smoke, but hey, ho, teenagers are dumb!

The day the Feb half-term started, I could hardly get out of bed – and that is where Mum found me when she arrived to take me away for the week's holiday.

We were due to fly to Scotland to visit my brother – and even Dad was coming! – for my 18th birthday.

We stayed the night with my grandparents, and because I was feeling so crap, she took me to their doctor. This doctor said he could hear nothing in my chest. "Not even a cold," he declared.

I couldn't eat dinner and hardly slept at all that night. The cough was so painful, and even breathing was hard – it felt like a broken rib was stabbing me in the lung.

On arriving at the airport, something happened – either the flight was cancelled, or we were late, I don't remember which –

that meant we had to get the coach from Heathrow to Gatwick. That was a nightmare journey: an hour on a bus with no water and nowhere to sleep. I felt so sick and tired I could barely take it.

Once at the airport, Mum asked for a wheelchair for me, as – by this point – I was struggling to even stand.

I had to dash(slowly) to the loo, but I didn't quite make it; I threw up green bile all over the toilet and the floor. I felt like I was dying!

It was suggested that, before I get on a plane, the paramedics should check me out. Mum agreed, and while I was being wheeled to the gate, I saw Dad waiting. I pointed him out, and she went and got him while they started their checks on me.

They began by giving me a really high flow of O_2 through a mask. It was way too much, however; it didn't allow me to catch my breath at all, so instead, I began to cry and panic. Mum did actually look worried at this point!

They said I most likely had a chest infection. They recommended that I not fly and advised me to go to the hospital for a proper assessment, as I likely needed antibiotics.

Now began the difficult task of getting everyone's cases off the plane and getting me to the hospital.

The ride to the hospital was a tough one; I was so tired but also in so much pain and discomfort that I couldn't relax. No one held my hand or reassured me.

Once at the hospital, I was assessed in a side room, sent for X-rays, and then left to wait for hours. My temperature was so high, but I felt like I was freezing, and I couldn't stop shivering. They took off all my blankets and put a fan on me. It was so uncomfortable.

To make matters worse, my period started, and I had diarrhoea. They wouldn't let me use a loo, and trying to squat over a cardboard bedpan was precarious and extremely difficult. The stench in the room really lingered!

I had to confide in Mum, asking her to go in my suitcase to get my tampons – no easy thing for me! It was all just so demoralising and humiliating.

The nurses finally came to move me to a 'proper room.' Thankfully, I was alone, and I had my own bathroom, but it was so lonely, and I felt abandoned when my parents left. But they didn't leave just then; they stood talking to the nurses, right in my line of sight, for ages. Eventually, I had to go and ask them to move, because it was so upsetting seeing them while sitting in my bed, all alone.

At the moment they did actually leave, I was moved to a ward. It was a room with three other people and a shared bathroom, which didn't feel so lonely.

That night, I experienced hallucinations; I saw a man with a moustache leaning over me. The next day, when I asked the nurses about it, they informed me that there were no male doctors or nurses who fit that description.

The next week was a blur of blood tests, IV antibiotics, doctor visits, countless different nurses, awful food, and pain. I moved wards so many times.

In one of the wards I was on, there were several older ladies with me. One was suffering from dementia and she would cry and scream for her Mum. They would put her in the corridor at night so she wouldn't disturb the other patients but, to be honest, it made no difference.

One day, she came out of the loo with diarrhoea dripping down her leg, leaving a trail all over the floor.

This same little old lady scared the crap out of me one day as she came over to my bed, all smiles, and bent down to me, getting closer and closer. I thought she was going to bite my ear off! Instead, she just kissed my cheek, and then one of the other ladies rushed over to lead her away. I felt bad for feeling the way I did, but I was just so scared. I'd never been in a situation like this and, when I was alone – without my mum with me – it was scary.

By this stage, my nerves were just so jangled by anything and everything. I was so untrusting of everyone around me and of my own instincts. I even told a male medical student that he could examine me – but I wasn't going to take my top off for him!

It turned out that I had a very bad case of pneumonia, which quickly caused septicaemia and anaemia. The anaemia wouldn't have been helped by the fact that I'd been trying to be vegetarian for the past year.

The doctors told me that if it had gone on much longer, I could have died.

So, instead of us going up to Scotland, I spent my 18th birthday in the hospital – with my brother coming down to spend a few days with us.

Laughing hurt. Breathing hurt. Lying in certain positions hurt. The IV antibiotics hurt while going in. They kept having to move the cannula as the veins kept collapsing.

First, they did it with a syringe in my cannula, which wasn't so bad. Then, once I moved wards, they did them by a drip, which took nearly 30 minutes for each dose to finish. This hurt the longer it went on. On the weekend Jeffrey was visiting, he tentatively asked the nurse if they could go back to the syringes. She angrily said they couldn't do it that way.

They often seemed annoyed at me on this ward.

There were strict rules about the curtain. About when you were allowed to draw the curtain, and when it had to be open. Most of the time, it had to be open.

I wanted it closed for privacy, as I didn't want everyone to be able to see me all the time. I was young and sick... just let me close the bloody curtain!!

Eventually, I started receiving the drugs I needed in the form of pills, which was much more comfortable.

Mum would visit every day, staying most of the day, and she'd bring me food as I hated the hospital offerings. She would arrive around 10 am and leave about 5pm. They woke us every morning at 6 am and turned the lights off at about 10 pm. She did what was needed, but I had no emotional support.

I remember, one day, crying uncontrollably. Sadness was just flooding through me. The young, married lady in the bed near me was in tears that day as well, but she had her husband, Mum, and Dad there to give her cuddles. Why was no one loving me that way? There was no joking at my bedside. There wasn't even any talking.

Mum pretty much ignored me that day; she acted like I wasn't crying. But, then again, that was the story of my life. No one really acknowledged my emotions. My thoughts. My words.

I grew up thinking and believing I was inferior and unimportant. So, it was normal for my emotions not to be validated or even noticed. Maybe they thought that if they didn't speak of things, they would just go away.

I tended to speak quite fast too. I figured I always had to get my words out quickly because it wouldn't be long before I was cut off, or before the person lost interest in me and what I was saying.

Two weeks later, the doctors said I could leave. I wasn't feeling 100%, but I could leave the hospital if I really wanted to. I wanted to.

As I couldn't fly, we had to get the train to Madrid. It was a sleeper train and I felt sick for most of the trip. It was such a relief to get home!

Due to being ill, I missed a term of school and, on my return, the main comment I got was how the girls would love to have had pneumonia if it caused the kind of weight loss I'd achieved… what twats! All that pain and misery for a few measly kilos!

After my illness, I found that I couldn't cope at school; I was constantly tired and sick. Eventually, people started to listen, and it was decided that I would go home again to study for my A levels.

This time, it turned out that I had a nasty urine infection. I also needed some breathing physio, and as my eyes weren't focussing well, I needed some eye physio sessions – apparently, this was caused by the infection.

Teachers would fax Dad past papers and assignments, and after I'd completed them, his PA would fax them back to the UK.

So, instead of being at school, I sat at home and did loads of mock papers. I spent most of the time doing English Lit and studying nutrients for food tech. I, rather arrogantly, figured that as my spoken Spanish was alright – especially while drunk – and as I was actually IN Spain, I would be fine on that subject.

The end of the summer term saw me returning to school to take my exams. "Head down and just get it done," I told myself. I didn't have many friends at this stage, but I did have a boyfriend in Spain who was waiting for me.

I left school the same day as my last exam. Just packed up my crap and left. I said goodbye to one or two people, but that was it – I was outta there. No more room searches, no more prep, and no more feeling like I lived in a fucking prison.

I ended up with two Bs and a D in Spanish.

Being given my results over the phone and hearing the D first was devastating. I had failed! Obviously, I didn't get any comfort, commiseration, or reassurance that I actually did great.

After completing a few weeks of summer school, teaching five and six-year-olds in Spain, I changed my plan of becoming an English teacher… mainly because teaching them had been an absolute nightmare! Rude kids, moody teachers, no one telling me what I was supposed to do or what the rules were and then getting pissed off when I didn't know the rules… no, it wasn't for me.

So, I needed a new plan.

I had always set my heart on doing an English degree and becoming a primary school teacher, but now I was going to follow my dream of being a travel writer.

You have to remember that I had no guidance, no help, and no one to bounce around ideas about my future with. The most the school had done was provide us with a room full of university prospectuses and given us just half an hour per week to visit it in groups of four. Of course, as horny teens, all we'd done was flick through them while flirting and joking around.

My initial plan, when The Wank had been around, was to train up as a teacher while he worked and then live together. And then, of course, get married and live happily ever after. I even had a cheapy ring! I hadn't considered that there might be a need for another plan!

Back in the UK, I had looked around a few unis by myself. Figuring out train routes, organising the open days and the interviews, staying in B&Bs and finding my way around places... I did it all alone.

But now, with my new plan, I wanted to see other universities that offered a travel course. The internet was not exactly massive in 1998, so researching this stuff while in Spain was not the easiest, and Mother didn't want to go back to the UK with me to see any. So, I had to make up my mind, on a course and location, completely blind! I spent a day on the phone calling universities and asking questions... that would have to be enough.

It had been assumed my whole life that I would go to uni. There was never a question about it; no alternatives had ever been discussed or mentioned or visited.

Also, due to being so ill from the pneumonia, it was almost a given that I would take a year off to recover fully before going back to the UK for uni.

During this year, I was diagnosed with chronic fatigue syndrome. I was constantly fatigued; no matter how much I slept, I never felt refreshed. If I sat down, I would fall asleep within minutes; my head was always foggy, and I had no strength to do anything. Even walking from one room to another was exhausting.

I just hoped it would be better by the time September came around.

CHAPTER 13
BOARDING SCHOOL CONTINUED

At boarding school, we used forms instead of years. So, Form 1 was age 11, Form 2 was age 12, and so on. Lower sixth was the first year of A levels, and upper sixth was age 18 and the last year of A levels.

There was a very comprehensive uniform list, including how many pairs of knickers and bras we would need and what colours we were allowed.

There were also random hierarchy rules – for instance, only prefects were allowed to use certain pathways or gates. There was a prefects' lawn that was basically a shortcut; I dared to walk along the side of it once and was reprimanded by the kindly house tutor, though after Form 2, she stopped being our house tutor.

Sixth-formers were allowed to go straight to the front of the meal line, so if there was a big group of them and you'd been queueing up for half an hour, you didn't get any further along in the line. You could spend most of your lunch break in the refectory just waiting to eat!

The younger you were, the lower down and less regarded you were. Unfortunately, as I moved up the school, these unspoken rules were abandoned – so once I was in the sixth form, I had no more rights than a first former. This was desperately unfair in my eyes as I had spent so many years waiting to use these coveted shortcuts… and now everyone was using them!

I also didn't have the confidence to queue-jump.

The food we were given was often burnt or, alternatively, undercooked. I have no memory of having any favourite meal or food. It was either barely edible or totally not! Ketchup was my best friend; I would use it to make things manageable, so when it ran out, I went extra hungry.

Food fights in my first few years weren't common, but they were so much fun when they did happen. I recall at least three!

In the beginning, there were wooden benches to sit on. The unfortunate side effect of benches, of course, is that if you were sitting on the end and everyone else got up… you would go flying off, as if you were on a see-saw. This often resulted in the entire table coming crashing down, with you and everyone's trays going with it. The mess and embarrassment were hard to live down.

Thankfully, after a year or two, these benches were swapped out for seats.

As you entered the 'food hatch,' you would collect a dented, metal tray. They were often still wet from going through the industrial dishwasher and, often, they'd still have pieces of food stuck to them.

You would then take a plate from a boingy plate distributer thing. Again, you would need to take out a few until you found a clean one. It was all just so unappetising.

The boarding house provided bread for toast and huge tubs of margarine. There was nothing else. Matron would make toast ahead of break time, so by the time you got down to the house, it was cold and bendy. The tiny kitchen would be heaving with girls making tea and eating this cold toast, so even if you wanted to get some, it was a battle – and most of your break would be spent trying to get a snack. We only had 20 minutes to rush from our classes, return to the house to change books, go to the loo, grab a drink and a snack, and then hustle back to class before time ran out. It was all such a rush and so stressful. There were, of course, punishments for lateness.

All breaches were reported to the housemaster and, in the worst-case scenario, you would be sent to personally tell him about your offence. I would knock on his door and then stand in the hallway, my heart pounding as I waited for him to answer. His 'front' door was inside our boarding house.

He would then poke his head out and make you stand there until he was 'ready' – and who knew how long he'd make you wait!

Then you'd be ushered in and would have to stand in front of his desk as you told him what you'd done. It was worse than having to tell a parent.

If you ever needed a teacher at any break time, you had to go to the staff room. You could spend ages standing by the doors, though, having teachers walk right by you – they were purposely ignoring you as they couldn't be bothered to go and find whoever you needed.

Eventually, someone would come and ask who you wanted, and if you were lucky, they would actually come out to see you.

I hated going to the staff room.

All male staff were termed 'Sir', and the very few females were called Mrs X. I would often 'accidentally' call Mrs P 'Sir,' however, as she was so manly.

We had to stand whenever a teacher entered the room and stand aside if they walked past us in the hallway.

There weren't actually that many staff members, so if you didn't like a teacher, it was tough luck – you had no other options.

There was no calling out in class; you had to raise your hand.

I got in trouble many times for sitting on steps around the school.

"Do you sit on the steps at home?" I would be asked.

Well… no, but there are actual bloody places to sit at home! I would think.

The staff were authority figures, and there was nothing pastoral about any of them.

One would throw board dusters at the 'troublesome' students. Once, an English teacher struck a boy in my class. Corporal punishment had only been abolished in schools in 1986, so some of these teachers were old enough to be of the generation that had been allowed to hit children.

Our Latin teacher was utterly useless, but his classes were a hoot. He would lean on the front of his desk with his eyes closed while he droned on and on and on. Or he'd write things on the board, with his back to us, for extended periods of time – while we, of course, messed around something chronic… throwing biscuits at each other, swapping seats, sending letters, and laughing silently until tears ran down our faces. I loved these lessons as it was the only time I ever felt like I was having a laugh.

When it came time to choose GCSE subjects, you were limited in what you could choose as they put the subjects in groupings, and you could only choose a certain number from each group. It was all very difficult and frustrating.

The only toilets were back in the boarding or day houses, so you had to trek for ages to get to the loo – and it wasn't common to be granted permission to leave class to go to the toilet.

During my time in Sutton House, there were approximately 30 or 40 girls spanning across all the years. In the main corridor were the houseparents' front door, the big yellow phone, Form 1, 2, 3, and 4 dorms, the common room, the Head of House show, the kitchen, three toilets and two bathrooms, and the matron's day room.

The showers were down in the underground changing room, where there was also the washing machine for the matron to wash our underwear and other bits. This was a cold and muddy room. All muddy boots and shoes were stored here, and the floor – which was stone – was freezing.

It was a horrible place to have a shower. Because it was always draughty, the shower curtain would constantly blow around, sticking to your wet body.

We had a rota for 'knicker duty,' which was where we would have to distribute the clean underwear to each girl's cubby hole. This was not a pleasant job. The tights would all be tangled with the knickers and bras. And, with a house full of girls going through puberty, you would often come across stained knickers.

By the time I got to lower sixth, this was changed to everyone having a mesh bag in which their underwear was washed, so you just had to touch the bags, not the actual garments.

The regular washing – uniforms, towels, and sheets – went to the real laundry, which was elsewhere in the school. All the ladies in there smoked like chimneys, so everything came back stinking of fags.

New sheets would be placed in the cubby holes every two weeks so you knew when it was time for 'sheet change' day. This was the same for 'towel day,' although towels and duvet covers were our own, not provided by them. The sheets were flat sheets, so at the age of 11, I had to learn how to make a bed with proper corners.

The other side of the house – the other side of the main front door – was the newer side, so it was a bit nicer.

My fifth-form dorm – the biggest dorm – was there. It could sleep eight girls.

There was another laundry room there, plus the main shower room, which had eight showers, two baths, two toilets, and sinks. It was freezing in there too.

At the end of the hall was the storage for sports kits, and during the summer, the floor would teem with Daddy Long Legs. The trunk room was also over there, where we would keep all our trunks and suitcases.

Every year, you had to pack up everything for the summer – as, when you returned that September, you would be allocated a new room and new roommates. You had no idea who or where you'd be until the day you came back. At the end of some terms, we had to clean out our rooms as they would rent out our boarding house to visiting students while we were away.

Up the stairs was the sixth-form corridor and bathroom, which had three toilets, two baths, and two showers. No one was allowed up there except the sixth form. I was caught up there many times, looking for girls who had phone calls. Of course, I would get told off for being up there even though I was just trying to help! As the phone was in the corridor by the younger girls' rooms, it would be up to us to answer the phone and go racing around the house trying to find people.

Eventually, the housemaster decided that, during prep, the phone had to be off the hook – which upset a lot of people as that restricted the times people could use the phone.

As I've mentioned, the phone was in the main corridor, so if you were on the phone, you had no privacy – and, sometimes, you couldn't even hear yourself as the girls hung out in the hallway, especially after evening call over. Or they would line up along the wall, waiting for the phone, making you feel like you had to rush.

The allotted time was supposed to be just 10 minutes for each person, but many girls – particularly those in the sixth form – would take hours, and no one could say anything about it.

As it was a pay phone, Mum arranged for me to have a BT card, where I had to dial in 12 numbers and a PIN number before the phone number. It was like a credit card for the phone, I suppose; it meant I never needed cash for the phone. Stupidly, I gave this number to The Wank, and then had to change the PIN code after we broke up as he carried on using it. I'd only given it to him so he could call me, but he used it to call his family in France and goodness knows who else!

Before getting my phone card, I would have to have a 10p piece to use the phone. I would call Mum, and then she would call me straight back.

You were screwed, however, if someone else called while you were waiting for your call back.

What if you didn't have a 10p piece?

The phone was a source of comfort but also extreme stress.

Weekends were boring. The bells that ran our lives went off at the same time as during the week. 07.10 first bell, 07.20 second bell, and 07.30 final bell, before morning call over. Then it was up the hill to the refectory for breakfast.

On Saturdays, we still had a half day of school, but Sundays were a bit different.

There was morning chapel, in full school uniform, for those at school, and then the rest of the day was free for us to do whatever we wanted… but, of course, there was nothing to do!

We would smoke, wander around, watch TV, and just get bored.

Once a month, instead of Sunday morning chapel, there was evening chapel, where everyone had to come back early from exeat and get in full uniform to attend an hour-long service.

To go anywhere other than your lessons, you had to 'sign out' using the book by the front door, and if it was discovered that you hadn't signed out or not received permission, you would be punished. One of the punishments was to write the lines and titles in the sign-out book.

Not that there was anywhere to go, of course. The school was very rural, surrounded by fields. The tiny village had just a post office and one village shop.

So many students smoked, and we had all kinds of hiding spots, but the teachers were always on the lookout for us. Sometimes, they would launch an invasion; multiple teachers would raid these hiding spots from multiple directions at once in an attempt to catch us.

It would then be detention, and, for those in Sutton, we had to personally go and tell Mr P.

The housemaster of Margaret's was a big smoker and drinker and would often leave his classes in the middle of lessons, be gone for 10 minutes or more, and return red in the face and stinking of fags or cigars.

Once I got to form 5 or so, the matron would occasionally invite me for a sneaky fag out the back of Sutton with her. She even invited me to her house one day during the school day for an hour's break; we had a few fags and shared a bottle of beer.

I found it hard to trust her, though. Sometimes, she seemed 100% on the kids' side and other times on the school's side, so I learnt to be careful about what I told her – which, of course, drove a wedge between us.

I don't believe she had any medical training. If you needed medical attention, therefore, you had to go to the 'San' (sanatorium). The first nurse I met there was a scary lady. By Fifth Form, there was a younger, nicer nurse, but I could tell she often wanted to be left alone rather than do her job. I had to spend a few nights in the San in Second Form. It was so lonely.

We had to be inventive about where we stashed our fags and vodka, especially as we had sporadic dorm checks.

One weekend in Second Form, I decided to tie-dye some white cut-off jeans. Others had already done it at school, so I didn't think it would be a problem.

I prepared everything down in the laundry room: the dye and the jeans in a bucket. The instructions stated it had to be stirred constantly. So, when call over came around, I rushed upstairs to ask if I could miss it just this once to stir my jeans!

Once the jeans had been in there for the allocated time, I drained the bucket in the sink, tidied up, and laid my sopping wet jeans on a black bag outside to dry.

Come Monday, I was in trouble!! As I'd asked to miss call over, they knew it was me who had done the purple dying, and they accused me of using the washing machine to do it as, somehow, there was watery dye in there. I swore I hadn't used the machine. I hadn't. I knew I hadn't, but they were adamant I had. I didn't even know how the washing machine worked.

This went on for hours!

Eventually, one of the cleaning ladies realised that if you emptied a full bucket into the sink, somehow the water went down the pipes and into the washing machine. I was let off.

That was a stressful time, and, of course, no one apologised to me.

The uniform was stiff and scratchy and the blazer heavy and itchy. It was made of some odd tweed that stunk of wet dog when it got wet. You needed to ask permission in lessons to remove your blazer, and you were never allowed to be around school without it.

There was the PE kit too, which included Aertex polo shirts. If, like me, you didn't wear a bra, you ended up with very chafed nipples, especially during the winter.

After Sunday chapel, you were allowed to put your home clothes on, or as we called it, mufti.

Mr P would do fire alarm drills at ridiculous hours – 2 in the morning, 11 at night... all times when we would be in our PJs, asleep, or when the older girls would be in the shower. Then he would keep us out in the cold, drizzling night for at least half an hour while he 'checked' the house and told us off for being so slow.

There was never a moment when I wasn't on high alert. Consequently, my nervous system was a mess, and this led to me getting terrible stomach aches from about the age of 13. As the years went on, they got worse. It was put down to stress and constipation, and I was given Gaviscon. On occasion, I could barely move; I was in so much pain.

As more years passed, and I was still having these pains in university, Mum decided to take me to a doctor in Madrid. This lady decided I needed a rectal exam and told me to get on the bed on all fours. It was mortifying; I went head first the wrong way, so the bed started tipping up with me on it… with my trousers around my ankles.

The doctor then lubed up and stuck her fingers up my bum; it was horrific.

When I was all finished , I had some Vaseline on my trousers, and Mum kept asking me what it was, but I was too embarrassed and ashamed to tell her.

This doctor decided I had IBS, so I started taking Metamucil, a laxative drink.

By the time I moved to New York, I was still getting breathtaking stomach cramps that would come on all of a sudden and stop me in my tracks. I couldn't move or breathe, and it felt like my tummy was going to rip apart inside me.

I was too embarrassed to go back to any doctor, though, so I just hoped it would go away.

By 2012, a few months after Ivy was born, I was away for the weekend with Dickhead at a spa, and I had a go in a sauna. All of a sudden, I felt like I was going to faint and be sick at the same time. I managed to get back to our room and I barely moved for the entire night.

Once home, the diarrhoea started. I figured I had eaten some bad chicken, so I just carried on.

The diarrhoea didn't get better, though; it got worse. I was going through the night, through the day – up to 20 times a day – and feeling so weak, tired, and sick. At the same time, I was trying to look after baby Ivy and then Jacob when he got home from school.

Dickhead, of course, had to have it spelt out for him – on numerous occasions – that, first thing in the morning, he would have to get up and help with the kids as I was stuck on the toilet.

They would be crying in their beds, and I would have to shout to him from the loo, telling him to go to them because I was 'indisposed.'

After a few weeks of my symptoms getting worse, I went to the doctor. They wanted to send me to see a gastroenterologist, but the wait would be long. Thankfully my parents paid for me to go privately and within a few weeks I was having a colonoscopy.

Alone in my private room, I had to drink two litres of a laxative solution to 'clean me out,' ready for the camera. And, wouldn't you know it, my period started while I was there, so I had the embarrassment of having to tell them that too!

It was agony for me. Even though I was sedated, it was like I could feel every movement of the pipe going in and out of my insides. They said that if I needed another one, I should be totally knocked out for it.

I was diagnosed with Crohn's disease.*

*CROHN'S DISEASE

As described by https://www.mayoclinic.org/diseases-conditions/crohns-disease/symptoms-causes/syc-20353304:

"Crohn's disease is a type of inflammatory bowel disease (IBD). It causes swelling of the tissues (inflammation) in your digestive tract, which can lead to abdominal pain, severe diarrhoea, fatigue, weight loss and malnutrition.

Inflammation caused by Crohn's disease can involve different areas of the digestive tract in different people, most commonly the small intestine. This inflammation often spreads into the deeper layers of the bowel.

Crohn's disease can be both painful and debilitating and sometimes may lead to life-threatening complications.

There's no known cure for Crohn's disease, but therapies can greatly reduce its signs and symptoms and even bring about long-term remission and healing of inflammation. With treatment, many people with Crohn's disease are able to function well.

Symptoms

In Crohn's disease, any part of your small or large intestine can be involved. It may involve multiple segments, or it may be continuous. In some people, the disease is only in the colon, which is part of the large intestine.

Signs and symptoms of Crohn's disease can range from mild to severe. They usually develop gradually but sometimes will come on suddenly, without warning. You may also have periods of time when you have no signs or symptoms (remission).

When the disease is active, symptoms typically include:

- Diarrhoea
- Fever
- Fatigue
- Abdominal pain and cramping
- Blood in your stool
- Mouth sores
- Reduced appetite and weight loss

Pain or drainage near or around the anus due to inflammation from a tunnel into the skin (fistula)

Other signs and symptoms

People with severe Crohn's disease may also experience symptoms outside of the intestinal tract, including:

- Inflammation of skin, eyes and joints
- Inflammation of the liver or bile ducts
- Kidney stones
- Iron deficiency (anaemia)

I've conducted research on the correlation between childhood trauma and the prevalence of autoimmune diseases – it is a high percentage.

Once, I asked on my boarding school Facebook group how many people had autoimmune diseases – FYI, Crohn's disease is an autoimmune disease – and the response I got was astounding!

I knew it would be lots, but the vast range of diseases these people had was incredible. There are only about 500 people in this group, so for so many to be ill with long-term, incurable illnesses is quite something.

This was a very sick time for me. I had no clear treatment plan. I was given an iron infusion at one point, as my iron was so low that I was finding it hard to function; I couldn't even write straight as my hands were always shaking so much.

Every drug they offered had nasty side effects.

Eventually, I settled on one oral drug that seemed to help for about a year, but then it started giving me bruises up my legs, and my hair started falling out. I was taken off it, and that's when the chemo drug was suggested. This would lower my immune system, which was a worry, as I had young kids constantly bringing bugs home from school. I was also worried about catching something and then passing it onto my mother when she started her chemo.

For this reason, I had my children vaccinated against chicken pox. We had to pay privately to get this done. Mum never realised that the main catalyst for me doing so was to protect her. Or she just didn't care… because, of course, we should do that for her.

I have no doubt that my childhood, with the constantly raised cortisol levels, is what caused my Crohn's. No doubt at all.

We were raised in a culture of silence. If I ever did say anything to my mother, she would laugh and say, "It can't be that bad."

The whole British stiff upper lip was designed to protect the abusers and make the accusers doubt themselves – and have others not believe them. "Is my memory correct? Did it happen that way? Was it really that bad?"

This leads children to doubt their own realities, especially when being told, "It never did me any harm" by others who had been to boarding school. It made you feel weak and pathetic for having an issue with it. This is victim blaming.

I still struggle with the idea that other people do not live with constant flashbacks to their childhood. Racing thoughts, nightmares, and triggers are not staples for the average person. Coming to terms with the fact that the chaos in your head isn't seen as 'normal' can be a tough reality to grasp.

I do not disagree that boarding schools throw out independent and resilient teenagers, but being overly independent is a trauma response, and what young child needs to be that resilient anyway?

Chapter 14
Tom – Madrid

Having decided I was done with boys at school, I met a man when I was home in Spain for the summer holidays. My parents had moved from Milan to Madrid soon after I started boarding.

I was 17, and he was 26. Expats tended to hang out together, and one night, when we were all out drinking, we ended up in a group together. I fancied Tom immediately, but he was with another girl. When I asked her how long they'd been together, she said seven years – totally off-limits, then!

The following week, we met up again, but this time, she wasn't there – and Tom made it clear that he was into me. I, however, was confused… because of the girlfriend. He told me they weren't actually together; they'd known each other for seven years, and they only got together whenever she was in the country. Looking back now, I realise that she saw me as a threat and was trying to lay claim to this man!

Despite the age gap, we hit it off and began what became a three-year relationship. Although a lot of it was long distance, we lived together for one of those three years.

During this time, I was a jealous mess. Previous to us living together, he was still living in his childhood room at his parents' house and only had a temp job doing translating. He had no ambition, no direction, and no plans for the future. He also drank way too much.

I would have fits of rage when he and his friends, who were girls, would do things that made me jealous. These girls knew exactly what they were doing. They hated me, and I reckon it was because I upset the status quo. He wasn't theirs anymore. He was no longer at their beck and call. He was the only guy in the group and he was mine. A 17-year-old. who the fuck did I think I was?

On nights out, I would come back from the loo to find one of their heads in his lap or vice versa, or them sitting and talking, legs touching, all close up.

I am sure you can imagine how a young girl – with my insecurities, no self-confidence or self-esteem, and terrible jealousy issues – would have a massive problem with such things!

One night, when I saw this happening, I stormed off. I sat alone outside, crying as I tried to decide what to do.

When I returned, I was berated by one of the girls – she told me I was selfish and immature and that I just wanted attention. This girl actually worked for my Dad and was a friend of my brother. I believe she wanted both my brother and this guy, so – in her eyes – I was the enemy. Also, I always felt that she thought I wasn't pretty enough to have Tom but that she should have whoever she wanted.

A few of the girls in the office would join, or I would join them on nights out or to a concert, and I think the general consensus was that I was a spoilt little rich girl. I'm not sure what gave them that impression, however, because I was quiet and timid, and I certainly didn't flash the cash or make a thing of my Dad being their boss… but man, did they make their feelings known!

Occasionally, when I got drunk during those years, I'd start sobbing and crying as if my heart were breaking. However, other than a "You OK?" I would pretty much get ignored by everyone I was with.

I think they thought I was doing it for attention, and so the best thing would be to pretend I didn't exist. It was agonising to be feeling so much inner pain and turmoil and yet not be comforted or even spoken to. I would get evil eyes from the girls and eye rolls and "stop it" from Jeffrey if he was there. Tom would just carry on drinking as if nothing was happening.

It made me feel invisible and irrelevant.

I definitely wasn't doing it for attention. I wanted to be happy and enjoy the evening instead of feeling sad and desperate. These were the emotions that I couldn't always keep in: the sadness and loneliness and all the abandonment I'd experienced in my life.

Once I left school at the age of 18, Tom and I had a year of playing house, him being out at his new job, me being at home, recuperating and acting like a housewife. Not only was I recovering from pneumonia/septicaemia, but I was also now recovering from stitches in my arm and hand.

We had been at a housewarming party for Jeffrey and his flatmate when something had set me off. I don't know if it was the noise, the crowd, not feeling comfortable, or what… but I needed to leave the party in a hurry. Jeffrey wanted Tom (and possibly me?) to stay, so he made me feel bad for 'making him leave.' When we finally got out of there, we had a big argument, and – as I was storming down the street – I whacked my arm against a restaurant window in anger and it shattered! I stormed off and then slowly became aware of the pain. Tom was running behind me, calling my name and telling me to stop, that I was hurt. The pain hit me fully when I looked down at my arm and saw the blood flowing – and a chunk of flesh hanging off.

An ambulance was called from a nearby bar and a kindly lady held a wad of tissues to my wound with so much pressure it made me cry!

I think, in total, I had to have about 17 stitches. I was still covered in blood as I got a taxi home.

These massive arguments, where I would fly off the handle, were not uncommon. I simply could not control the rage. The feeling of not being loved and not feeling heard would just bring this red mist over me. I would do and say things I was ashamed of. I would cry hysterically. I would also remember how The Wank had made me feel and it would set me off all over again. It was all-consuming.

No one understood and no one tried to either. I would just be ignored or given dirty looks.

Once again, I was an outcast. An annoyance. A pain in the arse that no one cared about.

Because of this, my loneliness and my self-hatred intensified. Every single day, I would cry – often about how I looked. I was positive that if I were thinner, I would be loved more. If I were better at this or that, I would be loveable.

I'd had perfectionistic tendencies at school – my space was used as an example to others, I would strive constantly for the best grades, and I always tried to hand work in early. I would panic if I had too much work, as I needed to get it all done immediately.

Now, I had to keep a perfect home, cook new meals from scratch each night, and do all the jobs in the house 'just so.' If it became too overwhelming – like the time Tom's sister and her husband were coming over for lunch and I had to have the house 'perfect,' even though he wasn't helping at all – I would flip out. I was just so obsessed with it all, needing this perfection so deeply within myself; my whole self-worth was attached to this perfection, and his not helping… well, it just proved how unloved I was, how used I was, how unimportant I was. I often felt like I must be crazy.

We broke up a few months before I was due to start uni.

One day, in the flat – after yet another argument – he told me he no longer loved me. As he left, he said he would call my parents to come and collect me, and just an hour later, they arrived to take me and all my stuff back to their house.

Not much was said other than, "What happened?" I didn't feel like they really listened or cared.

That night, I told my brother that we'd been arguing a lot and that we hadn't had sex in a while.

He just replied, "Yeah, that would do it."

As I needed extra love and care during this heartbreaking time, I latched onto my mother. I would follow her around the house and try to hold her hand. I just couldn't be alone.

She tried to shrug me off and was obviously getting fed up of me.

I think if she had just sat with me and snuggled up to me, making me feel safe and secure, I might have healed quicker. But we didn't have that kind of relationship.

CHAPTER 15
UNIVERSITY

A week or so before I started at university, Mum and I went back to the UK to get all my stuff ready.

She drove me from Crowthorne in Berkshire all the way up to the Lake District, where I'd be attending uni. It took us about four or five hours.

On arrival, we went to find out where I was meant to be. Fortunately, the boys we met knew who I was from my photo, and two of them took me to my halls/house.

I was popular with the boys in the first few weeks. Maybe it was the strawberry blonde hair, I don't know.

One guy told me I would be perfect if only I had green eyes! This same guy ended up pursuing me later on in quite an aggressive way; after a few months, the other guys in my house had to physically remove him and tell him not to come back! FFS!

Life at uni was much like it had been at boarding school – meaning I felt alone and confused. I was always on the outside of everything. Despite my best efforts, I never felt cool enough or involved enough.

I made and lost friends, drank too much, didn't have enough lectures or work to do, and carried on with my eating disorder – in fact, I upgraded it to include doing way too much exercise.

I lost so much weight my periods stopped.

At my slimmest, I got down to 47 kg and was wearing size 6 jeans. When I went shopping with my mum and I showed her the size 6 jeans I was fitting into, she looked so pleased and proud of me.

Despite this, at the age of 19, I made an appointment to get liposuction on my hips and thighs. All I could see there was fat.

I saw three plastic surgeon consultants. One said there was no fat to take. Another told me that massaging would help with the appearance of cellulite, and the final one said I had 'saddlebags' and that he could sort them out for me.

Mum didn't come over for it, so I had to get a taxi to and from the hospital as part of the package.

I felt so sick and awful the morning following the op. I tried to shower off all the blood on my legs, but I felt so faint and dizzy that I just wrapped myself in a towel and lay on the bed, which had been stripped while I was showering. A nurse walked in and shouted at me for lying on an unmade bed.

I hobbled around campus for weeks while the bruising and swelling settled.

At uni, I looked – once again – for love and affection in all the wrong places and had some unsatisfactory and regrettable experiences.

During my summer holidays in Spain that year, a guy friend and one of my girlfriends joined me. For the first week, it was just me and the girl, and we had a good time. The second week –

when the guy arrived with his brother – I shut down. Even though I was the one who'd invited them, I felt like they were taking advantage of my parents' hospitality. They left crisp packets all over the floor in the lounge, they didn't clean up after themselves, they ate all the food, and they weren't overly polite. I kind of stopped talking to them.

The whole thing was just so awkward, and our friendship never really recovered.

Once they left, I started going out alone again, meeting lots of guys. I was also introduced to my brother's friend's brother's friend, Ivan. At one point during that holiday I dated five guys on the go at one time – just casual dating nothing sexual - and when Mum found out, she looked proud!

This was incredibly confusing for me because when – at the age of 12 – I had somehow let slip at the dinner table that I'd kissed two boys, she called me a slut!

We started hanging out in a foursome: me, Ivan, his friend (the brother), and his friend's girlfriend. Ivan and I quickly became a couple. We had lots of fun and my Spanish improved massively.

One day, we went out, and his ex-girlfriend was there. He spent so much time talking to her, looking at her, and smiling at her that I got incredibly jealous. That night, when he barely spent any time with me, I felt so ugly and sidelined.

We argued about it in the car, and – while very drunk – I tried to exit the car, even though we were driving very fast. He thought I was crazy and, after dropping me home, he never spoke to me again! I called and called, left messages and texts, but I guess I'd gone too far… Either that, or he'd gone back to his ex.

So, that was the end of my foursome nights out and the end of those friendships.

As I'd fallen out with my best friend over the summer holidays, it was awkward when we came back for our second year of university and had to share a house – while not speaking! There was one other girl who I'd been good friends with at the beginning of the first year, but we'd grown apart, so it wasn't exactly the best living situation… especially as the three-storey house had fleas!

Through booze and partying, however, my friend and I started talking again, and all seemed fine.

In the second year, lectures became harder. The introduction of new people and a change around who lived with who changed the dynamic, and life wasn't the same as it had been in the first year.

In the first week of the second year, I met this Year 1 guy; we had fun on a night out and hung out for a bit. The moment I found out he was a virgin, though, I backed off and stopped talking to him – there was no way I was special enough to take someone's virginity. I found this out while we were in bed, kissing. I stopped immediately and asked him to leave. I explained that I was not the girl to lose his virginity to, and despite him begging and sending me letters over the following weeks, I was adamant that I wasn't good enough for that.

Next, I met another year 1 guy who was in fact older than me. We slept together early on and spent all our free time together. My jealousy increased, however, as I saw how he interacted with other girls when I wasn't about. A few of his mates, who seemed to like me at the beginning, stopped liking me the longer we stayed together – maybe because I was taking his time away from them, or maybe there was just something about me that people hated…

He was strange in that he was very immature in many ways but mature in other ways.

Eventually, I met his family and stayed overnight at his family home. His parents smoked pot in the house, and he seemed to have a 'matey' relationship with them rather than parent and child. Maybe because of his age? I was 20 at the time, and I think he was 23.

The longer we were together, the lower my confidence became. Surely, it should have been the other way around? During this time, self-harming became a problem again for me, and soon, it became a regular thing.

He gaslighted and pressured me into doing sex acts I never wanted to do – but ones I felt I had to do or else I would lose him. I hated every second and swore that, from that time on, I would never again do something I didn't want to do with any guy. I would rather lose the guy than compromise my integrity.

I told Mum how unhappy I was at uni and how I wanted to live alone; would they pay for a flat for me? I said I would pass my driving test and drive myself to and from lectures each day. It seemed like the perfect solution. I would have my own space and privacy while still getting my studies done.

She wasn't convinced. "I'll come over and rent a place with you," she stated.

What?!

I wanted to say to her, 'I'm 20 years old, and now you want to be there for me? *Now* you want to come over to the UK and live with me? Where the fuck were you when I was 11 and needed to live with my mother? This is a fucking joke, right?!' What I said was, "I will be fine by myself." No solution was found and we left it there for the time being.

After a few months of more arguments with the guy, seeing him flirt with girls who were my 'enemies,' and generally getting more and more unhappy, I took a very drunk overdose of paracetamol and cut up my arm.

Annoyingly, he called an ambulance and I was taken to hospital. The first nurse I came into contact with told me, "What a stupid girl you've been!" I spent two or three days in hospital, and on getting out, my mother arrived.

We had dinner together – during which I cried – but she didn't really want to talk about it. She seemed to believe that her mere presence would somehow stop all of my emotions.

She joined me at my follow-up appointment with the hospital psych team, and it was agreed that it might be best if I left uni for a while. By now, my parents had moved to Barcelona.

The boyfriend gave me a letter from his mother, telling me how selfish I'd been to do this to him.

I knew in my heart that he would cheat on me if I left, but I was so unhappy that I simply couldn't stay. I even knew who he'd cheat on me with – a girl we'd met together on the train one day.

A few weeks later, after trying to maintain a relationship on the phone and hearing more and more about this girl, I couldn't get in touch with him and I just knew… I knew exactly what was going on.

He finally admitted that it had been going on for a few weeks by that point!

So … here I was, back living with my parents, with no boyfriend… starting again.

CHAPTER 16
BARCELONA

The house they had in Barcelona was by far the biggest we'd ever had. The grounds were vast and the house sprawling. The garden was home to noisy frogs, as we had a pond with a fountain. My father dealt with them by whacking them with a spade. When I heard about this, I wasn't happy at all. Surely there was a better way?

I have always been an avid animal lover and any cruelty to them upsets me badly.

When we lived in Naples, we would often see markets where bunnies were sold; they'd be hopping about in cages, wanting to escape. Five-year-old me thought they were for pets – until something happened that taught me otherwise. One customer pointed one out and the lady picked it up by the ears, took it behind a curtain, and then – the next thing I knew – there was a horrific shriek. Moments later, the skinned rabbit was presented to the customer, still steaming. I was beyond upset!

From then on, whenever I saw a rabbit in a butcher's window – which, sadly, is a common sight in Mediterranean countries – I would get very upset and remember that day.

In Barcelona, I partied hard, going out alone in an effort to 'make friends.'

Now, I can see that I was searching for acceptance, love, companionship – and yes, friendship too – in all the wrong places. Once again, I was making mistake after mistake, feeling disgusted and filthy the next day, and swearing I would stop… only to do it all over again the next weekend.

Surely, the right guy was out there somewhere? I just had to find him! I knew this wasn't the right way to go about finding my soulmate, but I had no idea what else to do. I was so lonely.

If, however, by some miracle, I did find a guy who was gentle and sweet, I would run a mile! It was just so far out of my comfort zone and I didn't know how to handle it; it wasn't something I knew what to do with or felt I deserved… even though it was exactly what I was looking for.

I just kept thinking that these guys must be freaks, that there must be something wrong with them if they liked me enough to treat me well.

A few of them lasted a few weeks or months, and some left me devastated when they ended; other relationships ended by me, and I had to be firm to stop them from pestering me after it finished. A few guys got nasty when I turned them down, and a few got mean and exasperated if I got upset when they dumped me… it was a rollercoaster of a time.

Eventually, I got fed up with living at my parents' house and wanted more privacy, so I asked them to pay for a flat for me. This time, they did. I was sad, though, that I had to leave behind Webby, my black and white bunny. She was huge and was allowed to run free in the garden.

About nine months after moving out, I got a call from my mum that I needed to come home as something had happened to Webby. It took me an hour to get there on the train and, when I arrived, I discovered she was dead.

I didn't get much of an explanation; Mum looked angry as she told me, quietly, "She was up on the balcony (we had a garden that overlooked the front of the house, so not technically a balcony) and I could see her as I reversed the car, but then I couldn't see her anymore. I got out of the car to look for her and I saw her behind one of my wheels. Think how awful it was for me, having to pick her up and get her to the vets."

I was devastated, though the story also sounded 'odd' to me.

I dug Webby a grave in the flower garden that she liked to hang out in and then sat with her on my lap while I sobbed into her fur.

After a while, Mum came over and brusquely told me to put her down as I couldn't sit there all day.

Her attitude hurt so much. Where was the compassion and empathy? The cuddles and kindness?

I put Webby into the hole and covered her with soil. I then lay some stones on top to indicate her final resting place before going back to my flat. I didn't want to stay with Mum any longer than I needed to.

By this point, I had completed my Personal Training qualifications and was starting a massage course, so I set up a PT business. It actually did well to start with. My clients were mainly expats, friends of my mum or brother, or people who'd seen my adverts.

Unfortunately, those same adverts also invited a few weird calls.

One was a guy with a foot fetish. I saw him as a client for one session, and then I received a 3 am phone call:

"Hey, next time we train, can you wear high heels?"

"Er, no… I need to wear trainers."

"What about sandals?"

'No, it needs to be trainers for the support."

"Can you go barefoot?"

"I'm gonna say 'no'… bye."

It took me a few minutes to realise what had just happened!

Another one was through texts; this guy said he'd met me at some bar and wanted to meet again… but I'd never been to the bar in question.

He messaged again a few days later, and as I was lonely, I thought I'd play along.

He said he wanted to meet and hang out, and then he told me his age – 40ish, if memory serves. He also said he was short and balding! As I didn't ever want to be shallow or discriminatory, however, I agreed to meet up.

It was OK. He came with four of his mates and they were all giving me so much attention and buying me drinks. There was no attraction on my end, but I thought it might be a fun night.

After a while, a young, attractive guy started talking to me. This pissed the older guy off, and a big argument ensued. The older guy was threatening to call the police (for what, I have no idea), and I was actually worried in case I'd done something that could get me in trouble!

I then randomly bumped into a woman who worked closely with my dad – expats hung out in all the same places, remember?!

In the end, I left with the younger guy, Moi. We dated for a few weeks until I realised he might be a good guy. He had a job, a flat, and he treated me well… so he had to go!

When I ended things, he asked if he could see me and then brought me a gift, trying to persuade me to stay with him. I explained that, in a few months, I would be moving to America, so I couldn't afford to get attached to him. I felt bad because he did seem like a genuinely nice guy – but whenever I was around these 'nice' guys, my anxiety went through the roof.

My experiences with men in all the countries I've lived in have been so confusing. I admit that much of it is on me, who I've chosen to hang out with, and how far I've gone with them… but in my defence, I was lost and searching. I confused sex with love and was always left feeling worse than before.

I just wanted affection and someone to love and care for me.

I had yet to find it.

My experience of men had been nothing but bad, and at that point, I believed all men were the same. Even if they didn't do it straight away, I believed they would eventually show their 'true colours' and hurt me.

They thought of women as sex objects, and they treated them as such.

Even my own father… I had noticed how his gaze would follow young women; the more scantily dressed, the better. He did it all the time, not just once or twice. So, I came to expect it; I knew his type.

One night, when we were having a family meal in a restaurant, I saw him eyeing a thong that was poking out the back of a woman's trousers. Why? He was married, and he was there with his family! Besides, he was too old for these girls; they weren't much older than me. Wasn't it disrespectful to my mother? To me?

I mentioned it to her once and she just shrugged it off and said, "It's just looking."

I, however, couldn't cope with it. Not from him or my partners.

My brother did it too; I would see him follow women with his eyes. His type was J-Lo.

How would I ever find a guy who didn't do this?

During this time, I made some very risky choices: getting in cars with strangers to go to other bars/clubs, walking off with groups of people I'd only just met, trying to start fights with people over ridiculous things... I was lucky nothing bad happened.

Even this Colombian guy, who I'd spent a summer with in Barcelona, and who professed his love for me over and over, and even proposed multiple times... even he would do it. We'd be sitting together, eating or drinking and chatting away, and his eyes would follow some hot young thing that had just walked past.

Another guy would comment on how pretty such and such looked – without giving any compliments to me.

I think it would be fair to say that every guy I've ever been with has either looked at or commented on other women, beaten me, or cheated on me.

Dickhead (more on him later) was the first to not do any of those things while also not treating me sweetly enough to put me off. Obviously, this made me believe I had to stay with him, as he was the only one who didn't cause me excessive feelings of jealousy.

Chapter 17
Working Out

At some point in my late teens, I became obsessed with exercising. My mood was shit if I didn't work out, and I couldn't start the day until I did my workout.

It started with one hour of a video/DVD. I had a Cindy Crawford one, and then an Elle McPherson one. Then I started adding in half of another video, and then working out on my mum's elliptical trainer. Then I'd do it all with added ankle and glove weights. Sometimes, I would do a run as well.

In my first year of uni, I carried on working out, though I only did two DVDs at a time. People were confused and mystified by my schedule.

In my second year, my room had mould around the windows, and after cleaning this off one night, I then proceeded to go for a run. Halfway around, I found that I suddenly couldn't breathe; I couldn't catch my breath. It was terrifying. It was so dark and I was all alone, though I managed to get home. The only person I told about this was my mum.

Despite this, I simply HAD to do another workout. Realising that it probably wasn't a good idea, however, I opted to do a strength yoga video instead of something more strenuous.

I would put my body through so much because my head made me do it. I was obsessed. I was controlled and dictated to by my mind and these 'rules.'

I was strong. I was fit. I would push myself so hard. I would cry from exhaustion, but I would still push through – I had to.

I wanted to try bodybuilding as I was loving my muscles and how strong I felt. Mum, however, was dead against it and discouraged me every chance she got.

Then, once I moved out of my parents' house in Barcelona and got my own place, I joined a gym that was a bus ride and a walk away. I spent about five hours a day there, and each day was based around whatever classes I wanted to do at the gym. I'd take classes, do rowing, lift weights, go on the stair climber, and then end with an hour's spinning class. By the end, I would be dripping with sweat, my hair limp, and my body full of endorphins.

Soon, I befriended one of the trainers at the gym – or, rather, he started taking an interest in me. I was never planning on taking it further, though, despite him asking me out. I wasn't very good at saying no to anyone – for anything – so I either just ignored his calls or made up excuses as to why I couldn't join him at a party or whatever.

One day, we were talking at the gym about working out and I asked him what he thought I should be doing, working out-wise, for my body. In response, he said that my butt was too big and that I should do more to slim it down.

I was devastated. What more could I possibly do?! I was dragging my tired body out of bed every day, I was falling asleep on the bus, and I was spending five hours in the gym… and it still wasn't good enough.

After that, I called Mum to get some reassurance that I wasn't fat, but she wasn't very helpful. Or maybe I just couldn't hear what she was saying.

Not long after this incident, I stopped going to the gym. Instead, I bought a multi-gym for my flat and started my private training business from there, rather than going to people's flats to do their sessions in their own homes.

Now, my workout was a DVD, an hour of weights, and a run or a bike ride down to the beach, an hour away. These rides would happen after dark and on main roads.

One time, I got lost on my way home. So, I called Dad, asking him to help me figure out where to go.

"I am on _____ Street. How would I get home from here?"

"No idea, sorry," he replied, and that was that. He didn't call or text me later either to check I'd got home safely.

I didn't exactly have a six-pack, but I was very strong; I had so much stamina and endurance for weights.

One client commented that my arms looked bigger than the last time she'd seen me; this would have insulted me before, but I took it as a compliment now. I felt able to protect myself.

Eating was still an issue, and I was still restricting, but it was less of an obsession; now, exercise had taken over.

I understood that my new obsession was an issue – the exhaustion, falling asleep, not really wanting to work out but HAVING to – but I had no one to turn to and no way of getting help.

Chapter 18
New York

It was time to move to New York City!

I wanted a life like the girls in *Sex and the City!* The confidence and glamour and friends… I wanted it all.

My family all thought I was so dependent and weak – well, I would show them. I could do it all alone. I knew I was strong and capable, yet deep down, I craved validation from someone else. I longed for reassurance, for someone to confirm that I was right, that I was strong. All I ever got, however, was the opposite.

For any plan I had, Mum would ask me the most basic of questions with the assumption that I hadn't thought of these issues or planned properly. I took offence to this. I would show her!

So, I found a massage course in New York City and off I went; I turned up with my suitcases and a week's booking in a disgusting rat and cockroach-infested YMCA, and I began my new life.

Why massage, you ask? Well, when I started doing my personal training, I also did a massage training course in Spanish. I got a distinction and mostly enjoyed the course.

Obviously, I have a story about one of my clients asking me to test my newfound massage skills on him, which I was happy to do to get into some practice. Suddenly, he turned over and asked me to massage his chest. I said we hadn't learnt that yet.

"Just the same as the back," he declared.

He then whipped off his towel, exposing his nakedness, and pulled me on top of him! To make matters worse, he lived with his girlfriend, and this was in their bedroom!

I pushed him away, stood up, and left. He was definitely not going to remain a client after that!

When I arrived in the US, I already knew two guys. The first I had met online; internet cafes were a thing at this time and, in my search for love, I started chatting with this guy in NY.

I then met him in person when my parents and I were over there for something or other – they actually let me sleep at his house for the two nights we were there!

I met up with him again when I moved to New York and he became my boyfriend for a little while – until it became clear that he had a porn problem. I would go into his flat and there would be porn videos, used tissues, and a pump bottle of lotion on the coffee table.

In the beginning, I let it go, but once it became clear that it was carrying on despite us being together, I gave him an ultimatum: me or the porn.

He chose the porn!

The other guy was someone I'd met when I went over with a friend to view the massage college; we had a night out and then I ended up going on a date with him.

I didn't seem to have any trouble meeting guys. My brother would comment how I was always getting looked at when I walked down the street, though I didn't see it; I was still far too hung up on the way I looked. I always felt too fat and ugly. For countless years, I would cry daily about the way I looked. I believe this is called body dysmorphia.*

BODY DYSMORPHIC DISORDER

From https://bddfoundation.org/information/what-is-bdd/:

"Body Dysmorphic Disorder (BDD) is characterised by a preoccupation with one or more perceived defects or flaws in appearance, which are unnoticeable to others. This perceived flaw is sometimes noticeable but is usually a normal variation (e.g. male baldness) or is not as prominent as the sufferer believes.

The older term for BDD is "dysmorphophobia", which is sometimes still used. The media sometimes refer to BDD as "Imagined Ugliness Syndrome". This isn't particularly helpful as the ugliness is very real to the individual concerned and does not reflect the severe distress that BDD can cause.

As well as excessive self-consciousness, individuals with BDD often feel defined by their flaws. They often experience an image of their perceived defect associated with memories, emotions and bodily sensations – as if seeing the flaw through the eyes of an onlooker, even though what they 'see' may be very different to their appearance observed by others.

Sufferers repeatedly tend to check on how bad their flaw is (for example, in mirrors and reflective surfaces), attempt to camouflage or alter the perceived defect and avoid public or social situations or triggers that increase distress.

> They may, at times, be housebound or have needless cosmetic and dermatological treatments. There is no doubt that the symptoms cause significant distress or handicap and there is an increased risk of suicide and attempted suicide.

This used to happen all the time, though it's less common now, and I'm working hard on it: I would feel repulsed in my own skin. Through research, I have found that this is usually caused by trauma and can go hand in hand with body dysmorphia.

> Most people with BDD are preoccupied with some aspect of their face and many believe they have multiple defects. The most common complaints (in descending order) concern the skin, nose, hair, eyes, chin, lips and overall body build. People with BDD may complain of a lack of symmetry or feel that something is too big, too small, or out of proportion to the rest of the body. Any part of the body may be involved in BDD, including the breasts or genitals.
>
> BDD usually begins in late adolescence (16-18 years). However, milder symptoms of BDD often precede this from about the age of 12-14. However, it may take up to 15 years before presentation to mental health professionals."

It is a horrific sensation to despise your own 'inner skin,' to feel like you want to rip your skin off and reach into your head and pull out all the thoughts and feelings hiding inside.

It is indescribable and utter agony.

My family didn't help me in this matter. Mum would just say, "You look fine," or, "Compared to other people, you aren't fat…" or, "There's nothing wrong with you."

One question that came up a few times when I first arrived in NY was, "Does the carpet match the drapes?" I found this offensive, and it took me right back to my boarding school days when people would laugh at me for the colour of my hair – and, obviously, the colour of my pubes. Evidently, only brown or blonde were acceptable pube colours! It was just another aspect of myself that I couldn't change – yet was deemed 'wrong' – and that contributed to my sense of not fitting in or being desirable.

Anyway, now that I was in the Big Apple, I needed to find somewhere more permanent to live. It became clear quite early on, however, that living in Manhattan was going to be beyond my means; my plan was to start working once I started college and to pay my own way, so I needed somewhere affordable.

I called Mum from a payphone, as I had yet to sort out a mobile (this was in 2002), and when I cried down the line, saying I didn't know what to do, her response was, "See, I told you."

This only made me more determined to sort things out by myself.

They might have been funding me financially, but everything else was me. I wanted to prove that I could do it all myself because they thought I was weak and pathetic and needy – well, I'd show them. I knew I could do it; I knew I was strong.

I arrived in October and my course didn't start until January. After realising that Manhattan wasn't the place for me, I started to look in Brooklyn. I stumbled upon an estate agent and this woman showed me a few places.

When I chose one, I asked her to speak to my parents on the phone, which she did – she assured them that the area I was going to be living in was good. As it turned out, however, it wasn't the greatest of neighbourhoods! I stayed in that apartment for a few months before finding a much nicer one.

Even though pets weren't allowed in this apartment block, I decided I wanted a dog. After all, I'd wanted one for so many years. Matron at school sometimes brought in her son's cocker spaniel called Webster. I loved seeing this little guy come in and would enjoy giving him a stroke. So, I promised myself that one day I would get a spaniel and call it Webster.

This was now my goal.

Of course, Mother told me it was a terrible idea.

I went around all the shelters, but none of them had pups or spaniels. So, I went to some pet shops – back then I knew no better! – and, in the last shop, I found a brown and white American cocker spaniel. I had finally found my Webster!

It took me five days to get together all the cash I needed to buy her; I could only take out $200 a day from the ATM and she cost $1100. So, I put a deposit down and visited her a few times while I waited.

When I finally got her, they gave her to me in a box, and I rather stupidly got on the subway with her. I had a backpack full of her stuff and then her in this box. At one of my stops, I took her out of the box to give her some love and then, of course, when the train arrived at my station, I couldn't carry her, the box, and the bag at the same time!

Luckily, some kind people helped me out, but even with that tiny bit of help, I felt:

1. Stupid for needing help.
2. Stupid because I had obviously made such a palaver that they had seen I needed help.
3. In their debt!

Looking back now, I can understand why they noticed me – after all, I had a teeny-tiny, adorably cute, eight-week-old puppy in my arms! Besides, people feel good about themselves if they help other people.

But even these small gestures of assistance made me anxious and made me question my worth. I was so conditioned to doing everything for myself and by myself that when help was offered, I wasn't sure how to feel about it.

On my first day at the Swedish Institute – where I'd be learning all about massage therapy – I realised I'd made the right decision. These were my people; they seemed so in tune with emotions and touch and kindness!

We would hang out and laugh, and I felt accepted (most of the time). We shared all kinds of things, and I could mostly be myself. We hugged each morning when we got to class and hugged again when we left each day. We'd text when we weren't together, and in general, we were all very close!

Once or twice a week we had practicals, where we had to practise massage on each other. I felt no embarrassment at all – until a boy I fancied joined our class. And, wouldn't you know it, the first time we buddied up to do a practical, it was on my worst area – thighs and bum! FFS!

He and I flirted something chronic during classes and in breaks. Then, one day, we ended up in the back lifts together – I'm not sure how – and he decided that I wanted to see his dick! I don't remember it, though, so presumably, I didn't look when he flopped it out of his fly! Why do guys do this stuff?! I guess it would be the equivalent of sending a dick pic these days.

Not long after this, my friends and I bumped into him at the movies – we were leaving while he was arriving. I decided to stay and watch another movie with him, hoping this would move our friendship on to the next level. Of course, I had to push it – I could see him losing interest, so I had to ramp it up to keep him interested!

We sat at the back, and after a bit, we started fiddling with each other's hands. Though, to be honest, he didn't seem very interested.

At the end of the movie, we both went our separate ways, and the next thing I knew, he was dating a girl in the other class. Obviously, she was tall and pretty and had a good figure. She was American and confident – I couldn't even compare!

We never worked as partners or flirted again. I would never cheat or be a party to cheating.

Outside of class, I made friends in the dog park. There were only certain hours each day that the dogs could be let off the lead, so every morning and evening, you would see the same people out with their dogs – and, of course, you gravitate to certain people. I made lovely friends this way.

Two much older guys asked me out on dates, and as I found it hard to say 'no' to anyone, I agreed – even though I had no interest in either of them. For me, the dates were awkward and embarrassing. They must have been in their mid to late 30s at least. I was 22.

One day, while walking Webster in the park, I ventured further than I had before and found myself in some woods. I saw movement out of the corner of my eye, soon realising it was a totally naked man who was hiding himself behind a tree!

Fuck! I thought. What do I do? Do I let on that I saw him by turning around and scurrying away? Or do I carry on walking like nothing happened?

I decided to take my cue from movies, where if you haven't seen the bad guy, it's OK; if you can't identify them, they'll leave you alone.

So, I carried on walking, staring straight ahead! Thankfully, I didn't get jumped on – or worse.

Around this time, I tried online dating – and started to learn about people being very vague and limited with the truth. Most people were not at all as they'd described in their profiles!

I met some weirdos and got some abuse when I wouldn't meet up with them again – until I met David. He was much larger than the usual types of guys I dated, but we got along well, and he seemed honest and nice, so I put any concerns about not finding him attractive aside.

We were going great, having fun, he met my mum, and I met his family – and really loved them. As things got more serious, we talked about moving in together, about getting married. On a trip back to Spain to visit my parents, I even told Mum about us possibly getting married and she was thrilled!

By this point, we'd been together for just three months and I was just 22 years old!

We made so many plans for him to move into my flat, but at the last moment, he would always find an excuse… his main one being that he didn't make enough money – even though he had a really good job as a manager and earned a good salary. I felt rejected. And the more rejected I felt, the worse the relationship became. In the end, it came down to an ultimatum: split up or move in together.

He moved in.

By that time, however, I'd had to fight for it so much that I just felt so unloved – I mean, if he'd really wanted me, I shouldn't have had to fight so hard, right?

Well, it all fell apart pretty quickly; we broke up within a week or so of him moving in. I felt so guilty as he cried while he was packing up his stuff.

Not too long after, I fell a bit in love with a guy called Graham.. He had a big husky dog and we would meet most evenings in the park to chat and walk the dogs.

I would practise my massage on him and then we would fool around. I was a lot more into him than he was into me, and I knew I couldn't pursue him because I would ruin the friendship – especially as many of his friends outside of the park were girls. We kept our friendship/relationship very superficial and, although I did invite him on a couple of nights out with my massage school friends, we kept it all very light.

He did seem to get a bit jealous whenever I brought other love interests to the park, though… which made me wonder why he didn't want something more serious with me?! I think we had a communication issue, and our matching low self-esteem stood in the way as well.

A few months before I was due to leave the US, he moved away and I was devastated. I wrote him a letter, talking about our missed opportunity and how I would miss him. We hugged goodbye and he even kept in touch for a few weeks after he'd left. We spoke more then than we had done in all the years in the park.

I explained how, if we got married, I could get my green card and we could try to have a relationship – I think the idea of that freaked us both out, though, and things quickly fizzled away. I had dreams about him, and our missed opportunity, for years. I don't honestly think we would have been good together, though; we were way too different. He's now married with two kids and looks very happy.

In my continual search for love, I 'met' a guy online. We texted, emailed, and eventually spoke on the phone. He was in his 40s and had a 16-year-old son. He was a therapist. He lived in San Francisco so, of course, I had to go and meet him properly. A friend looked after Webster and I hopped on a plane.

Within minutes of arriving, I realised what a mistake I'd made. He was a lovely, kind man, but... he was nearly as old as my father! I wasn't attracted to him at all, and when we went to dinner, I felt like people probably thought we were father and daughter. I was mortified.

I went to my hotel after dinner and cried. I missed my dog, I missed my lovely apartment... what on earth was I doing?!

The next day, he had to work, so I went exploring – though not proper exploring, as I had no idea where to go or what to do. I was all alone, and it was a long, cold day.

That evening, he took me to his house, and I saw all the photos of his son, who was only six years younger than me! He told me that his son's girlfriend was a contortionist, which – apparently – was a sexy thing. I thought that was a gross way to talk about his son and his 16-year-old girlfriend.

I wanted to go home. So, I apologised and told him that I missed my dog and that I needed to go back to New York.

Thankfully, he was very kind about it; he helped me change my flight to two days earlier than planned.

When would I learn? When would I feel complete just as I was instead of continuously searching for this unobtainable love?

When I arrived back in the UK after completing my massage course in New York, I met Mum at the airport. When we were on the tube, she started talking to me.

After a long flight, when I was exhausted and emotionally drained from departing the place where I'd been happiest with my best friends, she began criticising my career choice as a massage therapist, claiming it wouldn't bring in much money.

I was aghast. What? Why would she say that now? What possible point could there be to her words in that moment?

I cried and shut down.

Chapter 19
Medical

The first time a doctor looked at my vagina, I was 15 or 16 years old; The Wank had given me thrush, so the doctor wanted a little look. She was respectful and had a quick peek, and that was all.

My second internal gynaecological exam happened when I was 17 years old. I went to our family doctor alone because I had an ache low down in my pelvis. This doctor spoke English, but not always with the best use of words. And, no matter the reason for my visit, he would always find a way to get me to take my top off.

Mum was usually with me and never queried this.

It was similar to how, when I was around 10 or so, we went to see an English doctor in Milan and he felt the pulse in my groin. Why? I have never had this checked since, in all my 44 years. Maybe if he had checked all my other pulses too, it wouldn't have been so strange, but he didn't.

Anyway, I turned up alone and he decided he needed to do an internal. He didn't explain anything; he just walked down the hallway, with me following, to the examination room. He then pointed to the loo and asked, "You need to piss?"

I was disgusted at his terminology in this medical setting; I felt shame course through my body.

When we arrived at the room, thankfully, there was a nurse there to chaperone.

I think I knew to expect the speculum – though it was very uncomfortable and embarrassing – but what I wasn't expecting, and what he didn't explain, was that he would insert two fingers inside me and feel around.

I was mortified and felt violated and confused. The only other time I'd experienced this was with The Wank, when we were being sexual.

Eventually, he finished and told me to get dressed. The lube was still inside me and I felt disgusting.

I didn't stop to go to the loo and clean up, as I was desperate to get home and be somewhere I felt safe.

Getting in the shower at home, I tried to wash away the shame.

Had he been inappropriate? Will that happen again?

I sobbed and cried and cleaned myself as best I could.

A few days later, the doctor called and spoke to my mother; I don't recall why, but I had to go back for another examination.

Embarrassed and ashamed, I explained that I wouldn't go if he was the one doing the examination. I didn't give any details – just a few tears to show I was serious.

Mum agreed that it would be nicer if it was a lady doctor.

My next experience was in America. I believe it was a routine smear test, or perhaps I was having irregular periods again, I don't recall.

The doctor was a man, but he was gently spoken and respectful. As it turned out, I had abnormal cervical cells, HPV, and precancerous cells. Mother was visiting, so as soon as I heard the C word, I invited her into the office to hear what he was saying.

We had actually been arguing before the appointment about my having to leave the USA when my visa was up, as she didn't get how much I loved my life there.

The doctor said I would need an operation, and it all sounded easy enough.

David – who I was seeing at the time – said that he'd be there for me on the day, to take me to the hospital and wait with me. When I told him I had to be there for 6 am, however, he backed away and said that was too early – but that he would pick me up after.

WTF?

So, I had to get a taxi to my operation! The doctor was surprised when he saw I had no one with me, as everyone else did.

Everything went well. I would need smear tests every six months for a few years, then yearly, and then – if all went well – I could go back to having them every three years.

When I came back to live in the UK, I had to find a new gynaecologist to start the tests again. Having only heard negative things about the NHS, I was distrustful of it; I had only known private healthcare for most of my life. So, I found a doctor in London and went for an appointment.

He was an older man in a huge room with a big ornate wooden desk and a bed with stirrups over on one side. The rest of the room felt empty. I got up on the bed, and he inserted the speculum, and then he walked away from me to go and get whatever else he needed. I had no sheet to cover me.

So, I just had to lie there, flat on my back, legs splayed, feet in stirrups, with a speculum opening me up to the world. Even describing it now, my heart is hammering, remembering the indignity and embarrassment of it all. I was 24. I had paid £200 for this lovely experience.

Why did I keep getting treated so poorly? Why were these men so unfeeling in their execution of such a delicate procedure? Was it me? Or was this simply how the world was?

Most of my experiences since then have been OK. I moved over to the NHS, and ever since I've always been treated well and with respect and dignity.

At 31, I had issues with my fertility – which I will go into more later – but although I was treated well throughout the experience, the shame of over 20 people looking at my privates during a six-month period had a long-lasting impact.

CHAPTER 20
THERAPY

I have been in and out of therapy since I was 16.

It first started after I began self-harming when I got with The Wank. The sleeves of my school shirts would be covered in blood, and when someone asked me one day what had happened, I made up some crap about scratching my arm on a bramble. I got this idea from The Wank and his nose injury.

They bought it.

I don't know how it came to be, but I started seeing a lady in the village – apparently, a few kids from school were seeing her. The Headmaster, of course, had to be made aware. I recently found a report the therapist wrote to the Head saying how she wasn't sure if my behaviour was just normal adolescence or if I was 'unstable.' She said that my insecurities and vulnerabilities were causing me to 'act out' and that she was concerned.

She was nice enough. But I hadn't exactly been honest with her. I protected The Wank; I left out all the details of the abuse.

Obviously, I had trust issues. One day, she allowed me to use her house phone to call Mum so that the three of us could decide something. She then made me a peanut butter sandwich and gave me a can of Coke to take back with me. I was touched but couldn't understand why she was being so kind – or why she always looked so concerned.

I allowed the abuse from him to continue. I was put on Prozac. Then the therapist took me to see a psychiatrist – and he took me off the Prozac, saying it increased the risk of suicide in teens.

I didn't trust him either, so I didn't open up in the one session I had with him. I didn't feel understood by either of them.

The next therapist was a lady at uni. She was nice enough and compassionate, but yet again, I didn't feel understood.

Just before I quit in my second year, we had a joint session with my mother and another with my uni boyfriend. In both situations, I felt like a child, as if I was crazy and everyone could see it except for me.

Once again, I was the odd one out.

When I was living in Barcelona, I found a nice English-speaking therapist. We analysed my dreams, talked about my fear of being sent to the mental asylum, and did some sand play.

I don't know how much she helped, but I was overwhelmed by her kindness when I arrived with a tummy cramp one day and she made me some mint tea. You can see how small acts of decency and kindness were so foreign to me, and in sharp contrast to my daily life.

My next experience with therapy was in New York – there I found a lovely lady called Sharon. We worked together for the two years I was there and I learnt to trust her. Perhaps it was because being in this country had been my choice. It was all on my terms.

I told her things I guess one usually tells a best friend. I opened up about my eating issues, my fears, and my anxieties, and she helped me change my view of myself.

We also had a family session with both of my parents when they came over for my graduation. A few minutes into the session, however, my father's phone rang and he took the call – explaining that they were in the middle of buying a house.

When he left the room, Sharon looked shocked, and I – once again – felt abandoned. My heart hurt. Mum looked angry at my and Sharon's reactions, saying he was a busy man. In response, I started crying quietly.

Throughout the session, Mum appeared visibly pissed off by my audacity to speak my truth.

On the subway, on the way back to their hotel, Dad made a space for me to sit between them. He was trying to show care and love and that I wasn't the lowest thing on his list of priorities. I knew it would be a one-off. I was right.

We were supposed to go out after graduation with my friend and her family, but at the last minute, she changed the restaurant where we had reservations. This was too much; I couldn't deal with the uncertainty of a change of plans, so I got up the guts to tell everyone, including my parents, that I was just going home.

The whole day had just been far too much – 1.5 hours of family therapy, the graduation, and now a change of plans… no way. I had to be alone.

I didn't care that they'd travelled all the way from Spain to spend time with me; they didn't want to talk to me anyway, right? Besides, they didn't seem at all fussed about my leaving early.

One day, Sharon suggested I join an eating disorder therapy group. I had an interview to see if I would 'fit' into the group dynamic, and then it began.

There were about eight other women there of all different shapes and sizes. By this time in my life, the eating had become a way to control my weight, control my figure. My worth came from my clothes size. After all, since the age of 16 I had learnt that small, slim girls were pretty and worthy. Big boobs were not nice… big anything wasn't nice. You didn't want to be bigger than a 32C or a size 8. Or so my mother said.

We would go around the room, telling our stories, our issues, and our fears. I found it validating that I wasn't the only one going through all this.

After each session, I would feel good and get myself a strawberry milkshake and a chocolate chip cookie from Starbucks for my ride home. It was a reward – and proof that I was healing.

Mum, however, didn't see it this way. During a visit and a joint session, she complained to Sharon, saying it wasn't healthy that I was eating these cookies and not much else.

Sharon backed me up; she got that it was a win that I was eating anything at all. So much for Mum's "You would never have an eating disorder; you enjoy food too much!" comment when I was younger.

She would always comment on how much people 'enjoyed' food. For her, this was a negative for sure. In her mind, food was only for sustenance, not to be enjoyed… did she enjoy anything, I wondered?

I always felt I had to show so much restraint around food with her. I couldn't eat too much – or enjoy it too much.

Years later, when I was seven months pregnant, she asked me if I wanted to share a sandwich with her for lunch! WTF?! No, I didn't want to share a sandwich; I wanted my own fucking sandwich – and some crisps and a chocolate bar!!

If I ate what she did in a day – which I tried doing for a few holidays – I was just constantly hungry. She always looked so frail and skeletal. If you put your arms around her, you worried you would snap a bone and break her.

Her clothes looked stiff and uncomfortable and, as if she should be cold. She wore thermal vests, but she didn't radiate warmth. Her hands were always frozen. Her shoulders always had a dusting of dandruff and were covered in strands of her short hair. I didn't like to touch her too much. It wasn't a comforting or nurturing feeling.

The most nurturing thing she ever did was stroke my head when I was about seven years old when I couldn't sleep. It was always in the same spot – on the forehead, above the bridge of the nose – as she had read that it helped sleep. However, as she just rubbed and rubbed in the same spot, after a while, it got sore and uncomfortable. It wasn't relaxing or pleasant, but I daren't move or tell her to stop because she touched me so rarely, comforted me so rarely…and I craved touch and love.

On leaving America, I postponed finding a new therapist as I felt I was doing pretty well after Sharon's help. I felt strong and stable.

Unfortunately, like they say, you gravitate towards what you know… Enter Dickhead.

Chapter 21
Dickhead & Baby Number One

I had been back in the UK for a few weeks now, and I decided I needed to make some friends. So, I put a post on some online forum, looking for people to meet up with. About six people turned up – all boys apart from one other girl.

It was a weird night. I was instantly attracted to this one guy – Dickhead – and I felt the attraction back. Still, after a few hours of flirting, he started talking more to the other girl, Freya.

That night, one of the boys slapped me across the face for mixing up the Swiss with the Danes (or something like that); I was too shocked to react, but no one around me reacted either. Maybe it was OK to be slapped? I guess I didn't deserve much better… so who cared, right?

On leaving the pub, we all walked to a club and, along the way, he put his arm around Freya. I figured that was that: he had made his choice.

While the others got McDonald's, I waited outside with Dickhead. He had his hand on a bollard and, while flirting again, I put my hand on top of his. He removed his hand. I felt like an arse!

Why I didn't give up right then and there, I will never know.

After being ignored by him in the club for quite a while, I decided to go home. I told one of the other guys and he asked if it was because of Dickhead. I replied that I had no idea if he liked me or not and that I didn't play games, so it was best if I just left.

He assured me that it was me Dickhead liked. So, I decided to be brave and just go and ask him what was going on… and he also assured me it was me he liked! It was just so confusing; his actions had told a completely different story.

This was the beginning of the end.

The confusing behaviour, the hot and cold, the lies – it was all so familiar, though far more obvious than in any of my previous relationships.

A few months into the relationship, he wanted to do something sexually with me that I found degrading and disrespectful. Remembering my promise to myself to never do something sexually I was not comfortable with I held my ground and said "no". He wasn't happy about it but thankfully didn't push it.

All of my growth and all of the self-esteem I'd gained while living in New York, started to get stripped away. The self-harm began again, the erratic eating, the self-hatred, the self-doubt… the fight between my heart and head was stronger than ever.

After Dickhead and I had been together for around a year, I found my fifth therapist. This one was a man. We met early in the morning before my shift at work. The room was always cold and I found it a bit too oppressive.

I didn't stay with him very long. I didn't feel like he got me at all – I felt my issues were beyond his comprehension.

Dickhead lacked any desire for affection. If I tried to cuddle up to him, he would shrug me off, ask me to give him more space on the sofa, and just generally not be open to kissing and cuddling.

He didn't help with the dogs or the housework.

One day, we had an agreement about walking the dogs after work. Due to my work rota, some days I'd get home earlier than him, and the other days he would get home first. On the odd occasion when it was his day to walk them, I would get home earlier and I would do him a favour and walk them for him. I felt that I was being kind and thoughtful and saving him a job and that he would appreciate it. Nah.

He didn't show any appreciation for it whatsoever and he never returned the favour. He started to expect it, and more.

One Thursday, after work, I needed him to take me to a hospital in London. The main doctor at the private surgery where I worked was sending me there with suspected pneumonia. Again.

As he drove me there, he kept huffing and puffing and looking at his watch. "I have work to do and I need to go to work in the morning," he told me.

I felt like such a burden. I sat there silently crying for how unloved and uncared-for I felt. I was already feeling so ill and was finding it hard to breathe... now, I also felt like I didn't even deserve to be taken to the hospital.

Thankfully, the pneumonia was mild this time - I spent 3 or so days in hospital and Mum came over.

As we – him, me, and Mum – all arrived home from the hospital, the lady I'd arranged to walk the dogs while I was away arrived at the same time. She asked if we still wanted them walked, as we were home now.

Mum and Dickhead just looked at me like, 'Well, if she isn't gonna do it, we aren't – you can.'

As I was still feeling weak, I asked her to continue. I was shocked. Really? You both expect me to walk the dogs on the night I get out of the hospital after having intravenous drugs to help me breathe due to pneumonia?!

This became a common theme throughout our whole relationship. If Dickhead was poorly, he would take time off work, relax at home, and do nothing. If I was ill, I was still expected to clean, cook, and walk the dogs.

There was one occasion when I had the most horrific pain in my eye; I could barely see and was in agony. He begrudgingly took me to A&E, where I sat crying in pain in the waiting room. I couldn't get comfortable in the hard chairs; my head was pounding, and my eyes were incredibly sore and blurry. He looked so embarrassed as I squirmed around and cried. No offer of support or comfort. Nothing. I was an inconvenience and an embarrassment.

I was diagnosed with a rare eye complaint called iritis. It can be dangerous and, if left untreated, it can cause blindness due to the pressure behind the eye. After being given drops, I was told to return if it happened again. For a few days, my pupils stayed a different size than normal, which made it very hard to see clearly!

Another time when he showed his utter lack of care for me was when I woke up and felt so weak that I even couldn't stand. There was hardly any strength in my body, and every time I moved my head, I felt like I was going to throw up.

I called 111 and they sent me to the hospital, giving me an appointment to see a doctor. I think it was a weekend. I asked Dickhead to help me shower and get dressed. Oh, the eye rolls and huffing!

It turned out to be a nasty ear infection.

I threw up as we left the hospital and he just stood there again, looking embarrassed and not helping me much. He did hold my arm as we walked to and from the car, though, so I guess I should be grateful for that!

As much as his behaviour hurt me – and, in reality, made me love him less and less, and feel less safe with him – I felt I didn't deserve any better, so I expected no better. I must be so flawed and crap if this was all I deserved!

As he told me many times over our 14-year marriage, "You're lucky to have me; I could be one of these guys who spends every night down the pub or looking at other women."

He made it clear no one else would put up with my 'crap'.

Obviously, he knew of my past, with my jealousy and with my boyfriends with their roving eyes. He also knew of my body issues. He would tell me things like, "Yes, your legs are big," or, "Your eyebrows are weird," or, "Why are your jeans so tight?" And – when I was pregnant for the first time – he told me, "You don't need that chocolate."

I never felt good enough. Pretty enough. Sexy enough.

I would guess that in our entire time together, we had sex maybe 20 times. On our two-week honeymoon, we did it twice. There was no passion there.

Any request I made to do things or buy things was always met with a no. He even made a 'rule' – whoever says 'no' to something, gets their way.

He was weird about certain things in public. For instance, I wasn't allowed to eat in a queue or while walking around. I also got told off for calling his name out loud in a shop. "People will know my name!" he told me. What?!

I would encourage him as much as I could. He told me he had imposter syndrome, so I would big him up by telling him how he had as much right to be at business events as everyone else. I would tell him how clever he was, how amazing his business ideas were, how if anyone could make it happen, it was him.

I never got similar reassurance in return. In fact, he outright told me, "I'm not going to reassure you; you have to do that for yourself."

We tried to get pregnant as soon as we were married; I had come off the Pill in May for our July wedding. I just wanted to be a Mummy so badly. Ever since I was 15, I had wanted to be a mother.

As we weren't having sex regularly, though, it was pretty hard to get pregnant – as I'm sure you can imagine.

Each month, when my period came, I would get upset – despite the obvious lack of sex or the 'once a month' sex!

One day, I was so upset that I called Mum. Her helpful reply to my tears at not being pregnant was, "I thought you were going to wait till you had some savings."

I started randomly doing pregnancy tests. One day in November of the year we got married, I received my usual negative test. My period was late, though, so I did another one the next day… and it was positive!

My breath caught in my throat. No way!! I did two more tests and they all showed positive!

How was I going to tell him? I wasn't sure, but I knew it had to be special. So, I went shopping and searched for something romantic and memorable. I even started to feel dizzy and breathless while doing it – OMG, I thought, I really am pregnant!

I bought a baby blanket, put it in a pretty bag, and then waited for him to get home from work.

He was smiling as he opened it up, but then he just frowned in confusion. "What is it?" he asked.

He thought it had something to do with my brother's wife being pregnant. He had no idea what I was trying to tell him! So, I explained what it meant, and – thankfully – he was happy too. We had a hug.

He came to all of the scans and appointments. He spoke to my belly and seemed to take an interest. What he still didn't seem to care about, however, was me.

I recall one day when we'd gone shopping in Kingston. We had taken the train and, when we'd finished shopping, we were walking up to catch the train back home when he realised we were going to miss it. He wanted us to run. I was carrying most of the bags (what a gent!) and I couldn't run as, being pregnant, it was too uncomfortable for me; I wasn't that far along, but I needed a wee and running wasn't that pleasant at that point. He started getting angry at me, losing his patience.

When we finally sat down on the train, I turned to him and said, "I am pregnant, with your baby. Life is going to change now. My body is changing and I can't do the things I used to be able to do. If you can't understand that, if you can't get on board with that, then that's fine. You can leave; I can bring up this baby alone."

He said nothing. He – we – were pretty immature as far as 27-year-olds go.

After that, he didn't get annoyed at me, but he still didn't help me with groceries, jobs around the house, or carrying things. Even after a few episodes of bleeding, he still didn't lift a finger. My duties remained the same and, when at home, he still did nothing.

Towards the end, when I was very heavily pregnant, I had a bout of nesting one night. Mum was over for a visit and was staying with us for a week.

I wanted to clean all of the inside windows. It was late at night and it was making me very anxious that it needed doing. I had to do it now as, after the baby was born, I wouldn't have time.

They both watched me frantically spraying and cleaning windows, going up the ladder and getting more and more worked up. They told me to stop, and then they spoke amongst themselves about how I 'get like this' when I'm least able to do things.

Why wouldn't they help? Why not take a window each? Then it would have been done quicker! Why just stand there bloody watching me and telling me to stop instead of doing something useful to help me out? I felt so unsupported, alone, and – to be honest – crazy! Why couldn't I just leave it? Why was it so important I get it done, right now?

Mum used all her past experience with birth and midwives to tell me how I would be treated, now, in 2008. "You will be shaved and given an enema," she told me. "Then they will inject you with drugs even if you don't want them."

"No, I won't, that stuff doesn't happen anymore," I told her.

"It will – of course they'll shave you," she insisted.

"They aren't allowed to do anything these days without my permission. No drugs or shaving or enemas. Times have changed, Mum."

She looked miffed.

It is awful that women had to go through things like that in the late '70s and early '80s, but why would she scare me just before my time? Surely she knew things had moved on?

A few days after giving birth, while washing up, I told her that I felt all fat and wobbly.

"Suck it all in; hold your tummy tight," was all she said in response.

I didn't want to be told to 'suck it all in'; I needed to be told to be kind to myself. To relax, and that my body had just done an amazing thing. I had created, grown, and birthed a baby! I wanted to be told that I needed time to recuperate and recover. It had taken nine months to grow this baby, so I needed at least that, if not more, to get back to how I was before.

It just added to the pressure to go back to 'normal' quickly.

Now, back to the birth.

On the due date, I sensed something different, like something was finally happening. With a scan appointment scheduled, Mum and I (she was visiting for the birth) headed to the hospital. That's where we met Dickhead, and the medical staff confirmed that I was indeed in labour!

So, Dickhead went back to work and then on to his parents' house, as it was his Dad's birthday, and Mum and I went home.

We had arranged a doula as I was distrustful of how much attention and care I would get in the hospital – you hear such horror stories.

The labour progressed throughout the day and, at 2 pm, Dickhead called to see how I was. I told him he should come home soon.

I wanted the TENS machine on, but Mum didn't know how to use it.

At 4 pm, he called again, but I was on my knees and couldn't speak to him. He arrived home soon after with magazines and prawn cocktail crisps – the last things I wanted!

I told him I wanted a bath, so he got that ready for me, and then he timed my contractions. They were pretty irregular, so – despite the pain – we didn't think much was happening.

Next, we took the dogs for a little walk, as I was told that walking helped with labour. Once we got back, I lay on the sofa and almost immediately, I felt and heard a pop – my waters had broken!

I had a bit of a panic then. I'm not sure why, but I did. I called him, all tearful and upset, and told him what had happened and that I needed to get up NOW.

He helped hoist me up and I managed to change my wet trousers into something dry. He then called the doula and she arrived within 30 minutes. By now, it was around 7 pm, and she thought it best that we get to the hospital.

As we were walking out the front door, I had a massive contraction and she told me to lean on her. I was so huge and she was so small, however, that I didn't dare put much weight on her!

The doula got in her car, Mum and Dickhead got in the front of our car, and I got in the back – with the bloody car seat in my way!

By this point, I was on all fours, as I couldn't sit down. Oh, the pain! At least the TENS was helping a bit, as I had it on the highest setting and with the boost on as well.

I was grunting and moaning.

"Nearly there!" they said.

"How long?" I pleaded.

"I can see the hospital – not long," Mum lied.

On arrival, Dickhead got out of the car and looked around; I think he expected someone to be waiting for us. I know he had called ahead to say we wanted the water birth suite, though I knew they wouldn't get it ready until we arrived.

I was wheeled into the ward and put on a bed, and the next thing I knew, I was being examined by a nurse. It felt like she had her whole hand up inside me. I pleaded with my eyes to the doula to get the nurse to stop.

"You are 9 cm dilated!" the nurse exclaimed. "We need to get you to the labour room!"

I was wheeled out pretty quickly, with just a sheet covering my modesty, as I zoned in and out of awareness.

They were preparing the pool for me, and the second they said it was ready, I got up off the bed and lumbered over to it.

"Stop, stop!" everyone cried. I still had the TENS machine attached to me.

Free of the wires, I finally got into the soothing, warm water, which helped a little. It was easier to move about and change position, at least… but oh, the pain! I felt like I was being ripped in two. I thought I would die from the agony of it all.

How on earth do some women describe this as nothing more than bad period pains?!

They allowed me to use the gas and air, and I clung to it like my life depended on it. When one canister ran out, they had to take it from me to replace it with a full one. That was a long few minutes!

At that point, however, they said I couldn't have any more, as the gas and air was slowing down my contractions. They took it away.

Suddenly, I had the overwhelming desire to push; my body knew what to do and that I needed to push. Right now.

"No, no, don't push!" said the midwife. She wanted to check I was fully dilated first.

Have you ever tried to overrule your body when every fibre of your physical being is telling you to do something? It was like that. I tried to breathe through each agonising urge to push, just waiting for her to give the word.

"OK," she said eventually, "you can push."

About an hour later, however, there was still no sign of the baby – despite me pushing with all my might.

The midwife took Dickhead aside and told him that if there was no baby within half an hour, they would need to take me out of the water. Unbeknownst to me, they wheeled in a Resuscitaire.

"If she sees it," the midwife told him, "just tell her it's a towel warmer."

At one point, I slurred, "Are the puppies OK?" And then, looking at Mum and Dickhead, "Are you OK?"

Mum was too busy scooping poo particles out of the pool to reply – something she would forevermore delight in telling everyone about!

Every time I pushed, I felt the baby descend but then go back in... I felt like I would never get him out!

At one point, his little head got stuck, but thankfully, I managed to push the baby out without any intervention. I grabbed him up from the depths of the pool and he came out screaming, with his arms wide and angry. I held him to me and stroked his little face. The top of his head was blue from where he'd been stuck.

We wanted the umbilical cord to stop pulsing before it was cut, so I snuggled him under the water while we waited.

The pool soon began to fill with blood, however, so I had to get out in a bit of a rush; I handed my boy to someone and staggered out with blood dripping down my legs.

Lying on the bed, I delivered the placenta and they assessed the blood loss. I had lost approximately 500 ml – just under the amount that they worry about.

Stitches were needed, and I had another suck on the gas and air – but, this time, it immediately made me nauseous. My head started swimming.

The male doctor was down there and all I could see was my legs in stirrups and a needle and thread dripping with blood; this consultant simply walked in, didn't say a word to me, put me in stirrups, sewed me up, and then left.

I felt faint!

Throughout this, I was holding my new baby, and I was so scared I was going to pass out and drop him.

It was after 10 pm now and, after some jammy toast, it was time for everyone to leave and for me and baby to go to the ward.

Mum had made the toast. She'd been gone ages to get it – as it turned out, she'd spent ages tidying up the kitchen area. That's lovely, I thought, but I'd just given birth and had lost loads of blood. I needed her. I needed help and I needed some food! Why was it more important to tidy up and please the midwives than to be with me?

Dickhead had been out of the room, calling his parents, so I had been all alone.

I requested a private room; I had heard awful things about the wards being so noisy that you got no sleep. Dickhead was allowed up to settle us in, but then he left. As he went, I felt a deep fear, like I was being abandoned. I had no clue what to do with the baby. I had never even held a baby before!

This little bundle didn't let me sleep at all. He wouldn't latch, if I put him in his crib, he made noises, and I was scared to cuddle him in the bed as the sentence, "You mustn't ever fall asleep with a baby in your arms," had been rammed into us at the NCT classes.

I buzzed the midwives twice in the night to see if they would help me with feeding him. They just had a quick peek and said it was all fine. It wasn't, though; I could tell he wasn't latching and wasn't getting anything.

Dickhead was supposed to arrive at 9 am to take us home. He didn't arrive till after 10.

I was so annoyed and disappointed. I was tired, I wanted to go home, I was alone, and I felt incredibly weak.

When he finally arrived, I asked if he would look after the baby while I went for a shower.

"Oh, err, yeah, OK," he replied, "but be quick."

What?! I had been up all night while he'd been asleep in his own bed. Not to mention that I'd just given birth. And he wasn't happy to look after his son while I went for a 10-minute shower?!

While washing, I felt something strange down below. Oh god, I thought, what if it's a prolapse? I had heard about women pushing so much that their uterus falls out of their vagina!!

So, when the nurse came to discharge me, I asked her to have a look.

She looked at me like it was a waste of time, then said, "Just haemorrhoids. Use this cream."

Once we got home, we watched some TV. I was falling asleep, though, so I said I wanted to go and have a lie-down.

"Me too," he said.

Once we were all settled, the baby started crying.

I wanted to cry I was so tired!

"I'll get him."

Oh, thank goodness, I thought, I can sleep!

Nope!

"I don't know what to do," he declared five minutes later. "You'll need to take him."

So, we swapped, and he went to sleep while I dealt with the baby.

By night two or three, I figured there was no point in even getting into bed, so I took a blanket and tried to rest on the lounge armchair.

"Why aren't you going to bed?" he and Mum asked.

Neither of them offered to help in any way. I guess the thinking was that as I was trying to breastfeed, it was up to me to do it all, alone.

I sat crying that whole night, feeling so exhausted and so alone. I still hadn't had a good sleep since the birth. He still wasn't latching and he cried a lot.

Those days are a blur to me now, but I remember the doula coming and telling me that, no matter what, I couldn't bottle-feed him.

I told her I wanted to learn to swaddle, but she didn't know how to do it. She also didn't know about breastfeeding…

She did tell me she could come and help out, though, on a postnatal basis.

"How much does that cost?" I asked.

"Oh, don't worry about that," she told me.

"Yeah, but how much?"

"£17 an hour."

Well, that was out, then! Anyway, I was supposed to be able to manage myself, right? Besides, Mum was going to stay for a month (some of that time with us and some in a hotel), and Dickhead was having two weeks of paternity leave.

By day three, we got an appointment to see a cranial osteopath who specialised in breastfeeding positions. She had me remove my tops and then show her what we were trying to do.

With my boobs out in this strange room with a stranger looking on, I felt beyond embarrassed, but I was also desperate for help – and, anyway, my dignity had pretty much left the moment that nurse had put her hand up inside me!

She declared baby had a headache from where he'd become stuck. The pressure had squashed his head and this, in turn, was stopping him from being able to open his mouth properly to latch.

She did her thing. He cried lots.

I would carry on going to her for two years!

She told me that all the symptoms he was having stemmed from that moment in the birth, and that it was also causing his fists to be very tight and closed – he rarely opened his hands, and his body was always tight. By the time he was a few months old, I could stand him on his legs and he would stand solidly upright.

None of this helped his feeding. The doctor queried multiple sclerosis, which of course caused a huge panic! I had to take him to a private consultant to be reassured that he was just fine.

One evening, I caved and gave him a bottle of formula. He gobbled it all up; he must have been so hungry!

By the fifth day after the birth, I got my first hot meal – one I had to prepare myself! No one was feeding me or looking after me.

After the success with the bottle, that night I lay in bed – crying, as usual – and came up with this brilliant plan. I was staying in the spare room with the baby and Dickhead was in our bed, sleeping soundly.

I decided I would pump – I would pump my milk and give it to him in a bottle! Win-win!

So, the next morning, I excitedly told Dickhead about my plan while I got the baby ready to go to another osteo appointment.

"No," was all he said.

"What do you mean, no?" I asked. "Why not? He still gets my milk, but this way we can see how much he's taking – and you can give him feeds too."

"No, you'll regret it," he replied. "You wanted to breastfeed and you're giving up too easily."

I was distraught. I thought I had this great plan, but he was having none of it.

So, I kept on at him, crying and telling him I couldn't carry on like this. The baby wasn't eating and he wasn't putting on weight.

Eventually – and angrily – he told me he'd ordered "the best pumping machine there is" for me.

"You'd better use it now 'cos it cost a fortune," he added.

I was relieved, but also upset by his attitude.

Fortunately, it worked! I still had to get up all through the night, however, and for double the amount of time – I'd read that you must pump whenever baby eats, so I would feed him, by bottle, and then pump.

I'd also read that you must only give night-pumped milk at night, and only day during the day, so I had to label them all with the time etc. and then wash up the bottles and the pump parts too.

Of course, sterilising was now needed as well.

On occasion, I would be pumping, and Dickhead would bring me the baby and expect me to be able to hold a pump on each breast and hold the baby at the same time. One time, as I had no hands free, he put him on this soft pouffe thing in front of me. It was so dangerous; "he might roll off!" I objected.

"He isn't rolling yet… it will be fine," was his response.

With a pump in each hand, I tried to manoeuvre myself so that I had my legs on either side of the baby, to keep him in place until I was finished.

When the baby – Jacob – was a few weeks old, I developed a terrible, painful earache. I was in so much pain that I was crying as I tried to feed him. Dickhead walked into the lounge, looked at me, and walked straight back out again. He didn't care, didn't help, didn't take the baby off me, didn't even go and get the antibiotics for me. I had to go and get those for myself.

Dickhead had ridiculous rules regarding everything I did. At one point, I wasn't even allowed to buy new clothes.

"None of my clothes fit," I told him. "My pre-baby stuff is too small still, but my pregnancy clothes are too big. I need new clothes."

"No," he replied, "you'll just have to make do."

I felt so uncomfortable in my body. Nothing fitted, everything looked crap, and I felt crap. Eventually, I secretly bought a £10 pair of trousers. I never wanted to have a relationship where I had to hide purchases or anything like that, but I was desperate. Weeks later, I told him. Thankfully, there was no big reaction to this news.

On and off, I had milk supply issues. After doing some research, I found that fenugreek is supposed to improve production. So, off I went and bought some.

After taking a few pills, there was more milk, but it stank of curry! I had to throw it all away. I started to sweat and stink of curry too; I felt repulsive.

Sitting alone in the lounge one night, pumping away, I looked down at my body. I saw big, swollen, ugly boobs, a hideous old lady bra, and my post-baby tummy bulging out at the bottom. I was disgusted. I had never looked so awful in my life.

I tried to cover myself with a blanket, but I couldn't unsee it.

A day or two later, after six weeks of pumping, I told Dickhead I was done. I wanted to stop. I was so depressed and just felt so awful in my body.

"If I can stop breastfeeding," I told him, "then my hormones and body will return to normal. I will feel better, I'll have more energy, and I'll be happier."

"I knew you would give up," he replied. "You have to keep feeding him. If you don't, and he gets cancer when he's older, it will be all your fault."

The shock I felt at hearing these words stabbed me in the heart.

"It's having a massive impact on my mental health," I insisted. "I need to stop."

"I don't care about you. I only care about Jacob." Those were his exact words.

I believe it was in that moment that any love I had for him disappeared. I also knew that I was totally alone.

I carried on with the breastfeeding for a few more days, but I developed mastitis. On my first visit to the doctor – a male – he had me pull down my bra to completely expose my breasts.

"It will clear up on its own," he told me. "Use a hot flannel in the bath."

A week later, it was no better and I was feeling terrible. When I changed nappies, Jacob would kick my sore boobs and send shooting pains through me.

I went back to the doctor and, this time, I saw a female. She just looked and touched the top of my breast – no bra removal for her – which made me wonder what had happened with the male doctor. Thankfully, she gave me antibiotics.

I think it was after this that I finally said 'enough is enough' and stopped pumping.

For a good week or so, my breasts were incredibly swollen and sore; they were rock-hard and tender to the touch. I developed a fever. Dickhead seemed to think it was my fault for stopping – that I deserved the pain.

The first year of Jacob's life was pure hell for me.

I had wanted a baby so much, had planned so much, and I was as ready as I could have been… but I was hating it.

I was constantly on edge, I hardly ever slept, I couldn't eat much, I was crying all the time, and I wasn't enjoying my baby. It was like my body was coursing with electricity the whole time.

I felt guilty for not enjoying him and because I didn't feel a bond with him. I knew I loved him – and that I'd do anything to keep him safe – but I didn't feel anything else. No swish of love that they go on about. No immediate connection.

It didn't help that whenever he would cry and Mum was around, I would go to pick him up and she would say, "Leave him. You can't pick him up every time he cries."

I was torn. Do I react how I think I should, how I wanted to, or how she – a mum of two – was telling me was best? I was sick of the tuts and the head-shaking, the eye rolls and the looks of exasperation.

I felt like I was in way over my head, I didn't know what I was doing, and Jacob wasn't responding well to me. It is highly likely that he was feeding off my anxiety. I was a mess.

I couldn't read his cries, I had no idea how to get him into a routine, and since he wouldn't eat or sleep well, it was impossible to predict what he would want and when he would want it.

When he was a few weeks old, I ventured to Tesco to get a few bits and Jacob started howling at the checkout. The lovely lady in front of me let me go in front of her as I only had a basket.

"Well, that wasn't very clever to bring him out now, was it?" announced the checkout lady.

I was shocked. This was one of my first times out alone and I'd been proud of how I was dealing with things – proud that I wasn't crumbling.

The nice lady said to her, "When is a good time with a new baby?"

"When they're asleep!" the nasty checkout lady spat back.

"Well, he was asleep when we left," I mumbled.

The nice lady told me not to worry about it and that it was very hard to know with such little ones. I was so grateful to her, but this incident had such a big impact on my confidence in terms of leaving the house.

The one time I verbally asked Dickhead for help was one morning when he was getting ready for work. Jacob was just a few months old.

Once again, I was in tears and struggling, and I bit the bullet and summoned up the courage to say, "I need help; I'm finding this so hard."

He glared at me and simply said, "Go back to work then."

I was stunned. I didn't want to go back to work; I didn't want to give up. I just needed help.

The conversation soon turned into an argument about how I'd wanted to be a mum so much but, now that he was here, I couldn't do it. I felt like such a failure. I didn't know what to do with myself.

I remember changing Jacob's nappy after Dickhead had left and telling him, "It's just me and you."

Around this time, my left wrist became incredibly painful. It had a sore swollen lump on it and, no matter what position I put it in or what splints I used, it was still agony.

The doctor diagnosed De Quervain tenosynovitis – a painful condition affecting the tendons on the thumb side of the wrist. I had some ultrasound therapy to try to ease it, but after a few months, it was worse, not better.

We still had private medical insurance, so I went to see a private consultant and she suggested cortisone injections. These didn't work, so the next – and last – step was surgery.

Mum came over to help me with Jacob for a bit while I recovered, but I found her presence difficult to tolerate for too long.

By now, Jacob was quite advanced. He was walking unaided by 10 months old, was speaking by 12 months, and had stopped having naps by 15 months.

He wouldn't, however, eat or sleep or poo normally. He cried a lot and, when he did poo, it was a total poonami. It went everywhere!!

When he was two months old, I took him to my parents' house in Spain. I wanted to get away from Dickhead and was hoping Mum would help me out so I could get some sleep.

Nope! The only morning she took him off me so I could get some extra sleep, I could hear her tutting and mumbling while he cried.

She did cook for me, though, and I didn't have to do laundry or walk the dogs, so in that respect, I did get a break.

When we returned to England, Dickhead was an hour late collecting us from the airport.

When Jacob was 10 months old, we both took him to my parents' house while they went on holiday themselves. I was hoping the sun, the pool, and no dogs and no cleaning would help.

Nope. I was more worried than ever about messing up their perfect surroundings; Mum was quite particular and liked everything left exactly as we'd found it. Or maybe that was my impression due to my need to show her I was the perfect daughter.

I had to do all the cooking and most of the baby care. Dickhead was disappointed because he thought the food was going to be amazing.

I'd been put on sleeping pills by this point, but I'd waited until this holiday to try them so that Dickhead could look after Jacob. I went and slept in my parents' room while Dickhead and Jacob were in the downstairs bedrooms. The house was huge, so I was hoping I wouldn't hear the crying from up there.

Nope. The pills didn't work and I could still hear him crying. I kept waking in the middle of the night, groggy and still half asleep, so by morning, I was no more rested than usual.

Of course, Dickhead got angry with me because he was tired and I was having "all this sleep."

I confided in him one day, while Jacob had a nap, that I was desperately unhappy and that I wanted to die.

"No, you're just tired," he replied.

This was far more than just being tired, but what more could I say? He wasn't listening.

Back home, Mum joined me at one of my doctor visits to discuss Jacob's poo issues.

"Grandma, what do you think the issue is?" the doctor queried.

"Just teething," she declared.

So much for the backup I'd hoped she'd provide! I knew it was more than teething. I knew there was something else going on with my boy, but no one would hear me. It wasn't until he was two years old and I took him to a paediatric gastroenterologist that I was finally listened to.

He prescribed medication to help Jacob go to the toilet and explained how to use it to effectively treat his faecal impaction. Going forward, Jacob would need to take this medication for years.

A few months later, on one of her visits over, I stood in front of my mother and tearfully told her that I hated my life.

She laughed. "Don't be silly."

I felt so alone again.

Soon after this, after a big argument with Dickhead, I drove down to the river and took over 30 paracetamol and ibuprofen. I was planning to take more, but I started to feel really sick.

I sat there and wrote in a notebook about how desperate I was feeling. About how Jacob would be better off without me. About what a crap mother I was, and how I loved him – but that he would get over me.

I poured my heart out onto those pages as I sobbed and sobbed.

This whole time, Dickhead kept texting me, telling me to come home.

Eventually, I did go home and immediately went into the toilet to try to throw up what I'd taken. As I turned around, I was met with two paramedics. I was angry that he'd called them.

Apparently, he'd also called the police when I'd left. Now I was scared they were going to take my baby away from me!

One of the paramedics was gentler than the other and seemed nice. Unfortunately, he was the driver, so I ended up in the back with the one who looked pissed off at me.

"Why did you do it?" he asked.

Sobbing, I replied, "I've been diagnosed with postnatal depression." This was true; my therapist at the time said he believed that's what I was suffering from. The trauma of the birth – plus getting no sleep, help, or support – had left me feeling utterly alone and abandoned.

If you spoke to either Mum or Dickhead they would undoubtedly tell you that they helped loads, did loads, and were super supportive. My reality is the opposite.

I felt so judged by that paramedic.

After triage, I was put in a curtained cubicle and left alone. I just sat there, sobbing out loud. My heart was broken, my head hurt, I felt sick, and I was scared for the future. I knew that this would have changed nothing in terms of how I felt, but what if social services got involved? That would make life even harder!

Was everyone going to be angry at me? Did this prove what an unfit mother I was?

I had so many questions, and I was so, so tired.

When Dickhead arrived, he brought me some biscuits, which helped with my tummy pains a bit; it was so empty after all the throwing up.

The psychiatrist tried to talk to me, but he was hard to understand. He stood so far away, and I was concerned that everyone else would hear my business. I just didn't warm to him at all. When I started throwing up again, he just stood and watched me. I had to ask Dickhead to tell him to leave.

Why would you even need to ask someone to leave? Wouldn't a respectful person stop staring at you at this point?

I got home and tried to sleep, but I jumped out of bed when I heard Jacob waking up. All I wanted was to cuddle him and hold him close.

Dickhead's parents had stayed the night with Jacob and were also going to take him for the weekend so we could sort things out. To be fair to them, they then started taking hi every other weekend, allowing me to rest.

He also started going to a childminder so I could have some time to myself – though some people couldn't understand why I would need any time to rest.

One day, I was walking the dogs and our postman stopped to talk to me. He asked where the little man was.

"He's started at a childminder's so I can get a break," I replied.

"A break from what?" he questioned with a roll of his eyes.

Was I utterly useless?

My parents were visiting, so I wrote them a letter, explaining what had happened that night when I ended up at the hospital.

Dad responded with a cuddle and, "Let me know if there's anything I can do to help."

Mum responded with anger. She looked incredibly pissed off. "Why would you do that?" she asked me. "When you did it at school, you told me you were tired. What is it now?"

I was exasperated. Really?! I had tried to talk to her – I had told her how miserable I was – but she hadn't paid any attention.

Later on, Dickhead used this incident against me.

Life got easier once Jacob was with the childminder a few days a week, though I still felt guilty as I was paying someone else to look after my child when I wasn't at work. I stayed home, walked the dogs, cleaned the house, and worked out to try to get my body back.

If I got my figure back, I thought, maybe my mood would lift?

Chapter 22
The Wedding

I suppose I should tell you how Dickhead and I ended up getting married in the first place.

A day or two after meeting Dickhead, I got a text from him (I don't remember if we had exchanged many texts or even seen each other again since meeting). I asked if he wanted to hang out, but he said he was busy with a girl he'd recently met online.

I was crushed!

As I began to cry, my self-hatred loomed its vicious head and I looked around for anything I could use to cut myself with. I took apart a foot knife/scraper thing I had and I ran the blade over my arms, watching the blood bead up.

Before getting his text, I'd been trying to teach myself to relax by meditating and by colouring to distract myself.

Now, the blood dripped down my arm.

Suddenly, another text came in telling me to look out my window!

He was out there – it turned out *I* was the girl he'd met online. Well, no… technically, we'd met in a bar! He knew where I lived because the taxi we'd shared on that first night had dropped me home first.

Upon seeing what I'd been doing, he told me to never do it again or else he wouldn't be with me. There were no questions, and no discussions of emotions or feelings or what he could do to help. Sounds just like my mum, right?

The relationship progressed, with him calling many of the shots about where and when we would meet. He would surprise me by waiting for me outside my work with a teddy, or coming to my house when we hadn't arranged to meet, and – as he knew London better than me – he would always choose where to meet up.

A few months in, he told me he wasn't sure he wanted to be with someone who suffered from depression and anxiety. I wish I had walked away right there and then.

He would tell me lies and half-truths, and he certainly had some odd ways about him.

One day, when we were walking around a shopping mall, I turned around and he was nowhere to be seen. I searched the whole shop and still couldn't find him. I was certain he'd changed his mind about wanting to be with me and had simply walked away – abandoning me.

I found him a few shops away. It hadn't even occurred to him to tell me he was leaving the shop!

All these 'little' things put together left me on edge and doubting my sanity. One day, I wrote in a diary I was keeping: 'Why do I always feel not good enough? Why can't I just feel loved and safe? What is wrong with me?'

As much as I was insecure in our relationship, however, this was all familiar territory to me.

I just kept telling myself that I didn't deserve better – that I wasn't someone who would ever experience safe, unconditional love – so I'd better just be thankful for this guy, for the crumbs he would occasionally sprinkle on the ground for me.

A few months into our relationship, my parents were over in the UK, so we went to the movies with them and then had dinner. He tried to impress them by paying for dinner – and it worked. Mum was smitten! But they were worried about how Grandad would react to the fact that he was of Indian descent; we'd have to tell him gently.

At first, my dog, Webster, didn't like him. She would growl and bark at him, especially when he started taking up her side of the bed. I wish I'd paid attention to her! Over time, however, she got used to him – probably because he would sneak her food when I wasn't looking.

Very early into the relationship, we went on holiday to the Maldives together. It wasn't the best holiday ever, but it was the first I'd ever been away with a boyfriend. I thought it would feel special. It didn't. On the way home, we spent the whole flight arguing about something or other.

I told him I'd always wanted a Bernese mountain dog and that I thought we should buy one together. He agreed. We met a breeder, chose a dog, and that was that.

The agreement – that we would do this together – well… that didn't happen! Christmas rolled around and he spent weeks at his family's house and didn't come back to help me with the dog.

I was alone.

We argued.

We had moved very fast. We got together in July and by Christmas, we had been on holiday and bought a dog together.

He was supposed to move in that February, but one night in January, at 1am, he knocked on my door. He wanted to move in right there and then, as he had seen a mouse in his room at his shared flat!

A few months later, we decided to move to a new place – one that would be 'ours.'

During the actual move, I saw his frustrated side. It was not pleasant and he took his anger out on me.

After being together for two years, we went on holiday to the Maldives again (I think we went there because of the prestige of going somewhere so expensive and elite). I was recovering from my second bout of pneumonia, and we were hoping that the rest and heat would do me good.

Cuddled up in bed one night, I asked Dickhead when he thought he was going to propose. Would we ever be getting married?

"Maybe September," was his reply. This was May.

I was happy with this response, even though I was already 26.

I'd been longing for marriage for quite some time. I wanted the stability, the partnership, the love. My timeline was strict – I HAD to be married by 26, with a baby by 27. I don't know where this came from, but I felt I would fail if I didn't hit these deadlines. No one ever suggested to me that there might be another way to go about things – that even if I waited a bit longer, I would still be young and still be able to have babies.

Besides, I knew Mum would be proud of me if I got married.

The next day, Dickhead wanted to go snorkelling, but I didn't fancy it. I wanted to read quietly.

He had quite a strop about this. "Is this what my life is going to be like with you? You always ill and me having to do things alone? Are you always going to be so ill and weak all the time?"

Other vile, hurtful things were said as well. He berated me and belittled me. I was devastated.

I thought he was my soulmate, the guy I was going to marry! Who talks to people like that?!

I recall crying my eyes out that night, alone in the bathroom, while he slept.

A day later, while still feeling down, we were walking along the beach when we found a sandbank disappearing into the sea. As we strolled down it, with me in the lead, he started calling my name. On turning around, I saw him down on one knee, holding a ring box out to me. He was proposing!

What was happening?! I thought he pretty much despised me!

Maybe I was worthy after all? Had he forgiven me for being so weak and pathetic?

With the sandbank disappearing and the water up to our waists, I accepted and put the ring on. It was a beautiful diamond solitaire from Tiffany – what a lucky girl I was!

He later explained that he'd only been so mean and condescending to throw me off the scent; he was worried I'd guessed that he was going to propose soon.

I was confused. Is that acceptable behaviour? Is that how people who love each other act?

Mum was delighted, though she knew already because he'd asked my Dad for my hand in marriage before the holiday.

We decided to have a year-long engagement and get married in July 2007. It would be beautiful!

Now we just had to find the perfect venue.

I am sure you can guess that Dickhead did not participate in the planning very much. This, of course, caused many arguments, and I was left feeling that he didn't care. And, if he didn't care about the wedding, then he mustn't care about me, right?

We argued about many other things too: his lack of helping around the house, not doing anything together, not going anywhere, not having any affection or intimacy, not helping at all with the dogs… the list was endless.

Our sex life had never been up to much; issues had started to show in that area very early on in the relationship. I would guess that we did it one or two times a year at most.

A few months before the wedding, after yet another argument, I was sleeping in the spare room, and as I sat there – crying and alone – not the life I wanted or deserved. But why was no one treating me better? Did I not deserve better? I couldn't talk to my parents about it, I had no friends, no job, and no house other than the one we shared. The expensive wedding was already paid for.

I had never experienced the love I desired, so I started to think it must not exist. Was what I wanted a fairy tale?… we all know they aren't real.

I was already 27, so if I left now, I would have to find a new boyfriend and then spend a few years together before having babies. I'd wasted three years on Dickhead already… I was fucked! I was trapped. I had no options. This was the life I had to live.

After all, that's what life was, right? Disappointment and hurt. My dreams were outlandish and unachievable.

When I saw myself in my wedding dress after collecting it from the shop, I cried. I sobbed my heart out. I was not beautiful. I was not happy. I was so sad and alone. I shouldn't be feeling like this, not when I was about to get married. I was sure of it.

After we met, Dickhead and I never went out socialising again. I wouldn't have been able to relax and be myself, as I could never be myself around him. This was very evident on our wedding day. He and my family sucked all the 'me' out of me.

My wedding day was not the best day of my life.

The venue – the orangery at Kew Gardens – was gorgeous. We had the use of the garden, a dining room, and this lovely, open, airy, light room. I had ordered lots of beautiful flowers and the tables were presented just so. My favourite colours – bright yellow and lilac – were everywhere. Dad had paid for everything and I couldn't have asked for a more beautiful setting.

But I felt uncomfortable all day. I felt like a stranger at my own wedding. I had nothing to say to anyone and felt like I wasn't really present.

By the end of the evening, I was utterly shattered, and things weren't feeling all that romantic; we didn't even hold hands in the Bentley that took us to The Dorchester in London.

Once we got into our huge, beautiful suite, Dickhead got ready for bed and I ran a bath. He then went straight to sleep while I sat in the bath, alone, pulling the painful bobby pins out of my hair and sobbing.

The sadness of sobbing alone on your wedding day did not escape me.

We didn't consummate the marriage for many months.

In the end, after the divorce, I donated my wedding dress to a lady who made it into little outfits for babies born sleeping. I chose not to keep it for my daughters' weddings, as it held no positive memories for me. This act felt like a meaningful and beautiful way to repurpose it.

Dickhead's response to my telling him this? "That's creepy!"

He was always telling me how I felt about things.

"You were happy that day..."

"We have loads of happy memories..."

This wasn't the truth – not for me – and it was confusing to have someone tell you how you felt when you remember it so differently.

It was gaslighting*; it made me doubt my own reality. It made me question if I was asking for too much, and made me wonder if it had all really happened.

*Gaslight

https://www.medicalnewstoday.com/articles/gaslighting

Gaslighting is a form of psychological abuse where a person causes someone to question their sanity, memories, or perception of reality. People who experience gaslighting may feel confused, anxious, or unable to trust themselves

Countless times, over the past six years, I have asked Mark: "Did all that really happen? Have I made it up? Have I embellished it and made it worse than it was?"

But every word is the truth. It is a hard reality to get your head around – that the people closest to you distorted and controlled your world so much that, now, you are confused about everything.

Chapter 23
Child Number Two

Jacob was a bit of an ill baby. He would get regular colds and things, like usual, but with him, it always seemed worse. I am sure some of it was my first-time mum anxiety, but he would often have a high temperature, not eat as much, and show more symptoms than friends' babies.

We had one visit to A&E for suspected meningitis, and they kept us in for a few days and nights. I slept in a foldaway bed next to Jacob's hospital cot and cuddled him when the nurses woke him every two hours to do their checks.

I was shattered, especially as we weren't allowed out of the room for the first two nights; after all, if it was meningitis, it would be contagious. It was a tough time.

Dickhead wasn't overly helpful. I remember him arriving one evening so that I could go home and have a shower, and when I returned about an hour and a half later – we lived more than 20 minutes from the hospital, and I had also walked the dogs and gone food/baby milk shopping – he was staring daggers at me because the nurses had arrived to take bloods. And, of course, he didn't want to have to deal with it.

The next day, he came to visit for less than an hour, saying he had to leave because his boss was going to have a phone meeting about him and he'd found a way to listen in to the call. That was more important than being with his wife and poorly baby in the hospital.

He made me feel bad for being mad about it.

As I was used to my father always putting work first, however, this just seemed like something I simply had to put up with. I was very disappointed and felt incredibly unimportant and alone.

Dickhead's job, it would seem, wanted him gone. So, he took redundancy and decided to work full-time on a project he'd been working on since university. I was happy for him to do this, but his working in the house while I was trying to look after Jacob just wasn't going to work. So, I organised for the 'summer house' in the garden to be insulated and made more comfortable for him, and this became his study.

If I ever took Jacob down the garden to see him, or if we walked past to go to the trampoline, Dickhead would quickly change his computer screen.

I asked him a few times what was going on and he just said he was working on something and had been about to change screens anyway. I didn't really believe him, but I wasn't going to argue – and, to be honest, I'm not sure how much I really cared anyway.

Dickhead would come into the house at the most inconvenient times. I'd just be settling Jacob down with a story so I could chill, or we'd be about to quietly watch some TV, and he would come in, rile him up, and then leave. It was infuriating and exhausting. Once again, I had no control over my environment, as he would just come in and disrupt it whenever he wanted.

Later on, I discovered that instead of working and trying to make money, Dickhead had been content to let us live off his redundancy money while he played video games! I think he believed he was safe because my dad would bail us out if anything happened.

So, I was keeping house, looking after Jacob and two dogs, and dealing with my poor mental health while he relaxed and played games!

Then, my grandmothers would tut at me when I told them, "No, I don't make him a packed lunch or have his dinner waiting on the table when he gets home."

Somehow, I was the one in the wrong!

My mother was always chastising me for not ironing the bed sheets. I just thought it was such a waste of time – something I had precious little of, considering I had young children.

On occasion, we would talk about saving money and he would say we needed to not spend so much, but if he fancied a takeaway, it was OK – because he'd been the one who had decided to spend. It was very hypocritical.

By the time Jacob was two, we started talking about having another baby.

"Oh no, you don't need to do that," my mum told me.

But I wanted to!

I questioned why she would say that. Was I not a good enough mum? Had she regretted having two?

My periods had never returned to normal after having Jacob, and I figured it was because I'd gone back on the Pill. So, I stopped the Pill, but they were still irregular.

I bought an ovulation kit, which I had to pee on every morning with my first wee of the day, and it would tell me when I was ovulating – and then, of course, that would be a good time to have sex to try for a baby.

With us, however, there wasn't going to be lots of 'trying,' as there no doubt is for other couples.

I did my sticks for 45 days, but there was no ovulation, no period for a few months, and, of course, no pregnancy because there was no sex. Eventually, I went to see the fertility doctor, who had worked at the same private practice I'd worked at all those years before.

I had scans, bloods, and examinations. Nothing was found.

The next step was a hysteroscopy and a laparoscopy to see what was going on inside; I was booked in at his clinic in Dorset, a few hours' drive away. I got knocked out and, while I was under, I had this vivid dream of meeting a toddler boy.

When I awoke, I was crying as I asked, "Can I have children? Am I OK?"

They went to get my lovely consultant and he held my hand and calmly told me they'd found nothing. There was no physical, medical reason why I wasn't ovulating.

The next few days were very painful, as the air he'd had to pump into me as part of the procedure escaped. It leaves you with a terrific pain in the shoulder and pain upon breathing.

One day, I explained to Dickhead that I was scared of giving birth again.

"Why do you struggle with everything so much?" he replied. "Other people give birth all the time and it's no big deal… but, for you, it's a whole thing."

I was shocked – really?! Isn't childbirth supposed to be like the worst pain there is? And I had done 90% of it with no pain relief – and, even after that, I'd only had gas and air. Was I making a big deal about nothing?

After the birth of my son, I had asked Dickhead if he felt bad that I'd been in so much pain. "No," he replied, "it's natural. You had to go through that."

"Yeah, but did you feel bad for me? Or sad for me? That I was going through so much?"

"No."

I was shocked by his lack of emotion and compassion. Surely you should feel something when the person you love – or even just anyone, really – is going through agony right in front of you?

Eventually, I went to visit a kind lady GP and asked her why I was struggling so much with the idea of giving birth again. We chatted for 45 minutes, with her reassuring me that I was in the right and that of course it was agony and of course I would be worried. Men know nothing about the pain of childbirth, and how stupid of him to even suggest that the problem was me!

I felt so validated!

The next step was to test Dickhead, and he tested fine – he kept boasting about his sperm count.

So, obviously, it was me who was the problem.

I was started on Clomid – a pill that's supposed to stimulate an increase in the hormones supporting the growth and release of mature eggs. Then, after three months with no success, the dose was upped.

The side effects of hormone drugs are abysmal... the mood swings, mainly. I would be screaming at either my boy or Dickhead, and even though I knew I was out of line, I was unable to stop myself. I felt like an awful, guilty, crazy mess.

One day, after I'd just cleaned the house and changed the bedsheets, Dickhead let the dogs out into the rain-soaked, muddy garden – and didn't monitor them coming back in.

Of course, they ran their muddy paws all through the house and straight onto the clean sheets.

I hit the roof! I picked up the hoover and threw it down. It broke. I felt like the Hulk, utterly wild with rage.

One evening, as I stood putting the clean clothes on the airer, sobbing and feeling hopeless, I called my consultant's mobile at 9.30 pm and cried down the phone to him.

He made an appointment for me in a few days' time and, at that appointment – which I attended with Dickhead – he reassured me that things would work out. At the end, he added, "And if you (meaning Dickhead) can be more supportive, that would go a long way in helping."

Funnily enough, I later had to remind Dickhead that the consultant had said this, as he apparently "didn't hear it." Or, as he said, "He was only joking; I'm really supportive!"

The Clomid was a bust, so the next step was injections; I was given daily jabs and, every few days, I had a scan. This meant a lot of trips to London, by myself.

Unfortunately, my eggs just weren't maturing, and they had to be a certain size to be viable. The dose was upped again, but still no joy.

On the next cycle, one or two eggs were big enough, so I was told to go home and get into bed with my husband.

Wouldn't you know, that was the week Mum was visiting, and she asked if we wanted her to go to a hotel. How embarrassing! I said nah, it was fine. After all, I knew it wasn't exactly going to be some passionate affair.

Anyway, we did the deed and then I lay with my legs up against the wall and a pillow under my hips for a good half hour.

Come on! Work!

Nope! Nothing.

Next came the big guns.

I was also referred for acupuncture. Although I knew this lady from the same surgery, she seemed to be pissed off with me the minute I arrived. I'd heard how she spoke to her other clients, but with me, she took a very brusque, harsh tone.

She told me that my breakfast of a banana was not healthy enough as it had too much sugar. She then told me what I should be eating. I explained about my history with eating disorders, but she just brushed that aside, saying, "Well, now you need to eat properly to make a baby, so you can do it."

She then put the needles in and left me alone for half an hour.

A week later, I emailed her to ask if it was normal to have a bruise on my tummy.

She called me soon after, enquiring why I'd asked such an odd question. "In all my years of doing this, no one has ever asked me that," she told me. "What is wrong with you?"

I was saddened by the question. I told her that, until the acupuncture, I'd been feeling OK in my body, but now I was feeling sick and ill – and I was fed up of feeling crap.

After that, she was a little gentler with me.

I had to have Dickhead inject me every night and go for scans every two or three days. If there were any good eggs, I then had to have an extra injection at a certain time and then go for another scan the next day. The HCG jab was a proper plunger injection, not a pen one like the daily doses.

Unbeknownst to me at the time, Mum delighted in telling people all about my IVF journey – I was so pissed off when I found out! She wanted me to show my grandparents all the injections and needles, and she smiled the whole time I explained it to them.

I'd also been referred for some therapy. This lady managed to get out of my subconscious the reason I was terrified of getting pregnant again: I didn't want the same things that had happened last time to happen again this time. We also did some EFT tapping – this is a technique that stimulates acupressure points by pressuring, tapping, or rubbing them while focussing on situations that represent personal fear or trauma. I released a lot of tears and fears here.

It was after just three sessions with her that I became successful.

My honest belief is that my body was stopping me from getting pregnant; it didn't want the trauma of the postnatal depression to happen again.

Finally, after six months or so, I had some eggs that were worth harvesting. We did the injection and then went to retrieve the eggs at the London clinic. I'd had acupuncture the day before.

I was sedated for the procedure and, before I'd even properly woken up from it, they tried to explain what had happened. I had to have it all explained again afterwards, however, as no matter how many times I had her repeat it, I just couldn't understand the nurse.

Eventually, I understood that they'd managed to get just four good eggs. As there were so few, they told me, it was best to do ICSI – which is where they inject the sperm directly into the egg to get the best chance of fertilisation.

I then heard that the lady to the left of me had 20 eggs harvested! What a failure I was!

Three or so days later, we had a call. The doctor told me that two of the eggs had died and two were multiplying, but one was doing better than the other. He wanted to implant this one. We were to go in the next day.

This was it!

There were about five people looking at my nethers as they implanted the embryo, and I watched on a screen as they placed it high up inside my uterus. Straight afterwards, I went for acupuncture to maximise the chances of giving this baby the best possible start.

Now we just had to wait for two whole weeks…

It worked! I was pregnant! That one embryo was my baby! We only needed one!! I was delighted.

While I'd been undergoing IVF, a friend I'd made at the dog park down the road from our house, was also going through the same process. She was about 10 years older than me, and although she'd had a baby a few months before me, she had suffered lots of miscarriages previously.

I was careful, therefore, when I told her about my positive result; I knew it would be hard for her. I wasn't expecting her to totally stop talking to me, though!

At 20 weeks, I was in the shower when I collapsed with pain.

Oh no, I thought, please... *Please* don't let there be a problem with the baby!

I told Dickhead, and we agreed it would be best to go to the maternity ward and see what was going on. They decided to admit me so they could keep an eye on me. There was no one available to give me a scan to check on baby, so I had to wait a day for that.

In the meantime, they dosed me up on painkillers and I had to stay in bed. I felt so guilty that I'd be away from my little boy for a few days. What if he needed me? What if he missed me?

I knew I missed him like crazy.

I tried to take advantage of the bed rest, but I found it hard to settle. I was just so overcome with guilt and worry.

After two days, they let me go home. They told me to have lots of rest, no sex (not a problem!), and to come back if I had any issues.

Because the pregnancy was via IVF, I was given lots of extra scans; they wanted to keep monitoring the baby's growth as well as my own progress. They said an IVF pregnancy brought extra risks and, although I was only 32 years old at the time, they were treating me like I was a 40-year-old.

I was glad for the extra care, though, especially as this pregnancy had been so hard-won.

Heartburn and anaemia reared their ugly heads, so I needed medication for those, and at one point, there was concern that I wasn't eating enough and wasn't putting on enough weight – but I couldn't eat because of the heartburn.

Mum would come over every few months and stay in a hotel nearby. She still wasn't helping much; she would watch me struggle to get on the floor to play with Jacob but wouldn't offer to play with him or for me to go for a lie-down or anything. The one thing she would always do was my ironing. That was about it.

As my pregnancy progressed, I was told there was no way I was going to be allowed to go even one day past my due date. If it got to that, they would induce me.

This scared me. I had heard that the pessaries they give to induce labour made everything much more painful. It also meant that more interventions would likely be necessary.

From 35 weeks onwards, I tried acupuncture to bring on labour. Then, a week before my due date, the acupuncturist did some 'extra' – and, after that session, I knew something had changed.

The next day, I felt weird. I spent the whole day in a fog and, by evening – as I was giving Jacob his dinner – I told Dickhead I thought I was in labour.

"Like really, really?"

"Yeah, I think so. I could be wrong… but something's definitely happening."

My contractions hadn't started, but I just felt so different.

Dickhead doubted me, so was hesitant to react. This, in turn, made me doubt myself too. Somehow, however, we agreed that Jacob should go to the in-laws that night. The plan was for Dickhead to drop me at the hospital on his way to taking Jacob there. And, if I was in labour, I would stay.

As I sat all alone in the waiting room, with other couples coming and going around me, I shed a few quiet tears.

Not only was I all alone and scared, but I was worried about how Jacob would feel when we brought a new baby home. Obviously, I'd thought of this before, but it was about to become very real.

What if I was ruining his life – like my birth had apparently ruined my brother's life? Would he ever forgive me?

I was 2 cm dilated and declined a sweep. They said that, ideally, I would stay in the hospital – considering my high-risk status – but just then, Dickhead arrived and we managed to persuade them to let us go. We would return when I was further along.

So, we went to Tesco and stocked up on supplies. Dickhead had no idea what we needed, and to explain it all was too complicated, so it was just easier if we both went.

All of a sudden, the contractions heated up. I couldn't walk through them anymore and I had to hold onto the shelves to steady myself. People were giving me very weird looks.

The checkout lady asked if I was alright, and when I told her I was in labour, she asked, "Well what are you doing here?!"

When we finally got home, I decided I wanted a bath. I figured that if we stuck to what we did last time, it should all progress nicely.

"I hope it doesn't happen tonight," Dickhead said. "I'm so tired from cleaning the sofa yesterday." He had hired one of those wet vacs to spruce up the sofas before the baby arrived.

By now, Mum was here, and I went and lay with my head in her lap (I think this is the only time I ever did this) while he got in the bath, I'd just got out of.

"Where is he?" she asked me.

"In the bath; he's tired."

She looked incredulous as she rolled her eyes.

He didn't appear for ages – he had fallen asleep in there!

The contractions were very regular, but as they'd been so irregular with baby 1, I was waiting for that to happen.

Dog walk next!

About 500 metres down the road, I realised I'd made a massive mistake; I could barely walk! I wanted to be on my knees, but the poor pups needed walking! Everything was my responsibility and no one else ever took the initiative – even when I was in labour!

We managed to get home and I declared that all was well and that we should all go to bed and get some sleep.

"I really think we should go to the hospital," Mum insisted.

"No, it's fine," I replied. "Go to bed."

Within minutes of everyone settling into bed, I was on my knees, crying and in absolute agony.

"You need to go to hospital," said Dickhead. "Can we go now? You're obviously in pain."

"OK," I sobbed.

Mum came in then, tutting loudly and telling me she'd told me so.

I cried to her, saying I was so scared about how much it would hurt. I'd been hoping that if I ignored it, I could pretend it wasn't happening.

I waddled down the stairs and, as soon as I got to the bottom, my waters broke all over the floor. I was trying to clean it up when Dickhead came and told me to get in the car. At least this time, the car seat wasn't in my way!

But oh, the pain again!

On arrival, two midwives came out and asked me how much pain I was in. "It fucking hurts," was my response. I don't think they were impressed with my language.

They walked me through into the examination room and then I had a massive contraction that put me on my knees. I was holding onto the bed and they were all telling me to lie down. Hang on!! Let this one pass, FFS!

It was like they had never seen a woman in labour before!

There was no sheet to cover myself with on the bed, so I had to ask Dickhead to give me his hoodie.

"She wants a water birth," he told a student midwife.

"You should tell someone," was her reply.

"Errr… we are telling someone! You!"

It felt like they didn't believe I was in much pain – perhaps because I'd walked to the bed myself, or because I wasn't screaming?

It took a few minutes, but eventually, someone appeared to examine me, and to give me gas and air.

"Oh my god! She's crowning!" the midwife exclaimed.

After that, everything happened in a rush. I was wheeled out of one room and into the pool suite. The gas and air were taken away and they told me there was no time for a water birth. My bed was literally surrounded by midwives.

In the end, I had both the labour team and the triage team standing around me. As neither of them wanted to relinquish control, I was getting mixed messages about what I was meant to do.

"Remove the TENS machine."

"No – leave it on if it's helping."

"Push!"

"No, don't push yet!"

FFS!!

I was lying on my left side, which all my classes and research had told me was the best way to lie. They said it was a fine position to give birth in.

"Raven, roll onto your back."

I stared at Dickhead, telling him with my eyes that I wanted to be left alone, that I wanted to stay as I was.

"Raven, move – go on your back," someone repeated.

"No, I want to stay on my side!"

The next thing I knew, they all lifted me up and put me on my back. I was aghast!

As I started to push, I had no traction, so my feet were trying to find purchase.

"Don't kick my midwives, please! If you do that again, we're going to have problems."

What?! I wasn't trying to kick anyone; I just needed to push against something!

"Hold your knees up and push down."

Huh?? How can I push and pull at the same time?!

It was all just happening so quickly. I had only been in labour for six hours.

After just a few massive pushes, the baby slid out. I couldn't see much but I did see her head was purple and covered in mucus. I wasn't a big fan of this 'on land' birthing!

There was silence.

The greatest risk associated with IVF births is stillbirth.

The word flashed in my mind: STILLBORN.

"Why isn't she crying?" I asked, looking from Dickhead to the baby.

Nothing. They said nothing and did nothing to reassure me.

The nurses all moved, quickly blocking my view, and then one of them picked her up and took her away.

"Where is she going? Is she OK?" I asked.

Again, I received no response. Nothing.

After a few minutes, she was brought back to me. She still wasn't crying but, thankfully, she looked fine.

The nurses did their thing and, as they were leaving, I thanked them. One of them replied, "Ha, she just didn't want to breathe, did she?"

To this day, I still have no idea what she meant. It wasn't in her file and it was never documented.

"Breastfeeding?" the midwife asked.

We had discussed this at length – after the catastrophe last time – and had decided that I wouldn't even try. We had to do all we could to avoid the PND, so it was straight to bottles.

"Oh, no," the midwife replied, "you know what you're doing this time, so it will be fine. Give it a try."

I felt crap, like I was making a bad choice even though I knew that – for me and my sanity – this was the right decision.

Once the midwife left, Mum took baby and Dickhead helped me waddle to the bathroom so I could have a shower. As soon as I got in, I fell to the floor and threw up everywhere.

Eventually, I managed to have a wash and get back into bed.

I was suffering from shock. It had all happened so fast that my body hadn't quite caught up with itself yet. It seemed baby was a bit shocked too – she just wanted to sleep.

At least I felt more confident this time, and I was put on a ward of four, though only two other beds were taken.

She slept most of the night, but I didn't sleep at all as the other two ladies kept their lights on and talked on their phones, and one of them let their baby cry non-stop. I even heard a nurse telling her, "We don't shake babies." No idea what was going on there.

The next morning, I couldn't wait to leave. The plan was to get home and then for them to bring Jacob home and introduce him to the baby.

We decided to make a game of it. We 'hid' her in the dining room, by the window, and had him 'find' her. He was so cute!

"Are you having another baby?" he asked while looking at my tummy. That stung! I guess he thought that now baby was out, my belly should have totally deflated in an instant.

I was exhausted, but I didn't want to go to bed as I needed my baby boy to see that all was well. So, we took Jacob into the garden to play, and while Dickhead lay down on the trampoline, I was expected to entertain him.

Chapter 24
Time For A Change

Second time around was easier in that I knew what to expect. Plus, Dickhead was more helpful in that he tried to do the odd night shift, although – in order to 'people please' – I would often take on his allocated time and go the whole night through. Once again, he never returned the favour.

For a few months, Mum even came and did a night shift once a week as they were now living in London.

Baby had awful silent reflux, so she cried a lot and threw up most of her feeds. It was tough going, especially as when she did nap in the day, I needed and wanted to play with Jacob.

I would take him on the trampoline and bring the baby monitor out with me. The reception didn't reach to the end of the garden, though, so every few minutes I had to run up the garden, check on baby, and then run back and play with him.

He was so good and sweet with her. There was no jealousy; only kindness. He loved to play with her, and – as she got older – make her giggle. It was beautiful to watch.

I knew of people who'd had to deal with terrible jealousy when baby 2 came along. One woman told me how she'd thought her four-year-old was leaning into the Moses basket to kiss the baby, only to suddenly realise she was actually biting the baby! Her mouth was covered in blood and the baby had a mark on her cheek.

I figured this meant I was doing something right at least!

I enjoyed being a mum of two much more than I'd enjoyed being a mum of one. I felt more fulfilled and more able to cope. Dickhead's and my relationship, however, was no better.

One night, when the baby – Ivy, we named her – was still tiny, something set me off and I started screaming and I even punched him in the arm. I don't recall what Dickhead had done or said, but I certainly wanted him gone.

When I tried to take the baby off him, however, he wouldn't give her to me. I thought about storming out, but there was no way I was leaving without my babies. I was stuck.

Of the two, Jacob was still more work than a baby. Mum said that was normal, but there was always something in the back of my mind that was sure something was going on there. When I talked to Dickhead about it, he just brushed it off.

As they both got older, shopping trips became a nightmare.

If we did nothing all weekend, like Dickhead wanted, then the children would go stir-crazy. As he never wanted to have a trip out or do any activity, all that was left was shopping.

When Ivy was a little older, the two of them ran riot in shops. I was embarrassed by the noise they made and all the running about. I tried to 'control' them, but to no avail. Dickhead didn't do much to help, of course.

"He's just being a typical boy," he would say, whenever I queried Jacob's behaviour. "I was similar when I was his age."

Eventually, he was diagnosed as having ADHD.

I knew it! I knew something wasn't quite right. At last – a diagnosis! I wasn't going mad after all. At least now I knew I could help him.

As Jacob aged, however, he seemed to calm down, so I figured that maybe they had it wrong after all. Any blips and I would just get, "Yeah, I did that."

When Ivy was very little and I was struggling, I put a lot of it down to the house. If we lived somewhere nicer, I thought, it would be easier. There would be more space, and it would be a fresh start without all the bad memories. Besides, I hated the neighbour who was on the other side of the semi we lived in. I needed a fresh start.

No one would hear of it.

Dickhead hated change and he said we couldn't afford it anyway. I begged my Dad for help – he said no. It was laughed off by my mother.

By the time Ivy was 15 months old, I came up with a plan – maybe if Dad loaned us the money, like a mortgage, we could move. So, instead of paying the bank, we would pay him. I called and asked him.

"Well, I don't want to be a bank or give you a mortgage," he said, "let me have a think."

A few days later he asked, "How about I gift you the money you need instead?"

WHAT? Really?! That would mean we could be mortgage-free!

I started looking straight away. We could afford to have a small mortgage, so our next house could cost up to £500,000.

During my search, I certainly saw some dumps!

As Dickhead was self-employed by now, we weren't tied down and we didn't have to live anywhere in particular – though we couldn't be too far from his parents, especially after a situation that had come up years previously… when we'd said it would be interesting to move to Canada or New Zealand.

Looking back, maybe he was just humouring me, but he made all the right noises at the time, which made me think he wanted to consider moving too. His mum emailed me, however, telling me I was bad for trying to take him away from them and that he belonged here.

As my mum and dad were possibly going to move abroad again, I figured we should move to be nearer my grandparents, so I could be there to help them as they got older.

Then, after seeing at least 20 properties, I found the one!

Mum was with me when I looked, and we agreed that it ticked all the boxes. Big open rooms, high ceilings, lots of light, a great garden, four bedrooms, an en suite, lots of storage, and even some outhouses in the big garden.

I took Dickhead to see a few other houses, and the best happened to be last. That wasn't my doing; it was just what the agent had booked in. Dickhead agreed that it was great and we told the owner we'd be in touch.

Unfortunately, the next-door neighbour scared away our potential buyer by chasing them down the street! And we couldn't put an offer in without an offer ourselves. I was so disappointed; I was sure we would lose the new house.

A few weeks later, after a change of agents and a few tweaks and shifting of furniture, we got an offer. Not the amazing offer the prospective buyers had assured me it would be, but if we wanted that other house – and to get out of there – then we needed to accept it.

As the man of the house, Dickhead called and made the offer, even though it was me sitting there and confirming the amount we could afford – it was my dad's generosity that was funding this, after all!

Dickhead later changed his mind, however, and accused me of tricking him by showing him the house I wanted last! He said I was devious and had engineered the whole thing to suit my own desires.

I was devastated – the house was amazing. I didn't want to not move, or lose this house. His dislike of any change or doing anything even remotely different was ridiculous. We argued, of course, and I felt at a loss as to what to do with my life. I was stuck.

After a few days, he thankfully came around. His attitude, however, made me feel as though he was implying that if anything went wrong, it would be my fault for choosing the house. He actually said this much to me.

When moving day arrived, Dickhead was predictably useless. He begrudgingly sat in one of the bedrooms with the kids while I directed the movers. I had to keep going and checking on them, and he would grumble at me when I did. Honestly, he was like a third child.

Then, once at the new house, I had to direct everyone again while he tried to take care of the kids. Eventually, I had to take my daughter – who was 15 months old at the time – and carry her around with me while attending to the movers.

As usual, everything was my job, my responsibility. Unpacking the house and getting everything settled was on me too.

I thought the move to this amazing house would make me happy – solve all our problems – but, instead, I fell into a deep depression. I wasn't sleeping much and I felt fuzzy and swirly all the time.

"What's wrong with me?" I asked my therapist, Kim.

It may have been around this time that we spoke more about my 'needs.' About what I needed to feel happy and loved. She had me make a list.

I don't have that list anymore, but it said things like:

Affection

Feeling listened to

Getting help with the children

Feeling like I matter

I was to make notes on when these needs were being met in the week before our next session.

Shockingly, I noticed that they were being met very little, if at all.

So, I put a post on Mumsnet to question how much other people's husbands helped around the house and with the children. Again, I was shocked at the replies.

It seemed that many other men did their fair share around the house. I discovered that it wasn't 'doing you a favour' if they changed a nappy or put the dishwasher on. The words 'partnership,' 'joint effort,' and 'best friend' were used a lot.

Kim and I spoke more and more about my worth and how much I could be expected to cope with day-to-day. She encouraged me to hire a cleaner, to take the workload off me and to give me space and time for myself.

I was hesitant – it was a luxury we couldn't really afford – but I was just so tired and fed up with the constant, thankless, never ending-cycle of my life.

"It's cheaper than a divorce," she pointed out.

I went through a few cleaners; after a few months, I would tell each one I didn't need them anymore. They just didn't clean to my standards. It was frustrating.

Dickhead always had something to say about so many of the things I did around the house or garden.

"The lines in the grass aren't straight."

"Oh, I didn't notice you'd cleaned."

But, on the rare occasion that he actually got off his arse and mowed the lawn himself, he would take all day, having constant rest breaks – despite the fact that there were no children needing him. When I did it, I'd have to stop every two minutes as the kids needed a drink, or they wanted me to watch them, or they just wanted to talk to me. He couldn't be useful for even the 30 minutes it would take me to do the lawn.

He would still be in bed after I got back from the school run and wouldn't emerge until after 11. He would then leave his breakfast things all over the kitchen for me to tidy up.

If he did help with the school run, then he would be late getting ready, so I would have the kids waiting by the front door in their shoes, ready to leave on time, while he'd still be faffing, even though he only had to get himself ready.

When the children moved to a school about 30 minutes away, I asked if he could do a regular morning drop-off for me. Not every day, just some days. He managed for about two weeks then told me it was too tiring.

He was so paranoid about people earning more than him or being better than him. He googled people on our street to see what job they had and then tried to figure out what salary they might have. If his job title was more executive and impressive, he was happy. He felt superior.

He did the same with people from the kids' private schools (we could only afford private school thanks to the money I'd received from my father's inheritance, which I'll talk about later).

In 2014 or 2015, we attended couples therapy. We'd been going for a few months, but I didn't really gel with the lady. She seemed to always take his side over mine, though I'm sure they're supposed to remain neutral!

Dickhead just said, "I think our problems are going over her head." I am sure he meant the problems that I had caused.

She never seemed shocked or fussed when I told her the things he'd done and said, and he ended up looking and acting smug, with an expression on his face that said, 'See, I haven't done anything that bad!'

Perhaps it was working, though, as one weekend – when both kids were at his parents' house – I took a massive step and initiated sex.

I'd had so much therapy to help me overcome all my feelings of being 'invaded' with the IVF and all the other gynae issues that it had brought up from my past, but we hadn't had sex at all since the IVFcycles.

I figured that, if we were to work as a couple, then I had to get over this and we had to do it.

We did it once.

Soon after, I knew I was pregnant. Dickhead didn't believe me, but I just knew.

At six weeks, we told the kids they were going to have a baby brother or sister, and for the next week or so, Dickhead was so kind and sweet and attentive to me – so much so that even my mother commented on how affectionate he was being with me!

I felt so happy. I had the beautiful house, two amazing kids and one more on the way, and my husband was finally being attentive and loving! Perfect!

Bright red blood on the loo roll brought my world crashing down.

I called the doctor and had an argument with her; I wanted a scan now, but she wanted to examine me first. I didn't want to be examined and all exposed and 'fiddled with'.

I called around a few private scan places, but they couldn't fit me in for a few days. I needed answers straight away.

So, I agreed to be examined by the doctor – even though I knew she wouldn't be able to tell me anything useful – and she told me that my cervix was closed but that, yes, I was bleeding so I needed a scan. She couldn't get me into the EPU (early pregnancy unit), however, until the next morning.

So we drove to St Peter's Hospital, where we'd gone for many of the scans for the other two when we lived over that way.

"I see the sac but no heartbeat," said the doctor who was doing the scan, "but it is a little early to be hearing a heartbeat anyway."

OK, OK, I thought… so maybe we're OK?

The next day, we had our scheduled scan and they confirmed my worst fear. I had had a miscarriage.

While we waited to talk to the nurse about the next steps, we had to sit in a little side area – which was in the same room as all the pregnant ladies waiting for scans and appointments.

All I could see was heavily pregnant women. It was soul-destroying.

"We can give you a pill that will make you bleed heavily and have bad cramps," they told me, "or you can come in for an operation to remove everything. What would you prefer?"

I chose to go in; I couldn't bear the thought of sitting on the toilet at home, bleeding and cramping in agony.

During the few days I had to wait, I was still bleeding a bit. Devastatingly, on one visit to the toilet, I felt something and, as I looked down, I think I saw my baby in the toilet. I was so stunned and shocked that I had no idea what to do. That can't be it, right? I wondered. They didn't say that might happen…

It was the size of a bean. I panicked and flushed the toilet. What else could I have done? I was numb with sadness.

I wish now that I had picked the little thing up and done something else with it, but I was just in such a state. It's something I know I'll regret forever.

All the love and affection Dickhead had been giving me stopped immediately.

"At last, something with you was simple," he said. "We didn't need to go through something hard to get a baby. And now it's gone."

The day of the removal came around and it was full of sorrow.

The op went fine but, afterwards, they had a hard time stabilising my blood pressure, so I had to stay in a few extra hours.

Once finally home, Dickhead went to work and Mum stayed with me. My uncle called from Canada and his first question was, "Are you going to try again?"

It wasn't the main thing on my mind at that point, to be fair!

A few days later I developed a painful internal infection and needed examining again and antibiotics.

I bought myself a pretty ring with a butterfly on it to remind me of my lost baby. When I showed that ring to Dad on his next visit, he said, with a distracted, uninterested look in his eyes, "What's that?"

"To remember the baby."

"Oh." He looked annoyed and angry.

What now? Surely this was something he should be showing me love and care for? Not shunning it and showing no interest whatsoever?

Mum didn't want us to try for another baby. She said it was because I'd been through enough, but I'm not so sure. With her, everything was always met with a disapproving look, and – other than the usual anger and disapproval I saw there – I found her face impossible to read.

She seemed visibly uncomfortable whenever I brought up the recommendation I'd heard to try again within six months for the best chance of conceiving. Sex was a taboo subject with her – as were so many things!

After much discussion, Dickhead and I decided to try for a third baby. We both agreed, however, that we didn't want to go through IVF again, so if it didn't happen naturally, then that was that.

I took hope from the fact that I had gotten pregnant naturally before, and without even trying!

We tried one or two more times, and on the final attempt, I recall feeling incredibly uncomfortable and in pain. There was an absence of love between us, and in that moment, I made a firm decision: if this attempt failed, I was done trying. I couldn't do this again. Making love should be just that – loving – especially when trying to make a baby.

But – as I'd been told before by both Dickhead and my mother – my idea of 'true love' didn't exist, except in the movies.

Thank goodness that last time made my precious baby number three.

Other than the acid reflux, it was a good pregnancy.

After her birth and returning home following the C-section, it was back to normal duties – more or less.

Within three days, I was expected to be walking our elderly dog and picking up poo in the garden; I vividly recall having baby – we called her Chrissy – strapped to me and bending down to do poo patrol and then taking the dog down the street… at three days post-C-section!!

At least Dickhead was more helpful this time. He worked from home for a few weeks, made me lunches, and drove me to pick up the kids from school and nursery.

He tried to do night feeds but he was useless at it. He would get frustrated at Chrissy crying and he could never figure out how to 'wear' her – I think his big tummy was in the way a lot. Between her cries, I would hear him cursing, huffing and puffing and even shouting at her.

Often, I had to go in and rescue him.

She and I would often sleep together – her on top of me or snuggled into the crook of my arm. I 'wore' her almost constantly. We both loved the closeness.

My neighbour at the time said, "You have to put her down eventually," and I just thought, Why?

As my father was so ill at this time, I looked into putting her into my daughter's nursery so I would be free to go and visit him in London. On the first try – on hearing her sobbing at my departure and the ladies in the room not being able to settle her – I rushed back in and said I would leave it a few months.

Next, I emailed them and arranged a settling-in period… but, at the last minute, I cancelled it.

Having her with me was the only thing getting me through my dad's illness!

Dickhead was being quite strict about how much time he was willing to look after her so that I could go and see my dad.

Thankfully, just before my father died, I got up the courage to tell Dickhead, "I'm going to visit my dad every few days. He is dying and I need to be with him. I am sorry if this is a problem for you, but that is just how it's going to be."

He reluctantly agreed.

That weekend, my father passed away.

Mum moved in with us for a bit until the bungalow I'd found for my parents was ready. The lease began on March 4th. He died on February 29th. He nearly made it.

When Mum's cancer was diagnosed that May, Dickhead was fine with her moving in after each chemo session, and he even made a timetable for all the medication she needed to take. That was good and helpful.

He showed a different side of himself to my mum, and to my family in general; he portrayed himself as helpful and hands-on. Shame he was the opposite when it was just us!

A few months after my mum's diagnosis, I told him I wanted to separate. The realisation that life is short and that I was so unhappy had hit me hard. It also helped that I had my own money now from my dad's inheritance.

"If I leave, I'm not coming back," Dickhead told me.

"But what about looking after Chrissy while I take Mum to chemo?" I asked.

"No," he replied, "you're on your own."

I couldn't believe this. I couldn't take a 10-month-old to an oncology ward for the entire day while my mum had her infusions! It was over an hour's drive away as well.

I was fucked!

So, he had to stay.

We continued living together, but our lives were totally separate and I was constantly pissed off at him. He still didn't lift a finger in the house or do much with the kids. I couldn't go off and have a hobby or a social life because I knew that if I left him in charge, he'd just plonk the kids in front of the TV all day.

He was rarely home in time for a family dinner, and he didn't seem to understand that I didn't want to make two dinners – or that after 6.30 pm was too late to feed such young children anyway.

We argued a lot, but we also had days and days when we would literally not speak a word to each other.

There were countless talks of splitting up. I told him I would never stop him from seeing the children. He agreed that he would never touch my inheritance. But no agreement was ever come to and life carried on.

I would often lose my temper, especially at weekends when everyone would be making a mess all through the house and I would have to spend the day running from room to room dealing with fights or messes or just cleaning up after meals – meals I, of course, had made.

I couldn't sit down for a minute without somebody needing me. They never called on their father, just me; they would walk right past him and come to me in the shower or while I was on the loo to ask for something. It was like he wasn't even there.

Eventually, I insisted – after many arguments – that he learn how to take the three children out of the house by himself. He had never really done anything with any of them before and certainly hadn't taken more than one anywhere on his own. He was scared!

It was agreed that he would take them to Costa Coffee and then to Tesco to collect a few bits. They would be gone about an hour.

He did this on about three separate occasions, and he thought this made him a very hands-on, present dad! He had proved himself… in his eyes!

In June 2018, my friend in New York had a baby. It was the perfect excuse to go over and visit.

While there, I tried to remember who I'd been when I lived there.

I met up with an old boyfriend who I'd remained Facebook friends with, and though we flirted, nothing happened. To be honest, it made me want to try again with Dickhead. After all, I had these amazing children and I wanted the happy family life I deserved.

On my arrival back in the UK, I texted him to say I wanted us to have sex. He said that was great but he was ill with a bad tummy so it would have to wait.

In bed that night, I was feeling sexy, so – despite what he'd said – I went looking for him downstairs. I brought him upstairs and we started to do stuff.

It didn't go well at all! He couldn't get properly hard and, in crying frustration, I jumped off him and ran to the bathroom.

I was bleeding. It wasn't my period.

We didn't talk about it after that – though he reminded me of how he'd told me he wasn't feeling well, so it was unfair of me to have even tried.

We went to couples therapy again but, in my mind, it got us nowhere. I had wanted this therapy – with a new therapist – for a long time, but I had charged Dickhead with the job of finding one, and it took him a year to even bother!

I felt nothing for him.

He was damaged from his childhood and I was damaged from mine.

Our needs from those traumas were so different. I craved love and affection, and he didn't – he was robotic and unfeeling. I could never forgive him for the callous, hurtful things he'd said to me at my most vulnerable times.

A month later, I came down to breakfast one morning and told him, very seriously and calmly, that I wanted a divorce.

He just replied, "OK."

I think he thought this was just another 'nothing' talk that would lead nowhere and that nothing would change. I was deadly serious, though. I was done.

We had a family holiday booked already, which we all went on together, me sharing a bedroom with the kids and him having a bedroom to himself. But, then again, the two of us not sharing a bed was totally normal.

He was overly attentive on this trip, refilling my water glass and even helping with the kids more than usual. This did nothing, however, other than show me he'd been capable of doing these things all along but that he'd obviously chosen to take advantage of me instead!

Throughout our relationship, he couldn't even be bothered to help me fold clothes or iron his own T-shirts. "I don't know how," he would lament.

How bloody hard is it to pick up a T-shirt, fold it in half, and then put it on the right child's pile of clothes?!

Whenever we went on family holidays – not that there'd been too many – I had to do all the sorting, planning, packing… everything, really. His only job was to lock up the house and drive us to the airport. In the airport and on the plane, I had to be 100%

in charge of all three children while he read his book, listened to music, and picked his nose.

If I said anything about it, he would just respond, "But what can I do? They all want you!"

I was shattered.

Trying to settle a fussy baby and look after the other two was a juggling act that gave me no rest time at all – I barely had time to have a drink of water or go to the loo.

Then, of course, on the holiday, I was in charge of getting everyone their food from the buffets while he would just see to himself. I had to do any night wakings and bathing and anything else that needed doing. Those holidays weren't very holiday-y for me.

This man had never laid a hand on me in anger, and he'd never cheated – as far as I'm aware – but the damage he inflicted on me surpasses that of any other man in my life.

I believe he decided to stay with me once he realised I was from a well-off family. I think he felt safe in the knowledge that if his self-employed business ever went wrong, my father would bail us out. He used me for my family wealth. I think this was proved by how things went with the house and funding at the end, during the divorce, and with my mum.

He belittled me and stomped on what little self-esteem I had. He stopped me from growing as a person and stopped me from doing what I wanted with my body and my creativity.

For example, I had always wanted a sleeve tattoo. He told me repeatedly that he didn't want me to, that it would be a mistake, that it would be ugly and he wouldn't find it attractive. I felt stuck, as though I couldn't do what I wanted with my own body.

He had told me when we got together that, like me, he wanted to travel the world – but during any travelling we did, he just wanted to sit in the room and not go anywhere. He didn't like the heat, he said. Why the fuck did we go to a tropical country then? Later on, I reminded him that he'd said he wanted to travel like me.

"No, I didn't," he replied, "I don't want to travel the world."

I felt tricked!

I was stifled and squashed by him.

He made out that anything he had to do was incredibly difficult and took days to complete.

I found out later that he had taken a pillow and sleeping bag to his office so that he could sleep there!

Everything was always on his terms, with absolutely zero wiggle room.

For instance, my phone kept running of data. "Can't I switch to a better plan with more data?" I asked him.

"No, there isn't one," was his reply.

That seemed odd, but as it was one of the very few areas he was in charge of, I believed him. After all, why would he lie? I wasn't asking for much. Of course, there were plenty of better data plans. This was just one of many examples of how I spent years of my life being gaslit by him.

He made out that doing his VAT returns or taxes was incredibly difficult and took days to complete. Nowadays, I have to do my own self-assessment forms and it doesn't take long at all. Even Kim, my therapist, agreed that it isn't that hard and it doesn't take that long. He just wanted to make out that what he was doing was incredibly specialised, complex, and time-consuming. If he was so busy and important, then of course he couldn't be expected to do anything as mundane as cook a meal or tidy up.

One of my nicest memories from after the split was going into the O2 shop and choosing my own data plan – I felt so independent and in control of my own life! How silly and sad is that?!

All of this, of course, is very hard to 'prove.' Emotional neglect and abuse are practically impossible to explain – there are simply no words to describe the depths of destruction they cause.

A month or two after I told him I wanted to split, I went on a five-day birth doula course in London. The split had given me the confidence to put my needs first and do what I wanted for me and my growth.

I had to get up early and get the train in each day. It was a lovely course and I learnt lots about what my birth stories 'could' have looked like. I wanted to learn how to support other women to ensure they didn't have experiences like mine.

The most important thing I took from this course was that my treatment by Dickhead after Jacob's birth was horrific and unjustified. When I told my breastfeeding story, two of the ladies started crying.

I also received the most comforting and 'present' hug I had ever had in my life. This Portuguese lady opened her arms to me after my story and, as I mopped up my tears, she enveloped me in the most warm, calming, connected embrace I have ever had the honour to be part of. She breathed with me and reduced my ragged breaths, and it was as though her heart was speaking directly to mine.

This opened my eyes to what was possible, and it also made me cry harder for all the years I had never experienced such love.

I have no doubt that Dickhead knows what he did, and what he was doing at the time. I just think he didn't care. Besides, he believed I would always be too weak to stand up to him. He figured I would flounder without him and come crawling back.

In the final weeks before he eventually moved out, he said something like, "I don't want to think of another man in my house; I'll miss this place."

He didn't want me, or us – he just wanted the prestige and comfort of this nice big house… and the money behind it.

I don't believe he ever truly loved me.

As much as I loved this house, it wasn't yet a home to me; I hadn't been allowed to make it my home. Dickhead hadn't let me change much or buy anything to make it 'right,' to make it ours. I was told that if I painted anything, I would ruin it.

"You can't do that, just leave it."

Change was bad in his eyes, but in my eyes, change was the future – change was growing and evolving and trying to make things how you wanted them to be.

Now, with the divorce, I would get to change everything. Things would finally suit me and be on my terms!

Chapter 25
More Therapy

When I had my job at the private doctor's surgery, I worked with many great consultants, one of whom was a psychiatrist. Once I stopped working there, I went to see him and he suggested I go and see a therapist at The Priory. This therapist sometimes came across as a bit standoffish. And, again, there were some things that I felt he didn't 'get' about me.

He did help me with my anxiety, though. He taught me ways to change my thinking when catastrophising and worrying about things. For this, I will always be thankful.

Our time came to an end after five years, when I explained I needed a female therapist to discuss my body issues with. He sent me to Kim, who went on to be my therapist for the next 10 years – and who completely changed my life.

She showed me that I deserved more than I had received, that my needs were not being met, and that I deserved better.

I had to write a list of everything that had 'happened' to my body over the years – you know, illness, abuse, accidents… – and she said my list was the longest she had ever seen.

Kim allowed me to trust her and I felt like she really knew me. That she 'got' me. She could anticipate my feelings and thoughts before I said anything, before I'd even made the connections myself. As I had such a deep desire to heal, I opened up my heart and soul to her.

After many, many years together – and after various couples sessions involving Dickhead – I went to tell her I'd requested a divorce.

Her reply was, "I've been waiting for you to do that."

This is when I started EMDR. EMDR stands for Eye Movement Desensitisation and Reprocessing therapy and it involves moving the eyes in a specific way to process traumatic memories and events. The goal is to help you heal from trauma and distressing life experiences.

The torment of the last few years opened up a whole new level of therapy; the anguish, pain, hurt, heartbreak, and devastation just poured out of me. I sobbed from deep inside myself, letting out all the emotions I'd pushed deep down.

At times, Kim would need to sit beside me, holding my hand to help ground me – to comfort me and reassure me that I was not alone and that I was now safe.

After one such deep session, I spent the next two weeks physically shaking. I didn't realise it was the EMDR; I went to the doctor and they wanted to put me on beta blockers!

At my next session, I explained what had been happening and she explained it was my body remembering its trauma. We did a more calming session and the shaking stopped!

I was amazed at what my body was doing, what it had held onto and what it had been through. What *I* had been through!

It was at this point that I realised I would never be free until my mother died. That she had a hold over me and that she was an abuser.

Kim nodded. She understood. She agreed.

This was not, I knew, the normal way people feel about their mothers – but, then again, she wasn't a normal mother.

I had been grieving her my whole life. Grieving the mother I needed, wanted, and deserved. I'd been crying out for her for an eternity… and I'd never gotten her.

A week after my mother's death, I was still smiling and feel free and light.

A year after my mother's death, I stopped therapy.

I have now found somatic breathing – I use it to help heal the deep feelings inside me. I am done talking about it all. I can't tell all these details again to yet another therapist to try to heal more. It feels like, at this point, talking any more about it will just be re-traumatising me. I am bored of talking about it; I want it all in the past, where it belongs.

But the pain inside me still persists.

I still have to deal, every day, with what they did. Their betrayal.

Before I discovered the full extent of my mum's betrayal, I stumbled upon little snippets of the truth, such as when she gave dickhead the extra money to buy the house. There were two occasions when I actually threw up because of how much they hurt me with their lies and betrayals; I became physically sick from the emotions of what they were doing behind my back.

Then I found Susie.

Susie is an Emotional Trauma Healer; she uses conscious breathwork to help your traumas integrate into your body and nervous system.

I didn't know what to expect in our first session. We had already 'met' on Zoom and discussed my needs, so after chatting for a few minutes, we got right down to it.

She could tell from my breathing that I was a people pleaser and a perfectionist and that I was holding myself rigid from within. That I needed to 'know' everything and that I found it hard to let go of control.

I lay on the mat with a pillow under my head, and she told me to close my eyes and breathe only through my wide-open mouth. It felt odd to start with, and my mouth became very dry and my throat very sore. She offered me the use of a plastic mouth opener, which I needed to hold between my lips to ensure my mouth was open enough to do the full-mouth breathing.

Within minutes, I could feel a change.

Over the next hour, while music played in the background, she said things to me such as:

"You are safe."

"You can trust yourself."

"You don't need to have all the answers."

"You are safe now."

I think it was the word 'safe' that started the tears. It wasn't voluntary; it was all happening automatically.

When she laid a blanket over me and we switched to nose breathing – ready for the 'transcending' – it was as though I was in another world. My hands started to shake immediately and I went somewhere scary. All I remember was that I was jolted awake, at which point I became very shaky and upset. Susie reassured me that I was safe and that she was here. I was tearful, and Mark – my new partner, who I'll talk about later – was summoned to come and sit with me while I 'came around.'

Despite this scary 'trip,' I spent the next week feeling light and joyful. Something had shifted within me.

Our next session was two weeks later. We went straight into the session and, this time, the tears came quickly. Strangely, my hands felt like concrete, as if they were stuck to the floor. My whole body started to shake and convulse. I had no control over my body and, once again, my mind went somewhere else. I have no memory of where, and – once I came to – I felt crushed and down.

It was hard to bring myself back up after this session and, unfortunately, my next appointment wasn't for another month.

That was one tough month! No matter what I did, I couldn't seem to lift this weight off me.

When we did meet again and I told her what had been happening, she decided to go more slowly with me. I wanted, if possible, to avoid the sick sensation I'd been feeling at a certain point in the process; she explained that going slower would help with that.

She also explained that the sickness could be attributed to deep trauma and that it was as though my body was trying to purge it. It was rare for anyone to actually be sick, she told me, but I might retch. It was just the body's way of trying to rid itself of the trauma within.

We started with me lying on my tummy, doing nose and mouth breathing rather than just going straight to mouth only. Once I was settled into mouth-only breathing, she asked me to turn over and we started mouth and nose again before settling into just open-mouth breathing.

For the whole hour – which felt like minutes – all I could picture was that moment when I'd been left at school. The place where it all began. I have never forgotten the very spot where they left me and walked off.

The more therapy I've had, the less the feelings affect me, and the less they physically impact me, but the image and the knowledge of the pain has never left me. I see it as though I'm looking AT myself, rather than IN myself.

During my previous sessions, my mind would flit between images and flashbacks of present and past events. Her words would bring forth emotions and they would release the tears. But this time, no matter what she said, all I saw was that moment.

The whole hour was on that one moment of my life. It was like I was having an epiphany.

Everything in my life stemmed from that one moment, that moment of being left, at just 11 years old, on the pavement between the quad and the boarding house – watching my parents as they walked away.

That moment was when my entire existence changed when everything changed. That was the very moment I was abandoned and my heart figuratively shattered into a thousand pieces.

I know that my upbringing up to that point hadn't been the greatest, but that moment is most definitely where it all went wrong.

Abandonment by your family – your mother – leads to self-abandonment. It leads to not trusting yourself, not trusting others, bad mistakes, bad choices, and a desperate need for love and affection that you search for in all the wrong places.

The more wrong places you search, the more the cycle continues. And then, by the very actions you take to end the cycle, you are actually perpetuating the abandonment because that is all you know; it is what's familiar.

This carried on all throughout my life. It carried on through my first marriage, and it was only through Kim that I learnt that this wasn't normal, that this wasn't how I was supposed to live, that I deserved better, that I could have better.

It was then – when Susie said, "You are not an abandoned 11-year-old anymore" – that I slowly started to realise this darkness had to end.

This trauma was so deeply buried that she described it as being like a Jenga tower of trauma. All the other traumas were piled on top of it, and as I was dealing with the issues on the top, the ones on the bottom never got dealt with and therefore stayed hidden.

Somehow, in this session, I had gone straight to the bottom of the tower and pulled out one of the lowest pieces. I now realise this was the root of everything. This was the moment that changed the entire trajectory of my life.

I felt so good after realising and releasing this.

I knew I still had lots of work to do, but I felt like a huge weight had been lifted. I was not the problem. I had been subjected to all sorts of awful things because of the decision my parents had made when I was a child. Now, I had to heal from that.

Now, I had choices; I could choose the way I reacted to things and the way I saw them.

At my next appointment, Dickhead – who I'd been having issues with, as usual – 'came into' the session. I had gone into the trance and all I could see was him standing over me… leaning over me from above my head, looking at me.

I felt nothing. I felt no fear, no anger, nothing.

This was quite a change from my usual feelings whenever he 'appeared' in my thoughts, texts, or life. It was almost amusing to see him there, so impotent and unthreatening.

Later, Susie and I discussed how he no longer had control over me. Now, I was the one in control. I would choose when and if I answered texts from him. He would dictate nothing to me from now on.

My life, my choices, my decisions, my rules.

My next visit to Susie was less dramatic. There was some convulsing but no big revelation or emotion. I felt calm and serene.

Session 5 marked our first online session, and before we even met up for it, I'd convinced myself that she didn't like me. If ever I feel a shift in someone's energy, I immediately assume they no longer like me, that I have become exasperating to them – much like how my family acted.

Already feeling anxious, I'd had a bad dream about it the night before.

In the dream, we had to do the session on the floor of a busy restaurant. I was naked and had only a sheet covering me. Everyone could see what was happening in the session, but I couldn't hear what she was saying to me. It was far too noisy to relax and breathe, and on top of everything, she kept dashing off to deal with something in the restaurant. After a bit, we gave up, and I suggested that next time, we go somewhere more quiet and private. This was too much of a request and she got angry at me.

In the dream, I knew I was in the right – this was a private, personal, healing experience and she was allowing it to be conducted in an environment where none of those things were being honoured – and I was shocked and upset by her reaction to me.

Back in reality, 12 o'clock came around and I logged onto Zoom. I needn't have worried, of course; she was as friendly and welcoming as ever. More so, in fact.

We chatted a little and then she explained how it worked with me at home.

I positioned the laptop so she could see my whole body and then I lay on my front with my forehead resting on a cushion. I used the mouthpiece, as it had been so long since I'd done this type of breathing.

We began. My body remembered.

It wasn't long before she had me flip over.

The breathing was going well and doing its job.

Time didn't seem to exist during these sessions, so I had no idea how far along we were when my head started to hurt and my jaw started to ache.

There was the odd twitch here and there, and then I became aware of feeling like someone was holding my left hand. Then my right hand started to twitch and shake, though my left never moved. It felt warm and tingly and like a hand was resting inside mine.

Next, we got to the part where the breathing was done through the nose and the legs were down. The integration.

Slowly, my shoulders started to shake and convulse. Some convulsions were so big my shoulders were lifted off the floor and my breathing stopped.

Then, I was overwhelmed by a wave of feeling that 'I deserve kindness.' It was like I could see the words in front of me. They were for me. I should have them. I should have had them before; I should have had kindness shown to me my whole life.

Why wasn't it? Why did my mother not show me this?

As I questioned this, tears began to leak out of the corners of my eyes.

With the convulsing almost non-stop at this point, Susie had me take a deep breath and let it out with a hum. We did this three times.

My body calmed a bit after this, though I did have a sob as the waves of emotion engulfed me.

But the hand was still holding mine and, by the end of the session, I felt a warmth flood through my body. I was safe. I was kind. I was showing my kids a kindness I'd never received – and I could show the same to myself. I could surround my life with kindness. I was now in control. It was all going to be OK.

We ended the session in the usual way and I told Susie what had happened.

I was so pleased as I hadn't been sure the online way would work as well, but it did.

A feeling of happiness and understanding stayed with me for a while after that, as did a feeling of lightheadedness – not an unpleasant feeling at all.

As I was at home, I could get myself a snack and chill afterwards, instead of having to deal with the hour-long drive back. I also had a massage booked for later that day, which I was hoping would do me even more good.

In that moment, I was full of feelings of hope. Of good things for the future. Of my ability to make my own life happy.

I was doing great with my healing journey.

Susie was pleased with my progress.

Chapter 26
Dad

My dad was an ambitious man, with – I believe – low self-esteem.

He and my mother met when they were in their late teens, living on the same street. The mothers didn't like each other and the families never became close. He worked in the corner shop and was so taken by her that he gave her the wrong change; her mother had to send her back to get the correct money. Was it a mistake or was it to ensure she returned to talk to him?

They were married at 21 and had babies at 24 and 27.

His first proper job was at and International bank. He started at the bottom – with no degree, just some A levels – and worked his way to the very top.

He didn't believe in his ability or that he was liked, and I think this drove his tendency toward being a workaholic. He worked every possible hour. He would be gone in the mornings before we got up and he wouldn't be home by the time we went to bed. On weekends he would sleep late and then work in his study, before reading the paper or dozing on the sofa.

I didn't know him and I was a little scared of him. My mum would often say, "Wait till your father gets home," and, on occasion, he would spank me on the bottom.

Mum was basically a single mother.

Dad would travel for work for weeks at a time, but it made no difference to our daily lives when he was gone.

He would play with us in the communal pool in Naples, though. Before his back injury, he would throw us around in the water and we would climb all over him and laugh and giggle. It was so much fun.

Mum would read her book or watch from her chair.

Dad smoked like a chimney – he always had a fag in his hand. As a young child, I got burnt lots of times; running into him, jumping on him, or just brushing past him would leave me with a circular burn mark on my hand or arm. Man, that hurt!

Once we moved abroad, he left my mother with a lot to deal with, on her own. She had to acclimatise by herself. New country, new language, new side of the road to drive on… it was a lot.

To be fair, she did amazingly well. She proved herself to be very competent and independent, in many ways.

We weren't a very jokey or laughy family. We played a fair few board games at Christmas – and occasionally at other times of the year too – but most of the games were very adult-like and to do with politics or banking. Think Poleconomy, Shogun, and Risk.

Whenever we got a new game, Dad would spend an hour or so reading the instruction manual and then he'd explain it to us. I was around eight years old at this time, so it would take me a little longer to understand than the others.

We played until someone won, but only he ever won. He never let us win and never dumbed it down for us.

In many ways, this was good, but it was also disheartening. I always, always lost.

When talking about money, I didn't understand the way he said the amount – 'thirteen hundred' instead of one thousand three hundred. He would look at me like I was stupid if I repeated it my way back to him.

Before I left for boarding school at the age of 11, I remember us walking along, arm in arm, chatting away. So, maybe – despite everything – we did have a bit of a relationship.

The older I got and the longer I was away – and the longer we would go without seeing each other or even speaking on the phone – the less we knew each other. The more distant we became, the less Mum would ask if he'd like to come to the phone to talk to me. And, as he never asked to speak to me, the less I would ask if I could talk to him.

Men were a mystery to me – something to be feared, almost.

I was wary of him and his moods; he could have quite the temper and, on occasion, I saw him lose it. This scared me – I never wanted to be on the receiving end of it.

Mum was always telling him he was fat, but he wasn't. He was just a middle-aged man with a sedentary lifestyle, that's all.

Both of my parents were quiet, withdrawn, and lacking in both humour and emotion. Consequently, I felt I had to squash my personality around them. They didn't appreciate or enjoy me – I was too much. The looks I would regularly have to endure… the disapproval, the exasperation, the knowing expectation that I was a fuck-up… I felt like I was constantly walking on eggshells around my family. I was emotionally controlled – mainly by her, as he was never around.

Dad could be sweet too though. One night, when the three of us had gone out to dinner after The Wank and I had broken up, I asked if I could get my fortune read by a gypsy. He agreed and asked the price. She told him a price, and then said she needed a tip on top.

She did the reading, saying I was very close to my father (upon hearing this, Mum's face showed anger) and that I was healing from a broken heart. She told me I needed to gather a little bag and put all these little bits inside – a grain of rice, a coin, etc. I must keep these under my pillow, she told me, and I would be fine.

Dad paid the full amount she'd said, plus the tip, but she told us she needed more – she'd bloody conned us! Eventually, he paid the extra and we went on our way. I felt very bad that it had cost so much.

Dad looked happy, though, and he took my arm as we walked ahead of Mum, enjoying the glow of the gypsy saying we were close. Mum lagged behind, looking very put out indeed.

I decided I could deal with her later; right now, I wanted to enjoy this special moment with my dad.

The next morning, Mum presented me with a little bag full of all the trinkets the gypsy had prescribed. It was sweet of her.

After that, life went back to normal, with me having practically no contact with my father and only talking with my mother.

Although I'd stopped cooking three-course meals for my parents once I went off to school, I did, on occasion, make cakes or meals to practise my food tech skills and try to impress them.

I would look through my cookbooks to find a dish my father would like – something like a vindaloo curry or a dark chocolate cake – but he never seemed impressed or appreciative. I don't know why. Maybe it was simply because he expected someone to cook for him. He was just used to it.

My parents' marriage was very traditional; he went to work and she stayed at home, cooking for him and serving him. They also had a cleaner as the houses were always pretty large.

I'm not sure what she did all day, with no job, no kids to look after, a husband out until late, and the house being cleaned for her.

He didn't have to lift a finger once he was home. He let her know he was nearby and she would have a cup of tea ready for him the moment he stepped in the door. Dinner was served on a tray on his lap; he would sit and read his paper and she would bring him his meal and tea. Then she would remove it after he was done.

In the evenings, he would read and watch TV. They didn't talk much, I don't believe. She must have been very lonely and craving someone to talk to.

After they left Madrid, she told him he could only smoke in certain rooms of the house, usually in his office or out on the balcony. This, of course, restricted further the time they spent together as he would spend much time alone in his study, smoking.

I was never sure how much she shared with him of my news from school, and I knew he wouldn't want to hear the same bit of info twice, so I just didn't say much.

It was like we were strangers.

I can remember one day when I had to leave for the airport to go back to school. I was crying and, as usual, didn't want to go. This moment sticks in my head as it was the only time I remember him giving me a long cuddle, not just a quick hug. He pulled me to him and he rested back on the counter – and we stood like that, together, for a while, with him wrapping his arms around me while I sobbed.

I was distraught. If he was cuddling me like this, surely that meant he must feel my pain? He must see how hard this was for me? In which case, why would he carry on sending me back there?

I think there was a small part of me that hoped he would say, "You know what? Stay. Don't go back."

Of course, that didn't happen. Instead, I pulled away from him and looked at the patches where my tears had soaked into his shirt.

Another time, they dropped me off at the airport and I went through security. Once I got to the other side and was trying to find somewhere to sit and wait for boarding, I heard an announcement saying my flight was delayed by an hour.

In that moment, I felt like I had to get back to them; no way could I sit there for an hour on my own when I could, in fact, be spending more time with them!

So, I raced back to security and asked how I could get back to the other side. They said I had to go through arrivals as if I'd just landed. So, I raced through and explained my situation to the staff. Luckily, they let me out.

When I found my parents, I cried! I think it was out of relief at having an extra hour with them, but also sadness about the situation and knowing I was going to have to say goodbye all over again.

Mum looked concerned and worried, and Dad just looked annoyed. What a waste of time for them; they could have been at home enjoying the rest of their weekend!

We sat in awkward silence, waiting for the hour to be up and for the tannoy to announce that my flight was ready.

At age 13, I got in trouble at school for sneaking out of the boarding house in the middle of the night. Then, during a school holiday, Mum received a letter informing her of my terrible indiscretion. Dad didn't usually get involved in my school life, so I was surprised when my mother insisted I tell him what I'd done.

A few of us had planned to meet some boys in the middle of the night on the field. We were bored teenagers with way too many rules and no freedom whatsoever; of course we were going to find ways to rebel and break the rules.

So, we jumped out of the utility room window and snuck up the lane to the field. We just wandered around with the boys, scared of getting caught but feeling exhilarated as well. After a while, one of the three girls decided she wanted to go back to the house. I seem to remember her saying that if we weren't back within a few minutes, she would tell on us.

Great! Cheers, mate!!

Once we were done, we started making our way back, but we stopped suddenly – we'd just seen three adults leaving the boarding house in a hurry!

Shit – were they looking for us?

On getting to the window, we discovered a big flaw in our plan: without help, only one of us could get back in through the window!

And we had already sent the boys away, saying we didn't need their help!

I pushed my friend through the window from my place on the ground, and once she was inside, there was silence.

Shit! What now?

Just then, my brother's girlfriend's head appeared at the window… fuck! I was in trouble!

She and her friend pulled me through and we all stood there, staring at each other. She told me she was going to tell Jeffrey, and then asked me what I'd been thinking… blah blah blah. Who the fuck was she to tell me off?

The next thing we knew, we were in the tutor's house and she was shouting at us, telling us she'd been out looking for us and did we know how much trouble we were in?

We were sent to bed in disgrace and, of course, we blamed the girl who came back early for telling on us. She apologised, but I still can't understand why she grassed us up so quickly. After all, she'd done the same thing!

The next day, more reprimands arrived – not only from the housemaster but also from my darling brother. He looked down at me like a disapproving father.

What had I been thinking? What was I doing? Did I know how disappointed he was in me… blah blah blah.

I thought this was crazy! Yeah, I had broken a rule, and yes, it could have been dangerous, but bloody hell… had he never been young? Never broken a rule? He was probably 16 or 17 at this point.

So, once I was home, my parents got the letter and my mum made me go and tell my dad what had happened. She didn't tell me off, but she had that 'I'm disappointed in you' expression on her face and an angry glint in her eye.

Slowly, I climbed all four staircases to get to the attic-type room where my dad's office/ home computer was. Then, sheepishly, I explained.

Once I was finished, he just held my hand, looked at me, and said, "Will you do it again?" I replied that I wouldn't and that I was sorry.

"It's OK," was his response.

I was shocked. No telling off, no lecture, nothing. It felt like he understood and, instead of having a go at me, he was commiserating with me! Confusing... but good!

I think Mum was angry that he hadn't told me off or gone mad at me. She liked to control me by saying, "Whatever you do reflects on us – so behave!" It was like with every move I made, every decision I made, I had to think of her before myself.

Like I said, he was pretty absent from my life; in many ways, he was just the 'wallet,' so to speak.

Occasionally, I would get an, "Isn't that skirt a bit short?" comment, but there would never be any follow-through, so I'd just ignore it.

Sometimes, Mum would say to me, after a night out, "Your father was angry you weren't home before he went to work." I was under the impression that I had no curfew; she'd just told me to leave my shoes by the front door so they knew I was home. But now I was coming home too late?

I seemed to cross this invisible line many times. There were no warnings and no rules, but then I'd get told off for breaking these non-existent rules!

After I moved to New York in October 2002, I saw my dad once in March of the following year and then not again until I graduated in July 2004. I'm not sure we spoke at all during that time either.

Mum visited a few times, but it always felt a bit awkward, like she was entering this life I'd created without her – a life where she didn't belong. This time, she was the outsider.

In the 35 years I had with my father, he called me just one time, and we had a total of five meals alone together.

When I was doing my Spanish massage course, my school was just around the corner from his office. So, sometimes, I would call him after class and see if he wanted to meet for lunch. This was a risk on my part, as the likelihood of being turned down was high. I so wanted a better relationship with him, though, and – on and off, through the years – I kept trying to connect with him more. I think I'd even asked my mother if I should ask him to lunch and she said he was too busy so I shouldn't even bother asking.

Of all the times I called and asked him, I believe we met three times. We would have a quick lunch around the corner; I usually had spaghetti. We chatted about nothing much and, although it was a little awkward, I always enjoyed our time together.

Mum was just jealous as he never met her for lunch, just the rare cup of coffee.

The other two times we ate together, just the two of us, was once I'd moved back to the UK and he was in London for business. He just had enough time to meet up.

The one and only time he called me was in my second year at uni. We chatted for 20 minutes. I'm not sure what made him call out of the blue like that, but it never happened again.

In fact, after we stopped having our lunches, whenever I called him, he always sounded fed up, or he would try to 'outdo' me in the who-was-more-stressed stakes. It never seemed right to me that my own father would rather moan about his crap than listen to why I felt stressed. But that was a common theme with both of them.

From the age of 15 onwards, I had certain little phrases I would say, such as, "If that's all you have to be stressed about, then you're lucky." I think I said it in the hope that someone would kindly ask me what was going on – why was I stressed? But they never did. They just looked exasperated and said nothing.

One holiday, just before the self-harming took hold, we were talking in a restaurant and I showed them where I'd dug a compass into my hand and left a big 'X.' They did at least ask why I did it, but then they just shook their heads and tutted at me. It was never mentioned again.

Once Mum found out about the self-harming, all she said to me was, "Promise me you won't do it again." There were no questions about why I did it, how I was feeling, what was going on… nothing.

It was as though emotions and feelings were alien to them. They didn't want to deal with them. They couldn't.

I believe Mum was happy when I had serious boyfriends because it took me off her hands – the emotions were no longer hers to deal with. This guy could deal with me instead. Brave them. Good on them! What a hard job they had taken on, being with me!

It always seemed to me that Jeffrey and Dad were quite close – something Jeffrey denied, saying he felt I was closer to my dad than he was. But they could talk politics and business. They were proud of Jeffrey because of his career. I was rubbish – both job-wise and then later, as a stay-at-home mum. Certainly not something for Dad to shout about.

When visiting Jeffrey and his family, Dad would always get involved. He'd talk to people, play with the grandkids, push the pushchair, and generally help out. With me, in my house, he would sit quietly, read, and then go outside for ages to smoke. He seemed to be there just to humour my mother rather than having a genuine desire to be involved.

In fact, they both got super involved with Jeffrey and his kids – taking them on days out, buying them new shoes, and being a big part of their lives. With us, they would just sit and watch. The most we – the grandkids – got was a bit of a kickabout with a football on the odd occasion.

Mum was different around my dad too. It was like she was protecting him from having to deal with me; she served him and was attuned to him to the point of ignoring everyone else. In her eyes, he was the star.

She was not, however, the apple of his eye. He would snap at her, ignore her, and walk on ahead without her. I never wanted a marriage like theirs; that was something I knew very early on.

I was never given the impression that my dad liked Dickhead very much. Despite his efforts to suck up to him, my father remained standoffish. He was certainly not a man who enjoyed arse-licking!

Dad even commented on his fatness a few times – I tried to protect my husband when he said this, but facts were facts.

Dad occasionally played with my son, but he thought him too soft. At two years old, he would comment on him being a bit 'girly' and 'weak.' "Is he gay?" he would query. He was a tearful, sensitive boy who didn't like to play rough. I don't think Dad could relate.

In the summer of 2010, we went as a family of three – plus my parents – to visit my brother and his family in Florida, where they now lived. My parents went ahead of us and we all stayed in a villa that my sister-in-law had found not too far from Disney World.

This would be the first time that Jeffrey had met Dickhead, and the first time he had met our son, Jacob. He and I hadn't seen each other for six years.

I was overcome with emotion on seeing him at the door. I had a huge smile on my face but was surprised to see nothing on his face. I went to give him a huge hug but got a lukewarm one in return.

I was so tired – after the nine-hour plane ride with a two-year-old – that we went straight to our room to unpack. Not long after, Dad started shouting angrily up the stairs, asking for our pizza takeaway order.

We felt rushed and unwelcome. We had been put in the two smallest rooms – the only ones without en suites.

Prior to the holiday, I'd been messaging Jeffrey's wife about what we'd be doing. I'd also explained that Jacob was fussy with food, so it would be great if he could eat with his cousins; maybe that would encourage him.

Well, she pretty much blanked me the whole trip. The agreements we'd made about the kids sharing meals never happened.

Mum and Dad spent more time with Jeffrey's kids than with Jacob.

It had been arranged that, one night, my parents would babysit and us four adults would go out to dinner together. I was really looking forward to it.

A few days before, Jeffrey and I were messing around and teasing each other – or so I thought – and then he said, "Not knocked up yet?" This was around the time I'd found out I was having trouble conceiving. It seemed a callous thing for him to say, but I let it slide. I just punched him playfully on the arm as we wrestled a bit and he punched me very hard back.

While we were messing around, I jokingly said something about him being a bitch.

I thought no more of it, but later that day at the park, he came over to me and said, "Let's forget the meal out, OK? We don't need to do that now."

I was crushed.

From that moment on, he didn't talk to me for the rest of the trip, and all I could put it down to was the bitch comment.

Anything else I did on that trip was either glared at or commented on.

His wife called Jacob a "scrawny little runt."

On Thanksgiving, it had been prearranged that I would go shopping while Mum and the sister in law cooked, and then I would do all the washing up. I imagined coming home to a lovely meal that we would all share as a family at the dining room table. There was a beautifully dressed table waiting for such an event.

Upon my return, however, everyone had already eaten and it ended up with just me and Dickhead eating this awful, tasteless, bland meal at the sad kitchen table while trying to get Jacob to eat something – anything.

Jeffrey was slagging me off, saying I'd done nothing to help, and Dad was still in a mood from the day before.

The day before, I'd been struggling terribly with the rejection from Jeffrey, and I'd been getting no sleep as Jacob kept waking throughout the night and then early every morning. As usual, Dickhead wasn't helping with his son, and I was worried that Jacob wasn't eating enough. The atmosphere in the house was terrible and it was just a shitty time.

I was fed up with Dickhead not pulling his weight and I spent the day feeling sad and angry.

We went off to show something to Jacob and, unbeknownst to me, my dad was calling us; we didn't hear him. He then rushed up to us really angrily and said, "I've been shouting to you – why didn't you answer?"

I said I was sorry, but I hadn't heard him.

When we started walking together, he muttered something under his breath – it was something about being stupid.

In response, I shouted, "Oh, you know what? Fuck off!" This was the first and only time I had ever sworn at – or even shouted at – my father.

He looked furious! He stormed off and didn't speak to me for the rest of the trip.

Fuck me, it was a shit holiday!

On the second to last day, we all went to this Disney BBQ show. We sat down and Jeffrey's wife started complaining straight away about our seats and how they weren't good enough etc. My father was mortified.

We each got up to go and help ourselves to the buffet and then came back to sit at the table. Then, suddenly, Jeffrey accused me of taking his seat! They were benches rather than seats, and I'd deliberately sat away from his family so that there'd be room for him to sit with his kids. I was sitting with Dickhead and Jacob.

"This is just like you," he said to me. "So selfish and thinking only of yourself. Pass me my beer."

I hadn't seen his beer so had no idea he had 'claimed' this bit of the bench. I was so tempted to throw the whole beer over him, but I managed to control myself. Instead, I explained why I was sitting where I was, but he just continued to verbally abuse me.

Instead of rising to the bait – which I really wanted to do – I picked up my and Jacob's plates and moved us to another table. For a moment, I wasn't sure if Dickhead was going to join us, but he did.

My parents stayed where they were and said nothing.

I tried to show Jacob a good time by pointing out things in the show and then taking him up to dance and meet the Disney characters, but it was so hard trying to pretend everything was OK.

After a while, I asked my parents if I could have the house key as I wanted to leave.

Dad, in an angry and very obviously pissed-off way, stormed off with us to drive us home.

I tried talking to my mum about what had happened, but Dad just shouted at me.

As soon as we got in, I started to pack. I was going to move us to a hotel where we could wait until our flight in two days' time.

Before we could leave, Jeffrey came back and my mum called him out to the patio, where my dad wanted a word with him. I stood at the top of the stairs, trying to hear what was being said. I only heard snippets.

"She's just the same now as when she was six. She's selfish; it's all about her," I heard Jeffrey saying. His wife caught me listening from the stairs and glared at me.

Thankfully, they left the next morning. His kids had been given strict instructions not to say goodbye to us, which was a real shame as we'd gotten along really well. His daughter and I had been holding hands in the queue the night before. We'd played in the pool and had started to develop a lovely friendship.

Once they'd gone, we actually had a pleasant day out. We visited another park and, the whole time, it felt as though a huge weight had been lifted. I hoped my parents could see how the stress and strain had been due to them, not us.

Other than when my father was dying, my 'brother' and I never spoke again.

Around the time I was heavily pregnant with my third child, I started to see a change in my dad – it was like he mellowed a bit. For instance, he started playing with my two little ones. They made up a game called Bed Monster. He would lie under the bed while they sat atop the mattress, and then he would push the whole mattress up to try to knock them off. They giggled with delight every time.

When it came to the kids, suddenly, the eye rolls and fed-up expressions were nowhere to be seen. He always had more time for my little girl, however, he would pick her up and carry her around more than he had my son.

One time, I was expecting my mother to come over for the day. I was eight months pregnant at this point, and although she never actually did anything to help – other than doing my ironing for me – it was company, at least.

I was still under the impression, at this time, that she was my best friend. After all, she was pretty much the only person I ever really spoke to… aside from Dickhead.

Then, she texted to say she couldn't come as she was waiting to hear from my dad. He was in Egypt on business and no one had heard from him for a whole day. His PA could see that he was looking at and deleting emails, but no calls were being answered.

I was pissed off with my mum because it wasn't like we were reliant on house phones anymore; what difference did it make if she was at her house or mine?

The next thing I knew, she was saying he'd had a fall and had hit his head. The doctor had been called to his hotel room and they suspected an ear infection.

Ear infections were common and he often needed his ears syringing, so… no big deal, right?

Well, time went on and he still wasn't getting any better, so it was decided he needed to go to hospital.

My mum wanted to fly over to be with him as the new diagnosis was a bleed on the brain! What the fuck?!

And here I was, eight months pregnant, so I couldn't go with her to Egypt to help with my dad, even though I wanted to go so badly.

Jeffrey met her over there and they spent the next five days in what was supposed to be the best hospital in Egypt, though it sounded horrendous!

I remember sobbing to Dickhead that there was no way I'd be able to give birth while my dad was so ill. "How will I find the strength to push this baby out?" I sobbed. "I can't think straight… I can't do it!"

I could hardly breathe due to all the overwhelming emotions I was feeling. I was just absolutely terrified. How would I do this? How could I possibly find the strength to birth a baby while dealing with this grief?

"Well, you're just going to have to, aren't you?" Dickhead angrily replied.

My heart felt like it had been punched.

I couldn't believe the lack of compassion, understanding, and kindness. Here I was, heavily pregnant, and I had just learnt that my father was incredibly ill – potentially dying – in a foreign country and that there was no way I could get to him.

Of course, it wasn't exactly a surprise that Dickhead was being so unfeeling towards me, but that didn't make it right.

So, I went to my bedroom and locked the door. I was hyperventilating and distraught, with tears streaming down my face. What was I doing? What could I do? I just felt so incredibly stuck in this life. My heart ached!

While all this was going on, I was also having a few health issues of my own. I felt uncomfortable down below, so I went for a check-up – I figured it was thrush. It turned out to be herpes! Type 1, contracted through mouth cold sores.

Dickhead had cold sores! The night we conceived this baby was the night he had given me this awful disease. I felt disgusted and devasted – especially as my plans for a home water birth had now gone completely out the window! I was no longer allowed a vaginal birth. I had to have a C-section, as the risk of the baby contracting herpes on the way out was too high.

Two pretty massive things to deal with, right?!

Well, after my appointment with the midwife to discuss the next steps, I had a phone call to make.

Mum, Dad, and Jeffrey had all been repatriated the night before, and I had texted my mum so many questions that it made no sense to me that they would allow someone with a brain bleed to fly – surely the pressure would be too dangerous?

She had no answers to my questions, so I remained utterly confused. She wouldn't tell me anything. Instead, she asked me to call that night.

I called her mobile, but Jeffrey answered.

"He has a brain tumour and stage 4 lung cancer," he told me. He would probably need an operation to remove the tumour.

I didn't know what to say; I was stunned, to say the least.

My whole life, I'd been anxious about his smoking. I had asked him to quit so many times, but whenever I did, he'd always become incredibly angry with me. Now, here we were!

I burst out crying and managed to blurt out that I was having a C-section, so I wouldn't be able to go back and forth to the hospital.

It felt like so many blows all at once.

As I wanted to go visit him in the hospital, I needed to arrange for someone to look after the kids. Dickhead wouldn't do it, however, as he said he had to come with me. Fortunately, the people next door obliged.

So, first thing in the morning, I dashed to M&S to get food for the kids and some meals for the neighbours to thank them for having my two kids for the day. They had two children of very similar ages, so they would just play all day. We had shared many play dates over the years.

The bank sent a car to pick us up and take us to the hospital in London. I had also picked up sandwiches for everyone there, to feed us all in the hospital room.

What was going to greet me when I arrived? I had no idea. My anxiety was high.

We found his floor and Mum met us at the main door. On getting to his room, a stream of doctors emerged and they all greeted me with smiles – and 'oohs,' on spotting my bump.

On entering the room, I gasped and tears immediately sprang to my eyes as I saw my father lying in a bed, with wires and tubes all over his body and a very big black eye.

Mum bustled me out of the room in a hurry and dragged me to the room next door. What was happening?

She put her arms around me, which I felt was more for her benefit than mine. I needed answers, not to be dragged out and hugged.

A nurse came in and started offering me tea. I didn't want tea; I wanted bloody answers!

I didn't answer her until Mum told me, "It's OK, she's nice, she's helping."

I raised my eyes to meet hers for the first time and realised she wasn't an enemy.

"He's just been for a PET scan, so he has radioactive particles inside him," she explained. "Because of the pregnancy, you can't go near him."

What?! I couldn't believe this. "Can I give him a hug?"

"A quick hug, and then you need to sit at least two metres away from him."

I wanted to sit and hold his hand! I wanted to let him know I was there for him.

Where were my answers?!

I eventually found out that when he'd fallen in the hotel room, he had totally blacked out, hitting his face – hence the black eye. They had diagnosed the cancer in Egypt but had obviously not staged it. They hadn't wanted to tell me anything because of how I would react and because of the pregnancy.

I could see where they were coming from, but bloody hell! When would I be treated the same as everyone else and not like I was some weak simpleton?

I was on the sidelines yet again!

Dad was talking and drinking and we all had a bit of a giggle – it was awkward and grief-filled, but it was a giggle nonetheless.

He needed the tumour to be removed, but as it was a weekend, the surgeon was away.

As he was acting 'normally,' I figured it would be fine to visit again the next day, and this time bring the kids with me. After all, Jeffrey's wife and kids were going to be there tomorrow too.

So, the next day, we arrived by private company car again, loaded down with two car seats and all the crap two young kids need.

Unfortunately, Dad was not having a good day; I could tell the moment we walked into the room. He was dazed, and drifting in and out of consciousness.

This was not what I had expected. I wish someone had warned me so I could not have brought the children. No one else seemed too concerned.

I pointed out what I was seeing and the nurse was called. She, thankfully, seemed to pay attention and called a doctor. However, Dad's normal consultant was not around – he was away for the weekend. FFS!

After a while, a different doctor appeared, though he didn't seem too fussed about Dad's decline.

I carried on watching him attentively.

The kids were nervous around him as he was mostly 'asleep' – and, when he was 'awake,' he was slurring and not making much sense.

Every time the nurses came into the room, I kept urging them on, asking for the doctor to come back. Eventually, he took his BP and evaluated him again, and although he admitted that his stats had changed, he would not acknowledge that this meant his condition was worsening.

By some amazing luck, a bit later on, the original consultant came to check on Dad – he had popped back to collect something, I think. He was immediately concerned by Dad's state and declared that the tumour – which was pressing on something – needed to be removed ASAP or he would die!

We discussed him being moved to an NHS hospital, but that was ruled out as he wouldn't get seen soon enough.

We had to keep taking the kids in and out of the room, to allow us all to talk – and so the doctor could examine Dad.

I told Dickhead to take the kids home so they could relax and stop being moved about, but also so I could concentrate on Dad rather than worrying about how they were. He refused.

A therapist was brought in to offer us help in processing this significant news. I explained that I had my own therapist, but Mum wanted me to sit in on her session. The therapist then explained that, in situations like these, she was there for the family to talk to, to cry at, or whatever they needed.

Mum's first words were, "He's left enough money, so I'll be fine."

I immediately looked at the therapist to check her reaction. She definitely looked shocked! That was certainly not what she expected to come out of my mum's mouth. Personally, I was surprised, but not shocked.

Next, there was a meeting to discuss whether Dad would want life-saving measures in the operating room. I had to explain to my mum what that would entail – the CPR, the likelihood of it not working, but his body being put through so much stress, the breaking of ribs, and so on.

She decided that she couldn't make that decision by herself, so she went to wake my dad up and ask him. In his groggy, slurred speech, he said that 'yes,' he wanted life-saving measures to be taken.

He was to have the surgery and then, assuming all went well, he would be moved to the ICU.

Once it was known that the consultant would be doing the op within the next hour or so, I was told to go home… or, rather, Dickhead decided I had to leave.

I wanted to stay! I knew there was nothing else I could do there and I also knew that I needed to rest – I was having my C-section in two days! – but, my god… once again, they would all be there and I had to leave!

The next morning, I woke to a swollen and painful leg. A car was coming at 10 – to take me straight to the hospital to see Dad – but now I had to go and see my own doctor about my leg. After all, this kind of pain and swelling this late in the pregnancy was not something to be ignored.

He immediately sent me to the hospital for a scan to check the blood flow and to ensure I didn't have a blood clot. When I explained the situation and that I was in a hurry to go and see my father, who had just had life-saving surgery, they were so, so good to me – I was in and out within the hour! All was well; they just told me I had to rest and put my feet up.

That morning, I'd also managed to drop off my son at school and my daughter at nursery. Just as I was preparing to meet the driver who was taking me to London (I had already postponed the time twice), however, the nursery called to inform me that Ivy was ill and that I needed to go and collect her. She wasn't actually ill; she'd been constipated, so I'd given her some medicine days before and she had finally 'let it go.' They decided it was diarrhoea and that she needed to be off now for two days.

Dickhead was 'working from home' so I negotiated with him about collecting her and looking after her while I was with my dad. He didn't look impressed and said he had work to do.

"What if I leave there at 2 and be home by 3? Can you just look after her till then?" I asked, exasperated.

He agreed, making out that he was doing me a massive favour. I had been rushing around like mad all morning, not taking a breath or having time to eat; I'd even had my planned therapy session by phone while driving to the hospital for my scan. Looking after his own kid, therefore, was the least he could do. I went and collected her and thanked him for looking after her at home.

My therapist told me to go and see my dad and to stay as long as I wanted – that was very important!

On arrival at the ICU – which is different to normal wards – I was unnerved by what I saw. My dad was all the way down the end, with a massive bandage around his head and a tube coming out of it – a drain. He was much better than the last time I'd seen him.

Shockingly, I was the first in my family to visit him that morning. It was already after 11… where was my mum?

We didn't have an awful lot to say to each other. I wasn't sure how tired he was and I was well aware of not pissing him off or talking about crap he didn't want to hear about. I also didn't want to concern him with my pregnancy issues or my other worries, so I just sat with him quietly.

He asked a nurse to bring a TV over for me so I wouldn't get bored. I know he meant well, but I took that as a sign that he really didn't want to talk to me. Then, of course, there was the issue of what to put on the TV! Something I wanted or something he would want to watch?

I was so uncomfortable; my leg was throbbing but there was nowhere for me to properly raise my legs, so I just kept trying to move to find a more suitable position. It was so tiring.

As it got closer to 2 o'clock, I messaged Dickhead to ask permission to stay a bit longer – as, apparently, Mum wasn't coming until 5. He said I could have 'just a bit' longer.

I was torn – do I go home to my family, like my husband was pressuring me to do, or do I stay with my dad, who I'd nearly lost yesterday?

At about 3, I told my dad I had to leave. I never bad-mouthed Dickhead to them, so they had no idea that it wasn't really my choice to go. Just like I never told them the real reason for needing a C-section. They just thought it was down to my Crohn's. "Yes, I thought that might be the case," Mum had said when I told her what was happening. HA!

I always protected Dickhead. I never told them what he'd done, or any of the awful things he said and did to me over the years.

Anyway, when I said I was leaving, Dad's face fell. He looked so hurt and confused, and I was crushed!

By the time I was able to visit Dad again, I think he was back home; having had a C-section and a new baby, I wasn't very mobile for a few weeks.

I would call the hospital all the time to check up on him and get real information about what was going on, as Mum never seemed to have the proper details. I don't know if she couldn't take it in or if she was in denial or what.

Going against my and possibly my brother's advice, Dad tried a second chemo drug after the first had no effect. We thought he would do better to enjoy the time he had left rather than spend it feeling shit, in and out of hospital… but what do we know, right?

At some point, I wrote him a letter. It detailed how much I loved him, how this was so awful and devastating, and how I was there for him.

He didn't mention it to me.

A few days later, I asked him if he had managed to read it.

"Oh yes, sorry… yes, thank you," came the reply.

I wanted more. I wanted to hear how he loved me too. I wanted to have a heart-to-heart and hear any advice he had, any regrets… anything.

I never got anything from him.

Nothing improved. He wasn't sleeping or eating. He'd lost so much weight by this point that he was basically a skeleton.

It got to a point, about five months later, where he could no longer manage the stairs up to their London apartment. So, I suggested I find them somewhere near me, but my dad replied, "I can't afford to rent two places to live."

What nonsense! I don't know why he was so against it.

He'd actually been against quite a few things since getting ill: sharing a bed with Mum, us sorting out an anniversary present for her from him, holding the baby…

It was put to him that he would either need to stay in the hospital, live in my house, or get a place of their own (which I'd find for them).

So, I began my search. First, I called every nursing home within a 25-mile radius of my house. I visited a few too. But it soon became clear that these were not places I would ever put my dad.

Next, I looked on Rightmove for a suitable house/apartment. There were only two to look at.

Around this time, Dad started to pee blood. He also developed a lesion on his cheek. I told his palliative nurse that I feared it was skin cancer.

"No, no, lung cancer doesn't spread to the skin," came the response.

As it turned out, it *was* skin cancer. It had also spread to his kidneys, hence the bleeding. He had radiation to try to help with this.

Why did they keep fussing with him? I wondered. Why couldn't they just let him go with peace and dignity?

I think both my parents were in denial that he was going to die soon.

One weekend when I visited, Mum and I entered his room to find him sitting on the side of the bed, struggling to remove his oxygen tubes from his nose. He was delirious. I went to get the nurse.

It was also the weekend that his two brothers were due to visit.

I knew we were close to the end.

I had a car go and pick up my overnight things from home and told Dickhead I wouldn't be home that night.

Back with my parents, my dad chatted a bit with his brothers in a slurred, faraway voice, and then started coughing up a pinkish phlegm.

Jeffrey wanted to know when the end was near as he'd said he wanted to be there for him. Over and over I texted him, telling him to come.

"If he can spit then he is strong," Jeffrey replied. "What's his BP?"

He never came.

I took it upon myself to mop Dad's brow and to try to keep him comfy.

While watching the rugby, he fell asleep. I gently removed his glasses.

He never regained consciousness.

He kept reaching out his arm as though he were touching things – I hope he was meeting his mum and dad, joining them in the afterlife.

He hung on for another day, and the next night, while Mum and I were once again top and tailed in a single bed, the nurse woke us at 3 am. "His breathing has changed," she said quietly.

I jumped up to be by his side.

"Is he even breathing?" Mum asked dispassionately. It was said in the oddest tone – an uninterested, 'what are you even talking about?' tone.

He was gone.

I carefully removed his wedding band and his watch.

We were then ushered into another room and brought some tea.

I had the worst tummy ache and was finding it hard to move much; my Crohn's was flaring up due to the stress. Mum seemed very calm, but I was feeling so many different things… relief that it was over, and so much aching sadness that he was gone. I was incredibly tired and exhausted too.

After maybe an hour, we were taken back to his room. He was covered with a sheet up to his chin and his mouth was being held closed by a bandage around his head. He didn't look like him anymore. He was just a shell now.

We weren't allowed to stay there alone with him, so there was lots of hanging around as we waited for the coroner to come and collect him.

I think they distracted Mum somehow while they put my dad in a body bag. I waited outside his room and then followed the gurney to the lifts. It felt like my heart was being ripped out. I would never see him again. I didn't know what to do with myself.

We decided it would be best to register the death now so that it was all done; then, we wouldn't have to come back to London again.

It was around 7 am by this point, so we drove to a café and waited for it to open. When it did, we went in for coffee and pastries. It felt surreal to be going about such ordinary activities while everyone else carried on with their day, especially after such a monumental event had just occurred.

After breakfast, we met with the lady who was to register the death. It was upsetting, of course, and we realised that the cause of death had been written wrong on the death certificate given to us by the doctor: it said kidney cancer, but it was lung cancer. We had to decide whether to carry on with it as it was or go back to the hospital to ask them to correct it.

But what did it really matter? He was gone. That was the only thing that mattered now.

I drove us to their London flat and Mum started to pack while I went for a nap; I couldn't drive the 1.5 hours home after not having much sleep the previous two nights.

We decided she would come and live with us until their bungalow was ready in a few days, and then she would return for the day in a week or so to organise the movers.

Soon after this, she got ill with a sickness bug – it was probably due to all the stress and grief.

It was tough for me too, though, as I was grieving, looking after three children, and trying to look after her with her illness and grief.

During a conversation I had with Jeffrey, he suggested she go and live with him in America for six months. I told him to ask her; I was pretty sure she wouldn't go, but I didn't want to tell him that. I didn't hear about it again, though, so I presume he never even asked. It was all big gestures and offers with him, but never any follow-through.

When Father's Day came around later that year, I bought a lovely candle with an inscription on the glass, and I also wrote a card for him.

When it got broken the following year – it was knocked off the table – I planned on replacing it, as I was so upset when it cracked and chipped. But I never did. When I started to realise the part he'd really played in not being the father I needed, I even took down the photos I had of him around the house.

Mum obviously kept his wedding band. She, unbeknownst to me, gave his gold chain to Jeffrey. I got nothing.

She tried to appease me by giving me his glasses.

I had wanted, at the very least, his watch. I was just so hurt that everyone got something they could wear and keep close to them… everyone except me.

Upon telling her this some months later, she took me aside, and – with tears in her eyes and a hesitation in her hand – she gave me his watch. I handed it back. If she needed it so much, I told her, she could keep it.

My father died in February, and in August – when it was their wedding anniversary and her birthday – we tried extra hard to be there for her. Jeff even came over to England!

While Dickhead and Jeff were moving some furniture into her bedroom, they asked her something about where she wanted it. Her reply was some awful comment about "in the bedroom with a man in it."

I was disgusted! It was callous and ill-thought-out. Not only was it too soon for such comments, but this was also my father she was disrespecting.

There was a time when she and I were sharing a bed at my house – perhaps a few weeks before my father died – and I was trying to comfort her. She was very stiff and not accepting of my warmth, as usual, and then she said, "My husband is going to die before my mother."

Again, an odd thing to say, in my mind.

She seemed to have so little care for others; it was all about how things appeared and how she would personally be affected. Her feelings towards her own mother were so callous and cold.

Dad's funeral was so full, people were standing at the back, and it even had to be live-streamed for those in other countries who couldn't make it.

These people talked of a man I had never met. Apparently, they had a saying at the Bank – WWAD. What Would Al Do? Who was this patient, caring, calm man that they'd all been so happy to go to for advice and guidance? This stranger who'd apparently had all the time in the world to explain, re-explain, and share? That guy sounded like he would have been a great dad.

We were all upset and angry at the treatment my dad had gotten at the private hospital from his oncologist: false hope, no proper answers, and seemingly little care. In fact, the night before he died, this consultant came in – while my dad was unconscious – and said, "Oh dear, he's a bit poorly, is he?"

So, I took it upon myself to get hold of all my dad's medical files and then I researched the life out of them to see if any errors were made. I wanted this consultant to be accountable for his lack of humanity and for pushing so many drugs onto someone who was never going to live very long.

It took me five long days to read it all. I had the baby and the two children to look after too, but I was determined to get answers. I then wrote a five-page complaint letter to the hospital, detailing where this man had gone wrong in his behaviour.

I'd become close friends with one of my dad's nurses and she confirmed that he was a rubbish doctor who lied to his patients about the seriousness of their diseases.

After some back-and-forth emails with the hospital, I finally demanded a handwritten apology, to my mother, from this man.

When the letter arrived, it was incredibly passive-aggressive, but at least it was something.

No one seemed to be at all pleased that I'd managed to get this hospital and this doctor to semi-admit he had fucked up. I guess it was upsetting to my mum, but I think it just confirmed to me that I'd known all along what was going to happen – and no one had listened to me.

As a result of my complaint, the hospital revised its procedures. A new directive was issued requiring consultants and palliative nurses to provide clearer explanations of a patient's prognosis. They also implemented a standardised method to ensure patients were well-informed about their condition.

CHAPTER 27
BABY NUMBER THREE

I had a million things to get done before this baby was born.

The day before my C-section was spent going here and there, cleaning, preparing, making beds, and getting my hospital bag ready. I was crying for some of it as I was so tired; I desperately wanted and needed a rest, but there was still just so much to get done!

That night, Dickhead's mum came over as she was going to stay with the kids while I was in hospital. As she reheated the dinner she'd brought over for us, she told a story about someone else she knew who'd had lung cancer – they had died!

Oh, great, thanks!! Just what I needed to hear right now!

I took my dinner and ate it alone in my bed.

Dickhead came up an hour later and I told him why I'd chosen to remove myself from the situation. "Yeah, I know, sorry," was all he said. He didn't bother saying anything to her while she was doing it, though!

When I arrived early to the hospital and was shown into a cubicle, the reality of the situation hit me. I was first on the list of the day, and I had my birth plan ready – not that I imagined anyone would read it.

I had planned a home water birth, so this was as far from that as you could get. Hopefully, they would at last read the beginning bit about how I might be a bit emotional because of my dad… maybe treat me a little extra gently?

Despite having taken a course of drugs and despite all my symptoms having gone away, they still wouldn't allow me to give birth naturally in case anything remained of the herpes and got passed to the baby.

I understood and, of course, I didn't want to take any risks, but I couldn't help but feel disappointed and ashamed. I just felt so dirty. If I ever get a flare-up these days, I feel filthy all over again. Dickhead never apologised for passing it to me, or for my having to go through a C-section because of it.

Before I knew it, it was down to the operating room, and even though I'd been assured a midwife would be with me at all times, she kept disappearing.

They exposed my back while I sat on the side of the table, leaning and hunched over. As soon as I felt the needle touch me, I flinched.

"You mustn't move!" the anaesthesiologist told me.

I started to cry. This was so real – so far from what I wanted, so medical and clinical. I was heartbroken for the birth I wanted and couldn't have, for the start I wanted my baby to have… but she couldn't.

Why was it so unfair?

They swung my legs up onto the bed and quickly set things up… and then they all disappeared!

How long were they going to be? Where had they gone? They could have at least told me!

The drugs made me feel sick and like I was going to pass out.

Thankfully, they came back soon after and gave me some other drugs that wouldn't make me feel so ill.

Dickhead did a good job of distracting me, talking nonsense while they did their work; I could feel them pulling me, rummaging about inside me.

After a few more episodes of feeling like I would rather die than feel so sick and woozy, they suddenly held up a baby dripping in blood.

I was so shocked! I'd been so busy dealing with my father and the impending C-section it was like I had momentarily forgotten there was going to be a baby at the end of it! Right from the start, she took my breath away.

While they cleaned her up, I told Dickhead to go be with her, to make sure she was OK. If Mum had been there she would have been with me while he saw to baby, but I was all alone, lying immobile, unable to do anything.

Finally, my baby was placed in my arms, all wrapped up. I tried to kiss and snuggle up to her, but it was hard as she was lying on my neck and I didn't want to drop her.

Dickhead held her while they sewed me up, and then I was wheeled to a recovery room.

I was naked, as was she, so we had some lovely skin-to-skin.

We drifted in and out of sleep for a few hours, and then we were taken to the postnatal ward. We spent two days snuggled up together. I barely put her down.

Mum came to visit for a few hours with Grandad. Stupidly, we all decided it would be best if Nanny didn't come as there wasn't much room, her balance was off, and I was too tired to deal with having to talk so much, especially as I knew I'd have to keep repeating myself; she had dementia.

I felt so guilty about this later on. I know she was upset by it.

The nurses decided it was time for me to attempt getting on my feet for the first time. Well, I took two steps and then I threw up! Back to bed for me.

Later that night, after everyone had left, I had an issue...

Due to wanting me to get up, they had asked me to put some knickers on, to hold my sanitary pad in place. Later, as I was lying in bed, the knickers must have dislodged the tube for my catheter – I realised the wee was bubbling up and was about to go everywhere!

I was holding the baby and had no way to move. I couldn't reach the call button, and after calling out a few times with no reply, I realised I was a bit stuck!

I managed to – painfully – put the baby in the cot and then wiggle, reach, and stretch as much as I could to pull the call button to me.

The nurse that arrived was not very friendly; she was annoyed about the knickers that were now covered in blood and was a bit short with me.

As much as I'd hated the idea of the C-section, and as much as I missed my kiddies at home, it was lovely to just lie there and bond with my new baby for two days, with no need (or ability) to get up or attend to anything else.

I wonder how things would have been if I'd been allowed – and was able – to do that with the other two.

CHAPTER 28
ME

My self-doubt and low self-esteem have been prevalent throughout my life.

Even now, at the age of 44, I don't believe in my ability to do much. If I achieve anything, I simply dismiss any accomplishments because 'it was easy,' 'it's no big deal,' or 'such and such made it possible.'

I cannot take credit for anything because I don't believe I'm good enough to achieve anything worth giving credit for.

I second-guess every decision I make, be it in my life or with my mothering.

I'm constantly asking myself the same questions:

Do they love me?

Am I doing good enough?

Am I spoiling them?

Am I teaching them the right things?

Is he doing it better?

Are they happier there?

Am I good enough?

How am I supposed to know how to parent when I never had a good parenting role model myself?

What looks 'normal' for a child, a teenager, a mother?

I have no idea!

I have no trust in people – in their intentions, in their motives, or in their ability to be good. Whereas once I clung to any hint of kindness and gentleness, now I distrust it. Why are they doing that? What do they get out of it?

I keep myself to myself. I don't talk to people, I have no social life, and I avoid groups and crowds wherever possible. I replay conversations in my head. Was there a tone? Did I interpret it correctly? Were they mad that I said what I did? Did they take it how I meant it?

And these are just normal conversations with regular people: shopkeepers, teachers, passing strangers… so can you imagine the replaying that goes on with conversations with my family?

It takes me right back to the past. One thought leads to the next and, before I know it, I am deep inside my head and all my memories. I start disassociating, and this bleeds into my day.

If I have to talk to Dickhead, I later replay every sentence in my head, second-guessing my choice of words. Did I say something that could be twisted and used against me? Did I give too much information? What will he do with what I said?

Therapy is work. It takes effort, patience, and so much energy. It is exhausting.

You have to retrain yourself to think differently, look at the world differently, react differently. Constantly trying to remember how best to behave, what was said in the session, and how to try to heal from within while still living through every day… like I said, it's exhausting. It isn't just chatting and complaining, which is what some people think therapy is.

At one point, I learnt that Jeff had received a financial gift from my parents one year of $195,000, whereas I'd received nothing – because "we paid for all that therapy for you!"

Yeah, "cos those are the same!"

She later denied this had happened.

I learnt at the ex-boarders' meet-up that it is quite common for us to not know how to parent, especially from the age at which we were sent away. We simply have no basis to start from.

I find that I also have no idea of what is 'normal' childhood behaviour. I had to stop playing at age 11 – and, even before that, I was so bothered about pleasing my parents that I'm not sure my behaviour could be considered 'normal.'

Would it actually matter if I wasn't here?

Sometimes, I think my children might miss me – I am their mother, after all – but then I worry about whether they love their dad more. If they have a better time at his house. If they're happier there… if it's just better.

My son hardly comes out of his room when he's home, which I figure is pretty normal for a teenager… but, often, he won't join in with family activities, preferring to retreat to his room at the first opportunity.

Everything I do, I try to do it with love and with their best interests at heart, but what if it isn't enough?

What if I'm doing it all wrong?

Until Dickhead and I split up, I did all the night waking and all the parenting – literally 100%. Even to this day, I still do all the kid 'admin' and everything else. Dickhead has more emotional energy than me – I presume because he didn't have to deal with any of the stuff I've had to deal with in life, and because he's been able to sleep properly for the last 15 years! He is, however, still pretty robotic in his demeanour and, I presume, execution.

I often feel like a failure.

Dickhead tells me how things are supposedly done at his house, but then I see evidence that these must be lies. Why lie about such innocuous things? Then again, nowadays, I don't believe a single word that comes out of his mouth.

My first go-to emotion is always the desire to just kill myself. To escape. To end the pain, the tears, the suffering, and the self-doubt. The arguing and not being able to fix anything.

This is going to be my life. The highs not being high enough, the lows being so low I feel suicidal, the doubt excruciating… and all the while knowing I can't kill myself because of the effect it will have on my children.

My heart literally beats for them. If I don't have their love and reassurance, I wither and die inside.

What is the point without them?

I have many ADHD traits, but not enough for a diagnosis. I believe I also have many autistic traits, but – again – not enough for a diagnosis. I don't believe these are genetic or things I was born with; I think they were caused by trauma.

Your brain chemistry changes as you grow up, and if you don't get the nurturing love you need, different areas shrink while others enlarge – kind of the wrong way around to encourage 'normal' social and necessary functions. In other words, I feel fucked and damaged, and these things are so deep inside me that I don't see them ever going away.

In 2023, I was diagnosed with Complex PTSD* and disassociation*.

> ### *COMPLEX POST-TRAUMATIC STRESS DISORDER
>
> The NHS describes this as resulting from recurring or prolonged traumatic experiences such as childhood abuse or neglect, domestic violence, and sexual abuse. It's also more likely if you experienced trauma at a young age, such as being harmed by someone close to you whom you trusted, when you were unable to escape the trauma.
>
> This differs from PTSD, which many people will have heard of. Whereas PTSD arises from one traumatic event, CPTSD comes from a series of ongoing traumas, usually stemming from childhood.
>
> * Feelings of worthlessness
>
> * Shame
>
> * Guilt
>
> * Flashbacks
>
> * Problems controlling emotions
>
> * Finding it hard to feel connected with other people

* Relationship problems
* Trouble keeping friends and partners
* Being distrustful of the world
* Anxiety
* Perfectionism
* Memory problems
* Problems with concentration
* Headaches
* Depression and crying spells
* Suicidal thoughts or attempts
* Mood swings
* Agitation
* Obsessive-compulsive tendencies
* Panic episodes
* Paranoia
* Shakiness
* Hypervigilance
* Nightmares
* Sleep disturbance
* Unexplained stomach upsets
* Chronic health conditions
* Depersonalisation or derealisation
* Autoimmune conditions.

* DISSOCIATION

This is a mental process of disconnecting from one's thoughts, feelings, memories, and sense of identity.

As Betterhealth.vic.gov.au states at https://www.betterhealth.vic.gov.au/health/conditionsandtreatments/dissociation-and-dissociative-disorders#bhc-content:

"It is believed that the underlying cause of dissociative disorders is chronic trauma in childhood."

The symptoms I experience include:

* Feeling disconnected from yourself

* Problems with handling intense emotions

* Sudden and unexpected shifts in mood. E.g. feeling very sad for no reason

* Depression and anxiety problems

* Trouble concentrating

* Significant memory lapses

* Feeling compelled to behave in a certain way

* Identity confusion. E.g. behaving in a way the person would normally find offensive.

This is the best description I've found of how I feel when this is happening to me.

As Betterhealth.vic.gov.au

(https://www.betterhealth.vic.gov.au/health/conditionsandtreatments/dissociation-and-dissociative-disorders) states:

"Depersonalisation disorder is characterised by feeling detached from one's life, thoughts and feelings. People with this type of disorder say they feel distant and emotionally unconnected to themselves, as if they are watching a character in a boring movie.

Other typical symptoms include problems with concentration and memory. The person may report feeling 'spacey' or out of control. Time may slow down. They may perceive their body to be a different shape or size than usual; in severe cases, they cannot recognise themselves in a mirror."

This is also a wonderful description of what I experience:

*DEPERSONALISATION

DEREALISATION DISORDER is a mental disorder in which the person has persistent or recurrent feelings of depersonalisation and/or derealisation. Depersonalisation is described as feeling disconnected or detached from one's self. Individuals may report feeling as if they are an outside observer of their own thoughts or body, and often report feeling a loss of control over their thoughts or actions. Derealisation is described as detachment from one's surroundings. Individuals experiencing derealization may report perceiving the world around them as foggy, dreamlike, surreal, and/or visually distorted.

> Depersonalisation-derealisation disorder is thought to be caused largely by interpersonal trauma such as early childhood abuse. Adverse childhood experiences, specifically emotional abuse and neglect have been linked to the development of depersonalisation symptoms. Feelings of depersonalization and derealisation are common from significant stress or panic attacks. individuals may remain in a depersonalised state for the duration of a typical panic attack. However, in some cases, the dissociated state may last for hours, days, weeks, or even months at a time. In rare cases, symptoms of a single episode can last for years.

I feel like I'm constantly living in my own private hell, with constant flashbacks to all the awful things people did and said to me. My hope is that writing this book will purge it all from my system. Every day I write, I remember new things I had previously locked away.

I was never convinced about my major depression, dysthymia, and generalised anxiety disorder diagnosis. The antidepressants have only ever taken the edge off – never enough for me to feel 'well.'

My constant need to stay busy – to always be on the move or else be left utterly exhausted and too fatigued to do anything other than lie on the sofa – has left me feeling bewildered. My thinking was that if I stopped, I would have time to think, and thinking leads to feelings and tears and sinking into a deep depression. Keeping busy stopped those thoughts.

Often, these days, I just feel numb. Not much gets my pulse racing or the tears falling.

I am amazing in an emergency, however, as I can remain calm while others are panicking.

Mostly, I just feel disconnected… from almost everything.

In terms of CPTSD episodes, the website https://www.medicalnewstoday.com/articles/322886#symptoms states that they include:

"Recurrent distressing memories and dreams of the traumatic event.

Persistent avoidance of stimuli that relate to the traumatic event.

Hyperarousal, which means being in a continual state of high alert.

Persistent negative beliefs or expectations about oneself, others or the world.

Difficulty sleeping or concentrating."

ACEs are also mentioned – Adverse Childhood Experiences. If you look at this list of what constitutes an ACE, you may query if this was me:

* Childhood exposure to violence, abuse or neglect

* Substance dependence in the family

* Mental health disorder in the family

* Having incarcerated family members

* Chronic poverty or neglect

* Housing instability

* Growing up in an unsafe or crime-heavy environment.

If you look closely, you will see that most of them WERE me!

I was exposed to neglect. I had mental health disorders, and I would hazard a guess that most of my family did too. I was incarcerated at school – it was like a prison – and, again, I was neglected there. My housing situation was unstable… school, home, different rooms, different houses. I never felt settled or safe or at home, or like I belonged. I was also sexually and physically abused at school.

The website goes on to explain the coping mechanisms people with CPTSD use:

* Misusing alcohol or drugs

* Becoming people pleasers

* Lashing out at minor criticism

* Self-harm.

https://www.hanleycenter.org/mental-health-disorders/complex-ptsd/ goes on to say:

"What happens with CPTSD is that your limbic system gets flooded with stress hormones. As a result, it stays stuck in fight, flight, or freeze mode.

With CPTSD, you constantly feel on edge; nothing seems to help. The emotional trauma gets physically stuck in your body. Professional care is needed.

Complex PTSD profoundly impacts the health of our nervous systems because our difficult memories feel like they are happening to us in the present moment. Over and over, our bodies relive the trauma from decades prior. This type of complex trauma is not related to a single accident like an attack or car accident but rather a series of traumas over a long time."

I don't make progress with people, and I've become so attuned to their fakeness and insincerity that it's nearly impossible for me to make friends. I trust no one, always seeing their ulterior motives, and quickly recognise the selfish bullshit that comes out of their mouths.

I know I come across as cold and distant, and potentially like I feel I'm 'better' than them, but I have lost all ability to care about this.

I did have a friend once who I thought would become a lifelong best friend. We met through my middle daughter; they became friends at nursery so we started hanging out too.

To start with, I got weird vibes from her, but as I tried to include her in things and we got talking more, I realised we had several things in common. We started texting every day and, once our kids started going to the same infant school together, we began seeing each other most days at pick-up.

For years, our friendship grew. We told each other almost everything – or so I thought.

Dickhead wasn't overly keen on her; I wonder if he didn't like the closeness we had. I thought we were like sisters. She would say as much – she called us 'soul sisters.'

After my dad died and she moved up north, she asked me to lend her £9,000 to pay off her credit card debt. She said she would start to pay me back when she could.

I agreed. I felt guilty for having so much money now and I wanted to do some good with it. Help my loved ones.

A few years later, she told me of the trouble she was having trying to pay for the wedding they wanted. I sent her £2,500 for her to put towards her venue or food or whatever, just anything she needed for the wedding.

As it turned out, she spent the money on other things.

She was always telling me how little money she had, but that never made sense to me because her partner was a CID detective. When I would query this – as I had googled his supposed salary brackets – she would just shut me down.

Now that I think about it, when it came to her, nothing made sense. Clearly, she was using me.

I was always sending her little gifts to cheer her up, but she would never let me know that they'd arrived or thank me. Every single time, I had to ask if she'd received them.

She asked me to be her maid of honour, and of course I agreed. I took the role very seriously. I sent her a bouquet of beautiful roses for her wedding bouquet, as she said they couldn't afford to buy a nice one. I would arrange it when I arrived. I spent ages choosing her something old, something new, something borrowed, and something blue.

On arriving at her house – which was a six-hour drive away – we were greeted well, but the next morning when her family were present, it was like I didn't exist. It was always like that when other friends or family were around; I was pushed to the sidelines and practically ignored.

I had thought that, being the maid of honour, this wouldn't happen this time. I was wrong.

I was happy to do little jobs and helpful things all day, but when I realised I was literally there to do that and nothing else, I started to get annoyed. I was being used as a dogsbody.

I was there to drive her around in the nice car, supply the money to buy things, and generally help her out… but I wasn't there as a friend.

We barely said five words to each other in the two days we were there, but she had plenty of time for everyone else.

One night ,a few months later, she started texting me. She said that she and her now husband – married just a few months – were arguing, so she was taking the kids to a hotel for the night. It was 11 pm.

Her next text simply said, 'Send me some money now.'

I tried to call repeatedly but there was no answer. I didn't know what to do, so I sent over £500.

She never answered my calls, but I managed to get hold of her son by text and he told me she was just driving around.

A week after she'd gone back home, I asked for the remainder of my money back.

"I was going to use it for food," she told me.

Still… I wanted it back. So much of my money was going on paying solicitors these days and I wasn't earning much at all.

I was fed up with her telling me how little money she had, while at the same time she'd be getting her nails done, having takeaways, and getting Botox and lip fillers.

I had been duped!

I could understand her wanting to get away from her husband, especially after I learnt what they'd been arguing about. Things hadn't been good with them for a while, and I knew before they got married that it was a bad idea. But she assured me she was happy and that it was the right thing to do. They'd already been together for 15 years and had three children together.

I just didn't trust him. They'd started their relationship when he was still married; he'd cheated on his previous wife with my friend.

What I wasn't on board with was her dragging her kids into it – ripping them from their beds in the middle of the night, on a school night, driving around for hours, and then going to a hotel for two or three nights, while telling them all the details of their arguments.

She later found out that he'd cheated again. His behaviour was despicable and unforgivable. It was a mess.

But I won't defend her actions either. She used her children against their father – and to turn herself into a bigger victim than she actually was. She then began to stalk the 'new woman,' sending emails and texts. I felt I didn't know this person and I didn't feel safe around her.

In the end, she chose to take the kids out of school and move back down south, where her family was.

As she was now living with her brother and his family – in total, there were eight of them living in a small three-bed terraced house – I offered her our house while we went away on a week's holiday.

She accepted my offer.

I cleaned and tidied, made it all nice, and left out clean sheets. I simply asked that she feed the fish and water the plants while we were away.

On our return, I found such a mess!!

I had assumed she would look after my things – after all, she was always talking about how much cleaning and tidying she did, and her house was always nice when I visited.

But that wasn't the case here. There were food wrappers under the beds, board games strewn across the floor, wee on the toilet seats, empty boxes put back in the cupboards, and so much food eaten out of the freezer and cupboards. I had requested that no one go in my middle daughter's room as she'd stated she didn't want anyone in there – but things were broken in there. The floor was filthy. I had never seen my house so dirty! I was so angry and upset.

She knew how much time and money I'd put into making this house 'just right,' that it was my one and only safe place. And she'd still ruined it.

My upset must have shown in our texts, as one day she asked me what was wrong. I was honest and told her how upset I was that she'd left it all so dirty. She blamed the kids and then turned it around on me, saying she shouldn't have accepted the offer because she knew I would act like this – and now I'd made her have a panic attack.

She also said we should take a break from the friendship.

WOW. I hadn't expected that! Although, to be honest, it was a relief.

After that, life became a bit calmer. I expected to miss her – to feel lost without her to tell my woes to – but I didn't. I haven't missed her at all.

For a few months she sent me £100 a month, I assume to make a dent in the money I'd given her, but then it stopped.

This experience massively added to my distrust of people.

We were 'friends' for nine years. I thought I could trust her. I thought she cared about me. Now, I can't help but think I was nothing more than a cash cow to her. I was always the one who paid for coffee or nights out. I even took her to Barcelona for a weekend and paid for everything.

I gave everything of myself to her – I laid myself bare – but I didn't get the same in return.

I am very much an all-or-nothing person. If we are true friends, I will give you the world. I will treat you as I want to be treated – with love and kindness, generosity, and care.

These days, I won't take that risk again. I take nothing from surface-level, small-talk acquaintances. I need depth and connection… but I won't open myself up to that again.

Mark and the children are the only ones who will get all of me.

After what I went through with my mother, I feel I can survive anything now. If I can live through my own mother showing me she didn't love me, I can live through anything.

I actually liked lockdown. Not having to go out, not having to talk to other people, not dealing with randoms. The selfishness of people astounds and fucks me off every bloody day.

I reckon I could live quite happily alone, with my dogs. I feel alone even when surrounded by people anyway, and at least this way I wouldn't have to deal with their crap!

I am sick of being so polite and accommodating to people, only for them to either ignore me, blank me, or screw me over. At least if I'm alone, the drama and hurt are next to zero.

When I'm alone, I feel at peace.

Chapter 29
Mother

As a child, I felt very protective of my mother.

There's one day in particular that sticks in my mind. I would have been about eight years old, and we were living in Italy. She, my brother and I were out.

There had been times in the past when she'd had her handbag stolen – ripped from her neck, even. Well, on this day, while we were on the bus, she said she felt someone pulling at her bag. Immediately, I wanted to shield her.

I stood very close to her, legs wide to give me good balance, and I was ready to defend her at a moment's notice. Then, as we walked down the street, I stayed close and surveyed our surroundings with sharp eyes. I would have done anything to keep her safe.

It is such a shame that I didn't ever get the same protection granted to me.

I was often told that whatever I did would reflect on her. So, I needed to behave and act a certain way so that SHE would be seen in a good light. This haunted me throughout my entire life;

every action, thought, and word was shadowed by this. Would she approve? What would she say?

This even got carried into the bedroom – I would imagine her disapproving face, watching what I was doing. Not a great turn-on, let me tell you!

When I was young, maybe 13 or 14, she was shouting at me and some spittle flew from her mouth and landed on my cheek. I wiped it away and she, trying not to laugh, sniggered and then slapped my arm hard before walking away.

I guess that was an improvement from a few years previous, when something similar had happened and she'd shouted, "I will spit on you if I damn well please!"

When I was six or seven, I had my mouth washed out with soap for saying a swear word.

My father also spanked me on the bottom by bending me over his lap. This only happened a few times but, of course, it added to my fear of my father.

Back in those days, mums would often say, "Wait till your father gets home," as a threat. Well, it worked.

She had this odd idea that 'everyone is a millionaire on paper.' I pondered this notion for years, trying to wrap my head around it. It's a clear example of her delusional thinking about money.

When I was in a relationship with Tom, he had to take something to my house one day while I was away at school. I knew my mother would be there, and I suddenly had the urge to call the house because I was worried about what might happen.

I had so little trust in my mother that I believed she might be cheating with my boyfriend!!

That is very sad.

No one else in my family had strawberry blonde hair, just me – yet another way I felt like I was different from them, and not a real part of the family, although people would often comment that I looked like my mother. This upset me on two counts: I didn't think she was especially beautiful, and she would always tell me she had an ugly face. So… did that mean I had an ugly face?

When I was little, I did think she was beautiful, but as I grew up and saw the person she really was – and how she made me feel – I guess I started to see the real her.

In my teen years, I would often see her staring at me – not in a loving, tender way but in a more assessing, critical way. She especially stared at my boobs. I found it all very uncomfortable. I would sometimes ask her what she was staring at, but she'd just say, "Nothing."

When I was in my late teens, she told me one day – while walking around a supermarket – that I had 'put on weight.' We then agreed that I should see her personal trainer, who would come to the house once or twice a week. This trainer made me strip to my underwear while she assessed me. She then took all my measurements and told me that my taste in food and vegetables was 'unsophisticated' and that I needed to lose weight. She made comments about what I ate in a day and showed me lots of exercises I should do to battle the weight.

It was shortly after this that I started working out relentlessly; I had to do a workout each morning before doing anything else.

I would judge my worth and size by how much I could feel my hip bones sticking out when I was lying down. If they were prominent, I was doing OK. If not, then I needed to work harder and eat less.

Being around my mum would rob me of my energy, my joy, my hope, and my laughter. I would feel weak and listless. Angry and helpless.

I was unable to talk to anyone about how I felt, because it made no sense, right? Surely, my mother loved me? So then why would I feel this way around my own mother? Surely, I was the bad one? Surely, it was me?

I must be the problem – that's what everyone else thought, right?

I was the black sheep, the problem child. I was too emotional and overly sensitive. I was selfish, and deserving of nothing. I would only ever get what I deserved.

She always told me I'd been a horrible teenager, that I'd put her through hell. Really? Well, for nine months of each year, we hadn't even lived together, so there's that.

Also, I wasn't out doing drugs or robbing people. I was never in trouble with the police. I was mostly polite. I did well in my studies. I didn't have a teenage pregnancy. I was polite and courteous to all her friends. I was loving and caring to her and to animals… so what about me as a teen had been so awful?!

During my time away at school, she would send me letters and occasionally baskets of flowers. I would take these flowers for 'walks' in the garden. I wanted them to live as long as possible, and I thought that some fresh air away from all the girls' aerosol body sprays would do them good.

They were like a lifeline, a connection, to her.

She declared to me that she was more caring than most as she would often call the matron to check up on me. She often mentioned that other people had said we seemed close, as if their observations somehow validated or confirmed it.

> From: Raven —
>
> What did u honestly think it was like there?
>
> From: Mum —
>
> A school where you studied and then lived with your class mates. Obviously there were rules as in any school. When we visited it all seemed friendly
>
> From: Raven
>
> That's it? No deeper thought?
>
> Nothing about who wud be looking after us in the evening? When we were ill?
>
> From: Mum —
>
> You were with housemates in the evening after prep watching tv etc. If you were unwell there was that lady, the house tutor and school nurse. I used to ring the house tutor quite often to see how you were and especially if you weren't feeling well. I probably had more contact with her than most of the other parents. She used to say we were obviously very close.

When I was 15 or 16, during the school holidays, she made me babysit for all her friends. They were all going to a talk in a hotel and they had hired a room. I earned a measly amount. I was given no instructions, no help, and no idea of how many kids it would be. I think she told me three or four originally. It ended up being a baby who was just a few months old, and at least 10 kids under the age of five.

They just kept being brought in, more and more of them! The mums would literally bring them in, tell me their name, and leave. Then, the kids and I – all of us in shock – were left alone.

One kept crying and calling out for his mummy. I gave him my watch and showed him where the hands would be when Mummy got back.

One child opened the door and ran out. I followed, calling him back, but since I didn't have a key to the room and all the other kids were inside, I had to return.

Had I done the right thing? Sacrificed one for the many and all that. I just hoped he found his mum or they found him… Oh shit!

By the end, I was absolutely frazzled!

That was a lot to put on anyone, let alone someone so young – and especially someone who had never babysat at all before. I appreciate that my mum was trying to help me earn some money… but bloody hell!!

One evening, when I was 18, and when I was home after recovering from pneumonia, I wanted to go out to see my boyfriend. I agreed that I shouldn't stay out late or go drinking; I just wanted to see him. I'd been with Mum for so long since getting ill and I desperately needed some space.

She put her foot down and said no. Feeling upset, I screamed at her and leaped onto my bed to get around her, as she was blocking my way.

She looked at me, incredulous, and asked, "What is WRONG with you?" Her face was one of disgust and disbelief.

There were so many times when my emotions were ignored or brushed aside.

I can vividly recall being at a party thrown by Dad's work colleagues one summer. It was held at their home and included both colleagues and friends. I was encouraged to bring my Colombian boyfriend and the friends I'd been spending all summer with.

I got a bit drunk at the party and ended up getting tearful. I was dripping with tears but my mum kept pushing me away, telling me to 'pull myself together.' I was obviously an embarrassment to her.

Not once did she, or anyone else, ask me what was wrong. Why was I crying? What could they do to help?

When my boyfriend said he would take me away, she jumped on that and pushed us to leave ASAP. She seemed relieved that someone else would have to deal with me.

As I've said, I often got this impression – that they were waiting and hoping that someone else would 'deal' with me… hence wanting to marry me off as soon as possible, I imagine.

We were not an affectionate family, though I craved touch.

When Jeffrey would come home, he would lay with his head in our mum's lap and she would stroke his hair. I was jealous of this; I couldn't do this with her. Was that on her or on me?

Throughout my life, but more specifically in my early 20s, she seemed to delight in upsetting me with tidbits of news. When Tom and I had broken up, for instance, she told me, 'Oh, by the way, such and such is getting married.'

Once, when I told her I wasn't pregnant yet, she followed it up with, 'Oh, by the way, such and such is having a baby.'

The list goes on and on.

It felt as though she wanted to kick me while I was down, to stick the knife in, twist it, and see just how much pain she could inflict.

If anyone in the world is supposed to love you unconditionally, it's your mother, right? The person who created you, who held you safe in their body for nine months. But not for me.

She destroyed me.

I found her demeanour – even around her friends – not very warm.

Since her death, multiple people I know who met her described her as 'cold.' And I'm not just talking about one person here; these are numerous separate individuals who don't know each other.

Even Dickhead often said, "She isn't a mother; she's just a woman who had kids."

She would protect her father's toxic and bigoted behaviour by saying, "That's just how he is."

Personally, I found my grandad's treatment of his wife – my grandmother – and myself, and women in general, very offensive. He once stated, "I would never read a book written by a woman" – despite the fact that one of his favourite authors was P.J. Tracy, a name that is actually a pseudonym for two women!

His views on women were/are archaic and wrong.

One evening, when I went to visit my grandparents to check in on them, he asked me, "Where are the children?"

"At home in bed; their dad is home."

"Well, that's good of him," he replied, "to look after them so you can come here."

"He IS their father!"

"Well, you're the one who wanted them."

What??!!

His and my mother's attitude towards my children after the death of my father, my grandmother and my dog – and the birth of my youngest – was abysmal. This all happened within the same year!

They expected them to be quiet and well-behaved at all times.

The reality, of course, was that they were suffering from the events that had been unfolding during their young lives. They were acting out by being loud and not listening to instructions very well. They were never naughty, just loud and a bit crazy – but they were only three and seven!

I can't even describe all the tuts and disapproving looks I, and they, would get.

It was soul-destroying to have them make out that my babies were bad, naughty, and unruly. I tried explaining that they had feelings and emotions too, but it all fell on deaf ears. It made me fiercely protective of my children, but it also tore me apart trying to balance what was best for them while also keeping my mother and grandfather content. I wanted them to see that I was trying my best, and that my little ones had needs too.

Mum was rude to wait staff and even to the nurses administering her chemotherapy. Maybe they didn't take her attitude as rude, I don't know, but I would go out of my way to be overly polite and accommodating to them to try to make up for her lack of warmth, politeness, and smiles.

She rarely said thank you or please to anyone.

She would regularly talk over my children and, if we were interrupted while I was telling her something, she never asked me what I'd been saying afterwards. I felt like what I had to say never mattered. Have you ever experienced that feeling? It's crushing.

She never listened to my advice, even when – nine times out of 10 – my advice was backed up by professionals, doctors, or her beloved Jeff or Dickhead.

I was unimportant; I was simply there to accompany her and be useful.

She always described herself as a very chilled, cool, calm person who was easy-going and who never judged people. My experience of her was vastly different to this. The exact opposite, in fact. I found her judgemental, very critical, cold rather than calm, and so hard to read.

Mother's Day cards and birthday cards were tricky. I never wanted to give her a card that said how she was the most amazing mother in the world or something equally untrue, but very few cards say anything but.

I guess the world finds it hard to believe that a mother can be anything other than giving and doting, while supplying unconditional love.

I've always had a fascination with observing other people's relationships – people watching but as an extreme sport! I watch how they interact, how they look at each other, how they touch, hug, speak… Is there love and affection there or anger and resentment? How are the mothers and daughters treating each other?

I know that, on the surface, our relationship looked close. The shopping, the walking arm in arm… and, for many years, I even said she was my best friend.

Text from my auntie, my Dad's sister in law:

"In almost 40+ years I can hardly say I know either of your parents. As you know we've never been close. Both polar opposites. Absolutely nothing in common I'm afraid. nanny said your mum was kind to her when grandad died. You seemed close at one time although I have to say you were the only member of your family that I felt closer to.

She is very interested in our family but rarely offers ANY news or info about their life or yours or Jeffery."

She also said:

"Bless you. Just didn't want you to be as unhappy as I suspected you were. You had so much on one hand and nothing on the other. All about balance."

She also called my mum "scary".

My uncle, Dad's brother, commented to me after her death that he thought we were close. The truth is, I knew no different. He remembers, when I was nine or so, us sitting on Nanny's sofa, whispering to each other. I don't recall this particular scene, but I do remember other times when she would keep me onside.

For example, the time we were all at Nanny's house (Dad's mum) when she was on her deathbed. The doctor came to talk to us about what was happening, and I wanted to hear what she had to say, but Mum got up and dragged me off with her. I wanted to be with everyone else, listening to what was going to happen to my beloved Nanny.

She whispered to me that my uncle's wife was being two-faced, that she had never liked Nanny but now she was being all caring and thoughtful.

Eventually, I persuaded her to go back to the lounge with me so we could hear the rest of what the doctor had to say.

I was talking to my Dad about trying to choose flowers for Nanny's funeral, I wanted to get them just right, this was the first loved one I had ever lost and the first funeral I had been to; what I got in return was "Come on that's enough now' in an exasperated tone.

My emotions shut down immediately. No crying or emotion was allowed - message received.

I was often seeing sides to my mother that I didn't like. I don't remember ever thinking, 'Wow, this lady is amazing. So kind and thoughtful and generous!' She was not someone I looked up to or wanted to be like.

I realised later in life that no one in my immediate family was someone who I would choose to hang around with, or be friends with if they weren't my family. That was a hard realisation.

Once the babies started coming, Mum made it very clear that she wouldn't be looking after them, even once she'd moved back to the UK. "I am not going to be one of those grandparents who regularly looks after the grandchildren, you know," she told me. "I don't want to commit to anything."

If she did ever babysit, it was only in the house; she never took them anywhere. If she looked after Jeffrey's kids, however, she would take them out places or take them shopping.

When Jacob was about two years old, I was out with him and he started choking on a Cheerio. His lips even turned blue. I was smacking his back, trying to dislodge it, and – as I began to panic – my vision started going in and out of focus. No one around me noticed.

I took him straight home and, once he was better, I called my mother in tears.

Her response? "I'm with friends. He's fine now… I will call you later."

So much love and support! I felt so let down and alone.

When her mum's Alzheimer's got worse, she told me she didn't want to go over each week to do stuff with her; she didn't want to make the commitment to take her places on a certain day or anything like that. Poor Nanny. Even her husband wouldn't do much with her.

I was being brainwashed into thinking my grandmother she was some pain in the arse old lady – sad and tearful and so needy.

I would visit occasionally and take the kids over to see her, but now – looking back – I believe that, like me, my nanny was a Highly Emotional Person*.

* HIGHLY SENSITIVE/EMOTIONAL PERSON

"A highly sensitive person (HSP) is a neurodivergent individual who is thought to have an increased or deeper central nervous system sensitivity to physical, emotional, or social stimuli.[1] Some refer to this as having sensory processing sensitivity, or SPS for short.

We're all sensitive about certain things—that is human nature—but an HSP is understood to be a different level of sensitivity. While highly sensitive people are sometimes negatively described as being "too sensitive," it is a personality trait that brings both strengths and challenges.

The term highly sensitive person was first coined by psychologists Elaine Aron and Arthur Aron in the mid-1990s. Elaine Aron published her book, "The Highly Sensitive Person," in 1996, and interest in the concept has continued to grow since then.

How Do You Know If You're an HSP?

Have you ever been told that you're " too sensitive" or that you "shouldn't think so much," particularly by people who strike you as too *in*sensitive or who you believe should think a little more? You may be a highly sensitive person, or HSP.

Sometimes, people assume HSPs are being "dramatic" or "attention-seeking" You aren't defined by other people's perception of you, and your experience is valid!

— AMY MARSCHALL, PSYD

> What Causes High Sensitivity?
>
> Research also shows that a lack of parental warmth growing up may cause a child to develop high sensitivity and carry this trait into adulthood. The same goes for negative early childhood experiences. If you experienced trauma as a child, you may be more likely to become an HSP as an adult.

My therapist Kim told me I was an empath, and the lady I did my Soul Midwife training with told me she could see a bright white light around me – and that I had to be careful as people would try to take it away from me, and take advantage of me.

I think Nanny's emotions were just 'too much' for my mum and grandad, and they couldn't find it in their hearts to reassure her or love her like she needed. I wish I'd seen this then and done more with her.

Once she died and my grandad was alone, Mum started visiting him regularly. She started doing for him all of the things she should have done for her mother.

Why was she always so willing to help the men of the family but never the women?

From: Mum —

I know you are hurting and think I was (am) an uncaring awful mother. When you (and J—) went to boarding school it was also a difficult time for me and Dad, we, especially me, missed you very much but thought it would be better to give you a stable and good education. We didn't send you off because we didn't want you around or didn't love you. Don't judge us too harshly. When we lived in Naples I was told by the Vice Consul's wife that we were irresponsible not sending you both when aged 7. I cried for a week after that.

Obviously if we were still living in the UK you wouldn't have gone.

I appreciate that you had a hard time settling in but I was always there for you. Every time I left you at school or the airport I was upset. Hindsight is wonderful but at the time we thought we were doing the right thing. I wish Dad was here as he could explain things better than me. If I knew then what I know now I would have talked to you more about how you were feeling and encouraged you to go to the American School but was never sure you would have been happy there either with the education system being so different. With hindsight I also would have insisted Dad stopped smoking so that all of us wouldn't have suffered so much and that my life wouldn't be so empty now and we could enjoy old age together.

We have always been there for each other - you for me especially over the last 2 years. I miss you and the children.

XX

I had stopped talking to her for the first time in my life a few months before my separation from dickhead. I came to realise that she – along with my father (who was deceased by this time) – was responsible for me being sent away and everything that transpired during that period of abandonment. Despite having the option to intervene and prevent her children from being sent away, she didn't take any action.

I emailed my mum with questions about why I'd been sent away. The replies pissed me off. First, she defended herself and tried to make out she didn't do anything wrong – because she didn't send us away at the age of seven.

She said she was always upset but I never saw or felt it. If it was so hard and if it hurt her so badly – and if she missed me so much – then why send me away?

She constantly told me that the American school would be a terrible choice for me.

How can she have 'been there for me' when she was in another country?

Then turning it to my dad's death and mentioning how she missed me and the kids… that was manipulative.

From: Raven

I think we all know and knew that sending me away was never a good idea. I was always a affectionate girl who needed you. what would Dad explain better right now?

Did you ever consider you staying in the UK while Dad went abroad?

I would have been happy in the American school cos i would have been at home. I was told many times by you that the education there would be no good and that i would never be able to go to a UK university with american qualifications and that in turn would affect my job prospects. When i was unhappy you told me to find myself a new boarding school.

The thing is how ever hard you think it was for you, believe me it was over a thousand times worse for me! I was 11 and totally alone in a strange place all day and all night!! Those were my formative years.

You may believe you were there for me but unless you were these everyday to collect me from school and tuck me in at night - you cant have been there. A phone call is no substitute.

From: Mum—

We never considered me staying in the UK. I can't change what happened and I honestly didn't think it would affect you as much as it did. I don't know what to say to make things less strained between us.

Jeffrey got in touch – to tell me off for not speaking to her – and when I asked him if he realised that all his issues in life stemmed from being sent away, he told me he'd never thought about it… and wasn't going to.

Once, during this period of not talking to my mum, she came over to my house one late Sunday afternoon with no warning.

I said nothing, and she just stood there watching me prepare dinner. Then she left. What had she expected? Had she wanted me to apologise? I was the one who wanted that from her!

She had said how the housemaster "always seemed friendly when I was there." Seriously? Of course he was – to the parents – and, let's be honest, how often did she actually see him?

It sounded like she was trying to say I was making it all up!

I think I lasted a week or 10 days or so before I calmed down and allowed her back into my life. Our dynamic had shifted slightly as I began to realise that my existence perhaps wasn't as intertwined with hers as I had always imagined. I started to notice more about her reactions to things and how I felt and reacted to her, realising I had more power in the relationship than I'd thought.

One day, we were in town with the kids and I told her, quietly, "We're separating. It's fine – it was my choice and I'm happy with it. This will be better for everyone."

Her face registered anger and then tears started to well in her eyes. I assured her I was fine – stupidly thinking that the tears were for me. They weren't; they were for her. After all, how would it look, her daughter getting a divorce?

She barely spoke to me again that day… or much afterwards, really.

As I embarked on a journey to 'find myself' and discover my true identity while striving to live life on my own terms, I decided to sign up for an online 'meetup' group and join them for nights out.

I would put the kids to bed and then go out, making sure I was there again for when they woke up. They had no clue I was gone, and their dad was home with them, so they were safe.

At this point, we were still living together until we could figure things out.

A month or so later, we were all around Mum's house and I was telling her about the new people I was meeting and how I was going to spend the night at a guy's house who I'd become friends with. I assured her it was friends only; we had plans to go to London for a night out so it was just easier this way. This was 100% the truth and nothing ever happened between me and this friend. I wasn't attracted to him; I just enjoyed the laughs we had together and he seemed like a genuinely nice guy. A friend. With other friends too – a group.

Obviously, when Mum heard this, her lips pursed and she looked pissed off.

The morning after I returned, she showed up at my door without warning.

I was hungover and tired and annoyed that she'd come over. I just wanted to chill with my kids and rest; I could never relax with her around.

She looked annoyed – but, then again, when didn't she?

"I wanted to make sure you were home," she told me. "You should be home with your husband and children, where you belong. The kids wonder where you are."

"Who told you that?" I asked. "The children are always asleep by the time I go out, so who said that?"

"No one... I'm just imagining; you should be at home."

"I am here for the children, they have everything they need, and he isn't my husband – we're getting a divorce!" I replied, utterly exasperated.

"Why?"

I sighed. Loudly.

This was the first time she had asked me this and I was not in the mood.

Many times in the past, I had gone to her to tell her how unhappy I was in my marriage; I even questioned if she would help me and the kids financially if I left him. She had never asked me any questions then. She only saw the fake side of Dickhead – the goody-goody 'do you need anything? What can I do to impress you?' side of him.

I knew that anything I said to her wouldn't, in her eyes, be a good enough reason. She would never understand my point of view, or how crushed and defeated I felt in this marriage. She would never know how mean and uncaring he was.

I was also pissed off that I even had to defend my choice. She was my mother; I should have her unwavering support no matter what.

I wanted her to tell me that, as long as me and the kids were safe and happy, all would be well. That I could count on her. That she had my back.

She had questioned me like this before, when I'd tried to tell her about the awfulness of boarding school. Her one-word questions elicited feelings of not being believed, of my issues being unimportant and irrelevant.

I told her I didn't want to discuss it, but she kept pushing me. "Tell me," she said, "what is so awful about it?"

I was tired and pissed off. "I'm tired. Can you leave please?" I asked her. It was the first time I'd ever asked her to leave my house.

"NO!" came the reply. "Tell me – I'm not going anywhere."

"I would like you to leave my house," I insisted, as the argument moved from the lounge into the hallway.

In that moment, everything collided: the years of therapy, the hard-earned lessons I'd learnt, and the inner strength I'd gained. The injustice of feeling unsupported by her, the recent revelations about my boarding school experience, and now, the realisation that she didn't have my back. And, on top of that, I was exhausted and hungover. I felt deeply insulted by her assumption that my place was at home with my 'husband.' It was all too much to bear at once.

I opened the door and asked her, yet again, to leave.

She said no.

I shouted that I wasn't going to carry on living in this fake bubble of a world where we pretend that everything is fine when, in reality, we all have emotions and needs. She told me to shut the door or else all the neighbours would hear. I replied that I didn't care, that I was done pretending. That I was now going to live my life with full emotions – and be honest about it.

As she stalked to the cupboard under the stairs to get her coat, she told me, "Your father would be so disappointed in you."

Then, for a few moments, she just stood by the open door and stared at me, a look of defiance in her eyes.

I can't remember the exchange we had after that, but she still refused to move, so I literally had to put my hands on her back and slowly push her out of the door. In response, she leant back into me as though trying to push back. As I was trying to close the door, she tried to lean into it to stop me closing it. I want to clarify that there was no forceful pushing, no shoving, nothing aggressive.

The look in her eyes was pure hatred.

Once she was finally out of the house, I closed the door and ran upstairs to my bedroom. What the fuck had just happened?!

I realise now, a few years later that this 'meeting' was set up!

She had never once before come over on a weekend at that time of the morning. It was too coincidental that I had only been home about an hour when she arrived. Why didn't the kids come out to greet her as they normally would?

I have no doubt that dickhead kept the kids away so she could 'talk some sense into me'. So already, at that early stage they were bonding against me.

Dickhead followed me up to the bedroom, and I said to him, "I'm not asking her for any help to buy you a house; I would rather sell this house and get two smaller ones than ask her for anything."

"That's OK," he replied. "I have no pride; I'll ask her."

I shrugged. I wanted nothing from her at all. I was done.

This is important to remember because this was used against me later on.

As soon as I told her of the divorce, I did ask her if she would help us buy Dickhead a house. I don't deny this. What I did do, however, is change my mind after this incident.

I never told anyone of all the awful things Dickhead did and said to me. I carried on protecting him – probably because I figured that my mother, or anyone else, wouldn't see what it did to me. Or they'd just say it "wasn't that bad." I had no illusions about other people in my family giving a shit about me.

This is an email between my mum and me regarding this incident:

From: Raven

Hi,

I just wanted to get in touch to explain the situation we have found ourselves in.

I am concerned that you think I am distancing myself from you simply because of your reaction to the divorce.

If that were true it would be quite an excessive reaction - unfortunately I felt let down and without your support at a time when I needed it and was vulnerable. This is something i have experienced many times in our relationship and this was one too many times.

I do not want to cause you any hurt or rehash the past but I would like you to know that moving forward I would like us to be able to be civil to each other and for me to bring the children over to you.

I hope you understand now.

From: Mum

The comment I made to you was not about the divorce (which I had accepted) but your behaviour. I was concerned for your welfare and safety as you were spending the night away with people or person you hardly knew. No one should have been spoken to or pushed out your door the way you did to me.

I know I have never let you down, if this is all about boarding school we had been over this so many times.

Presumably the fact a few years ago you apologised for being a horrible teenager - your words - was meaningless and the Ducky Duckerson list of what I had done for you was insincere. You have always received support from Dad and me.

I had always thought we had a close relationship.

Moving forward I would like to see you and the children. On tuesday I am taking the cheque to my solicitor so you need to make a future appointment to sign and collect it.—. Mum

We did bump into each other once or twice over the next few years, either in town or outside the large supermarket nearby. I was always polite.

> No

> She was at the hairdresser when I went on Tuesday !

> Did she say hello?

> She was already sitting down so I went up to her and said hello. She looked surprised! I finished before her so went to her to say goodbye. Got one in return but no warmth

> Well it's something

On her deathbed i looked at my mothers phone – over the next chapters are samples of the texts i found between her and Jeffery and her and dickhead.

When she texted me to tell me she was in the hospital, I asked if I could visit.

This was in 2020, however – during COVID – so, of course, I wasn't allowed to go. Instead, I went out and bought anything I thought she might need, dropping it into reception. She thanked me.

I called the hospital each day for an update until, one day, I was greeted with, "Oh, you're her daughter – she doesn't want you to call anymore and I am not to tell you anything."

I was so shocked! What was going on?!

It seems that she and Jeffrey had decided I had no right to know about anything that was going on – and that he was to be in charge.

> Have told R she can ring hospital for updates

Did she ask

> Yes.

The nurses will get fed up of we're both ringing

Just tell her I'll give her 1 update each day

> R isn't happy about it

About what

> Hi Mum
>
> A different patient liaison person will have to bring it to you on Tuesday. In the meantime you can tell the nurses/palliative team to not discuss your situation with xxxx and have them direct her to me

Jeffrey was furious with me for calling the hospital when he'd told me not to.

So, instead, I emailed a nurse I'd been in touch with to tell her I was my mother's LPA (lasting power of attorney) and that I would like to discuss her treatment. My concern was that she was being kept in too long and would die in the hospital, when she'd told me many times that she wanted to die at home. I was just trying to ensure she got her wish!

As it turned out – unbeknownst to me – Jeffrey was also registered as her LPA. I have no idea when this happened or why I wasn't told.

> Ok hold on. I'll look in my electronic files

> I've found 2. One for health and welfare and one for financial. They're old though, and name both my sister and I. They were updated in March 2016.

> I'll email to you.

I don't know whether to update them or how easy it would be.

> Did u see?

> I think they're fine unless you want to remove xxxx, or me

As long as you can act jointly. Don't want her in control of my finances

> Well the lpa is just for decisions while you're alive. Shouldn't really be any big $ decisions while you're around.

> You could take the lpa to a solicitor

Exactly

I'm cheaper than your solicitor. Want me to see?

> Ok but there is no one apart from you and her

I understand. I'll look it up and you can decide if you want to remove her

> Might have to have someone in this country to act

I'll look

> Ok

Has she been in touch again

> Yes

... and

> Asking about me

Has she been Inappropriate

> 1) ring Grandad. 2) how involved do you want xxxx? She's trying to engage me more in conversation and I don't want to argue w her but I am very upset at how she's treated you and don't really want her much involved

> Don't ring G. It will be easier for her to get involved as she lives nearby. I don't want bad feelings between you two right now

> Let Grandad know we talked and thats why you're ringing so he doesn't think I forgot

> I will ring G is what I meant

> Yes. But let him know we talked

Jeffrey and Mum's brother then managed to persuade Mum that a nursing home would be a better place for her to go – and an NHS one at that, not even a fancy private one.

I tried my best to get her to answer my texts and calls to see if that was really what she wanted, but she didn't reply. So, I resorted to emailing Mum's brother to tell him how she would get better care at home – and how, due to COVID, no one would be allowed to visit her in a residential care home. As I believed she would get all the drugs and nursing she needed at home, I asked them to stop pushing the care home.

Thankfully, my efforts paid off; Jeffrey allowed her to have her wish of going home.

I was, of course, not allowed to be part of it. They didn't let me help get the house ready for her return or let me help choose a live-in carer for her.

Family friends were allowed to go to her house and move furniture around, Jeffrey emailed people to find a suitable care company, and I – who lived just seven minutes away from her – was allowed to do nothing.

Once she was released from the hospital, I went to take her some flowers. I had no idea it would be Jeffrey who answered the door – all smiles!

I gave him the flowers and asked him to give them to her. No way did I want to be around him, and I had no idea why he was acting like nothing had happened between us.

Of course, my rejection of him in that moment added to all his complaints against me – complaints that had apparently been piling up since my birth!

The timeline of the next few years is a bit all over the place for me, as I was dealing with so much. On top of COVID, lockdown, and homeschooling, there was also a car crash – and what happened with Mark's ex and his girls.

I could have forgiven my mum for my childhood, the boarding school, and any other mistakes. I could have believed she had tried her best and done what she thought was right at the time. But the final two years of her life – including her terrible behaviour and deceit and all the lies and manipulations – were and are utterly incomprehensible and unforgivable. I will never forget about them or forgive her for them.

Chapter 30
Mark

In July, I told Dickhead I wanted to split. Around this time, I had injectable methotrexate – a chemotherapy drug – stored in the cupboard, ready to hopefully get my Crohn's symptoms under control. I was delaying starting because I was scared, and there was also an underlying belief that I didn't truly have Crohn's disease. I know the scans and tests showed I did, but I still wasn't convinced.

The moment I told Dickhead I wanted a divorce, it was as if a huge weight had been lifted off my shoulders. I felt so light! And, one week later, all my Crohn's symptoms went away!

I will also tell you that, other than the odd small blip when things got very stressful with the divorce and Mum, I had no more flare-ups. I had to take extremely strong antibiotics a few years ago, and those set me off into a flare-up, but otherwise, I've been symptom-free for going on six years now. With no drugs at all.

The consultants are shocked!

It was after the split that Dickhead started making more of an effort. For one thing, he finally did what I'd suggested many times in the past: he didn't use his laptop or phone in the evenings in the lounge.

I was used to being alone in there in the evenings, watching TV by myself – or with him in there, paying no attention to me or what we were supposed to be watching together. But now he came in and sat next to me on the same sofa and told me off for being on my phone! What?!

Bit late for that! I was single; I didn't need to bother making any effort now, mate!

One night, he came into the lounge all smiles, sat close to me and all playful nudges and winks, he asked me if I had slept with anyone yet.

"You can tell me, we are friends." He declared with a smile.

I paused and considered. I did want a friendly relationship with him and I decided to tell him that yes I had.

He immediately jumped up saying, "well I would never want you back now." And stormed off. He had tricked me!

There has never been a moment when I have doubted my decision to leave him. I have cried and lamented missing the children and wanting to be with them permanently rather than having shared custody, but the idea of being with him… no. I could never go back to that.

For a few months, I basked in my newfound freedom and possibilities, allowing it all to go to my head. I went out at weekends to go clubbing and drinking. I got with a few guys, and although it did have a little bit of my past about it (with sleeping with people I wasn't in a relationship with), I felt more in control and, this time, it was a choice. In some ways, it *was* a choice, because I was choosing to do this to prove to myself I still had 'it' – an ability to attract people – and that I didn't need to settle for someone who treated me badly and who hadn't touched me in years. After all, I had years and years of no sex to make up for!

But there was also a desperation to it, a feeling that I was still searching for 'the one.' I was craving touch and affection, having had next to none for the entire 14 years of my marriage.

I met some arseholes, of course, and one made me cry a lot; I think that scared me a bit, knowing how it was still so easy to get hurt by stupid boys!

After that, I started to toughen up a bit, and then I decided to just have friends with benefits. This, however, was disappointing – sex without intimacy or affection is crap! No matter what people say, it is unsatisfying and leaves you with a feeling of emptiness.

After a couple of visits with this 'friend', always at his place, never at mine, I quickly realised I was worth more than this. It wasn't working for me and I deserved better.

I don't know what I was looking for, but I signed up to eHarmony and, as I was perusing the page full of profile pictures, I was drawn to this one photo. A guy called Mark. As far as profile pictures go, this wasn't a great one, but I felt compelled to say 'hi.'

Within a few minutes, I had a reply, and we exchanged texts into the early hours of the morning!

Our first phone call was a day or so later, and our first meeting was on September the 22nd, 2018.

Yes, it was only four months after I'd told Dickhead I wanted a divorce, but honestly, I felt like I hadn't really been in a relationship with him for years. I felt no connection to him, nothing. In my mind, I was free.

The moment I saw Mark, I felt comfortable.

"Thank goodness you're good-looking!" was the first thing I said, and then we gave each other a big hug – and it wasn't awkward or weird, either.

We went into the pub. As I was driving, I wasn't going to be drinking, and this worried me. What if he thought I was boring? What if I had no confidence to talk to him properly?

I needn't have worried.

The conversation was slow, as he was so shy and nervous. Unlike with other men, however, I sensed that his silence stemmed from a genuine fondness for me, rather than dislike. It was evident he liked me but was worried about messing up. So, we took it slow, with me taking the lead in the conversation.

We spent so much time just staring into each other's eyes, which wasn't something I'd ever done before. It wasn't weird or creepy, but very deep and connecting. It was like we were sinking into each other's souls.

I knew that night that this was the man I was meant to be with. I had never before felt anything even close to this. It was a bit scary, however, to feel so close to someone so fast. To feel this connection and comfortableness.

As the conversation continued, he told me things that were – in his eyes – potential deal-breakers. I knew he wasn't bad and that he wouldn't intentionally hurt me. I could see he was a good man. We laughed a lot too. We held hands at the table and hugged outside while having a fag.

When we had to leave the warmth of the pub at 11 pm, we carried on chatting and giggling by my car.

At 2 am, we finally said goodbye, and it hurt to see him go. I was worried I would never hear from him again. That would be just my luck! So like every other fake man I'd ever met.

He had a race meeting that day – the Sunday after our Saturday night date – so I wasn't holding out much hope of him having much time for me; he would be too busy with his hobby. I had a friend coming for the day with her kids, anyway, so I was going to be busy too.

Fortunately, I was wrong – he messaged me loads all day!

He'd had just three hours of sleep – if that – but he was walking in the clouds with happiness, he said.

We made a promise to each other that day: no secrets, no games! He still makes that promise to me to this day, whenever he goes to that location for racing.

We have both been hurt by our previous spouses. We are both sensitive and caring. We both need a lot of affection and care. We just make sense together.

There have, however, been some issues along the way. How can there not have been, with my history? His history? The baggage we each brought into the relationship certainly took its toll. After all, we were both going through very acrimonious divorces with narcissistic exes. Neither of us had very supportive family around us, and we'd both been damaged – albeit in different ways – during our childhoods.

His parents had divorced when he was nine years old, after many years of screaming and fighting. Then, from the age of 13, he'd had to battle with extreme bullying at school. Consequently, he was under the impression that relationships looked like hatred. Arguing and accusations. Fighting, shouting, and physical abuse.

I taught him what kind, nurturing love looked like – how someone who loved you should really act towards you.

When he would cry and feel like his mind was shattering from grief and overwhelm, I would hold him and tell him I loved him.

When I would push him away, putting my walls up high and shutting down emotionally, he would tell me he was going nowhere and that he loved me. That he had me and that he was there as soon as I wanted a cuddle. He showed me what unconditional love looked and felt like.

He moved in as soon as Dickhead moved out. In hindsight, maybe this was too soon, but I was just struggling so much with leaving him each night; it felt like a smaller version of when I was left at boarding school. Every night I would feel like crying when we had to say goodbye after spending a few hours together chatting in whatever pub we could find. It was exhausting... for both of us.

After a few months, he got really ill from it all. Mark had to get up at 4 am every morning for work, so hanging out with me from 8 until 10 or 10.30 every night, getting home after 11, and then getting up just five hours later... it really took its toll.

I deserved my happiness, I knew he was my future, and I wanted him close. I had been so lonely and miserable for most of my life, and now – finally – this was my chance. So, I grabbed it with both hands.

It must have been confusing for the kids.

I was so in love with Mark and I knew that if I was happy and doing well then they would thrive too, but it took my eldest a little longer to get his head around the idea.

They loved seeing us so happy. After all, they were finally witnessing an affectionate, caring love. When the older two were having fun with Mark, though, I could see they felt guilty. They were torn. They liked him and enjoyed his company but, thinking about their dad, they couldn't help but feel guilty.

I got it, and it was made harder for them with the way Dickhead, his family, and my mother were behaving. I dread to think what they overheard.

I have a gorgeous video of Mark and Ivy playing together on the swings. They are laughing and giggling, just enjoying each other's company and messing about. An hour after this fun time, she came and told me that she hated Mark. The guilt was a lot for her to deal with.

We made it clear from the beginning that Mark was not trying to take the place of their father; he was not a father figure but my boyfriend. They were to call him Mark. On the few occasions that Chrissy – being so young – mistakenly called him daddy, we corrected her immediately.

I was still in charge of all their discipline. The only time Mark got involved was when Jacob became very disrespectful. It wasn't Jacob's fault; he had never seen anyone treat me with any respect over the years, least of all his father. Now he was going to learn the hard way that I deserved to be spoken to with respect.

He found this difficult and, consequently, he decided to go and live with his father. After a week away, however, he wanted to come back and live with us. This happened another time a few years later, and again it wasn't long before the novelty wore off and he wanted to come back. The grass isn't always greener.

I tried to make the transition as easy as possible. I went out and bought double of everything for them to have at Dickhead's house. Same pants, vests, bubble bath, shampoo, sippy cups, Calpol… everything. It was also so Dickhead would see what they had and then know what brand to buy when it ran out – otherwise, he wouldn't have a clue.

He has now totally forgotten I did this! As usual, he's oblivious to the efforts I made to try to make it easy for both him and them.

Looking back over that first year after splitting, my time was spent either in dire stress or blissful happiness. There was no in-between.

I made such efforts with Mark's children – he had two daughters, aged one and five – but perhaps trying to act motherly toward them was a mistake.

Whenever they stayed over, I had to take over the night waking. I rocked the little one to sleep, gave her milk, changed the odd nappy, and gave Mark advice on how to parent, as their mother had been hell-bent on pushing him out from the moment the eldest was born.

During the marriage his ex undermined him in front of the kids – threw things at him and screamed at him. If he tried to parent his child and teach her even something simple like manners, the ex would tell him off, right in front of the kid. She belittled and berated him. And, the whole time, this little girl would have a twinkle in her eye as though she enjoyed the fact that he was being punished instead of her.

As time went on, however, the dynamic changed.

It became as though the ex was deliberately sabotaging the time we had with them. She wouldn't tell us if they were ill. She wouldn't send Calpol. She wouldn't tell us she'd started potty training. She wouldn't let us know nap times or food preferences.

We later found out that she'd actually told the older one not to talk to us at all.

This became more obvious as time went on and she would reply, "I don't know," to even the most mundane of questions.

"What did you do at school this week?" – I don't know.

"Do you want a sandwich?" – I don't know.

"What's your favourite colour?" – I don't know.

"Do you want carrots?" – I don't know.

"Do you want to play?" – I don't know.

It was agonising trying to have a conversation with her. I had never met a child like her before; she was so guarded and closed down.

For the first six months or so, things had been OK. We chatted and hugged and I thought we were going to be this big happy family of seven. The kids mostly got along and it seemed like they were becoming close.

Then, we believe their mother got wind of this happiness, and did everything she could to make sure it stopped. Her texts to Mark became accusatory and nasty.

Things in the kids' bedrooms started to get broken, water would be spilt at night, and arguments would start, but we never got a clear idea of who was at fault. My kids or his.

It caused a rift between us.

Then, Mark's eldest started acting very oddly around my son – sitting so close to him on the sofa she was practically on his lap, following him around, giggling this odd laugh she reserved only for him, liking what he liked…

We figured that maybe she saw her mother acting this way with men?!

One weekend, we managed to get it out of her that her mother had told her not to tell us anything. To keep everything a secret, to not even talk to us. And one of those things she wasn't allowed to tell was that Mark's best friend was now living with them! The man they had previously called 'Uncle' was now her mother's boyfriend!

We are 99% sure they began an affair while she and Mark were still married. We even did a DNA test on his youngest!

The bitch swore her five-year-old to secrecy from her own father – told her not to get undressed in front of him, even. The damage this did to not only this little girl but to her relationship with her dad is still in evidence today.

The youngest was encouraged to call this guy,'Daddy.' You can imagine the heartbreak this caused Mark. It still angers me now.

After about a year of going out of my way to include his children, to make them feel welcome and as though this was their house, something happened that was the last straw for me.

Thanks to all the fighting with their mother, the stress of the pick-up and drop-off where she would invariably come out to shout at him, the obvious neglect towards the mental health of these girls, and the lack of any communication between us and them, I was always anxious during their visits.

They were sleeping over one night when we noticed odd bruises on his daughter's leg. Due to the spacing and size, they looked like fingerprints.

We questioned her but just got the usual, "I don't know."

So, Mark texted their mother and she texted back, 'Arm or leg?' That alone set my alarm bells ringing.

When we dropped them off, they stood there 'discussing' it, and she started to get very angry and defensive. I stepped in and said, "To be fair, they do look like fingerprints."

She spun around to face me with hatred in her eyes, before starting a tirade of abuse of which I've never heard the like! I was a bitch, a slut…a red headed slut no less, the list goes on. She got right up in my face, her own filled with hate and anger.

Unfortunately, Mark just stood there, cowering.

I was so sad and angry that he didn't defend me.

After a moment, we got in the car and drove off. I threw the engagement ring he'd given me at him and told him that, once we got home, I wanted him to leave. I was devastated he hadn't stepped in to help me as I had done for him.

He begged me to let him stay.

I didn't want such hateful people in my life. The stress of dealing with all this was too much. Don't forget, I was still going through my divorce and dealing with my mother.

I just wanted some peace, and this kind of stress was not conducive to a quiet, happy life.

It took a lot of talking and upset but, eventually, I realised just how much this woman had abused Mark; she was more horrific and narcissistic than I could have imagined. We agreed that, after this incident, I would never go with him to pick up the kids again. He also negotiated to pick them up from down the road so he could avoid seeing her again.

Mostly, this worked, other than the odd time when she still came out to scream at him. Like the time she came out to shout that the girls couldn't bring their Christmas gifts from him back home. The eldest just stood there, crushed, pleading with her.

From that moment on, he decided to do something different for Christmas and birthdays, to ensure these situations didn't keep happening. To save them from her.

She will not admit to any wrongdoing whatsoever.

The youngest has super hypermobility and her feet turn in at an alarming angle. She can turn both her feet around the wrong way. Would her mum admit to an issue though? In the end, when she was around two years old, we had to pay a private consultant to get an opinion about it.

Oh, the anger we got from her when we sent her the report and asked her to get in touch with the NHS! She even declared that I should pay for another appointment.

Now, at nearly seven, her feet are still turning inwards and her mother's done nothing about it at all.

The eldest – and possibly the youngest – most definitely has ADHD, just like their father. Will the mother hear of it? No way. "I am an early year's provider; I would know these things," was her response.

Oh, please! You are one of the dumbest, most ignorant people I have ever met!

Unfortunately, the stress that the girls' visits started driving a wedge between us. We would start to get anxious on the Wednesday before the weekend visit, and then it would take me until at least Tuesday to recover from the weekend. It was too much.

We fought about this a lot. Maybe blended families really can't work?

We consulted doctors and child therapists, hoping for some answers to the children's behaviour – mainly the eldest's – but we got no joy. They all said the same thing.

To me, it seemed like the mother was a narcissist. We could only ensure that the kids knew their dad would be there if and when they realised they needed him.

I simply couldn't be a part of all this anger and hatred and difficulty – not any longer. The impossible nature of trying to form any type of relationship with these children was just too much.

I also couldn't keep trying to teach Mark what he should care about concerning his own children. He should know which dentist they go do, he should be getting school reports, he should know if they've been ill or been to the hospital, etc.

It took me a long time, but I am now at a place where I've learnt 'not my circus, not my monkeys' – in other words, it isn't my business, so I should just back off.

I have my own children to nurture, so I leave Mark's relationship with his children up to him. It is still strained, but some weeks he feels like he's making some progress. It went from him seeing them weekly and having them sleep over one weekend a month, to now seeing them one day every two weeks.

Their mother never prioritises their visits to their father, and he can't keep fighting and risking his mental health to deal with this woman.

He does his best for these children who've been taught that he is the enemy. At least they now show him some degree of respect – and the occasional act of care.

These days, when they're in my house, I mostly keep out of the way. I say hello and goodbye but generally I have nothing to do with them. It started as a way to preserve my sanity and mental health, as it had got to the point where their very presence would make me feel suicidal; seeing and hearing them would drain my energy completely.

I would just feel so much stress and unhappiness the moment they walked in the door, and I couldn't understand why my body was having such a strong reaction to them. It was devastating for me, especially as I've always thought of myself as a caring, kind person, particularly to children. But something about hearing their voices would trigger something in my body.

One winter, I even googled how fast you can die from hypothermia while walking the dog. I was that on edge and unhappy.

Now, thankfully, I can be in the same house as them and just feel neutral. My relationship with Mark is stronger now that we keep them separate.

Mark and I were both so conditioned to seeing the negative – to trying to figure out where the next 'hurt' was coming from – that we often misinterpreted each other, getting offended when there was no cause.

We had very explosive arguments. I've even thrown him out a few times.

My heart always comes back to him, however, and although I know I CAN live without him, I truly do WANT him in my life. I am happier with him in it and our love is unbreakable.

My mother, on the other hand, wasn't convinced. She figured lockdown would end us.

In fact, the more time we spend together, the stronger we become.

Due to all the health concerns over COVID and the divorce not being finalised, I was worried that something would happen to me and that Dickhead would get half the house, as his name was still on the deeds.

I told him I wanted him to sign the house over to me ASAP, just in case.

These texts show his thoughts on the matter.

The first are between Mum and Dickhead;

Yesterday she had a go at me because I wouldn't sign house over to her before the lawyers said

Because if something happened to her I would have half the house

The fact that that's her priority tells me she's going fine

Of course you shouldn't sign yet

Exactly I said I'll sign when the lawyers say so

Obviously worried if something happens to her M would be out on his ear

She should be thinking about the kids

These are between him and me:

> Will u sign something ASAP to release ure share of this house?

Why?

That happens when the consent order is signed which should be soon?

> Cos life is changing and who knows what is gonna happen.

> Who knows how long that will take?

Thigns are complicated and stressful enough without side deals, everything gets signed with the consent order and lets focus on getting that done, and this ended asap.

> If I died tomorrow u will get half my house!

> You are still on the deeds to this house! Even if I changed my will tomorrow I can't change that!

Because I am not signing anything without my lawyers approval. So if you really want it, then send it your lawyer to send to mine, and if she approves, then fine. Otherwise, it happens on the consent order. I have enough going on without having to think about this as well!

[photo] Show this to xxxx it's for the Roman gods work she did

> If something happens to me all my money and assets are going to the kids so there will be plenty to pay for schooling

If you remarry will that be the same?

> That is what my will will say.

> The kids are my priority always. U imagine for a second I wud leave them without ????

No, but your new partner will also be your priority. I wanted to make sure that hmrc isnt going to turn up and take 40% of the school money. Anyway lets hope this never has to be considered.

> How on earth wud I stop them taking 40%?

> Kids are top priority always

What cream are you using in xxxx legs? Dipobase?

> No been doing the big bottle

> Bringing them over about 4 tomorrow?

It had nothing to do with Mark; it was simply the fact that I detested Dickhead so much that there was no way I would risk him inheriting half my house! It was to go 100% to the children. His attempt to twist this and suggest that my loyalty and priorities weren't with the children reveals more about him than it does about me.

My life before was dark. There was no colour. When I tried to think of the future – to look at where we might be or what travels we might go on – all I saw was grey, darkness, and misery.

Now, I see sunshine and colours. We have fun, I feel free, I am me, I am my own person, and I make decisions that are supported. My victories are celebrated, my body worshipped, and my affection appreciated and reciprocated.

CHAPTER 31
SUICIDE

There were a few attempts.

Mostly overdoses with paracetamol.

The last one – in 2019 – was, my most desperate and serious…

The day had been stressful and exhausting. The stepkids had been over, and both Mark and I were anxious and overwhelmed.

I was putting my three to bed after tidying up the mess, while his two were being taken home. My guys wanted to share beds, which always resulted in hours of chatting, giggling, and throwing stuff, invariably followed by an argument and tears. I couldn't relax and I didn't get any downtime.

Halfway through dragging a double mattress from one room to the other, I suddenly thought, 'Hang on, why am I doing this? I don't want them sharing; this is only happening because their father lets them share all the time!'

So, I stopped dragging the mattress and told them no – the rules here were different. I don't honestly remember much about what happened next, other than I asked them if they would rather be with me or their father.

They shrugged.

In hindsight, of course that's how they would have reacted; I was shouting at them and they weren't getting what they wanted!

In the moment, however, this devastated me. I was in the midst of being torn apart not only by my ex but by my mother too. I was doing all I could to protect these kids and give them a better life, and now they were rejecting me as well.

Upon seeing them shrug, my heart broke.

"Fine," I said, "let's go."

Chrissy said she wanted to stay with me, so we left her favourite teddy behind.

I got them in the car and drove to Dickhead's house. Ringing the bell and banging on the door didn't summon him, though. I called too – no reply. After more ringing, Dickhead finally came to the door.

I angrily told him he'd got what he wanted – that he was ruining them and making my life harder.

Chrissy now decided she wanted to stay with her brother and sister, of course.

Consequently, he and I had a huge argument outside his house where I told him I wished I'd never met him, and he said the same. This shocked me, as I felt I'd done nothing wrong. It was him! He was the abuser, the neglecter, the one making all of this so unbearable and long-winded and horrific. He who had lied and manipulated.

How fucking dare he!

I think it was on the drive home – to collect the teddy for Chrissy – that I decided I couldn't live thinking my children had chosen him over me. That they didn't love me. What was the point? What was there to live for if not them?

I went back, handed the teddy over, and on the second drive home, I felt sure. All I wanted and needed was them. They were my world and life.

I did a loop of my road – almost as if, subconsciously, I was going home to safety. Then, pulling over, I called Mark. Over the phone, he could hear the beep of my seatbelt not being engaged. I told him what had happened. I knew I could ask him for help, but if I told him exactly how I felt and what I was planning, I knew he would stop me. I was sobbing and telling him what had happened.

Maybe I could call my therapist? I thought. But would she even answer at this time on a weekend? Besides, I didn't want to explain the entire situation to someone else.

I just wanted to die.

I drove down the hill, picking up speed – probably reaching 70 mph – and then purposely swerved my Land Rover into the big metal skip sitting on the road outside my house.

I had envisaged being thrown through the windscreen and dying on impact.

Instead, I ended up with bruised ribs, a bruised head where I hit the airbag, and a bruised, twisted ankle from where it got caught under the pedal. This was followed by police, an ambulance, lots of nosy neighbours, 12 hours or so in A&E, scans, X-rays, a psychiatrist, and many, many tears.

As I lay there in the hospital, I worried that Mark would no longer want to be with me, this set off my fears – my fear of abandonment, of not being good enough… of not being enough at all.

By now, this exact same feeling had reared its ugly head so many times in my life. When would it stop? When would I ever feel enough?

Doubt set in hard – doubt of everything in my life.

I know my mother was aware of the crash because I later saw it in one of her text messages from Dickhead. She only asked about the state of the car. Between them, they decided I did it for attention.

At the time, Dickhead just texted me and asked, "What condition are you in?" I didn't bother replying.

Mum and Dickhead:

> R just turned up at the door and dumped the kids here! They were all crying, they were messing around at bed time and she said "they would prefer to be at your house because you have no rules" and drove off

>> Goodness

>> Are you expected to have them during the week?

> I am disgusted

>> Don't blame you

> Yes they were all crying

> I've calmed them now

>> Did they say what happened?

> Looks like they were messing around at bed time, then she was shouting at them and did do you want to go to dads houses and then they didn't say no immediately told them to grave their things, put them in the car and brought them here, in their pjs, no coats, crying

>> Unbelievable

> Just got a phone call from xxxx, swearing at me, saying that she has just crashed her car into the skip out the house, and it was all my fault

Omg

> Unbelievable

Incredible

What did you say?

> I told him to calm down, tell me what happened and when he started swearing at me, and blaming me, I hung up

She must have been driving fast to do that

> After she dropped the kids, she came back to give me a teddy and swore at me, saying I was a liar and wished she never met me etc and I said that's how I feel about you, and she went off

> She needs to calm down

> Wonder who bad the car is

> How bad

As I was hanging up I heard xxxx say it's because of you she's tried to commit suicide, so I don't know if he was saying that to be horrible

He sounded very emotional

But my thought is if it was serious he wouldn't have called to shout at me

> Always someone else to blame

Always. These poor kids.

> Exactly

They will be nervous about staying there again

> Wonder if she will want them back tomorrow
>
> If she is happy with him why try to commit suicide?

Attention and to make me cave on the divorce?

I think she used the same tactic when she had post natal depression

> She has so much in life - more than most

I know

Have you heard anymore?

> Nothing

The hospital psychiatrist, Kim, and my GP all stated that I'd had a breakdown from the stress. Kim knew it was also from my past and the struggles I'd lived through all my life. The sadness and rage I felt at always being dismissed and ignored. The gaslighting from Dickhead. The way I was being treated by everyone for finally standing up for myself.

Dickhead's mum had been slagging me off to the kids and telling them how they mustn't tell me about things that happen at theirs or their dad's house. She told them how tattoos were evil and how Mark was basically an interloper.

I was sick of the unfairness of it all.

Then I found out my neighbours had been texting Dickhead before he moved out. They texted him about 'a man' coming into the house one night: Mark.

I had explained about the break-up to the lady neighbour and Dickhead had explained it to the man, but it would seem some couples don't like people who get divorced. I think they feel they can catch it!

Case in point – years ago, I had a friend who was getting a divorce.

"I don't think I want you to spend any more time with her," Dickhead had told me. "I read that if one person gets divorced, their friends are more likely to get divorced too."

He was worried her happiness would rub off on me!

They all took an aggressive dislike of me and Mark. I'm not 100% sure why, but it certainly made life very unpleasant for a few years! These days, I couldn't give a fuck; I just ignore them all and go about my business.

Back then, though – and all through my life – it was tough. I felt like I was always in the wrong. That I could never get it right. If I tried, I failed. If I tried less, I failed. Being polite didn't get me anywhere either; it seemed to be seen as a weakness. Smiling usually wasn't reciprocated. Not smiling got 'cheer up; it might never happen' or 'don't look so worried.'

If there was even an ounce of kindness or attention, I would grab it and hold on tight. But kindness would sometimes make me cry. Or cause me to make rash, bad choices. 'Wow, if this person is being kind/saying something nice they must really, really like me! I must do everything I can to keep them liking me!'

I constantly worried about what other people thought of me. It was exhausting.

In May 2018, I had my ensuite redone by a lovely, friendly couple. The work was full-on and took five weeks to complete. During those five weeks, I would go and chat with these lovely people and, as the weeks went on, I started to realise that I enjoyed their company.

Chatting to them was not awkward or embarrassing. I didn't feel ashamed or guilty. I wasn't made to feel 'less than' or 'not enough.' We laughed and told stories. I was being myself!

Once they'd finished, I missed their presence.

This was the first time I had truly enjoyed someone's time and felt like they'd enjoyed mine in return. There was no ulterior motive and they seemed to genuinely like me.

A revelation!

This realisation made it even more obvious how little I enjoyed my husband's company, and how little I felt like myself around my parents and family. The fear and anxiety I constantly felt just weren't right!

So, it wasn't 'normal' to always feel so disconnected and unhappy around people?!

This revelation added massively to my decision to divorce that July; it helped me see how wrong my life was and how truly unhappy I was.

To illustrate how indoctrinated I was – after the split, I asked for Dickhead's permission to buy a flat with my own money! I explained how I needed the rental income to help pay my bills. He shrugged and said 'no.'

What fucking business was it of his?

I was so powerless with my own money – this probably helps explain why it was so easy for him to take so much and dictate so much during the divorce.

In terms of my suicide attempts, my father seemed more compassionate than my mum, perhaps because his own father had killed himself when I was just two years old. My father would have been around 29 years old at the time.

My grandfather drove somewhere secluded, I believe, and put a hose pipe – connected to the exhaust pipe – into the window of the car.

Even this massive event, early on in their marriage, did not encourage my mother to be sympathetic to those with mental health disorders.

One time, when I'd grown up and learnt what had happened, I mentioned that depression must run in the family.

"He wasn't depressed," she stated.

Chapter 32
Divorce & Nastiness

Divorce is never easy or nice, but when you do it with someone who is intent on controlling the situation – and trying to screw you over in the process – it becomes 10 times harder.

Add to that the dynamic that was going on between my mother and me, and between her and Dickhead, and you have a true shitshow – and I was the main attraction!

I had never wanted a marriage like my parents… but it was pretty close to the crap I ended up with.

During a visit to my mum with the kids, she made it clear to me whose side she was on. Even though we had our differences, after our falling out, I'd told her I was happy to bring the kids over and maintain their relationship.

While I was at her place, I went into her spare room – to get the kids' toys that lived there – and saw loads of boxes from Simba. Mattresses… I guessed for his house.

"What are those mattress boxes for?" I asked her.

"Oh, just spares."

"Hmm, really? Why?"

"Just 'cos."

"They're for him, aren't they?"

"Yes," she eventually replied.

"Why would you lie about that? Why not just tell the truth? What's the big deal?"

She shrugged.

We left soon after that.

We didn't tell the kids about the divorce straight away, as I didn't want to confuse them while we were still living together.

Funnily enough, they didn't notice anything different during this time, as – by that point – we hadn't shared a bedroom in five years anyway. Nor did we spend any time talking, being in the same room, or doing much of anything together.

Back in 2010, when Jacob was two years old, I sat next to his father on the sofa and he commented: "Mummy, what's wrong? You and Daddy never sit next to each other." A two-year-old noticed it was odd that his parents were actually within touching distance of each other! That's not good.

For a few years, Dickhead slept in the spare room. Then, when Chrissy came along and she took up one room, this fiasco began:

The baby was in one room and each other kid had their own room.

It began with the older two taking turns to come and sleep in my bed with me. So, for at least a year, I shared my bed with one of my children.

One day, I put my foot down and said I deserved to have my own space and my own bed.

Then began a bed-hopping mess – every night, once each child had fallen asleep in their own beds, Dickhead would lift one out and put them in the bed of the other child so that he could sleep in their bed.

Once Chrissy was over a year old, I decided that if this was to be a long-term thing, something had to change. So, I put both girls in one room. Then Dickhead could have his own bedroom and there would be no more disturbed sleep for the children.

We didn't share a bed primarily because of his god-awful snoring, which had plagued my life since a few years after we'd got together. The doctors attributed it to the fact that he'd put on a lot of weight.

So, add his snoring to my already light, crap sleeping, and that meant I pretty much never slept! Not to mention having to deal with one child or another waking me most nights.

Plus, he'd started to repulse me. He smelled; I couldn't stand the smell of him. I read somewhere that you have real problems if you're really put off by the smell of your partner.

We never had sex anyway, so what did it matter?

We didn't ever go to bed at the same time and he never got up in the night or in the morning for the kids. We lived a separate life in so many ways, so why not this way too?

After the split, I was still doing everything around the house and for the kids, and then most nights – after they were in bed – I would go out and meet Mark until about 10 before coming home.

After a few months of this, I tried to stop doing Dickhead's washing. After all, why the hell should I?! He came up with some bullshit about saving money on the washing if it was all done together. I didn't argue, but instead of folding it neatly on his bed, I started leaving it in a basket by his door, unfolded.

Then I decided it was time for him to take on more of the fathering responsibilities. After all, soon he would have to step up anyway, considering he needed to move out.

First, we alternated nights we were 'on,' and by nights I mean bedtimes! Next, I declared that, on his days, he needed to start picking up the kids from school, doing dinner, and everything else. This gave me a little more freedom and it got the kids used to him actually doing some things!

Up until this point, he hadn't done much of anything with the kids or around the house; he was next to useless. His only job was to put the bins out once a week!

The closer I got to Mark, the more I wanted this arsehole out of my house!

He said he would be gone by the November. That didn't happen. But, because he'd told me this, we decided to tell the kids about the divorce in the October half term. To be fair, they didn't seem too fussed at the time, though I think it sank in more once he eventually moved out.

The lawyers – who were supposedly working away in the background – were useless. Nothing was moving along.

Dickhead requested that I remove from my list of 'divorce reasons' the fact that he never got up in the night to help with the children. It was 100% true, but my solicitor said that, 'as a gesture of goodwill,' I should remove it.

Against my better judgment, I did – illustrating once again how I'm always bowing down to others' needs and desires!

Ironic considering that when Jacob was a baby and he was 'babysitting' he wouldn't even sit in the same room as him.

This next part is a mistake I still regret. Again, I wish I hadn't trusted someone so fucking evil.

Without involving the lawyers, we agreed that if I signed over my rights to his company, he would not touch my inheritance from my father – or any future inheritance from my mother.

I signed this, and I also signed to say I didn't want his pension. In exchange, he signed a letter from my financial adviser, putting all my money and the kids' money in my name only.

Before I'd hired this financial adviser – and when I received my inheritance from my dad – I'd split it all up into £75,000 chucks and invested them. As I was doing this, however, I stupidly put one of the chunks in his name. I was scared of what he would say if it was all in my name as he had decided the money was also his.

Dickhead called the investment and they told him that the name on the account couldn't be changed. He swore that when it matured, in two years, he would hand it all back over to me. Why I didn't get this in writing, I will never know. There's that stupid trust again!

My heart is pounding while I write this, as I still feel cheated. He stole from me!

That's right. He never gave me that money back. He decided that it was his and, consequently, much of our arguing through the divorce hinged on this moment.

After two years of back and forth with solicitors, and with him taking over a month to reply to each exchange (whereas I got back to my solicitor within a day), I was utterly exhausted – and £20,000-odd lighter!

He also had it written into the divorce that I was never to go to him asking for school fees. He wanted them in private school, of course, but he didn't want to pay for it himself.

My mother apologised to him for my behaviour, as you saw in previous text exchanges between them. Funny that, because as far as I could tell, she wasn't around for nine months of the year, each year between the ages of 11-18! I had to raise myself! I was under constant attack in some way or another and I always had to defend myself.

I believe that my mother was paying his solicitor fees.

He moved out, finally, in January, and just before Dickhead left the family home, he hugged me and apologised that things hadn't worked out.

Now, I knew this was not a genuine apology – and it did not, even for a second, make me second-guess my decision or wish I'd made a different choice – but it did upset me in a way I didn't understand.

I told my therapist Kim about it and she explained that I was having a reaction to the fact that this would have been the first time ANYONE had ever apologised to me, for anything, in my life.

On the day of moving, my mum didn't text or call or anything; she was too busy helping him settle into his new place!

Mum and Jeffery:

Yes. All ok.

How r u

Ok going to help xxxx will move later

Still chilly with you?

Make sure you dont do too much

> That's nice for him to have them there first night. Do they all have their own rooms

> Is it far?

All have own rooms xxxx has small en-suite too. xxxx has en-suite. About 5 mins in the car

New man already installed

> From you? That's better than before. How often. will xxxx have them?

Yes not far from me. There is a rota I think he will have them 4/5 days then to R

> Sad really

Yes

> 😟 xxxx parents coming to help too

What about my sister?

Any big blokes to help?

> No idea about her. Don't know about other help

Nice of you to help

Weather is crazy. It's getting hot then will be cold again monday

> Mattresses and bed frames have been delivered here so xxxx has to collect them. 9c here. Yesterday xxxx swimming pool was frozen!

Oh wow

I can't believe xxxx is going through e this

How is xxxx taking it now

> Can't wait to get out

Good for him

Tell him there are support groups, in person and online, for people who deal w border line and narcissistic partners, ex partners

Co parenting w a narcissist will not be easy

> His main priority is children. He is seeing counsellor. I will tell him

We got the magnet and postcard. Thank you.

It turned out she had bought all his furniture for him – she had given him her credit card details and allowed him to buy anything he wanted! She even paid for him to join a friend on his 40th birthday in Las Vegas – the flight, the hotel… everything! She also paid for a family holiday for him and the kids, which I know cost at least £6,000 (I know because I bought the same one for all of us a few years previously).

Evidence that she bought his furniture and paid for holidays.

> Hi xxxx
>
> Just got back from furniture village and they have a corner sofa on offer there that would fit the play room
>
> its £795 plus £45 delivery
>
> can I buy it on your card?

> If course 👍

> than k you

> Find anything else?

> just looking at a few I saw, but it was difficult

No rush get what you really like

> its asking me for the 4th, 5th and 6th characters of your Verified by Visa pass phrase

---

> but having to buy xxxx a cricket uniform as they play cricket in the summer terms

> lol. private school life!

Think R should help out

> Hmmm, maybe, but we'll see

I was paying half for school uniform! Of course he neglected to tell her this!

About a holiday to Lanzarote:

> Im not sure, xxxx has mentioned how great it is, but Ive not had a chance to look at dates etc
>
> Are you still ok to pay for it if we do go?

> Of course

> thank you

This one is about the Las Vegas holiday she paid for.

> Hi xxxx you home ?

> Might be good idea just to check that the BA flight is in your name

> Have checked and ticket is in your name! Jut need to add passenger information and get xxxx

> Hi xxxx
>
> Just landed back in the UK
>
> Just wanted to say thank you for making Las Vegas possible, it was amazing

Welcome back. So pleased you had a good time

> Just got an email from next, and it looks like they had an technical problem and so the for the sofas didn't go through

---

Fine just jet me know the total

> The total is £2871 including assembly

Ikea? That's fine

> No Next

> Hi, Im just placing the order for dining table from next
>
> they are going to send you a security code to your phone via text

>> Ok
>>
>> 165822
>>
>> HSBC fraud alert but ok to reorder

> thank you, i think its gone though

She was paying for the kids' school uniforms as well... goodness knows what else she paid for.

She also lent him £350,000, interest-free! Repayment just £800 a month.

So with the £400 000 advance on my inheritance and now the £350 000 he bought his 5 bedroom house.

> Im not sure, *** has mentioned how great it is, but Ive not had a chance to look at dates etc
>
> Are you still ok to pay for it if we do go?

Of course

> Thank you

Wonders why owners want to sell as market lower

Once you know the asking price and think you would like to buy we should talk

Probably best not to tell xxxx

> Thank want to but somewhere cheaper in Scotland now the market is down there as well

> Good idea

They replied rejecting my offer, they were looking for £615k

Im going to give a day or so to think about it and then raise the offer a bit

> How much you going to offer?

Maybe £603k

>

My offer of £606k has been accepted!

> Fantastic news. So pleased for you x

> Have you got to pay a deposit ?

Not yet

> Let me know when you need the money so I can let my financial advisor know

Thank you

> Does *** know you are buying?

No

More trouble on that front will tell you when I see you

> When do you have the children this week?

> I will be in Camberley tomorrow if you want to meet for coffee 12.30?

> See you tomorrow. If the subject of your house comes up there's no need to say anything about my involvement

Be there in about half an hour

Have just told ***

About the house

> Yes I have received some unpleasant message

Just ignore them, she will calm down in a whilr

> Yes but upsetting

I am very sorry that this has happened and you've been caught up in it, but am very grateful for your help

> Apparently she is struggling !

> Hi xxxx, lawyers should be sending you paper copies of everything in the post

> That's great thank you. She calmed down yet?

> Hard to tell.

> That day she was horrible, she then said she wasnt feeling well and asked if I could pick up the kids

> She will be getting the proposal from my lawyer today or tomorrow

> and that will kick off everything again

>

> She was going on about having to pay inheritance tax ! I cut off contact and asked for my house key back! Stand well clear then over next few days !!

> Yep!

> Im not sure if I already

So not only had they been doing all this behind my back, my own mother had no interest in helping me out in any way shape or form but was practically throwing money at Dickhead and my brother.

Text between mum and Jeffery

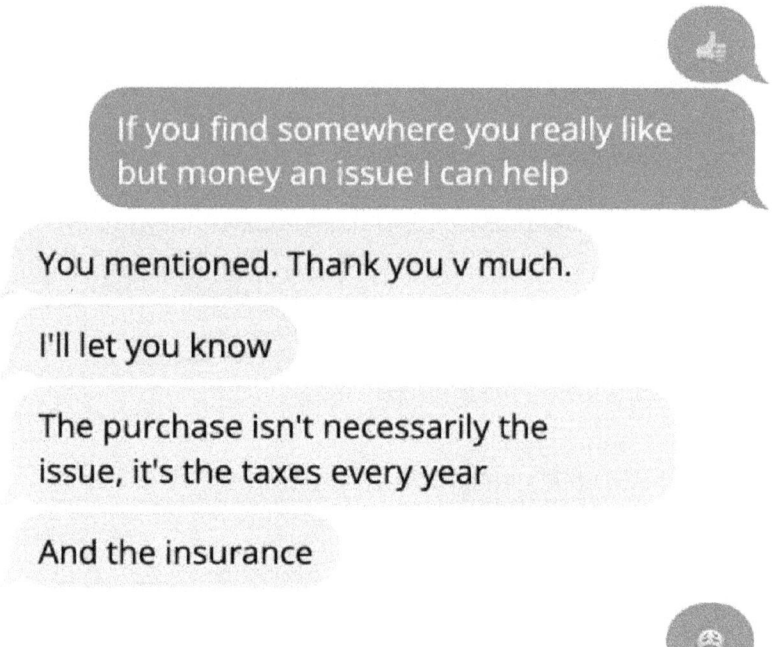

When I found out about this, I changed her name in my phone from 'Mum' to her Christian name. She was no mother to me.

Dickhead did, however, have to pay this money back a year after she died; I was shocked Jeff didn't give him longer just to antagonise me.

At the time of all this fighting, she also signed a cheque giving him £400,000 to buy a house. This cheque was waiting for me at her solicitor's office with a letter I had to sign. This said that I was accepting this money as an advance on MY inheritance.

Again, this was a cock-up of epic proportions – my accepting this money, and then giving it to him, would cause a legal nightmare for me through the divorce and beyond.

I had been set up.

Mum and Jeffery:

> the money?

> > Yes

> She signed the letter?

> Did she get it in person

> > Yes at my solicitor's office . He handed her the cheque

> :(

> So you've done the letter, did u change the will too at the same time?

> Not yet
>
> Still working through details
>
> I know she is worried about it and whether I will cut her out

Need any help?

I bet

Has she mentioned it

> Not to me but to xxxx

Got some nerve

> Weren't u there when she got it

No

> Oh

> No shame

I was on the cruise and didn't want to be there

> Good idea

A new man is on the scene and I don't want any of my money going to him or his children or any future children they might have

It's not the divorce I am Upset about but her opinion of me

> He has children?

2

> Oh boy

Don't worry about what hateful people think

Grandad told me she's going on a cruise

> No she and new nan are going to Barbados

Must he nice

How? With what money if she has no job

The money she got from you is for to pay xxxx isn't it?

> xxxx has given good child maintenance and she has mortgage free house , her inheritance and investments . Yes money for xxxx and she is in process of transferring it to him

She can't have that much left and it won't last if she's blowing it on nonsense. Does the new boy have a job

> He drives delivery van for Parcel Force but seems to have lot of free time. I am not sure I am supposed to know about him

> Ugh. I'll stop because it makes me angry and it upsets you

> I hope they will be happy and I wish him luck

> Let me know if u need anything with the will and when it's done.

The next are between Mum and Dickhead

> Hi don't say anything to your solicitor yet about the legacy to pay inheritance tax as my solicitor says it should be £80,000 half of £160,000

Ok, do you know why?

> Not sure going to have to talk to him. Might be something to do with donations to charity and if enough money available- he doesn't know how much I actually have. Will sort out but she will receive

> Hi xxxx, do you have a copy of the letter that xxxx signed when she received the money from you?

Yes you want a copy?

> Yes please

Bring it tomorrow night

> Warning you might get an angry message from *** she rang Grandad to ask about the funeral and what he was doing for Christmas- he told her he was seeing the children at your house!

> Oh well

Sorry

> No probs, I'm used to it 😄

Settlement sorted?

> Far from it
>
> Some progress

> I'll tell you more tomorrow

> I have found the text messages *** sent me asking to help you buy a house

Great can you keep it

>

[photo]

Hi xxxx, is it ok if I drop xxxx off to you a bit earlier tomorrow, about 11?

> Ok. Will xxxx be coming at all as I have her birthday cards?

Yes, she will bring xxxx a bit later I think

> Ok

Hi xxxx yes delete that email

Throughout the divorce, Dickhead tried to make it look as though that money went to me. Then, later on, my brother and that same solicitor tried to do the same thing.

At the time of agreeing to this advance, I was under the impression that I was still in my mother's Will – half going to me and half to my brother, as my dad had explained before he died.

I wasn't too worried about him getting £400,000 if I was going to be getting over £1 million at some point. The kids would have two lovely houses to live in and I would be set.

Little did I know that she'd changed her Will within a month of him moving out of the family home – before I signed this document.

It became clearer to me why Dickhead had been referring to me as 'little miss narcissist.'

> xxxx and I think * has narcissistic disorder.

Likely

> Maybe I shouldn't be too hard on her

You don need to walk around on eggshells. She needs to be self aware and get help

You haven't done anything wrong

> The disorder means she can't recognise she has a problem

> She knows I am going to change my will and concerned

She has been to a lot of therapists. I'm sure she's been told she has a personality disorder

> Not sure about that or if she has probably won't take notice

Mum you are too understanding. She has issues- we all have issues - and she's not doing anything about it and has deliberately hurt those around her

That's not your responsibility

> She is my daughter

Doesnt mean you have to be her punching bag

> I know but maybe she has mental issues

Doesnt change things. Like I said she had been given every opportunity and chance for treatment

People can get help and be stable w these disorders

> With narcissistic tendencies?

Yes. W therapy and sometimes medication.

Narcissism and borderline are similar and related.

> Person has to admit it first

You can only lead a horse to water. It's not your responsibility to fix her or cure her.

> Person has to admit it first

You can only lead a horse to water. It's not your responsibility to fix her or cure her.

> Difficult not to feel responsible

> In some way

Of course but u have to pet go. She's an adult now.

There's lots of research to show people like that r very difficult to live with but controlling it is possible

> Ok

Try not to dwell on it

It's v difficult

Almost time to go out

It also made sense how his confidence had increased; now, he had both her and her money on his side. And it explained Jeffrey's deep involvement with Dickhead and the subsequent outcomes.

Clearly, all three of them were out to destroy me. And for what? For sticking up for myself? For following my own wishes and desires instead of just blindly doing what I 'should' do?

I was strong enough to follow my own path instead of the predefined path they'd all followed and set out for me.

Did me gentle pushing her out my front door really deserve all this?

After everything I'd done…

Ensuring my mum was set after my dad died. Securing Dickhead's business, pension, and access to the kids, and providing him with a nice place to live. Trying to get the divorce done quickly and easily to save money and time so we could both move on with our lives. Trying to forge a relationship with Jeff despite his constant bad treatment of me over the years. And now this???

Honestly, I am still lost for words with it all.

On top of all that, my uncle – my mum's brother – was easily swayed to take their side, as was my grandfather, her father.

No one ever asked for my side of the story; it was just a given that I was in the wrong. A mother can never do wrong, right? It must be the child who is evil if they go 'no contact.' Does anyone ever think of the emotional toll and pain a child experiences when they decide to go no contact with their own mother?!

On one of my birthdays, after we'd stopped seeing each other, my mum did send a card with some money in. The card was blank. I texted her to ask her what it meant. She said she had forgotten. But then she laughed about it with Dickhead. I saw this in the texts.

I am officially the black sheep – the outcast – but, these days, I don't give a shit.

Jeff is still trying to exercise his control over me with the Will and his capacity as executor. I am not spending another penny fighting him or trying to get him and his unusually incompetent lawyer to do the correct thing.

I was put as an 'add-on' on the eulogy sheet. My name was last.

I bet it killed him that I had to be on there at all.

Years later, Dickhead told me that when people asked him what it was like to get divorced, he would say, "Imagine the person you trusted most in the world suddenly shooting you in the head."

Oh please. He was not the victim. He also berated me for "breaking the sanctity of marriage" by asking for a divorce. FFS, really? You wanted to stay married, did you? Happy, were you?

The vows are only good if you love each other and if you both work hard on the marriage out of love and respect. We had none of that!

He went on and on about how I had 'taken EVERYTHING from him.'

What had I TAKEN, exactly? He had a new house, all his furniture paid for, two holidays paid for, 50/50 access to his children, his entire pension, his entire business, and no maintenance or child maintenance to pay… he had it GOOD!!

This victim mentality of his carried on throughout the divorce.

For a long time after all this, when I had to spend any time near him – for example, in school meetings, or when we had to discuss the children – I would get awful headaches which, as time went on, became migraines. Soon, I was put on steroids to try to deal with them, as they'd become regular, daily, never-going-away things. I tried massage, head massage, an osteopath, and endless paracetamol.

The steroids worked for about a week – it was amazing! – but then the migraines returned. The dose was upped, but all that did was give me acid reflux.

On one occasion, I had to spend a good few hours in his company at school and, as I returned to my car, I started shivering and shaking. It was a hot day, so it was certainly not from the cold; I think it was my body showing signs of distress and trauma.

Thankfully, these days, I have overcome any anxiety I have about being near him. It no longer takes me days to recover and I do not feel so drained or miserable afterwards.

He has no power over me anymore.

Today, it's like he's just some random no one. His opinion, presence, and thoughts bear no significance to me or my well-being.

Of course, Dickhead made the divorce process a thousand times more difficult and lengthy than it needed to be. He'd take an entire month to answer one email. He would give incorrect answers. And he brought my mother and brother into the mix to be 'onside' so they could all make decisions together against me.

I told Dickhead how little most men end up with after a divorce – case in point: Mark. But he just looked at me and said, "I am not most men; I am different, I am me."

I've already included the texts where Dickhead asks my mum for information about my inheritance; I think he wanted to catch me out on the figure I'd declared on my consent order.

Originally, he said he would not leave the family home until the consent order was done. Thank goodness that, after I signed his business and pension over, he was happy to leave. His being there another two years would have led to my death, I have no doubt.

When I took him the paperwork to take his name off our joint bank account, I put a star next to where he had to sign and pointed it out to him as well; wouldn't you know, he signed the wrong bit! Totally on purpose.

Thankfully, I found a way to get it done without him.

His delaying tactics were all about control and him having the upper hand. As Kim would tell me, "He'll do it all on his terms, in his own time. As you began it all without his permission, he's now going to punish you and make you wait."

Once I realised Dickhead and my mother were having discussions about me behind my back, I told him to stop gossiping about me. His response? That I wasn't important enough to talk about.

"No one talks about you, you aren't important enough to ever mention."

It seems that, after finding all these texts, that was a lie.

Nice try, but your delusions don't carry water here. I am perfectly capable of taking care of my children, you need to start pulling your weight. the agreement was 50/50, but Im doing far more than half. So show some gratitude, or raise your game and actually do your half.

Just not taking them to school for a few months as I am unable does not mean I am not doing my half.grow up and stop pouting

Actually thats exactly what it does mean.

> I do need you to do it as I cannot drive!! Unlike you I do not have my mum to run to for assistance with the children

> Appreciation?? When in your life have u ever shown me any appreciation? If you want them at school u are gonna need to step up for once

Y0u are hilarious. What do you do all day? I appreciate things far more than you do. Youre the one who needs to raise your game and step up, you are responsible for getting the kids to school on your days

---

Kids coats have been left outside your house

I noticed that your car was gone, so I presume you're out and about, in which case Farnborough shouldn't be a problem for you.

> No I am not cos I can't drive! M took my car and I am with the girls

> Right. Onto this. You have a strange way of asking for a favour! How long will this be going on for? and why dont you use a mini cab to cover your days?

> A mini cab ??? Who is gonna pay for that? These are ure children too and then need to get to school.

> I do, however it would be nice if you acknowledged that is a favour, and therefore requested it instead of ordering it, and also a level of appreciation of the cost to me in fuel and time.

> Do u really want to go there? Please sir would you please take the children to school?

> I am giving up 2 1/2 hours each day to cover the fact you cant drive, for reasons you've not even explained to me, which means zero days off. There has been zero appreciation for this, further demonstrated by the fact that I didn't do this one thing gets you riled up. Why don't you return it online and buy a new one online, or solve the problem without expecting someone else to do it for you.

> If u can't manage them I am very happy to have my children full time!

> Originally you told me that "You needed" me to take them, and now you have told me "I need", neither is a question, which would have been "Can you take the kids to school this week please?", and a level of appreciation if the request is agreed to, its an extra tank of fuel per week, almost 3 hours driving EVERY working day with no off days

No off days? You are a parent!!

You can afford the extra tank - you have my £75000!!!

Are you gonna run to your lawyer now?

> Its unfortunate that you don't know what a decent person is.

You are so funny!! Shame no one is laughing!

> In any case, you ask and appreciate, just as if I need to ask a favour from you, I would ask, and then actually thank you if you could do it.

Hard to appreciate someone as malicious and conniving as yourself. I can't even look at you let alone speak to you

> Ha

> I am neither of those things

> but then again, youre hardly a good judge of character.

> I think that after years of you ruining my life it was time I stood up for myself and did the right thing for me and my kids. That makes me strong and right. Yes.

I am happier without you than I have ever been when married to you, and my home with my children is beautiful, something that could never have existed when I was with you. Your conduct during his entire process has been a disgrace, but not unexpected.

Now, if you can just cover your half of parental duties, instead of demanding my help and then getting angry about it.

> So petty! I wud love to spend extra time with the kids taking them to and from school. Such a shame you see them as a chore and things that waste your time

> Are you going to take them or not?

I see the fact that you don't appreciate it as a bore. They are never a chore, and you know that, but nice try.

Yes I will be taking them. I will pick them up at 7.45am on Monday.

> Oh I know that but you have never shown that. Always been Such a hands on dad haven't you

Don't project your insecurities on me

Raise your game, step up

if you require me to do it the week after, ask at the time. This is not a rolling agreement.

> I cannot drive till maybe mid feb. That will not change.

> I am all up and I am very secure in what I do for my children thank you

As I said, ask each week, you may find a way to change this.

> No. It won't change.

> Say what you like you have no effect on me. You are irrelevant and nothing. If you were so happy you would be so bothered that I had 'left you with nothing' You poor lamb

> I cover more than my parental responsibilities. I simply can't drive right now

I am bothered that you keep asking me to help with no concept of gratitude.

> So petty! I wud love to spend extra time with the kids taking them to and from school. Such a shame you see them as a chore and things that waste your time

---

> You will have to or else they can't go to school

Its is lovely how you off load your responsibility so easily.

As I have said, ask and show appreciation when you require help, I would show you that courtesy if the roles were reversed.

> Oh my goodness you are funny!!

Well I did develop a keen sense of humour when married to you.

> Lucky you

> Screaming at me on the prone, turning up at my door shouting at me, and your partner leaving me a threatening phone call and voice mail. Telling me not to come to your front door, and then in the next moment demanding my help. Your solicitor has sent proposals that are inaccurate, and unfair, and I will not accept, but continue to negotiate. When I am pleasant to you in person, it's not being two faced, its just treating you with respect

If that's what u wanna tell yourself. I totally disagree

Are u still coming?

> Passport posted

Haven't seen ure lawyer email yet but I understand u have rejected my proposal. Just want to be sure you understand the implication of keeping that money. If u keep it u mess with the whole investment *** has set up. Not only will it all be down £75000 but it will be unable to grow so it will be down the interest from all the years it wud be growing. There is more chance school money will run out. Do u get that? So effectively you are making it so there may not be enough money to carry on paying school fees in future

> Review it with your lawyer, the entire £75000 (including interest) is being allocated by me to school fees, with the same obligations you would have for your school fund. What I have rejected is your proposal to transfer £107,000 from the school fund to yourself, agreeing to £42,000.

> How do u figure that? I have paid £107000 from my money to school fees! Whatever u have set up will not be the same as what *** has put in place one reason of which is that his plan has been in place since 2016 always with the intention of it running its course. I understand u want to cause as much pain and damage to me as possible but doing it through the children is not right

> Your need for control cannot extend yo school fees.

> Do u remember saying you wouldn't touch my inheritance?

I do not understand how you have paid 107k from your money, especially when the vast majority of that time we were married. When it was received school fees money was put away for that, you are attempting to claim money from all the way back to 2016. You cannot warn me the school money will run out without my 75k, and then transfer 107k to yourself, making it certain it will. That is what is not right.

> You are misunderstanding how it all works Even when we were together this is how it worked. All school money was invested. I have been paying for schooling from my inheritance since the beginning. The idea all along was that I paid from my inheritance so the school money cud grow. Then when the Tesco acc matured it wud go to me as part of what I am owed. Once accounts mature they will pay me the £107 back. U keeping the 75 means money needs to be removed early from investments to pay me back what I am owed. Which means it will not be maturing. So it will be damaged in two ways. I am not making certain it will run out. This is the way *** has set it up from the start. If u mess with it u are changing what was agreed in 2016!

> Your lawyer should have shown u the list of fees paid... that is from xxxx

When married that inheritance was joint money. We always had joint funs, my *** salary, every bonus etc, was always shared and treated as "our" money, its only once the divorce started that it changed

> No my inheritance has been my money always. You just happened to benefit from it. You said u wud not touch my inheritance just like I said I wud not touch ure business or pension.

> I am not touching it, however you are rewriting history to make it seem like it was always like that, which it wasn't. We even used to comment how weird it was that other couples had separate finances

Yes but this was different. This was my money. Everything else was family money. Just like the pension is yours.

Were u with mum tonight?

> Nope

Pls explain how this is 'not touching my inheritance'. That money was worked for by my father and then given to me. Now for some reason u think it is acceptable that u keep it. How is that?

> I am not asking to keep it. u cant rewrite history to make out that our assets weren't joint, unless of course as far back as then u were already plotting a divorce. I do not want a single penny, and if agreement is reached the entire amount will be used for school fees. the original numbers had the school money at 330k and u had 300k. Now suddenly you want over 400k cash, and are reducing the school money to 280k. You already have everything! now you want more?!

I have never taken a penny from the kids. He is showing how he has no idea of the cost of private schooling or what money there ever was. He is making up figures.

> I want over 400k? I have everything? Joint?

> Crazy if u imagine for a minute that 4 years later there wud still be the same amounts in these pots!!

> And whatever u are thinking... that money is MY inheritance!!!

> If u r using that money for school why not put it where it belongs and allow it to grow and function as always intended??

> Your need for control and a dictatorship is ridiculous!! Oh and u have achieved what u set out to do. The wedding is cancelled due to the continuation of this stupid divorce so congratulations!

> FYI u aren't as clever as u think! Ure 'reasearch' into my flat is flawed!! No one pays the asking price!! So don't go calling people liars till u have the facts! We aren't all stealing and morally corrupt so don't taint us with ure brush!!

> No longer need ure assistance with school runs thank you

> I realise that it was my naivety that allowed that money to still be in your name but when you signed the st James places forms you agreed to sign all accounts back over to me. You must see how that money is mine from my fathers pension? You also know Mum is unlikely to live more than a few years which means u will never pay that money back!

> Don't need ure help March 8 anymore thank you

> But will need same deal on March 22 nd pls

Ok

> Are u gonna say anything ??

What is your fathers pension? Are you arguing that all the money is yours, including the school money, and you dont have to pay school fees????

> What?? No I am saying all the money is mine and I will pay school fees from the school pot!

> My inheritance includes everything in the school pot. I will continue to use the school pot for school fees as planned. You said u wud never touch my inheritance... you are by keeping the £75000 that is part of the 11:04 school pot

Under your last proposal youre taking money from the school pot, giving you over £400k, and leaving less than £280, including the 75k Tesco

> Do you need me to once again spell it out for u cos I have already done that quite a few times but ur choosing not to listen!

> I am walking the dog and free to talk... call me if u need to me explain it to u! I have not once changed anything... all I ever said was I couldn't trust u to keep paying the £1000 and needed a guarantee... u have changed so much

The cost of your flat, your lawyer provided the address, and the land registry listed the price.

> I have the paperwork to prove I paid 123!!

> Not 125

> Oh my god how can u be so stupid???

That's helpful

> I swear it is like ur trying to not understand!!

Get your lawyer to make it fking clear, and stop dicking around moving money around

Amend the last asset sheet and then we can at least work from the same numbers

> No money is being moved or any dicjong around happening! You r the one who magicked away £158000!! And deciding for yourself how much money my flat cost and how much money I have where!! I have not lied once!! You on the other hand!!

> We did!!! Where is the £158000 u should have left??

> Just stick to the original agreement, u take the business, ure house, ure pension. I have my house and all my inheritance!!

> Why have u never told ure salary despite being asked 3 times??

> I have been transparent from the start!

OMG! Ive told you, £4k at month before tax

> Put it in the letter!!!

> Where the £158000???

> She has cancer again!!

> She isn't gonna live too many more years!!

> Then what? They gonna make u sell the house to pay the estate back?! Pls!

I've already started repayments

> Doubt that cos u ain't gonna keep paying once she's gone!!

> Can you just do what we originally planned and let's d d this! If u are gonna use it to pay school fees like u claim then it doesn't matter if u don't have it does it?! It is just pettiness

> Then your solicitors filed the wrong price, look at it on rightmove sold prices.

It was listed as 125 but that's not what I paid!!

> In any case

Why ru investigating my stuff anyway?!!

> I'm not

> My lawyer had to put it on the asset sheet!

Yes originally the estate agent solicitor filed the wrong price but I have paperwork to prove what I paid!!

> If something happens to you that entire school fund gets IHT'd, if Im going to pay school fees from it, why does it all need to be with you? There also has to be complete transparency for the children's investments

It needs to be with me so it can grow and mature like it was originally intended!!

U imagine for a second I wud take from the kids accs?!!

I gave the kids acc figures to my solicitor yesterday in our meeting

Why is the £50000 not on your asset schedule? Trying to make it look like I have sooo much more than you!

Your first year costs wud have been £36000.

Also that doesn't make sense cos ure rent should have come from ure salary if ur on so much!

> It is, HSBC, £46k
>
> Send through revised asset sheet and will consider with my solicitor, I need to be sure that you will pay school fees. Needs to be absolutely clear how much is where.
>
> You think I will stop paying?? Then what they leave private school!! It was my idea in the first place that they go and I pay for it!!

> Why wud ure Stamp fury be £50000??

> It wud have been more like 20000

It was 40k because I still owned part of college ride

> So where is the extra 10000? U can't round up by £10000!!!

> **** needs his blue house t shirt

I am not rounding anything. I have declared what I have in my accounts. I am not going to justify myself to you, any more than you were willing to justify yourself to me. What I have listed is exactly what I have left.

> You said £50000 on stamp duty. Now u say £40000! That's rounding up'

> He says not in his pe bag

On the asset sheet are actual figures

Will check when home but it should have been there

> I had another look at assets schedule, where do u see it saying I have £300000?!!!

Add it together

> Yes.. spoke to lawyer and she also says doesn't add up to £300 000 too

> Maybe ur looking something else

> my solicitor is drafting a response to the letter yours sent. The asset sheet is still incorrect and a corrected version will be sent, along with the documents yours requested, other than that I believe we agree on the terms

How is it wrong? On whose side??

> on my side, its counting numbers twice, the 400k AND the 57k I have left from the 400k

So just an extra 57 then

And are u putting the school money back where it belongs?

> Your proposal has asked me to sign an undertaking to use it for school fees

---

That was written before we spoke and I still don't know if u mean what U say ... so I need u to write the reply stating ur happy to put the school fees back where they belong.

> I am happier to sign a legally binding obligation to pay the entire amount, which is what you've proposed

We agreed u wud put it back so it can grow!!

> right, but then you sent through this proposal! which has me signing a legally binding undertaking, why is that even in there then?

> This was the proposal before u agreed on the phone to put it back where it should be. So once again ure word is worth nothing?

Are you kidding me?

You send through a proposal that isnt what you want, and then you complain?

> U reply say that u agree to put it back as per a conversation we had.

> Oh bloody hell...

I am not complaining I am saying what is the big deal .. put the money back. Say it in the letter and be done with it. What is the problem ??

> What is inaccurate???

the fact youre not asking for an undertaking or funds to be ring fenced

I will have to tell my solicitor to re draft the reply tomorrow. You need to extend your 7 days deadline

> She should have reviewed it already!! Y have already said no to my proposal once..,

> I am tired of the back and forth. U need to agree to what we have said to each other and tell ures that. Let's get this done

thats what I thought we were doing!

> Transfer the money back to the school fund?

Yes

And have ure lawyer write it

> As I said on the phone, with the right undertaking or whatever, then Im not opposed to doing that! Will contact her tomorrow

Undertaking?

> legal promise or whatever, your laywer proposedd it

To put the money back?

Or to pay the school fees?

On the phone we agreed u wud put the money back. Have nothing to do with school fees and I wud let u know yearly how much is left. End of

> Right, in return you would sign a legally binding whatever to pay school fees, right?

Fine. I will obviously be paying the school fees till it runs out

> Fine??? Thats what we agreed on the phone!

Yes fine

> Right, enough of this for tonight, I will discuss with my solicitor tomorrow as stated it may not make your deadline, so suggest you inform your solicitor.

> Just please put it back so it can grow and last as long as possible.

> Have u had any more interest come through on the Tesco acc? You have changed the bank details they have so the intresr comes to you...??

Yes I did that a while ago

No interest, gets paid once a year I believe

> Are you going to return it?

Theres been no interest paid since the last amount you received.

Happy Birthday

> What are u doing with cheques the kids get?

depositing and holding until they are older

> Depositing where?

One of my accounts

> Are the cheques not in their name?

No

> So how does anyone know the money is not being spent by you?

> Why not open accounts for them?

This money is still 'held' on a spreadsheet. It is cheques from my mum and grandad for birthdays and Xmas. The kids have no real knowledge about it and I have my suspicions as to whether or he is keeping it for them. It would be worth about £10 000 by now.

When I suggested he open bank accounts for them years ago, he said, "I will think about it, I am busy."

> Did u bother to find out about the hearing test?

Did not get a reply

> So didn't bother to try to find out?

> I have called the school many times to find out

> Well Since you aren't asking as u aren't interested..., I shall I tell you. They don't offer it again and the nhs don't offer it either. So you missed it totally

> Was expecting kids at 5

> Don't lie to me in future. Be a grown up and tell the truth.

Explain

> Sorry already have plans What day that week r they free? Plans every day that week

> This was a conversation between us a few weeks ago

Firstly, don't speak to me like that.

Secondly, we did have plans, but in case you haven't noticed a lot has changed since then, and continues to change on a daily basis

> BS

> You should know right. Dont message me unless its important.

>> Don't project

> You really are odd. You have them for practically the whole holiday, yet you want me to give you even more time of mine. You know things were cancelled last week, but still want to fight about it. I can only presume you have too much time on your hands, or are just bored.

> Either way, dont bring your drama to me

>> So what was cancelled last week? Everything I have planned and booked for them is still on! That's odd isn't

---

>> Orng Wow

> Love how facts get changed to suit you isn't it.

> Please have the balls to text me ureself about a change to drop off time. I need them here before 11

> Wow!! Yiu are amazing!!!

> Getting your 13 yr old to fight your battles!!

Given your disgusting behaviour I try to limit contact. Jog on, not interested in your mentally ill adventures. Its like you wake up looking for a fight. Seek help, its not normal.

> Maybe stop lying. Start telling the truth. Just say 'no' instead of making up imaginary crap you are doing with them.

I dont answer to you and never will again. You really are simple if you think that things weren't cancelled, you yourself cancelled her appointment with the therapist. Maybe watch the news if you dont know what's going on. But then again when I warned u about this at the start of 2020 your expert opinion was it was just the flu. Recall? But dont let facts stand in the way of your feelings.

> No. But that isn't Ure business. All the agreement was was that u saw a statement. What wud u do if there was a withdrawal anyway? This is not Ure money. It is not Ure business. I allow u to know the figure of the accounts ex h year and that is it. U don't get to query it or question it or know any Thing about it.

Its not your money either. If there was a withdrawal I would expect there to be a valid reason Its absolutely my business to ensure that my children's money doesn't simply disappear!

> No it is not Ure business. I am Trustee so I will decide where and when it goes. It is nothing to do with u. Where is all the kids Xmas and birthday money? *** bank?? Please

> I won't be discussing this any further. This money is my business and not yours. You are lucky to get the yearly figure. You have no authority, rights or anything here. I don't care if you believe I am as untrustworthy as u and would take their money. This money is between me and my children. End of

> In future when doing your 10 days it needs to be your week plus some of mine. Then they come to me for the remainder of mine then back to the normal weeks. Easier and less faff and moving about for the children. Like I do it. Thank you

I agree, you should remember this as you have previously booked on my time, causing untold disruption. Furthermore your day trips should not be booked on my days. Thanks.

> Some activities are only available when u have them / or like with 'stranger things' it was only for ***. I would have thought regardless of whose day it is u wud want them to have the experience.

On that note there is a charity bike ride I want to take the kids to. It starts at 4pm at blackbushe on 16 september

> You just said we shouldn't do. Either it is allowed or it isn't... Make up Ure mind.

And you just said they shouldn't miss out. Since youre taking them in december and have done this numerous times already maybe its time you accommodated it

440

> I am not saying no and in December it will be the 2nd time only. I am merely saying u can't tell me how bad it is and it needs to stop and then ask for it yourself.

> If u want to get pedantic then u shouldn't take *** for haircuts on my weeks. Please stop being so ridiculous and try to see the bigger picture. I am not sure why u have suddenly become so aggressive and antagonistic but I assure you it will go nowhere

Uniform?

> I want to take the girls with me to the airport on Monday.

?

> What?

ask for what you actually want, not a vague statement

> I need the girls home by 4 ish

That's still not asking. That's telling.

> Can you bring the girls home by 4 tomorrow pls

ok

> So not going to farnborough then right. Can u deal with the maths grade pls

yes, no going to farn

what do you mean about the maths grade?

> Talk to teacher about if he can get a better grade

I thought you were going to ask *****?

> I am dealing with everything else for *** and ***. U can do that bit.

And I am dealing with four difficult GCSEs, but ok!

> Both were told to you many months ago

> I book holidays on my week and part of yours. Not all if your week and part of mine. See the difference

> I suggest this year they come to me on the 31st as that's New Year's Eve! And then next year they stay with me till the 30th and come to u on the 31st

> there is no issue on this end, but if send hostile messages you should expect a response.
>
> i will review this and respond when I have time.

> there is no issue on this end, but if send hostile messages you should expect a response. I don't start hostile or aggressive. Everything about you shouts hostility and anger and resentment. Move along

> your lack of introspection is interesting but expected. I'm not sure why you are still so angry and bitter but it cant be healthy. Get over it

---

> No. Can u agree that in future u take all of your week and half of mine so then the remainder of my week I can have the kids and then the wwwks can return to normal

> Can u??

> I am not entering into more pointless arguments with u. Can u do this? I am doing it.

> If u do, I will

> Do you approve the calendar?

> I havent taken them anywhere this year, so not sure what ur talking about. Historically you are the onlly one who are consistently booked holidays on my time. Its getting tedious reminding you

> july the problem you have is with the 2 weeks i have them, even though some days are schools days?

< I have no idea what u are talking about, and I haven't taken them away this year. Next holiday I am taking them on I am using only some of Ure week. With the 10 day allowance that has been agreed we will each have to take half of the others week. The 7 days of Ure own week then the remainder of the others week snd the time left over days of the week the children can return to the other parents and then things return to normal

< Yes there should never be a need for either of us to have them for a full 2 weeks as it is unfair on the other parent

> Attached change gives you 2 weeks as well. Suggested rule of preventing 2 weeks away from either can come into affect after next year.

> I will allow this this year only. Did u not understand the 10 day holiday deal? I need the children with me from July 28 afternoon to allow for packing

> I also need them this Dec on the 31st as per my having them for new years

Dickhead told me many times that I didn't deserve my inheritance, asking me, "What did you do to deserve that money?"

It was my money that bought him his car, which he still drives, and my money that fixed it when it needed a service before he moved out. He saw it as his, and a backup.

He's both a user and a manipulator, and he still becomes angry and blames me whenever I dare to request anything from him. He has never put his hand in his pocket to pay for the children's education, and he had it written into the consent order that he never would.

He told Jacob during the divorce that I had taken all the money and wouldn't give him any, which made Jacob come to me and ask, "Why don't you let Daddy have any money?"

They must have also discussed how I had perfectionist tendencies because – during a heated discussion – Jacob accused me of "always needing everything your way."

I hadn't ever put these needs onto the children so it had to have come from their father. My issue with this has only ever been directed at myself anyway. Never others.

I do not trust Dickhead in any way, shape, or form.

Among the shocking things that Grandad angrily said to me after I informed him of the divorce – and after my mum had started her smear campaign against me – was, "Why do you get to be happy?"

I asked him if he had been happy in his marriage.

"Yes," he replied.

"Well, I'm not, and I'm still young, so I want to find happiness," I explained.

He sneered down the phone and I was left reeling.

Following arguments, during the marriage, any 'changes' Dickhead attempted to implement were short-lived, with everything reverting back to normal within a week. It was a regular, tiring pattern.

CHAPTER 33
THE WILL

So, as you know, my mum changed her Will. Instead of leaving money to me, she left everything to the grandkids – which is fab, because now I don't need to worry about their financial futures.

I don't have an issue with her choosing to change it; my issue is that it was done maliciously and with bad intent., and after the 'advance' giving the majority of it to dickhead. I was forced into something without all the details.

She didn't tell me about her decision to change it, which meant that I continued with the divorce in the belief that I had money coming to me later. Even Dickhead was privy to bits of information from her that he tried to use against me.

Truth be told, I had always seen my potential inheritance as a reward/payment for the life of emotional damage they'd forced upon me... but now, I wasn't going to get that payout.

I was the reason there was even any money anyway. When my dad died, my mum was given a choice between getting a lump sum of £4 million or an annual payout of £80,000 for life (I think, anyway – I don't remember all the ins and outs), but having to pay income tax on the yearly amount.

She chose the yearly payout. I have no idea why.

Then, one night, it hit me – she had cancer; she would need to live 20-plus years to make up the £4 million. She needed to take that lump sum and invest it... ASAP!

So, I set it all in motion, and the next decision that needed to be made was where to invest it.

She declined to use the financial adviser my dad had used, because Jeff said he was no good. "He's a tool," were his exact words.

Jeff was angry that I had stepped in for some reason.

Email between me and Mum after she told Jeff about my changing the money:

>Had to tell Jeffery about asking if I can change option

> Oh dear, what did he say?

> Bit miffed as said we should be on the same page. I said I should have told him but

Angry?

>>> He said did he know about it and I said didn't tell him because might not be able to change anyway . I told him the yearly amount was taxed and he asked me who I had contacted.

If I hadn't realised what was going on... there would be no money now. But it seems Jeff had made the bad decision about what choice to make!

Funny because later on, I found a text between Mum and Jeff saying what an amazing guy with money he is and others wanted his advice too!

A week or so before she died – when I was allowed to visit – I asked her about it all.

It had occurred to me that there may be a big IHT bill to pay for the £400,000 she'd given Dickhead. She'd told him the estate would pay it, but I had my doubts now that I'd found out how close those two had become. At this point I still had no idea HOW close or about the discussions they had already had about the IHT (see previous texts.) So dickhead was working through the divorce proceedings with way more knowledge of these things than I did and was keeping them secret.

I worked out that £160,000 might be due – and, of course, I would be liable.

I told her I didn't have that kind of money to give away to the tax man.

Her reply was, simply, "Why not?"

WTF?!

Even if I did have that kind of money sitting around, I told her, did she really want it going out of my pocket – the pockets of her grandkids – and into the tax man's coffers?!

She then asked about Mark's savings! She also knew about the fight with Dickhead over the £75,000. As I've mentioned, she'd always had an odd idea of money, constantly telling me, "Everyone is a millionaire on paper."

After Dad died she'd even been anxious that the £5 million she had wasn't going to last for her entire life!

Honestly, I was astounded at how supportive she was of Dickhead over me – her own daughter! He had lied and told her he was paying me £1,000 a month for the kids – a 'good salary,' as she had declared in her texts to a friend. WTF? As a single woman, she was getting £6,000 coming in every month!

He did given me £1,000 for a few months, but then he reduced it to less than £300 for all three children. This was soon stopped, however, as we were sharing custody 50/50, which meant I was entitled to nothing. It was around this time that he asked me, "When you become a millionaire (when my mum died), I won't have to pay you anything anymore, right?"

He meant the CMS child maintenance. Remember, at this time, I wasn't earning. I later found a job during the hours when the kids were with him or at school, but it didn't pay much.

He and my mum expected Mark to be paying for Dickhead's kids! If this doesn't show his attitude to my family money then I don't know what does. This was also while he was fighting to keep my £75,000. His greed knows no bounds!

I ended up giving in to the £75,000 Dickhead had, as I was so sick and exhausted by the drawn-out nastiness of the divorce – but also because my mum had led me to believe, all the way up to her death, that I would be inheriting half the house plus half of the £600,000 investment.

After she wrote me out of the Will, I confronted her – by text – and told her how many life choices had been made on the presumption that I would be inheriting. She told me how no one made choices based on the future.

The whole divorce had been fought and based on what I thought I'd be getting. It was almost like she went out of her way to ensure I was left with as little as possible – while making sure Dickhead was all set and cosy.

Mum couldn't give me specifics, but she assured me that the lawyer would explain it to me and that there wouldn't be much inheritance tax to pay. Looking at the texts, it would seem that she and Dickhead had known about this all along – and had kept it from me.

I ended up paying £22,000 to the tax man.

She told me I would get half the money from the sale of the house and half the money from an investment she'd set up – there would be £600,000 in there, so I would get £300,000.

So, I believed I could relax, knowing I'd be receiving this money.

And, as I'd had (!) the £400,000, Jeff would get all the money in the USA accounts, which added up to about the same amount – she said. Funny that that £400 000 didn't go to me at all but whatever!

On discovering that Jeff was the executor of the estate and was, therefore in charge of everything my children were due to inherit, I literally got on my knees in front of her and begged her to reconsider. I told her he wouldn't do a good job where my kids were concerned. I pleaded for her to choose someone else – anyone but him.

"I am not redoing the paperwork," was her response.

"I'll write it – you just have to sign it. Please, anyone else… please!"

She shook her head. "Don't be so silly; Jeffrey will do his best for those children. No, I'm not changing anything."

I felt distraught. I was fucked. If Jeffrey had control, goodness only knew what would happen; I knew his hatred of me went beyond anything anyone could imagine.

One night, Jeffrey emailed me, telling me to print off and sign a form that stated I was no longer the sole trustee of her investment – that the solicitor would now be a trustee too.

"Doesn't she want me to do it anymore then?" I asked him.

"No… it's just that it must have two people now. Just sign it and then post it to the solicitor to sign."

I was still under his control at this point, believing I was inferior and nothing more than a burden who was always in the wrong. I can hardly remember doing this, but I did. I also have no memory whatsoever of printing off her 'wishes' and taking the paper to her to sign, which just goes to show how conditioned I was.

Having the solicitor sign that form was one of the worst mistakes of my life.

If I hadn't done that, the whole affair after her death would have gone a lot swifter, been a lot easier, and cost much less money. But they obviously had no trust in me and believed… what? That I would take all the money for myself?

I would have split it evenly, 50-50, between Jeffrey and me, just as my mother had instructed. Nothing more, nothing less.

I guess people judge you based on their own actions and thoughts of ill will, hence why I kept getting caught out by these people – I would never have even thought to do to them what they did to me.

During my visits to my mum, I was called in to do her nails, massage her arm (as she had fluid build-up), cut her toenails, go shopping to buy her more comfy clothes… you get the idea.

She mentioned that the wedding rings would be divided between us, that there were certain pieces of her jewellery that were meant for certain kids, and that there were some pictures here and there that she thought such and such would like.

She was giving me her Pandora bracelet, "You will want to get it extended though." she told me. I jokingly, but half seriously, commented," Are you calling me fat?"

"Well you always told me you are bigger than me and your wrists are fatter than mine."

Even now, even in this moment she had to say something mean.

In the end I split the bracelet and its charms between the kids, I wanted nothing of hers.

The ashes of her and my dad were to be split between us.

During my visits, she only showed me disdain.

I dealt with doctors, nurses, the palliative nurses, ambulances, and other things that the live-in carer couldn't deal with.

I went over at 11 o'clock at night to help get her into bed, I called people for her, I shopped for her, and I took the grandkids over to visit her.

I'd been useful when she needed a good oncologist finding, when she needed transportation to her chemo and radiotherapy sessions – instances where I willingly went out of my way for her. But, ever since I found my voice, I became the devil incarnate in her eyes.

One weekend, when I had the kids and Mark had his vasectomy, I was called to come over. I took the kids over and I could see that things weren't good, so I arranged for the kids to go to Dickhead.

I wanted to stay at home and look after Mark, but she wanted me to stay the night with her.

I knew this was it.

Chapter 34
Death

Suddenly, she looked at me, and in that moment, she seemed to stop breathing. Her eyes turned black as her pupils enlarged dramatically. She looked at me with a pleading expression and gasped, "Help me."

I held her hand and put my other hand on her heart. I offered comfort and love.

I tried to recall the lessons I'd learnt in my Soul Midwife course – this is a person who comforts the dying to enable them to have a 'good' death by feeling safe and not alone. I did this course after my father died as I wanted to understand how to be helpful and useful in death.

I held space for her and was present for her. I was determined to put aside my issues to ensure I gave all I could for her death.

Her heart was beating fast and she felt clammy – I was sure this was it.

But it passed and she went to sleep.

Later, when my mum woke up again, she said she wanted me to stay the night.

I was torn – my partner Mark had just had his vasectomy, and I wanted to be home to look after him. Fortunately, he understood, and he kindly brought my toiletries over to her place.

I organised final phone calls.

Jeffrey made an empty offer of coming over straight away – what bullshit.

She couldn't talk much by this point, so I had to translate her eye and head movements and her whispered words.

She did manage to tell him, "I love you all so much."

Never, in all my life, had she told me she loved me out loud – and definitely not 'so much,' and certainly not at the end. I always just got a 'you too' after I said, 'I love you.'

The pain of hearing those words in that moment sliced right through my heart.

All I had done.

All she had put me through my whole life.

All I had provided.

All the times I'd been there for her when she needed me.

Putting my shit on the back-burner for her.

All the support and love I'd given her during my father's illness and death.

Finding and setting up her new home.

Dropping everything at night, when I had a new baby to look after, because she said she needed a hug.

Taking her groceries during COVID, even after our falling out.

Dropping off mint tea and ginger nuts when she said she felt sick, even when she'd hurt me so badly.

All of that… forgotten in an instant.

According to Jeffrey, however, this was all just stuff a daughter should do. But where the fuck was he? What was he doing?

In his eyes, I was a terrible daughter, a terrible person, and I deserved nothing – he would see to it that I got nothing.

"You don't do things to get things," my mum had said to me months before.

No, of course not, and I never did anything to GET something, but I would have thought that my love and loyalty would have been honoured or even given a second thought at some point. Not just dropped the moment I found my voice.

On my mother's deathbed – rightly or wrongly – I went through her phone. I wanted to know, once and for all, what had been happening behind my back. What I uncovered (and while I write this, I'm shaking, remembering the discovery; my heart is pounding and I feel sick) was nothing short of shocking, revealing to me a level of betrayal I hadn't even imagined.

The lies, the secrecy, the manipulation… even my therapist, Kim, was shocked by all the secrecy and lies when I showed her some of the texts. Discussions I didn't even know had been happening. Whole relationships I didn't even know had been happening.

All the texts I found were proof of my lifelong fear and theory – that I was unloved, always on the outside, and an easy scapegoat.

Between her and Dickhead.

> I don't think she realises how lucky she is

No

Kids ok?

> If you need anything just let me know

> All good, got a pinch punch text from xxxx this morning

Thank you. She asked me if you had been getting me any food. Maybe kids told her

> Sure I don't mind her knowing

Don't know if she was annoyed or not!

> I've come to the conclusion that she will always be hostile so I don't care what she thinks. I'm going to do what I know is right

> I spent 14 years trying to please her, that's enough time 😂

> How are the patients?

Much better, jumping around and dancing

xxxx still got a slight cough, but temp has been good

> Well done nurse! Nursery tomorrow?

Yep!

> If you go to Ikea can you get me some paper

missed all the application deadlines for both

So not sure what we will do yet

> Nowhere that goes up to age 15?

Not that we have found but also most places are full or will make us wait

> R freaking out?

But the school today was very nice and I think xxxx will certainly be happier there

I never got any praise for looking after my own children!

> Or ***
>
> Have to see them first
>
> Just off to a meeting at *** about the closure

Good luck

You both going?

> Just me

Probably better !

> Hi xxxx, are you still coming over this evening?

Yes just shocked

> Are you sure you don't want to come over? If you change your mind and want someone to talk to just drop in

Thank. Will let you know if coming

Sorted out LV trip?

> No sorry was going to do it Monday but things got in

How lovely to have someone to talk to!

When my brother's 3rd child was born

> He said yes

> ok, you tell her, otherwise she'll be annoyed that I knew first

> I have just sent photo

> Had the reply- "oh he's early!" nothing else

What else did you want me to say? Look at how they discuss me!

More texts between them to show the extent of their talking about me and the development of the relationship between Dickhead and Mum.

> How was she today? Seeing her later

She was good

She was a little confused about your relationship, she wants to help you and care, but feels that you are being closed.

> Oh So I am supposed to forget what she thinks about me??

> She was the one who broke off contact with me!

I know. Its very confusing

> I don't want a relationship just when I have cancer.

> Hi can you order something on Amazon prime for me please ? Magnetic care phone holder. Mpow 360 rotatable sticky mount. £8.99

Sure

> Thank you

> How lovely thank you. Going out for lunch with Grandad

> Thank you for the beautiful flowers. Does * know you sent them? Had card from children via her and message this morning

You're welcome

No she doesn't know

> Ok. Can I come round Sunday late afternoon have my tyres checked

---

> Thank you

> * says she is at work - what she doing?

No idea! Far as I know she only works a few hours on a monday

> Said going to be all day. Maybe volunteer care work?

Maybe

Any news?

> Out of surgery - Half replacement - just ball went well.

> Can you take the presents xxxx sent to the children ? R is even more uppity with me for leaving them with you . She says lovely how close you and I are!!

> I just can't win - said I thought the children were with you and that she wouldn't want me going round to her

Just ignore her

She blames everyone else for everything

> She was the one who doesn't want a relationship with me!! Next time I will ask her where I should leave any presents- xxxx birthday.

Did she invite you to xxxx birthday party?

> No . I am not welcome I know that

> I will just need to know where to leave xxxx presents

> It's mentally exhausting know what to do!!

Yes, I've found it's best to just do what you want and not care what she thinks

She doesn't care what we think when she acts

If you want to bring the presents to mine on xxxx birthday do that that way you can see her open them

> Can I text you when *** has left?

Of course

> Don't say anything to the children about me coming - if Grandad is tired I help feed him and won't be home til 7

> R gone

---

xxxx might be contacting you about the new iPad she has just bought. Needs your expert advice

> No prob

Hope the party won't be too awkward for you

> Me to!

Don't let them intimidate you

> I won't,

My daughter was having a birthday party at my house and I thought the nice thing to do would be to invite her father. Look how they discuss it!

I tried to involve him and I served him drinks. At the end Mark's father had no idea he was the children's father as he had not interacted with them at all.

Was also hard seeing garden again

> So who were these people? Yes it must have been very difficult for you

Parents of xxxx friends

> They must have thought it odd then . Was xxxx there?

Yes

Everything go ok?

> Yes thank you had couple of rainy cooler days but warmed up

> Any further developments re settlement ?

Apparently her lawyer has replied yesterday but I've not seen anything yet

> She has been checking on me during the day

> Also she's having some sort of work done so his room had been moved around, so hopefully it's back to norms

> That's good

< What work?

> Electrical, I'm guessing she has had the all the lights in the dining room changed, she always wanted to

---

> Maybe ill ask what he thinks next time I see him

< Hope you didn't mind me saying - don't want to interfere

> Not at all, I'm hoping that the time away will give them both the space they need

< R let me know she was home and if I needed anything from Tesco! Do you know where I stand with her

> You heard if * and children arrived safely?

Nope

But presume so, I only hear when there's a problem

> Ok. Hope the children enjoy

> You ok?

> Have you spoken to xxxx today? Hope they are having a good time. I sent a message to * about xxxx birthday and she acknowledged it

Yep

They had a good day now going to watch some banger racing

> Think that's xxxx influence!

> Hi xxxx
>
> There was a change of plans I have then from tonight

> When does * leave? Can I come round tomorrow night to see you all ? - don't worry about supper

> Of course! And dinner is included!
>
> Friday morning

> Thank you

> I hope you're not sick of fajitas yet

> I don't have the kids this week so if you need me to drop in to check on him or bring shopping just let me know

> Thank you that's kind. After you were here I messaged xxxx to say she was welcome to come over but she replied that She doubted Grandad would want to see her. I replied he would but there was no reaction !

> R is dropping xxxx present on Wednesday evening

> How is your dad doing?

< what time should I come then to avoid any confrontation? Dad was having problems breathing but after he sat in a chair was finding it easier and looked brighter. Today is he having an angiogram. * was there when I arrived yesterday she showed us photos of the 3 dogs

---

> Hi xxxx, won't be going to the even tomorrow evening

< Ok but can bring round the ironing

> And stay for dinner!

< Thank you

> Completed! It's mine! 😊

> xxxx has given me cards for you and your dad, they were in the kids bag but she forgot to tell me

That's good. You be in late afternoon as I can come round on my way home ?

My card from xxxx thanks me for the voucher I sent her!

---

change the number of rings on his phone!

> will do that as well

Happy New Year. Let's hope 2020 is good to you .

> Happy New Year! Lets hope its a peaceful one for us all

Do you need anything?

> Can't think of anything thanks. How's it all going??

Got a first mediation meeting next week

series of nasty messages from her yesterday for no reason

>

---

they are supposed to be neutral

but Ill be watching carefully to ensure

The long and short is there isnt any more she can take from me, its now about her taking money from the school fund

> That should be solely for fund

Yep

> apparently the wedding is cancelled
>
> She said it was my fault because this "stupid divorce" is dragging on
>
> But xxxx said it was because it clashed with his trip to iceland
>
> and its been moved to next year

Sounds bit strange

> yep

Sounds more of a party than anything else

I think also she wants all her personal finances secure which is sensible - not sharing !

> yep

Next year is a long time away

> I know

very strange

she could have moved it back a week or so

maybe shes got cold feet

> Getting back to reality

> Don't want her doing anything to make things worse for herself

She just needs to calm down and stop attacking everyone

> Yes

> Sit back and consider

> Where you going for mediation? Solicitors be there??

Its in north camp

No solicitors

she wont be there for the first meeting

> Got some in Tesco's yesterday

> xxxx rang Grandad to see if he needed anything and sent me a text asking

> Received the amazon parcel thank you. You are welcome to come round and I can pay you . You ok for toilet rolls?

Have you got enough to eat? Need anything else?

> Plenty thanks . All fine for now

Happy Ex-Mother-In-Law day 😊

> 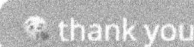 thank you

I have a delivery from Asda on Thursday, not sure how much will come, but let me know if you need anything

> Is * over her cough?

Not but it's become phlemy which corona doesn't and no temp

> That's good . She has been messaging me and put a card from the children through the letter box

---

> * has offered to do mine and Grandad's shopping so agreed . Think she wants to help

> Will you get money back from school fees?

Thats great!

Im not sure, they havent said anything

They are send homework, and the kids have video chats with the teacher occasionally, but hard to imagine they would keep

> Sure
>
> This bail out by government benefit you at all?

Not sure, long process to claim, but the self employment one won' because I'm a director

> You ok for now?

Yep!

>

Indeed. She has been asking me about my condition

I hope that's out of real concern, but I can no longer tell

> I hope so too and all this won't be thrown back at me later on

Doesn't ask how I am feeling though - pain etc

> Do you think something like this would help?

Can't win – if I ask it isn't good enough, if I don't ask it means I am bad!

> Hi no need to bring my order next week when you have the children as I don't want them telling her you are shopping for me so cross off the yogurts please . I don't need anything urgently . Thanks

are you sure? has she said something?

> No she hasn't said anything . She is going shopping tomorrow so I will give her a list for Grandad but I don't need anything. I can get fresh food myself from the local Sainsbury's

ok, so I can remove the items you asked for?

> There is one of xxxx I would like

Do you know which one?

> I think xxxx had it in your hallway

> Thank you so much for coming round last night. I have had a shower but not steady on my feet so back in bed. If you have time could you make me a hot drink and toast to see if that will stay down ? No rush

> Can you come round ?

Hi xxxx sure be there in 30 mins

> Do you have a thermos flask?

No, do you need one?

> I think I have one on a high shelf so maybe you could look for me

---

> I move and my arm hurts!

Hmmm, well hopefully he can prescribe something

> R knows I went to pain specialist and having side effects. If she says anything to act surprised

ok

She didn't even say hello to me when she dropped the kids off today

> They ok?

Yep

> Sorry about last night

> Feeling better and less tired . You all ok?

Why would I say hello to him after all he had been doing?

> Garden and plants watered thank you for the cards, I'll open them on Wednesday

> Will transfer birthday money when home 👍

> Thank you, no rush

She would have been giving him £200 each birthday and Xmas. My grandads would have been giving him £200 each birthday and £300 at Xmas!

They carried on giving him money, but not me.

> Happy birthday 🎂

Thank you!

Thank you for the card! Please can you also thank xxxx and xxxx (i dont have their number), and also your dad

> Welcome

How are you feeling?

> Very tired today

You friend xxxx called me, she seems very nice

> Yes she is

If you need anything let me know

Are you ok with me sending you photos of the kids, or would you rather I stopped?

> Love seeing them

Jeff didn't send him cards before the divorce!

Yes

Ok if I pop in to see you?

*coming Sunday

No WhatsApp message *

I hope she was sympathetic

Yes

Good. Maybe she's coming to her senses.

Better sooner than later.

I am trying to do the decent thing

> I actually have. Will sort it out but she will receive something towards the tax anyhow. You keeping warm?

Yep! Hopefully British Gas will be here soon

Had a heated exchanges with R yesterday, she needs me to do the school run again

These are now between Mum and Jeff:

> I will try not to take things personality. She is going to * on his birthday with children and cake. I will be there too

How nice of her to grace him

> Don't be unkind

I have very little sympathy for her. She's been given every opportunity in life

> Can u send or give xxxx a bday card from us please? I didn't realize in time and it wont get there. I just sent xxxx

Ok

> Thx

> xxxx didn't receive anything.... :(

Don't expect he did . I think you won't be receiving anything from her

Shall I write the card from all of you or just * and *?

> All of us please.

> I don't remember that last time I got a card from her lol

Is Uncle and Auntie or what?

> Uncle and auntie ues

> You alright?

Going down with a cold

> No better than yesterday?

> Yes awful

Didn't xxxx offer

> She did for the results when I first arranged the appointment but Monday is xxxx birthday. I don't want her talking me

ok

> If I let her down the last thing I want is her helping me

> Yes xxxx brought them round. They had been looking at sofas

For his new house?

> Yes

When's the move

> Gets the keys next Friday
>
> This Friday

When's the divorce

> xxxx offered to take me to hospital for appointments. I gratefully decline but at least she offered

Bare minimum

I have to ring the courthouse tonight to see if I have to go for jury service tomorrow. Have to do it every night 2 weeks

> Might be interesting

Lol might be yes

> Yes was checked before I left

Good

> Hope proves conclusive of whatever the problem is

> * texted me to see how it went

How thoughtful of her

Did they tell u how reliable the test or analysis is?

> No didn't say anything

Ok

* messaged me to see what results were. Wants to go with me next visit to oncologist so I agreed

Ok

She wants to come to all my appointments so I agreed

That's something

I think if I said no then out fragile relationship would get worse

Dont worry about that. You have to think about you. What you want, what you need. The rest will fall into place. She's a big girl.

I don't like unpleasantness

I know u dont, but sometime you have to what's right for you and put yourself first.

If u want her to be there, great. If not, tell her

You're not obligated to her.

These appointments, especially, are about tour health-physical and emotional- no one elses

> Hi mum

Hello

> You ok?

Yes. Has xxxx been messaging you about me?

> No. Why?

> Haven't heard from her since she told me about the divorce.

She think I am telling you and xxxx more than her and she has to find out things from other people

> Oh for goodness sake

> I haven't spoken to anyone about anything you've told me. One message between me and xxxx about how upset we are and how we'd try to Locke over for your treatment. That's it.

> There are bigger things she needs to worry about. And needs to jot worry you with this nonsense

I did text xxxx and told him maybe a little more as I had time to think about what the dr said so maybe that is it

I don't think xxxx will make it to Feb 12

She's living the life... she'll come to regret it

Did she take u to the scan yesterday

I'm in line outside the blood place to get xxxx blood test done. It's not even 7 am

> She is hoping to get some work after course. No she was away. Early birds.

> Ok well early to Waitrose shopping. Going round to xxxx this afternoon his mother and sister will be there and staying the night

They're staying the night? * the children there?

> Yes

Good

I was checking on them both.

I never got 'kisses' sent to us.

> took me to Waitrose. xxxx asked me round to dinner but not up to it

:(nice of him

> * has been texting me today and sent flowers in memory of Dad

Oh

She should have visited... but whatever

> She is in New York

Living it up

> Freezing there I think

I'm sure she's staying warm

> xxxx had a fall in her garden and bruised

Oh dear. Is she om.

Ok

> *had asked about my appointment so I had to tell her and she is going with me on Monday

If u dont want her to go u can say no. She's not in charge

> I don't want to make things worse

Dont let her get her way so as to not rock the boat. It's your boat

---

Wow! That's nasty.

> Now space at xxxx school so be easier all round

Good

What is xxxx training for

> At a nursing home I think . End of life care

You're being v nice to help

> 👍

> She takes me to my appointments

you're ill and her mother

> Don't expect her to especially now

[photo]

> Cutie

> But xxxx will tell her about the card

Oh

Ok

She can't control everything... its not a crime to talk to family. It's v irritating how manipulative and controlling she is

> I just want to stay out of the line of fire

I know

> 100% . Haven't got the same energy

Thinking of you cars since she was bullied

> Kind thought but probably not a good idea. If *gets to know she will be annoyed that I told you

I'll send it to xxxx.

Dont let xxxx control u

Good

Has xxxx done anything for today

> She gave me presents from the children and sent me a message this morning

Oh

Sorry we're not there

Do u know the fill schedule of the radiotherapy yet

Full

> Make sure you dry off

>> 👍. Going to look after xxxx and xxxx for couple of hours this afternoon

> What's xxxx up to then

>> Nursery

> Why do the older two need looking after? Mother getting another tattoo?

Dickhead left them with her, not me.

My son was struggling with the divorce and having two homes, so I suggested he see a therapist.

See the comments from Jeffery to Mum.

> * and * had to fill in therapist about what's been happening and xxxx will go to her next week

Does xxxx talk to you?

> No not to anyone

Not at all?

> Not about the situation

Does xxxx see how she caused all this nonsense because she wants to party more

> She isn't partying anymore! She has her man

For now... she's get bored in 5 mins

She did the same to xxxx.

> Didn't he finish with her as she went to uni in uk?

> I don't remember specifically but I do remember her wanting to go out more and mess about before the broke up for good

> She was too young to settle down. I hope now she has met someone to settle down with

> Stop making excuses. It wasnt about settling down it was about rebelling

Tom broke up with me! I always wanted to settle down. I, in fact, begged him, on my knees, not to break up with me.

Horrific how Jeffery has chosen to believe some fantasy that I am this awful, rebellious, bad person – yet he has no concrete evidence to support this. I just haven't stayed in the little box they all tried to keep me in.

> He lives there so is there when the children are there. His 2 girls stay over some weekends. I bumped into her and him in Camberley one day

> There children like him

No wonder xxxx is upset! OMG

Very inappropriate

Way too soon

> I am not commenting and want to keep out it as nothing I can do. I just do what I can to make sure they are ok

So sad for the children

She needs a good smack. She has no shame. And is obviously putting herself before them... no surprise

> The children always seem happy and laughing though

Don't always show it

It might not manifest now bit will. They learn behaviors from the parents and have a v bad example in her, the girls especially

I'm not perfect but try to do the right thing

> That's all we can do

Doesn't seem like she does though. Seems v selfish

> Who knows what she thinks. I have had enough thinking about it - too upsetting and I cant live my life like that any more

But she drags u in and expects you to help out and do what she wants

> I have little contact with her

> Going to bed now as tired

Love u mum

I was trying to do the right thing, I just wasn't doing what they wanted me to do!

> Has his grand daughter been see him

I said she was welcome to come but she said she doubted G would want to see her. I replied that he said he would but not reply to that

> :(

I can't do any more. She asked me when my oncologist appointment was

> No you can't. U needn't try any more. Shes grown and the decisions or mistakes are hers to make

When G was in A&E she wanted to be kept informed how he was

> [photo]

New car?

> Yes they all did . Children going on holiday on Monday with R and man plus his two . Caravan in Great Yarmouth

> xxxx changed. I dont see her as the caravan type. Will she marry him?

> Does she have a job

> They went to a caravan few months ago. Getting "married" but not legally so that she can ask for spousal support from xxxx! Seems she is giving massages from her house

> She's got some nerve.

> Is that Avengers that xxxx likes?

> Think so

All the info they are talking about it shared from dickhead – not me. And most of that info is then given to dickhead by the kids – lots of Chinese whispers going around!

I never wanted spousal support, it was never mentioned.

How

Visit to Florida sometime

W xxxx?

xxxx is up for it

What about his ex wife

Once divorce gone through

Won't she have to give permission

Don't know

K

Church today?

I can come help

> Giving him pain blocker now. See what xxxx says about coming. Have told R and she wants to come to hospital. Said I will her her know when he is in a ward

Shouldn't bother w her.

I can come, just let me know. See what trevor says.

How long will OP be?

Of course it does.

Did u leave when she got there then?

> No she was there when I arrived I knew she was going

Oh

> Bit strained but she is ok with G

I should think so too. She shouldn't be a victim

No idea what being a 'victim' has to do with going to visit my grandfather in hospital!

> Doesn't have any . xxxx just been

Good

> No warmth towards me

She is lost.

I thought she was in Greece this week

> Last week . Adopting rescue dog from Cyprus collecting her tomorrow

> Will then have 3 dogs

Keeping such close tabs on me!

Oh for goodness sake. Does she do things to be deliberately stupid?

She should focus on her children.

> Hopefully can do both

Uh huh

Ridiculous

Has xxxx arrived?

> Yes. Expecting a wet weekend
>
> Did Grandad go with you

Yes and we went with cousin xxxx and her husband. xxxx came with her dog wgich was well behaved

> Why would she take a dog to a wake ?
>

It was in a pub. Nut sure she can leave it for long and it acted as a support for her I suppose

> She needs a support dog to go to the wake of someone she barely knows? Ok

It was good she still wants to go to family gatherings

> Ok
>
> Had your dinner?

Having it now home made you soup

It was the wake of my dead grandmother's brother. I was there to show support to her. I took the dog as I knew it would be hard being around my mum and grandfather. While there, grandad told me to "just give her a kiss and say sorry". I told him, "You have no idea what she has done or what has gone on." We didn't have any communication after that.

> You're welcome. Xxx

At least one of my children loves me !

> one out of two ain't bad.

> ;)

> Don't let her into your head.

Just don't understand what I have done

> It's not you. That's what you have to know. It's her.

Busy making soups to freeze and for Grandad

How is xxxx doing with weight loss?

> I'm sure he'll be glad of them

> She's frustrated. Thinks it's not working. Too early to tell really

Frustrating

I sent a text to the birthday girl. No answer yet.

Me neither

She hasn't read mine although I know she is online

Surprised you bothered

Well... I know what day it is. I did it partially to see if she'd acknowledge it.

It's up to her - we have acknowledged it

Exactly

Can't be accused of abandoning her

Gotta keep on keepin on

I got a "thank you"

Me too

No mention of vouchers

I was never good enough! Even my 'thank you' wasn't specific enough!

> xxxx is staying home and the rest of us are limiting going out

> I don't expect to go out for the next few days

R has said she will help out with G as I am high risk. I said she was too but reply was she is fit and healthy

> Oh she surfaced did she

> Tell her to shove it

She has offered if I need anything. I might need her help with G

> Up to you.

> Desperate times...

> It's late... Are you sleeping ok?

Don't have much choice . Usually take something to help- taken codeine and will take paracetamol soon

> Ok

> R u watching anything good now?

As I read all those messages, I had never felt such rage, such hatred, such anger as what was coursing through me right then.

I was literally boiling – I felt so hot, and so full of energy, yet so very exhausted.

My body ached, deep inside my bones.

You always hear people say, 'Oh, I could have killed him/her,' but there is no way they felt like I did in that moment.

After a while, I considered my options. She was on death's door. I could put a pillow over her face and no one would suspect a thing. There would be no autopsy done, no evidence… it would be the perfect murder.

Mark and one of my friends – both of whom I'd been sending screenshots of the WhatsApp messages to – told me to leave. To just walk out. They said she didn't deserve me being there with her.

I stood by her head and wrestled with my conscience.

Could I live with myself knowing I had murdered her?

She was going to die soon anyway, so would it really make any difference?

But… I would know.

I would feel guilt and shame for the rest of my life. And then, she would have won. Forever.

Would I tell Mark if I did it? Could I bring myself to tell him? Put that burden on him?

After digging deep for a few moments, I stepped away.

Lying down on the sofa, I tried to sleep, but it was the shittest, most fitful night of my life.

The next morning, she started to rouse around 7.30-8 am. I watched her struggle with her water bottle.

She had no idea that I knew what she'd done and, in that moment, she looked more evil to me than ever before.

After a while, I helped her with the water. Then, 30 minutes later – after helping her with the water again – I got up and walked out of the house.

That was the last time I saw her alive.

The instinct to kill her was still strong, and I needed to get some distance. Besides, I needed Mark. I needed a hug, a bath, and to get away from her.

Within 30 minutes of getting home, the home carer lady called, informing me that Mum was asking where I was, and that she wanted me.

What a turnaround!

So, I got ready again and was just getting my shoes on when the carer called back… She had died!

On turning up at the house, one of the carers – who came a few times a day to change her – was crying.

I did not cry.

I called Jeffrey and his first question was, "Were you with her?"

Too honestly, I replied that I was not.

This, of course, was a big mark against me that helped fuel his hatred and his ongoing mission to destroy me.

When I was looking on my mum's computer, I found an email she'd sent to her friend in Spain. It said: 'I had to make a choice, and I chose him.' She was talking about me and Dickhead.

When, a month or so before, I'd confronted her about her not even messaging me on the day Dickhead moved out, I said it felt like she had chosen him. And what did she say to me? "No, not at all, of course I didn't!"

What a lie. I started to wonder if she'd ever told me the truth about anything.

She must have emptied her bowels on her passing, as the room smelled really bad. So, I opened the windows – this would also allow her soul to leave – and waited for the ambulance people.

They took a long time to do their paperwork.

Unlike when my father was removed by the undertakers, I felt nothing.

With him, I'd been filled with sadness and heart-wrenching grief, knowing I'd never be able to see him again.

With her, I felt empty. Numb.

I was just glad it was over.

I got this from Jeffery as he found out I was looking at her phone.

Can you turn Mum's phone off and put it on the desk in the office.

> Was gonna take that and laptop with me

Don't think there's any need. I have the numbers and docs needed.

> Just taking loo roll and fairy liquid, bubble bath etc . If thats ok with y?

👍

Chapter 35
The Funeral

COVID was still going on at the time of the funeral – July 2020.

Jeff came over, of course – always making grand gestures rather than being here for the actual 'event.'

I had wanted to get into her house and get things sorted and sold, but he made me wait until his arrival.

> And they may have them. When I get there. You have no reason to go round there anymore other than to put the key through the letterbox

> U r laughable!! Seriously!!

> On ure quest to collect things u might wanna get mums credit card / info from xxxx

Jeffery has all her credit card info and who knew if he would use it!

I was still so conditioned to follow what he said and was scared of him. I wish now I had just gone in and sold stuff. But who knows what the repercussions would have been to me!

He asked if my kids were coming and then said there was no space for my partner to come.

So, I called the funeral director, as I'd met her and spoken to her about things before Jeff waltzed in and took over. She explained that, as he was her client, theoretically, she had to do what he wanted. However, despite the law stating that only 30 could attend the funeral, she assured me there was no way she would ask Mark to leave, emphasising that there was most certainly a space reserved for him.

She explained to Jeff that she was my mother too and that I deserved to have someone by my side, supporting me, on the day.

My Uncle (Dad's brother) and I arranged to sit together. His wife opted out of coming due to Jeffrey's behaviour towards me.

I was nervous. I had bought a new dress and Mark had had the car cleaned.

Later, the funeral director, told me that, as I walked down to the crematorium, Jeff said, "Is that Raven?" and she replied, "It is – doesn't she look gorgeous?"

Thank you!

Before she got really ill, Mum had joined a cycling club. She can only have been in it a few months, but about six of the club members lined up in their cycle gear and, as the hearse drove by, they clapped.

It sounds like a nice gesture on paper, but in reality, it was so cringeworthy! As the hearse was driving so slowly, they had to clap for quite a while, and I hate to say it… but I found it hard not to laugh! I looked at Mark and my Uncle and could see they were holding in the giggles too. It was just utterly bizarre.

It was like they were honouring some world-class cyclist or something!

Much to Jeff's – and I'm sure others' – dismay, the funeral director asked me to lead the mourners into the hall. Jeff, my uncle, my grandad, Mum's friends, and Dickhead carried her coffin.

Jeffrey cried through his eulogy, and neither Uncle nor I recognised the person he described.

Her brother cried through his too.

I was listed last on the order of service – I guess I should feel lucky I was even mentioned at all.

There was, apparently, a small gathering at Grandad's house afterwards, but I'd only been told about it five minutes beforehand and I wouldn't have gone anyway.

Some family friends who I'd stayed with while at boarding school were there. I had chatted with them when they came to keep Mum company during chemo one time. However, during the funeral, they totally blanked me. When I finally mustered the courage to go and talk to them, they had already left.

She consistently used people. Years would pass with no contact other than exchanging Christmas cards, but as soon as she needed something from them, she reached out. Whether it was staying a weekend with one set of people or another, her pattern remained the same.

She supposedly didn't like my Dad's brother and his wife much. My mum was always bad-mouthing them to me – and, presumably, to Jeffrey too – but then she'd go and stay with them for a few days so they could look after her.

It made me sick.

No one but me bought flowers for the funeral. I ordered 2 gorgeous arrangements, one from me and one from the kids. Her wonderful 'men' hired fake flowers from the funeral home! She had told me many times over the years that she wanted her funeral to be full of colourful flowers.

I waited to speak to Grandad. I kissed his cheek and said goodbye… and I haven't seen him since. I have no intention of doing so either; after all, he hadn't spoken to me since my falling out with my mother, other than to say, "I have no idea what to say to you."

I had visited him in the hospital, taken him food during COVID (which he never thanked me for just stared at me), and even gone to collect him from hospital the night before the funeral when he'd become dehydrated. I did everything I could to still be 'there' for him and show care for these people – despite their treatment of me – but now, I was done.

The day before the funeral, Jeff had declared that I was to meet him at the bungalow the day after the funeral. I was to bring the £200 that I'd found in a drawer at the house and, if I didn't, he wouldn't let me take a mattress I'd asked for.

Prior to this, he'd demanded that I not go back to the bungalow and that I was to take nothing from it. He was in charge now and he had to account for everything.

No matter. I had gone back the day after she'd died and had taken a few bits I wanted for the kids. The only things I wanted were a freezer I had lent her, a mattress, the kids' box of toys, and the jewellery she had designated for each child. Oh, and my father's wedding ring.

There had been some back and forth about the ring via text and Jeff had left it kind of open – so I was supposing, hoping, it was going to be given to me that day.

Again, there had been back-and-forth messages about the jewellery for the kids, and he had also supposedly sent photos of items to Dickhead for the kids to choose.

> 2.30 on Thursday is a good time. Please confirm.

> Yes

> Ok. You might end up having to take the freezer with some things still in it.

> You can arrange with xxxx for the kids to choose jewellery. Please do it in the garden, they can go in the back gate so don't go through the house, please wear a face mask and pls don't touch them

Have you been round to the bungalow?

> Today? No

Since Mum passed

> What do u want?

To know if you've been to the bungalow since Mum died

> Oh let me guess... u sent xxxx over. He has seen... goodness what u have both decided I have done something awful. Close?

No.

Just answer. Have you been round there since Mum died?

> Just as what u do appears to be none of my business. What I do is none of yours . So no I will just answer cos it is none of ure business

Yes it is. That house and everything in it is my business now, so I need to know.

> Cos what? Has it been burgled? Is there something there of utter importance ?

Take the key you have and put it through the letterbox by tomorrow.

> Gonna have xxxx do the same?

> I need to know where all the keys are and I need it thro the letterbox by tomorrow. xxxx has nothing to do with this. He's not there and I've not talked to him about you.

Power trip or what!!

I don't have a key!

> Good

What is ure problem. Just get it all out. U will feel better afterwards

> Right now my problem is knowing where all the keys are.

And how am I then supposed to help my kids choose what they want ?

> You ask me

> I'll be there soon enough. So kindly put the key through the letterbox.

> through all the clothes wud be overwhelming and their father has nothing do wiry this!

> xxxx needs to look at the jewellery and choose something

> show me where it state you get everything in that house or get to dictate and choose what happens to it all

Do you have the Will?

> No I don't

Well, there's a reason for that. If you did, you'd see it written there.

> No I wouldn't... prove it

> I can abd will just contact the solicitor tomorrow

> Was gonna wait for u to be a decent person and tell me about the will but more fool me. All will go through the solicitor now

Decent. That's funny

> that is rightfully mine.

That's the way these things work. That's the point of a Will.

> right so then u should know what the kids have been left etc

> There are things in that house that are actually mine and I wud like them returned to me.

I've invited you to tell me what...

> I should have first choice of stuff before charity

According to you.

Very entitled.

If there are things of yours there that you want back you should make a list and send it to me tonight

> Me entitled!! Hark are you

> And then how will u get to me?

> What about their jewellery and what she left for me?

> The jumpers etc??

> Tell me what pieces they were told they can have and I'll look.

> Jumpers perhaps they can come round and have a look, or their dad can.

> Why do u imagine for a second you get to dictate everything ?

Yes! He did imagine he dictated everything!

> Where are the knitting things and true toys back?

> Be easier if I come get it

> If I find it I'll separate it then, but if not it might get taken out of you don't want to tell me.

> I don't know where the knitting is. The toys are in a box . So... just so we are clear u won't let my kids have what is theirs cos u won't let me come get it

> Ask u what?? Please sir can my children see her clothes?? And then what? Am I to stand on the doorstep?

It is not yours to take. I have responsibility for everything on that house and I need to account for it. I will not den her grandchildren but have to coordinate everything whether it's a simple pen or a pile of gold.

> Oh my god u r a joke!!

What's more I have instructions from Mum for many things, so need everything where it is

> I tell u now mum wanted each of my girls to have specific rings

I have instructions from Mum for many things, so need everything where it is

> Yeah... she tell u how many jumpers she had and what to do with them? The kids want an item of clothing each to make memory pillows!!

> Any particular reason why I can't travel 20 mins up the road to sign the *** paperback?

Is it ready?

> No

You're not the executor of the estate. I appreciate your help to this point. I will handle it from here.

> Fine

> Gonna be a struggle to get the dress etc there isn't it?

Well if you don't want to do that you don't have to. The only person you hurt is Mum.

If you want to drop it off you can, and I appreciate it. If not just let me know and I'll make arrangements.

> So I was enough to hold our dying mother's hand and see to her every need but now I am worthless to u again?

> You can pick it up
>
> > Like I said u can't choose jumpers for the children
> >
> > xxxx has a right to choose jewellery
>
> I'm talking about the list of your things, that are yours
>
> > Yes and I am talking about the other things too

> I'll have to confirm
>
> I've found the Pandora bracelet and a blue ring but no pink one after looking through several times, so I've picked out another nice one for xxxx. I'll bring them when you get the other things.
>
> > No you don't get to pick... they get to pick.
>
> Unfortunately for you, I do. The only other option is to look through with their dad.

Expect they didn't get to 'look through' with their Dad either. Jeffery took selected photos and had them picked from the few he sent. His kids got everything else.

> I'll look at the rings. I did see a Pandora bracelet.

and xxxx?

> Don't know yet.

> Don't know about my children either yet. Remember I have children too?

Mum told me the wedding rings are to split between us

> You may come to the bungalow to get the matress, freezer, box of toys, knitting and spinner tomorrow afternoon. I found some photos you might like to have as well. Bring the envelope of cash too (it had £250 in it) About 3 I think we'll be ready.

What about jumpers

> Yup them too

Jewellery when?

> When I get round to it

> I'll keep jumpers aside. Jewelry isn't at the bungalow.

>> All the jumpers? And then what? So then what happens about the jewellery?

> Not dealing with that now. Focus on your list first.

>> No. I need to know what is going to happen

He never 'dealt' with any of it. Simply ignored it and gave me nothing.

> xxxx has already chosen. xxxx is already separated. So I'll talk to him about xxxx. We're not at Mum's, we're at Grandad's, so we'll sort it out.

>> How did xxxx choose?

> I talked to xxxx last evening and sent him some photos for him to choose from. Quite civilised.

>> As long as they were safe

When I arrived, two guys in a van were just leaving, looking very happy with themselves.

It seemed that Jeff hadn't bothered trying to sell anything but had instead paid someone to take all her stuff away. I know for a fact that it all would have sold for thousands and thousands of pounds.

When my uncle invited me inside, I saw some bags on the floor by the door, full of the bits I'd asked for. I also wanted some of her jumpers to be made into memory items for each child. He had, of course, taken it upon himself to choose the clothing I was allowed to take!

Straight away, I clocked a wedding photo – from my wedding to Dickhead. I took it out of the bag and put it on the floor.

Jeff appeared then, and the first thing he said to me was, "Get out! And don't take stuff out of those bags; it's all yours!"

"Why would I want a wedding photo?"

"You're in it!"

"But I'm getting a divorce!"

I think, at this point, Mark said something in my defence.

In response, Jeff just looked at us both and said, "Get the fuck out now!"

I picked up the stuff and stood by the door.

"Get the fuck out!" he repeated.

I just stood there, staring at him. I wanted him to see that I wasn't intimidated by him and that he couldn't order me around like he had when we were children.

He just laughed and walked off.

I put the stuff in the van and rifled through it quickly. No wedding ring.

So, I went back in just as Jeff was pushing the mattress out the door with a family friend and our uncle's help. "Where is the ring?" I asked. "She said we should share the wedding rings and I want Dad's."

"No, she didn't want that," Jeff told me. "There is a letter of wishes."

I was shocked; she had said exactly that – regarding the rings – to my face only days before she died.

"She told me a few days before she died," I explained. "What letter of wishes?"

"I have a letter of wishes."

"I want to see it."

"No!"

We carried the mattress out. Then I went back inside, where the freezer was waiting for us.

I told him again that I wanted the ring.

"No," he said again. "I am the executor of the Will, and I say no."

"So the fuck what!" shouted Mark's dad – who'd come to help us – as he thumped the top of the freezer.

I started shouting – I don't know what, I don't remember – and tried to hit Jeff, but I missed. So, I tried again, though this was made all the harder by the fact there was a freezer between us! Eventually, I managed to knock his glasses off. He looked extremely shocked.

Mum's friend appeared then and told us to calm down. I shouted at him, asking him why the fuck he was even there.

He had shown his hatred of me years before when I'd decided to move to New York. "I can't believe you are leaving your mother," said the guy who left his mum in the UK when he moved to Spain. Go figure! He'd also shown utter contempt for me when I helped him move some furniture into the bungalow before Mum moved in. My dad had died only days before, and I was there with my six-month-old, trying to set up a home for her!

There was more shouting from both sides, and I told Jeff that Mark knew everything that had happened between me and Mum.

"I don't care. Fuck off."

Then, Mark – with good intentions, albeit ill-advisedly – declared, "I'm glad she's dead and I hope she rots in hell!"

Well, that was it. Jeff pushed the freezer out and slammed the door shut in our faces.

I banged and banged on the glass of the door, and then I gave up and fell into Mark's arms.

He and his dad got me in the van and we drove home.

I was shaking.

On looking through the bags, I realised he'd chosen crappy jumpers and none of the jewellery that had been destined for the kids. Two of the pieces were actually my grandmother's, and one was a ring I hadn't seen my mum wear in 15 years!

"I have children who need bits too," he'd told me – and now they were getting the pick of everything! And this was the guy who, apparently, had my kids' best interests at heart and would do all he could for them.

Yeah – well done, Mother!

A few weeks later, at my house, I was having a birthday party for one of the kids when there was a knock at the door.

It was a policeman – Jeff had filed charges against me for attacking him!

I had the choice of agreeing that it had happened and signing a form – which would give me a seven-year reprimand and which would show on any enhanced DBS – or going down to the station to discuss it further.

WTF?!

I signed the form.

Considering that the only jobs I could get would need an enhanced DBS, however, I was now a bit fucked if I needed to go out and get employment.

How pathetic!

Jeff gave his statement and then disappeared back to the US.

The policeman pretty much agreed it was bullshit – and that Jeff was a pathetic pussy! – but the law is the law. He told us that Jeffrey had said he wanted me taken away in handcuffs. "We don't do that over here," the policeman had explained to him.

Seriously! Arrested. Handcuffs. What the hell was wrong with this person?! He really was pathetic.

A few days later, my uncle called me to request that I legally 'hand back' the share of Grandad's house that my grandmother's death had left to my mother. Jeffrey was asked to do the same. My uncle asked if I was happy to wait on Grandad's death to get something or if I wanted it now. I said it was up to Grandad.

During this phone call, I told him about Jeffrey calling the police on me. "Oh, that was a horrible situation that day," was all I got in response.

The next I heard was that Grandad had decided to give me nothing as I "had had enough already."

I then received a letter removing me from being my grandfather's LPA (lasting power of attorney). Fine! That was good, as I wanted no contact. Funny how I was good enough to do these things when I was compliant.

Soon after this, I blocked my uncle on WhatsApp and I haven't heard from him since. He's one of them, never asking to hear my side of things, and never sticking up for me or wondering what really happened.

A few weeks before she passed away, he chose my mother's house as the setting to share his opinion of me. By then, my mum had deemed me fit to enter but not to stay and help; at this point, I was basically a runner. I was told what she wanted and I had to go out and buy it.

I was standing with him in the kitchen when he said, "If you have something to say to her, do it now, because soon it will be too late. This poor woman has lost her husband and her mother, she has cancer, and now her daughter has abandoned her. Raven, you need to apologise."

There was no way I was saying sorry; I had done nothing wrong. I had simply – finally! – set some boundaries and was doing what I should have always done, which was to fight my corner and believe in myself.

Did no one else remember that I had also lost my father? My grandmother, too? Had everyone forgotten everything I'd done for my mum during my father's illness and beyond? How I had been the liaison for her illness and my grandmother's illness, and how – up until the argument – I had been my mother's biggest support?

I was done talking to him; other than the odd word about Mum, I didn't bother with him after that.

And then the dance of the Will began!

Chapter 36
The Executor of the Estate

Jeffrey, of course, took his role as executor far beyond anything a rational person would.

He used it to gain control over me and dictate everything I could and couldn't do.

> We shall see

> I'm beyond fed up with you. You're childish, rude, disrespectful, arrogant, entitled, and thoroughly unpleasant. I'm trying to give you what you've described bit if you make it difficult then you'll end up with less. You forget these things are for he children, not you. You cut your mother out of your life and this is partly the

> your mother out of your life and this is partly the result of that. I'll tell you what you're getting in the Will and later send you the Will so you can see. You are every lucky in getting 50% of the house win Naphill, as Mum told you. You have 2 choices: pay me cash for my 50% and get the house or wait til it's sold and get proceeds due to you. The 6 grandchildren get the investment accounts and other bank accounts. I'm the executor of the estate and the trustee of their accounts. There now you know everything

During COVID; Jeffrey had broken all laws by coming into the UK, not isolating, and then being around my grandfather, my mother, and all the medical staff.

I did not want him to potentially infect my children.

There was no list of instructions from my mother and the children did not get what she'd wanted them to have.

Jeffrey left them five jumpers to choose from, all but one in the same colour, and I wasn't sure I'd ever seen her wearing most of them.

I never got the wedding ring or any ashes; he purposely kept refusing to discuss it in texts to make me think he was going to be reasonable about it.

My children missed out due to his selfish superiority complex and egotistical needs.

He was, is, and will forever be, pathetic and weak.

Over the course of the four years that this Will fiasco has been going on, Jeffrey has shown his constant need for control and power.

He has wasted hundreds of thousands of pounds by not distributing the children's inheritance in a timely manner. If the money had been invested, it would have grown significantly.

I have emails that illustrate his need for control and his manipulation of the weak, useless solicitor.

With there being two separate parts to the estate, and with Jeffrey being 'in charge' of one and myself the other, the solicitor should not have been sharing all the information and discussions I'd had with her, to him.

She actually liaised more with him regarding these issues than she did with me. But, of course, I was not privy to any of the information about the estate. It is a complex situation to explain, but let's just say that her behaviour was biased, unprofessional, manipulated, and manipulative.

At one point, Jeffrey was calling and emailing her multiple times a day, the cost of which was financially huge.

.

Email from Jeffery to solicitor.

> Please follow up with the other party on Monday for a response on both points. If there is no response or further delays next week I will petition to have my sister removed as a trustee, something that I, and we, should have done some time ago. When speaking with them, please remind them to be reasonable and to act so as to keep me onside, as you have done with me for them on other matters.
>
> This should have been simple and is causing me undue stress and delay. It's been more than 13 months at this point.
>
>   Regards,

He was not allowed to be the other trustee of the account I was in charge of.

> I am extremely well aware of the cost of delay and having to contact you, regrettably. The matter is very much not in hand having taken 13 months+ to still not be resolved. These are already undue delays and I expect them to be resolved forthwith because my patience is beyond exhausted, as you already know: I should have petitioned a long time ago for changes.
>
> Please respond to my questions above and push the matter forward with all haste.
>
> Regards,

> 1. 8 ways/2 ways. As far as I can see the request to split into two only confirms that there should be an equal division between her side of the family and ……. It doesn't say how those two shares should be further divided or held. My starting point would be that as both children and grandchildren are mentioned in the original Trust Document then all the potential beneficiaries should be treated equally (on the basis that "equality is equity"). From memory, … would be content with this.
>
> 2. I am not, necessarily, opposed to moving from that starting point. However, it would seem to me that there should be good reasons for doing so. The reasons that I know about If we are to move from that starting point would tend to suggest more should be for her children than her (especially her divorce and the risk that Trust funds could get caught up in that). Should we obtain Counsel's Opinion that any final decision is proper for us to take? There are a number of people who might make a claim in the future - including her children when they become adults.
>
> 3. Trustee
>
>   a. I was appointed at about the same time as her mother died. I know nothing about how that came about. I just received a document for me to sign which had already been signed by Raven and her mother..

As you can see the decision to split 8 ways instead of 2 was already decided. I am 100% sure that Jeffery had been in his ear and told him goodness knows what about me to sway his opinion.

When I went to the solicitor's office one day before he retired to take him some paperwork, I asked him what was to happen to the trust. Old Man Lawyer immediately said, "It will be split eight ways." There was no question, no 'we need to sit and discuss it as it is OUR job to do'… nothing.

This was the money my mother had been telling me for years was to be split between myself and Jeffrey.

As the children were getting the entirety of the estate, it would seem fitting that Jeffrey and I split it – but, no, the decision was made by Jeffrey and Old Man Lawyer to ensure I received as little as possible. I was told that the only way to split it two ways would be to spend lots more money on a barrister, give over all the details of my financial affairs, and then they'd decide if I deserved half.

I gave my solicitor all the information regarding where my previous inheritance from my father had gone. This was then used against me, which meant I was no further along in securing my rightful inheritance.

As I said previously, the discussions about this – and setting up trusts for the children – were all pointless anyway, as when Evil Lawyer bothered to read the policy properly, none of it was allowed. So, £30,000 or so was wasted, paying her to do nothing!

I hope that you are well.

As agreed, I contacted ………….. in order to ascertain whether they would be willing to replace you as a trustee. Unfortunately they have both confirmed that they would not be able to do so.

We have also written to *** to address all of the issues which she had raised in her emails to us. I attach a copy of the letter for your information. She has since come back to us to advise us to 'progress the matter as quickly as possible'.

Accordingly I advised her that the options were as follows:

You continued to act as a trustee alongside her. If we were to proceed on this basis, I advised that I would need her to confirm that she no longer believed that you were conflicted in your role. I would thereafter ask you if you would be still willing to act and subject to this, would thereafter organise a trustee meeting so that we could formally discuss a distribution of the trust assets.

We approached other suitable individuals in order to ascertain whether they are willing to act in your place.

Since then, I have had a number of email exchanges with her.

It would appear that she is questioning your appointment as a trustee by her mother before her death. I have advised her that if she feels that her mother was forced into appointing an additional trustee, then she would need to take this up with ……. directly.

- The solicitor who helped administer my late father's estate:. He met my late mother and sister a few times during 2016 and is obviously familiar with trusts and family law.
- We could ask my grandfather's solicitor in………. She is not familiar with our situation at all, I do not think, but probably met my late mother when she was helping my grandfather prepare his will.
- The company that manages the property my late mother owned in ………. knew her for many years: even though they're not professionals in this field, they are impartial professional people.
- In the U.S. there are people who act as professional directors and trustees does a similar profession exist in the UK?
- I am loathe to ask family friends, but could if need be. I suspect that my sister will resist the appointment of anyone tainted by knowledge of her past behaviour, in her opinion, however.
- If all else fails, we could potentially ask my paternal uncle, who my sister seems to favour. I am not keen on this idea because my late mother was not particularly close him and he was not active or present in our lives, and I suspect my sister thinks she can dominate him, if it'll break the logjam, however, it might be a last resort."

I look forward to hearing from you.

Best wishes

Emails between them that I should have been privy to – why the secrecy?

I simply wanted the money split into two, just as my mother had assured me it would be.

From Jeff to the Useless solicitor.

> I would defer on your judgement for that: if you think it'll annoy my sister or delay things, no. If it'd help, yes please. Does my sister understand that it is in her interest as well to resolve her own issues quickly?
>
> I might suggest that if my sister is insisting that she be given control of her children's share, that she be given the "win" to make her agree and relent. Again however, I defer on ***'s judgement. I can assure you and *** that my children's shares will be invested in their existing custodial accounts, which will soon be transferred into the control of trusts for their benefit.

> Thank you. I must say it is very frustrating to not know what's going on with funds of which my children and I are the partial beneficiaries, especially when the problem party is given information to which she is not party.
>
> It's hard to conceive what the conflict could be when there is a letter of wishes, and the wishes we're previously known as well.
>
> I'm just venting.

Frustrating to not know what is going on? You are telling me! This is the very definition of irony and pot calling the kettle black.

Jeffrey was also given over $1 million – it seems my mother had added to the USA accounts, and now he had significantly more than my mother said he would get – so he was not opposed to letting the situation unfold, even if it meant only a paltry £145,000 would go to his kids. I, on the other hand, really needed that money as I had spent so much on my divorce, my ex had stolen £75,000 of my money, and now I had to pay £22,000 in IHT – not to mention that I was paying all my children's private school fees, as I was obviously getting no help from Dickhead!

> Dear ***
>
> Many thanks for your emails.
>
> I have suggested the week commencing the 24 May for a trustee meeting. I will revert as soon as I have a firm date.
>
> I have also been liaising with – to let him know that the trustees are due to speak and had already suggested that we spoke before then so that he could give me full details of the below.
>
> He is becoming increasingly frustrated by the delay and so hopefully we can arrange a distribution following our meeting.
>
> Have a nice weekend
>
> Best wishes
>
> –

> Dear ***
>
> A thought for consideration: would it be a good idea to ask –
> for details of the accounts he is proposing to use for his children ahead of the meeting.
>
> [Including things like signatories, protections against money being taken out other than for his children's benefit and so on.]
>
> On the one hand this information will be needed at some stage so that the Trust can make the transfer funds knowing that it will be protected for the benefit of the children.
>
> On the other hand this level of detail is not needed to make a decision and complete a Deed appointing the funds in agreed shares. The exact Bank details are mechanical and could be left to be dealt with later.
>
>   What do you think?

I believe that this was to see if the money for my children could be 'locked away' in a more secure manner than the money going to Jeffrey's children.

There's no chance Jeffrey would 'take it on faith' for me.

Dear ***

I hope that you are well and enjoying the sun..

Please see the below email from – at ...... She has enquired whether you would agree to ***'s fiancée being the second trustee in relation to the share of the funds held for the benefit of her children until they reach the specified age. Of course, if you were to agree to this, then you would need some assurance that the funds could not be accessed until such time that the child reached the specified age. Please let me know your thoughts.

Whilst writing to you, I had asked *** to arrange to provide me with a letter of confirmation that the proposed accounts which will be used to deposit the share of the trust funds for the benefit of his children cannot be accessed until their 21st birthday.

I attach the letter for your information. *** has advised that Fidelity did not want to provide a letter that could be interpreted as giving legal or accounting advice and so his financial advisor has written this letter outlining the conditions/characteristics of the proposed accounts. He has advised that this is the same financial advisor that his late mother used during her lifetime.

The proposed accounts are exclusively for the children and can only be used for that purpose.

Is this letter sufficient to give you the necessary confidence that the funds will be reserved for the children's use and not be accessible until age 21?

As the joint trustee, this decision wouldn't have been solely Old Man Lawyer's; it would have been mine as well. I was never kept in the loop – the loop was Evil Lawyer, Old Man Lawyer, and Jeffrey.

See how they want different 'rules/allowances between us.

Dear ***

RE:

Thank you for your email. I was hoping to update you my the end of the week whilst I deal with the discussions between *** and ***'s instructed solicitor.

At this point, I am advised that the accounts may not be sufficient as there is flexibility for you to draw from the accounts, albeit for the children's benefit. I will be speaking with *** to ascertain whether he is willing to give the same degree of flexibility to *** in relation to the share held for her children.

I will update you further as soon as possible. I hope to speak to *** today or tomorrow and will then go back to ***'s solicitor.

Best wishes

From: –

This shows how they were attempting to grant Jeffery different rights and allowances than those given to me.

> Dear ***,
>
> I do not understand what you have said. While I am not a trustee, I hope that my opinion and input can be considered as Executor of the Estate and someone who knows my late mother's intentions for these funds:
>
> This should be wrapped up and not incur further costs or delay. Without knowing what my sister's intentions are for her share, or that of her children, I suggest simply splitting the trust assets between her and me and letting her do as she will with funds intended for her children. I certainly will deposit equal shares in my children's accounts. If R– elects to do that for her children, all well and good, if not, it's on her head and she can be asked to sign a release or waiver for herself and on behalf of her minor children to hold ***'s and *** harmless.
>
> Next week marks a full year since my mother died, and this trust should have been the easiest and quickest part of the inheritance to deal with. Please find a way to wrap this up without further delay or cost. The children deserve to get some funds invested immediately to avoid losing out on further potential gains.
>
>   Please advise.

Incredible that these are my very thoughts on the estate. Note how he tries to show his authority as 'Executor of the Estate'… when Evil Lawyer already knew exactly who he was!

Four years on, my children still haven't seen a penny from the estate.

> Dear ***
>
> If you wish to speak so that I may clarify anything, I am available tomorrow afternoon.
>
> Your comments are noted and I will relay them to the trustees.
>
> The issue is that the Trustees cannot simply pay out the funds due to the minor children absolutely in the circumstances.
> The concern (particularly expressed by ***) is the risk of being sued by a minor beneficiary at a later date if the funds are not properly managed on their behalf.
>
> I am considering whether we can work with what we have and amend the current deed in anyway. This would be the simplest option.
>
> I will revert ASAP. I spoke with ***'s solicitor today whilst she was on annual leave and she has advised that she will be letting me have her comments too shortly.
>
> Best

Amend the deed? So… twist it to say what you wanted?

How interesting, especially considering I would go months without hearing anything!

> Dear ***
>
> Thank you for your email.
>
> There would be associated tax implications of this option and would defeat the tax benefit of creating the trust in the first place.
>
> Whilst writing to you, sadly I am still awaiting to hear from ***'s solicitor. I chased again yesterday. I will call her this afternoon to see if I can ascertain the reason for the delay.
>
> Best ***
>
> From: ***
>
> Dear ***
>
> It would seem that a satisfactory solution to the distribution of the trust would be use the existing infrastructure: place the children's shares of the Trust assets into the Estate, from where they'll be distributed into restricted trusts until age 25. Surely, that'll negate the need for new subsidiary trusts to be created.
>
>   Kind regards ***

> Thanks –, please be assured that this is not the case. She has been on holiday as I had advised and since considering how we proceeded in the circumstances.
>
> I shall revert as soon as possible.
>
> Best wishes
>
> ***
>
> Subject: Re:
>
> That's a week since you spoke to her. This is another source of frustration: resolving this doesn't seem to be at the top of anyone's priority list.

Just put it all into the estate so Jeffery can be in charge of everything!

Dear ***

Please find attached the letter which I have now received from …. in reply to my recent email to them, also attached.

As you will note, they have agreed that there is no power within the trust deed to transfer the trust assets to a new settlement. Accordingly they have suggested the following two options:

- You retire as a trustee so that *** may appoint a replacement trustee of her choice. I do not think that you should do so in the circumstances nor do I believe that the indemnity would provide you with sufficient protection.

However an option could be that you agree to step down in place of ***. Do let me have your thoughts in relation to the same.

- The second option is that the Fund is simply appointed out to be held on bare trust for *** and ***'s respective children and their parents give valid receipt. However if you have genuine concerns at this stage that there is a risk that the parents may not use the funds for the benefit of the child, I do not believe that the indemnity would provide you with sufficient protection.

Please could you confirm how you wish to proceed.

   I look forward to hearing from you.

I have no doubt at all that Jeffrey told them I was some kind of thief who took money from my own children – and that I wasn't to be trusted.

This was probably confirmed by Dickhead's belief that I was trying to steal the money I'd put aside for the children's private school fees. This was my father's pension money – not money in a special trust – that I assigned to pay the fees. I never tried to take it and was adamant that the £75,000 that Dickhead stole needed to go back into that pot of money. It's funny how these people accuse you of the very things they themselves are doing!

> Dear ***
>
> Many thanks, once we have appointed out to R– and ... by means of separate Deeds of Appointments, we cannot then appoint Trustees of the bare trusts. This is because the appointment is absolute and the trustees will have no control once appointed.
>
> Are you available for me to call you at 4pm today?
>
> Best wishes
>
> Subject: RE: My client
>
> Thanks ***

This shows more phone calls and emails that I, the trustee, was not privy to.

> Subject: Re:
>
> Dear ***,
>
> Please advise the timeline going forward: when do you expect to calculate IHT and income tax? Have the firm's fees been calculated already (all time spent on the Trust should be billed to the Trust and not to the Estate)? When do you expect to make distributions?
>
> I confirm I have received the trust documents and letter of wishes.
>
> With respect to the Estate: one thing at a time as far as R– and her solicitor are concerned, let's get the Trust done first. Either way, I am not available next week as I have a long weekend away planned and then an educational course at the end of the week.
>
>   Regards, ***

Jeffrey purposely delayed doing or discussing anything until he had what he wanted from me!

Subject: RE:

Dear ***

We have recently submitted the tax return to deal with the capital gains tax position.

I will now need to register the trust for inheritance tax purposes and thereafter prepare a return. I will look to deal with this next week.

With regard to fees, the trust and the estate are treated separately. Accordingly all time spent has been allocated separately. We charge on a time spent basis and so our fees are ongoing.

I will let ***'s solicitor know that you are not available next week and so do not have instructions to update her. However I would prefer to keep them on side and so we should look to give them some update the following week at the latest.

Have a good weekend.

Best wishes

+***

> Dear ***
>
> I write further to our recent communication.
>
> I have been considering the inheritance tax implications of the appointment and will write to you under separate cover in relation to the same.
>
> In the interim, please find attached a letter which I have now received from ***'s solicitor.
>
> Upon my review I cannot see that there has been any undue delay on my part. I had been considering the potential exit charge which was slightly complicated by the fact that we will have to consider the previous chargeable transfers made before the date of the settlement.
>
> Before the recent agreement as to the distribution of the trust assets, we had awaited almost a month for ***'s solicitor to revert back to us and so it is unreasonable for her to now say that we are causing delay. I suspect that it is because she has changed her mind as to how the trust assets should be distributed.
>
> Please could we organise to speak on Monday as to your instructions.
>
> I look forward to hearing from you.
>
> Kind regards

Once most of the policy was dealt with (three years after her death!), I was then informed that the estate and the policy were the same thing!

All these years, they were kept separate and billed separately, but as soon as I pointed this out at a time when it no longer suited them… it changed!

> RE: My client:
>
> There is always the issue of a lay sense of timing and the reality.
>
> Bother anyway.
>
> It seems that this is where we were some months ago.
>
> Steps had been taken to get away from a situation that I am sure ***'s mother would have wished to avoid.
>
> Anyway I am content for this to be referred to Counsel - if *** now feels she wishes to go back on something that I had thought was agreed by both Trustees.

When I found this email, it was the first time I'd been made aware of any month-long delay.

They were delaying constantly!

Evil Lawyer would spend a long time 'considering' things – and, of course, she billed us for this time! She was so far out of her depth, it was almost laughable.

> ***,
>
> If ***'s solicitor is not responsive, you might give her the same arbitrary deadline she tries to impose on us. Being non communicative is a decision.
>
> Regards,

It is true that I changed my mind, and I did this for two reasons:

Firstly, I was under the impression that if I just shut up and agreed to what they were proposing, it would be resolved swiftly. This wasn't the case.

Dear ***,

I have been made aware that *** might be away on holiday from September 6-13, so please try to get instructions and final decisions from her before then.

Regards, ***

We did keep trying to impose deadlines because they always took so long to reply, make decisions, or do anything, really.

Again, funny how they can do it, but we can't!

Secondly, as this moved – slowly – along, I was gaining more confidence because I was seeing them all for who they were and what they were doing.

I realised that I deserved my money, so I wasn't going to 'cave' to their pressures any longer.

Dickhead was relaying my whereabouts to Jeffrey – they had set up an alliance after the split and after all this crap began.

Funny how, before, they never had anything to do with each other, having met only once. Then, the three of them – along with my mother – became a little gang.

As you can see from previous texts between my mum and Dickhead, she was 100% on his side, wanting him to get everything while screwing me over as much as possible.

It's hard to believe one's own mother would act this way... whatever terrible thing did she imagine I did to her?!

CHAPTER 37
DREAMS AND NIGHTMARES

I sleep very badly; it is practically unheard of for me to have a full, restful night's sleep.

I either can't fall asleep (despite being tired), I wake up lots in the night and then struggle to get back to sleep, or I have nightmares... sometimes all three.

This has been an ongoing issue with me for as long as I can remember.

In fact, I can still remember some of the nightmares I had when I was seven or so. There was this recurring one:

My family and I were in a cave-like, underground dungeon. Each day, the gaolers would take us out of our cage and we would have to line up to get whipped across our backs.

Surrounding us were cages filled with people at different stages of being thrashed – some just had bloody slashes across their backs, others had ripped-up flesh, and other cages were simply filled with chunks of flesh that had come from the people who'd been in there before.

We were trying to figure out a way to trick them into thinking we'd already been whipped for the day – red pen, pieces of sticky red tape?

The darkness and blood and ripped-up flesh were all seared in my mind.

I had this dream over and over and never told a soul – until I was 37 or so when I told my therapist, Kim. She said it showed deep anxiety.

My dreams/nightmares now range from mild – where I'm being verbally abused by Mark, one of 'them,' or a past boyfriend, being cheated on, or simply people being mean to me – all the way to extreme, the type of nightmares where you jump awake and lie there, terrified, as you try to catch your breath.

I also experience sleep paralysis, including vivid episodes where I'm certain there's something horrific in the room with me or just outside the door, and I feel in immense danger, yet I'm unable to move or speak.

It isn't uncommon for me to have a nightmare about school. I find myself back there – as a student but grown up – and I have to stay and finish my education, for another two years at least. I beg and beg and tell them I'm an adult now and that I don't need to be there… at the very least, I say, can't I come in each day and do my studies rather than board?

These dreams feel trapping, chaotic, heartbreaking, and frustrating. I am stuck, once again, in a situation I have no control over – and would do anything to be out of – but I have no means of escape. I struggle in these nightmares to figure out how I will survive another two years at that place. I'm not sure I could.

These nightmares can affect me for hours after I wake up or even all day; they follow me around and bring flashbacks and memories of things I thought were long buried.

It is very disheartening when you start having flashbacks of new things, events you hadn't thought of for 20 or so years, that now – for some reason – come flying into your consciousness and rip you apart anew.

Just when you thought you had cried out all your tears, you realise how deeply the past still affects you. Speaking these experiences out loud, your voice catches and tears well up once again.

Sometimes, I wake from dreams featuring my mum with a start. When I wake up, I find myself confused about what time period I'm in – and terrified that I have to see her again.

I feel for the young me so much; it was all so unfair and undeserved. I just needed to be loved and reassured.

Imagine what I would have become had I felt unconditional love! That in itself is a sad and sobering thought.

I recently heard a podcast (from an Instagram short by @marriagerecoverycenter) where a therapist described emotional abuse: "The more covert the abuse is, the more difficult it is to explain, the more difficult it is to describe, the more difficult it is to perceive from the outside. The abused will feel unseen, disregarded, disqualified, unequal in terms of status, demeaned and used. Not a person in their own right, but only as an extension of the other person and existing only to benefit them. It is an assault on personhood, an assault on values and worth. Aimed at control of another person."

This is how I have felt my whole life.

In a narcistic relationship the grief is from the death of oneself.

I also saw this from a lady called Tine,

"If you want to know what it's like to look evil in the eye, try divorcing a narcissist."

I spent so many years of my life just trying to survive – not developing or thriving – and now, in my 40s, I'm having to learn how to react to events without immediately switching into survival mode… into fight or flight.

I am someone who has always been easily startled by loud noises or people creeping up behind me. Hypervigilance is definitely something I excel at!

I notice everything. I overanalyse everything too: facial expressions, twitches, eye flicks, mouth purses… It was important for me to be able to read every piece of body language I could. Even now, I can tell you who is pregnant before they announce it. Who is mad at who in a room full of people. Who is secretly sleeping with who, etc.

When I'm walking into a room I'm familiar with, I can immediately tell you what is out of place and how. Why? Because noticing equals survival. If I see it, I can plan my next move. Should I appease? Remove myself? Fight?

To be fair, I'd often fight rather than appease because I was – and still am – headstrong. I have such a strong moral compass when it comes to right and wrong; Kim would always say I see everything in black and white. It's true.

Before, with Dickhead, my home felt like a prison. I couldn't relax as I felt like I always had to be 'doing.' I'd fooled myself into thinking it was my safe place, but I never felt truly at 'home' there.

I had to go out every day; I had to escape. To get any rest at all, I would have to take myself to a coffee shop with my book and 'allow' myself the time to sit and read. If I were at home, I would clean, tidy, or look for other jobs to get on with.

If I sat too long at home, my thoughts would wander and I would get incredibly sad and depressed. Being busy kept the thoughts at bay.

Now, I give myself permission to rest and relax. To just 'be.'

I'm happy to say that the home I have now is my safe place. There are days – weeks, even – when I don't leave it at all.

It is my solace. My peace.

After Dickhead moved out, I started replacing anything he'd used, or even touched. It might sound petty, but I needed things to be fresh, to be untainted. They had to be 'mine' – and have nothing to do with him.

If the house hadn't been so perfect, I would have moved. I've looked on Rightmove so many times over the years, but I've never found anything even remotely as suitable or lovely.

Now, I've created my safe haven – a bubble within my home – and the outside world feels unsafe, especially other people.

I love to travel and experience the world, but these days, I generally don't interact with anyone else. I go out of my way to avoid talking to people.

In my mind, if I just stick to the very few people who I know are safe, then I can remain more or less in my safe place – and not get hurt again.

CHAPTER 38
NO WIN NO FEE

When bad things happen, I turn inwards. I used to punish myself – with the eating and cutting – but now I, unconsciously and unwillingly, focus on my body. I feel my thighs rubbing together, I feel the weight of my breasts, I think of how slim I used to be and how not flat my tummy is now. I see fat pockets under my arms and hate that when I was in my 20s, I would cry about being fat – when I most certainly was not. Why did no one help me see how beautiful I was back then?

I become so conscious of every aspect of my physical body and how I'm supposed (?) to hate it. Where did this stem from? Why can't I find peace with this body that has done so much for me and that has gone through so much?

Despite disliking how my body looks, I've never felt healthier or more loved. This feeling pales in comparison to the self-hatred I used to harbour.

Back then, if I could have, I would have taken a large knife and literally sawn a piece of my fat body off. That was how I felt. I felt wrong within myself.

Looking in the mirror was torture. I would pinch and prod myself, proving I was ugly and fat – and, therefore, worthless.

In 2016, upon deciding I hadn't 'pinged' back into shape enough after and the C-section, I went to Harley Street to discuss getting some tummy liposuction.

"Oh yes," the registration nurse lady told me, "we can do your tummy, thighs, and flanks all in one go. If you sign up today, you can come back in one month and get it all done."

It sounded amazing!

Then, the actual surgeon – who was too perfect-looking for my tastes – took a look at me and decided he'd just do my tummy and flanks, as there wasn't enough fat on my thighs. I asked about other forms of fat reduction but he said standard liposuction would be the best.

A week before the op date, I had a minor Crohn's flare-up and got in touch to see about delaying my procedure.

"No, sorry, the operating room is booked," came the reply. "If you change anything now, you'll be liable for the full cost."

Well, shit!

When the op day came, I made my way – alone – to the private hospital in London. As I waited in my private room, contemplating what I was about to do, I started having second thoughts. The only mirror in the room was above the sink, so I stood on my tiptoes, trying to see my tummy.

'It isn't so bad,' I thought, 'I don't look that fat! But Dickhead will kill me if I back out now… it would be £5,000 down the drain!'

Not that he or anyone else tried to talk me out of it much.

"You don't need it," was the most he gave.

Mum just said, "You're silly – you look fine."

Not exactly enough to make me believe I was beautiful and wonderful just as I was.

Soon enough, the op was done and I was in a lot of pain. They told me it had gone well and that they'd taken loads of fat.

'Well,' I thought, 'I must have been a fatty then, right?'

My blood pressure refused to stabilise, so I was kept hours later than I should have been; instead of getting home at 8 pm, it was more like midnight.

I was shattered.

I had to wear a shorts-and-corset combo thing for nine weeks. It had a wee hole in and I could only remove it for showering. I guess this was to keep me all compressed, to help with the healing.

At my halfway check-up, it was noted that I had a few 'bobbles' of flesh. They were sore to touch. Other areas felt incredibly tight, particularly when I stretched; it was as if I'd been sewn up too tightly. There had been no sewing, though.

The nurse wanted the doctor to see these patches, but as he wasn't around that day, she took photos instead. It was suggested that I just do some massage to get things moving.

By eight weeks post-op, things were no better.

At my last nurse check-up, they signed me off, saying that, within a year, everything would have sorted itself out – and not to worry.

Life carried on, but I was uncomfortable. As the swelling went down and the months ticked by, I started to worry that these areas of skin that were so uncomfortable would remain so.

I visited my GP, who obviously suggested I return to the surgeon.

So, at nine months post-op, I requested to see the surgeon. I found it a little odd that I hadn't seen him already.

He looked a bit sheepish, and when I (acting out of character for me) spoke up and declared that, contrary to his belief, I would NOT look fine in a bikini, he turned red! In that moment, I knew the same thing he did: he had fucked up!

The suggestion was a course of treatment to break up the scar tissue. I was unsure if he was wanting me to pay for it or if it was complimentary.

Once home, I got a call to arrange the treatment, but all of the available locations – under their payroll – were so far away. The lady said she would investigate and call me back.

Wouldn't you know, I never got a callback!

About six months later, I plucked up the courage to call a 'no win no fee' solicitor and see if they thought I had a case. It seemed I most certainly did!

It took five years of fighting, several visits to an expert to assess the damage, and countless phone calls, emails, and Zoom meetings – but I won!

The surgeon obviously didn't want to go to court, so we settled for a good amount.

He was actually 'charged' with doing the wrong procedure! I should have had a minor tummy tuck, as I had stretched skin, and not much excess fat. I also had diastasis recti, which is where the tummy muscles separate during pregnancy. These, it seemed, needed repairing before the surgery.

He had used the wrong needle size and was too aggressive, going too close to the skin's surface – leaving me with internal scarring that was visible from the outside. He also did the wrong type of liposuction – it should have been vaser, not traditional. There were other things too, like not keeping accurate and satisfactory notes.

And, just to make matters worse, all of this was going on in the background during my divorce and all the crap with my mum. Talk about having a lot to deal with!

I wish now that I hadn't had the procedure done – and it has certainly scared me off any future ideas of having a little nip and tuck – but, these days, I like to look at the positives. If I hadn't had it done, I wouldn't have an incredibly cool tattoo covering my tummy now! I also wouldn't have had the money to treat me and Mark to an amazing, once-in-a-lifetime, luxury trip to the Maldives, and I wouldn't know all about the ins and outs of plastic surgery and no win no fee solicitors!

Chapter 39
Jeffrey

I was never close with my brother, and after he left boarding school, I obviously saw him even less than before.

I joined him for his wedding in Florida, though I wasn't asked to be a bridesmaid or to be involved in any way. In fact, I cried quite desperately after the actual wedding because I felt like he'd made a huge mistake. I was just so overcome with negative emotions that I couldn't stop the tears.

I wasn't asked to be Godmother or to be involved at all when his daughter came along.

Mum and I went to visit when she was maybe eight months old, and I wasn't allowed to pick her up or cuddle her – the excuse he gave was something about not wanting to ruin her schedule. This was very difficult for me, as I wanted to play with her and form a bond with her.

One year, I emailed Jeffrey, telling him I wanted to have a better relationship with him. He just replied, 'I'm busy, I don't have time to email with you.'

It was a hard blow. It takes just minutes to send the odd email, but he didn't even have the motivation to do that. I meant that little to him.

Years previously, soon after he left school, he said we were so close that we didn't need to talk often. I tried to make sense of this and hung on to the hope we were close. Bullshit!

This explained why he didn't come to my wedding, or visit my firstborn, and why he'd taken no interest in my life at all.

He belittled and dehumanised me by never calling me by my name in the texts he sent to our mother. It was always 'my sister,' 'his granddaughter,' 'the ex-wife,' or 'your daughter.'

You can see this throughout all his texts with our mother.

Their marriage was certainly not one I wanted to emulate. In a rare exchange, Jeffrey confided that he felt the same.

Funnily enough, after our father died, Jeffrey and I started texting regularly. He confided in me about his disastrous marriage and how he wanted to leave. He hired a solicitor and even went as far as telling his kids of the split.

Our exchanges went on for a few weeks, and then – all of a sudden – the divorce was off, he was staying at home, and our text conversations ended.

Once again, I was blanked and pushed to the side.

He used me. He took my kindness and my desire to help and listen, and then he discarded me!

On my dad's deathbed, my brother declared, "Raven and I won't be taking any of the money; it all needs to go to Mum."

Hang on! I hadn't agreed to that.

So, I sidled up to him and whispered, "But Mum might come and live with us, in which case I'll need to do an extension. Can I please take £250,000?"

"Yes, you can," he agreed, "for an extension."

Why the fuck was he making these decisions? And why was I asking his permission?

He had done this before when he'd made choices for the both of us – with no notice and no thought for me.

When going through emails for this book, I found an email between me and the solicitor dealing with my father's estate. In it, I asked about my share.

> Dear ***
>
> At present the only funds definitely coming to you and Jeffery, as far as I am aware, are in respect of the pension fund for your benefit (please see the second form IHT409) which passes outside the estate. As you will recall, it was decided that everything within the estate would pass to your mother and ++++++++ prepared documents in that regard which were duly executed by your mother and St Andrew Trustees Ltd and dated 15/4/16. It is then open to your mother to make gifts to the family and I do not know if that has been discussed further – of course, that is not really anything to do with this firm (unless advice relating to this is required).
>
> With kind regards,

I have no recollection whatsoever of agreeing to this.

Later on, my mother was advised to divide the money she received between myself and Jeffrey – this, again, would protect IHT (inheritance tax).

***

On your mother's death, if no planning is in place, then her total estate in excess of the nil rate band (currently £325,000) will be taxed at 40%.

On your figures below, that is £1,846,800 to be paid out of her assets before the inheritance is passed to the family.

That is why planning is so important!

She never listened.

***

I thought it might be useful to have a recap.

My advice was based on my understanding that you wanted to remove the potential IHT liability from your estate as quickly as possible.

If you die within 2 and 7 years of starting the plan, then this is the only strategy (that's BPR, not Octopus) which will work.

If however, on reflection, you expect to survive 7 years, then alternative strategies present themselves.

I give you one, as food for thought.

- Put £325,000 into the trust we have created.

- Gift a large sum (£1M?) each to *** and ***. There will still be more than ample to meet your needs.

Both of the above trigger no immediate charge to IHT, will be outside of your estate after year 7, and will have a reducing rate of tax after year 4. Of the £3M+ you retain, perhaps £1M into the octopus strategy we discussed.

The above is just another example of what we could do.

I am still available to call this morning if you wish, not to complete forms, but for a further discussion for you to help me understand what is important to you. Regards

***

The animosity between us heightened once more when I was arranging our grandmother's funeral. Apparently, I was choosing awkward dates just to piss him off.

The fact of the matter was that she passed away in December and I wanted to have her funeral before the New Year so that we could put this hellish year of death behind us. My father had died, my dog had died, Mum had cancer, and now my nanny had died too… all in the same year.

So, I wanted 2016 to start off fresh – not with a funeral.

Behind my back, Mum agreed to try changing the date to accommodate Jeff.

I don't recall if there were no suitable dates going forward or if my pleading my case made any difference, and I don't know why she was trying to change things just for him anyway, as the original date suited everyone else… but in the end, the first date stood, and now my relationship with him was in even more tatters than before.

The day after the fiasco at Mum's bungalow with Jeffrey, I hired a solicitor.

I explained the malicious nature of my so-called brother and that I wanted to ensure I got what I was due – and that he was removed from being in control of my children's inheritance.

The solicitor who was, at the time, in charge of administering the estate was also supposed to be a co-executor with him. Between them, they decided that only Jeff would be the executor. How convenient!

Obviously, all communication between myself and Jeff had ceased by this point, leaving me to try to understand things through this other guy.

The solicitor hardly ever answered my emails, and the one time I managed to get him on the phone – after a few weeks of trying – he was walking to the post office and spoke to me about all these confidential family matters as he went. It was hard to hear it all, but apparently, I was supposed to be happy with that!

A few months later, this man retired, and the most useless, incompetent 'partner' took his place. She wouldn't engage with me about the estate and was not very knowledgeable about the policy I was a trustee of.

One day, she organised a Zoom call between me, my solicitor, and the other trustee, Old man solicitor. It didn't go well because they asked me to allow Jeffrey to have things that he was not prepared to give me in return.

As it turned out, it was a pointless call, as none of the money was due to be distributed yet anyway.

We argued about what my mother's two lines of 'wishes' meant. Oh, and the 'wishes' letter Jeff had spoken about regarding my father's ring? That didn't exist.

This trustee was very involved for someone who was simply supposed to be a bystander to ensure things were done legally; I have no doubt that Jeff was in his ear.

Don't forget – he wanted me to have as little as possible.

Eventually, I gave in, as I just wanted this whole thing to be over with.

After a year of fighting and going back and forth – and, I think I should point out that this useless woman was getting paid a staggering £360 an hour! – she suddenly declared, "I have read the terms of the policy and what we are proposing is not allowed. We will have to come to a new arrangement."

What the fuck?! You have to be kidding me! But of course we had to pay for the 'work' that had been done and a year of wasted time.

After yet another year of fucking about, some money was finally distributed. Not all, mind you.

Then, I received a call stating there had been a mistake and that only my share – not Jeffrey's – had to be returned.

What???!!!

After much discussion and trying to understand what had happened, I sent back my share.

It turned out that my mother had not understood her own investment! She had assured me there was £600,000 in there to be split, but £500,000 of that had to be returned to the estate.

So, there was nowhere near as much money to distribute as we'd first thought, and a huge chunk of it had now gone on this bloody woman who'd spent the last two years fucking about and getting everything wrong!

More was taken for tax, and still, she only distributed half back to me. She was holding on to £10,000 in case there was more tax to pay.

This went on for so bloody long that, after the first lot of tax, there was then income tax to pay on it because it had earned interest in the meantime. This, of course, delayed things further – and, as I write this in February 2024, I still do not have all of my inheritance.

It took a year to sell the house that belonged to Mum and Dad.

Jeff tried his best to ensure I didn't get my half of that by going to a different firm of solicitors and trying to find a loophole to kick me out of inheriting! He and Evil Lawyer (the solicitor's name, in my mind) then had the audacity to try to get me to pay for half of those fees!!

Thankfully, my solicitor actually did her job here and put her foot down.

Jeff was still dragging his heels about who he would 'allow' to be trustee of the kids' accounts; it took him 2.5 years to finally declare he would allow me and Dickhead to do it. As they still haven't received a penny, however, who knows if that will actually stand?

I had tried to suggest that it be Mark, my friend, or my uncle, as I didn't want anything to do with Dickhead.

Evil Lawyer was very quick to update Jeff on all the goings on with the policy, but when I wanted an estate update, she wouldn't give me one. As the mother of the minors – my children – who will inherit, it is my legal right to know what's going on.

She ignores my emails and phone calls. She tells me she will ask Jeff if she's allowed to update me, and then she takes weeks to reply. Jeff's got her wound so tight around his little finger – and I think she's even scared of him – that I wouldn't be surprised if she's skirted around the letter of the law for him.

In July 2024, this will have been going on for four years!

The most recent news I've received is that Jeff believes HMRC's calculations on the tax are wrong, so he won't release any of the children's money until it's sorted.

I dread to think how much of my father's money has gone to this incompetent solicitor. I do know that nearly half went on inheritance tax – disgusting!

Nearly two million pounds of my father's life's work went on nothing because my mother couldn't admit she was dying, couldn't figure out the correct investments, and hired crap people to invest the money.

It turned out that the 'equal' share of my £400,000 that American dick got was not actually an equal sum after all.

He got nearly £1 million (in dollars). He had also talked to her about them sharing a credit card, but I don't know if that ever came to fruition.

So, Jeff did very financially well out of my father and my easily swayed mother. Me, not so much.

But the amount I got – plus the money from my father – allowed me to buy some flats to rent out and pay off my mortgage. I have also set up my own self-employed business (a dog boarding business, plus grooming) and have gone from not earning a penny to single-handedly managing to support myself, my lovely home, and my three gorgeous children.

I am stronger and happier than I have ever been in my life.

Who knows if the same can be said of all these other people?!

Right now, my only wish is to be done with Evil Lawyer, be done with that controlling prick on the other side of the pond, and be able to put it all behind me.

I'm amazed by the lengths people will go to in order to maintain and exert control; it shows weakness and an alarming sense of inferiority. For all of this overdominance, bullying, coercion, and lying, my so-called brother is really just a weak, pathetic little boy.

I have no doubt he treats his family similarly to how he treated me, and I wish his children all the best for their futures.

Chapter 40
More Boarding School

I had only visited the school once before I joined, and even then, it was only to go to the Headmaster's office for a talk – a chat I zoned out of completely and consequently have no recollection of. I do remember something, though: as we walked past some kids who were waiting to go into the science labs, they laughed at me. Was it the jean jacket, the colour of my hair, the luminous orange headband? What was so amusing about my appearance? It hurt my feelings, and it definitely added to my self-consciousness.

Boarding school is designed to spit out compliant 'adults,' devoid of independent thinking. Instead of fostering self-reliance, it breeds institutionalised children who often grow into emotionally damaged, unfeeling adults. The system aims to sever familial bonds, which are crucial for nurturing strength, resourcefulness, and resilience in adults. Being with Mummy makes us weak; they do not want the softness or femininity of the mothers to affect the 'training' of these future leaders of the Empire.

This hyper-masculine environment bred antipathy towards women and perpetuated misogyny and the patriarchy. Imagine trying to be a girl growing up amid such testosterone-fuelled boys! As young girls, we weren't shown any femininity. There was no gentleness, no nurturing. Our bodies were simply there to be used, discussed, and rated by the boys.

It is now recognised that simply experiencing boarding school life – even without additional abuse – constitutes a form of trauma. The separation from everything familiar, from all that provides a sense of safety, is deeply impactful.

To disassociate from the vulnerability of the missing Mummy, we had to suppress all our vulnerabilities. Any emotional outburst or display of weakness would be perceived as us having 'lost.' And where would we have had this breakdown anyway? We had no private places, no safe spaces to retreat to.

There was a 'splitting' between home and school. They were both so very different from each other, yet we had to find a way to exist in both.

Boarders, including myself, often experience a constant undercurrent of anxiety, leading us to believe it's simply a normal part of life; we assume everyone must feel this way. It is only as you enter your 30s and 40s that you start to query this and begin to realise that not everyone carries such burdens. Where did this come from? Why do I feel this way?

Personally, I figured I must be crazy, or that something else must be very wrong with me. Unfortunately, for me, CBT (cognitive behavioural therapy) didn't help much. No one else seemed to struggle as I did, but the more I look into this, the more I realise I'm not alone. Thousands and thousands of ex-boarders are now coming forward and discussing the hardship, the heartbreak, and how damaging it has been to them throughout their lives.

Of course, there's limited research on this issue, given that boarding schools constitute a multi-billion-pound industry and hold significant influence over the upper classes, MPs, and even the Royal family. So, we cannot simply 'out' the insidious devastation this institution causes.

According to author Nick Duffell, the traumatic memories of these experiences are stored in the same part of the brain as memories for tasks like riding a bike – memories that, no matter how much time passes, we still have easy access to. Simply put, we never forget them. These are called implicit memories – memories that come easily to us without much conscious thought.

Traumatic boarding school memories are also implicit memories, as they are easily triggered. We aren't only triggered by sights or smells; a flashback can be ignited by a feeling, glance, or thought. The trauma is constantly all around us and we cannot escape it. Therapists need to be specially trained to help boarding school survivors as it is such a tricky area.

I recall The Wank getting angry with me when he learned I was seeing a therapist. He was paranoid that I'd tell her what he was doing to me, and of course, he took this anger out on me. Consequently, I lied to my therapist and eventually stopped seeing her – mainly at his request, but also because I saw no point in carrying on with the therapy if I was lying my way through it.

The total lack of care from all adults was evident when a girl in my boarding house became so skeletal, through her anorexia, that you could pretty much see every bone in her body – every vertebra, every face and arm bone… it was so disturbing to see how emaciated she'd become. Why did no one do anything? Why didn't her parents take her home? She was obviously so distressed and suffering so deeply. I can't even imagine how hard it was for her to get through her A levels when she was in such pain.

We were never physically alone, but we were always alone. We were alone on the inside.

We had no privacy whatsoever. The only place where you had a door to yourself was in the toilet – but even then, people could hear you. It wasn't until the lower sixth that I got a room on my own when I was 16. The 'show' (bedroom) doors didn't lock, though, so anyone could walk in at any time.

This lack of privacy extended to the payphone in the main corridor. When sixth formers wanted to use the phone, sometimes they'd just come over and hang up on whoever was on the phone. I always had a low-level fear that the same would happen to me.

There was a Head boy and Head girl, but as it was originally an all-boys school, there was only mention of the Head boy in the school rules. He was allowed to grow a beard, smoke a pipe, and keep a goat! These absurd traditions persisted despite having no relevance in the modern world.

Even social workers these days try hard to keep families together. Even where there is neglect and abuse from the parents, they try to educate the parents to enable the children to stay at home. They don't seem to bother when it comes to borders.

For some of us, it heightened our empathetic side, but not for ourselves. We tend to over-emphathise with others while lacking the ability to recognise the sadness in our own situations. This often results in a significant lack of self-love and the inability to practise self-care. We neglect ourselves to give to others. We're all massive people pleasers.

There is a term used to describe people who suffer with the after-effects of boarding school – Boarding School Syndrome.*

SYMPTOMS OF BOARDING SCHOOL SYNDROME

The symptoms associated with being sent away from your family and your life at a young age (under 16) – and the ones I suffer with – are as follows:

* Struggling with emotional intimacy, and the anxiety that surrounds this

* Not being able to switch off; always needing to be on the go and having things to do

* Perfectionism

* Feeling like a failure or being scared of being seen as one

* Finding it hard to relax

* Being out of touch with your own needs; being happy to give to others, but not spending time giving to yourself

* Not feeling happy or joyful, and forgetting how to play and have fun

* Feeling alone even when in a group

* Fearing that you are unlovable

* Struggling with addiction

* Experiencing patterns of not committing to relationships

* When things aren't going well in a relationship, do you avoid conflict? Do you prefer to be secretive or covert in conflict if it does arise?

* Do you always take care of others but really struggle to take care of yourself?

* Finding it hard to bring up children

* Fearing exposure as a fraud or imposter

* Sleep disorders

* Getting easily stressed.

This is now being recognised as a specific psychological condition characterised by depression, problems with relationships, and long-term emotional or behavioural difficulties.

It is estimated that just 1% of the UK population went to boarding school, and the ones who did? We are known as Boarding School Survivors.

It's not something we're allowed to complain about – it's almost as if this silent prohibition has kept us silent all these years. Only now, in 2023/24, are boarders very slowly coming out to tell their truths.

Look up Boarding School on Wikipedia and you will be shocked by the issues it describes. Not only are you taken from your home and parents, but also from your extended family, your toys, your 'stuff,' and all that you know.

For me, I was taken from my extended family when I was just four or five, when we left the UK. I didn't often see my grandparents. Apparently, my mum's mum pleaded with her not to send us away. Mum said this was bad of her because it made her feel guilty.

It is common for boarders to not be able to tell you the age they were when things happened. They will say "I was 11 or 12… around there." This is because if you had your birthday while you were at school, it won't have been celebrated, so it's hard to remember what age you were – the years just kind of merge together. Personally, I judge things by what dorm I was in and then what form I was in.

I was never taught – either at home or at school – about taking care of myself or my mental health. I never gave myself permission to relax or to enjoy anything. It was all just work work work. Full timetables and being productive. This led to a life where I never felt able to just 'be,' to just sit and relax. I always had to be on the go.

Even now, I have no hobbies, as, unless I'm being productive for some reason, I find it hard to see the 'point' in something. I am quite jealous of Mark's ability to sit and make things just for fun, to relax and still his racing mind. I am trying to learn, though, as I want my children to know how to relax and how to take care of all their needs.

There was a culture of not complaining. Not making a fuss. After all, we were privileged! We should be thankful and grateful for this amazing opportunity provided to us by our loving parents. The gift of this amazing education!

Although we lived together and spent almost 24 hours a day together, we knew next to nothing about our roommates' lives outside of school. It truly felt like living two distinct lives, yet I didn't feel like I belonged in either.

I was constantly told to 'enjoy it' and that 'these are the best years of your life.' This notion, of course, was terrifying for me. To think that the years after leaving school might be worse! How could these be the best years of my life?! I was imprisoned in hell! I was miserable, being abused and neglected. I had nothing of what I needed, not even any food I liked.

But, deep inside, I didn't believe it – surely, after school would be better? At least I wouldn't be stuck in this prison; I would have some control over my life and my day-to-day activities.

As I've mentioned, if we wanted to go anywhere other than our normal lessons, we had to record it in the sign-in/out book – even just to go down to the village, or to go and watch TV with the boys at the weekend.

As I was a full boarder – meaning I didn't go home at weekends – I was still under the 'care' of the school every weekend. On occasion, I would go to my maternal grandparents' house, or a friend's house, but this wasn't common. There were only a few girls left in the house each weekend, maybe 10 or so. At least it was more friendly and cosy considering there were so few of us.

Sunday mornings, we still had the bells to wake us up at stupid o'clock for a gross breakfast. I seem to remember having to go in uniform as well.

By the time I got to sixth form, they relaxed the rules for everyone by allowing us a lie-in and the choice of attending breakfast or not. I would often stay in bed and just feast on a jar of Nutella while reading my book. This was bliss.

As a very conscientious person, I took my studies seriously. I wanted to please the teachers and make everyone proud. This, of course, led to me being mocked for being a 'square,' a 'suck-up,' or a 'swot.' Thankfully, although this hurt me, I didn't let it stop me from trying my hardest and getting my work done on time or even early!

Before my parents sent me away, I would often draw pictures and scenes, write stories, and daydream. This was 'scheduled' out of me at school. My imagination withered away; still, to this day, I find I have very little imagination or vision. I would love to create and design things – anything – but I simply don't have the ability to even think of anything.

The six-inch rule (where members of the opposite sex had to keep six inches apart at all times) was obviously designed to keep us from having sex, but maybe if we'd been allowed to hold hands and have a cuddle, we wouldn't have felt the need to sneak off and hide – and then allow things to go further. It was even frowned upon for the girls to give each other hugs; there was such a fear of anyone touching anyone. It felt so unnatural to never be allowed to touch or to have to look around you before you touched. I was once told off for hugging my own brother. Even once I explained that he was my brother – which the teacher would have known, with it being such a small school – we still received a 'look' and were told to move away from each other.

It is so damaging for anyone – let alone growing children – to have no human contact. To have no nurturing touch. No wonder I was so confused about nurturing/sexual touches.

Whenever I was unruly at home (like burping or being 'uncouth'), my mother would jokingly threaten me with Finishing School, usually in Switzerland. I have no doubt, however, that this was not actually a joke at all. She had a tendency to joke about serious matters, things she actually meant but could pass off as a joke if we took it the 'wrong' way.

She would 'joke' about my sending my kids away to boarding school, multiple times. I reckon if I did do as she suggested, it would absolve her of any wrongdoing because I was now doing it to my children.

She told Jeffrey that as his new baby was being 'difficult,' he should put him in daycare.

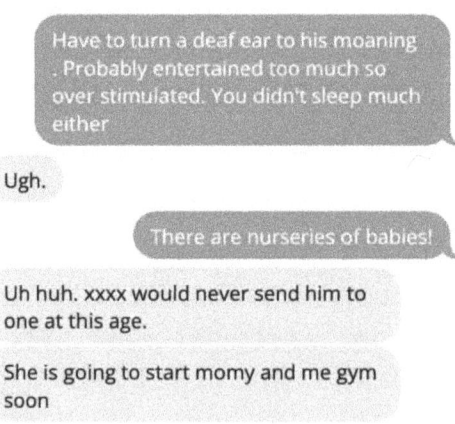

She was so ready to ship off anything that was even the slightest bit difficult.

Over the years, I was often told to 'get rid' of my dogs as they were a lot of work once kids started coming along. She couldn't comprehend that the dogs were part of the family and that there would be no 'getting rid' of them!

As we didn't grow up together as a family, we didn't know each other as a family. For instance, I would hide my true self, and if I ever did confide in them or show a part of my real personality, I would get berated, shunned, or receive disapproving looks.

Once I was sent away, there was no connection between parent and child.

In a podcast between Piers Cross and Tom Greaves, Tom stated how his parents standing on the touchline at his rugby matches was supportive, but it was not love. How even though parents may think that, at the time, they were 'doing their best,' sending a child away for nine months of the year is not love.

The damages done to the child, the bond, and the relationship are so deep and so profound I would say they are irreparable.

I find it staggeringly difficult to be without my children for the week they spend with their father; I cannot imagine it being longer. I know their teachers, their friends, most of the classrooms they're in, and a lot of what goes on in their day-to-day lives when we're not together. It would destroy me to not have that connection with them.

I am overly independent and find it very difficult – often impossible – to ask for help. The drive to 'do it all myself' is very ingrained. After all, I've been left alone to deal with the majority of life's issues and trials.

There was an incident a year or so after Mark and I got together. I was in the middle of mowing the lawn when I had to go out. By the time I returned, he had finished the lawn, put the mower away, and hoovered the house.

I burst out crying! I had never had someone do something so helpful and kind for me before – and for no other reason than it needed doing. I was just so grateful. He was quite shocked at my reaction, at how happy and thankful I was for him doing something so small and menial.

It was reactions like this that showed him how badly I'd been treated in the past.

Male authority figures – well, any authority figure, but mainly men – have been an issue for me most of my life, up until maybe a year or so ago.

The intimidation, the superiority, my feeling so inferior and unable to have any kind of voice… I would just shut down and cower while, at the same time, I'd be silently simmering with rage.

I was so against any kind of authority. I saw it all as so oppressive, taking away my rights and thoughts. The school, the teachers, my housemaster, my father, my brother, and even my ex-husband… they all took from me, quietened my voice, and dismissed my opinions. I was made to feel as though I was nothing in comparison. I was taught no sense of self. To not be me.

With Mr P patrolling the halls during prep and after lights out, listening at doors and trying to catch anyone out of their desk or bed, talking or even whispering, we felt trapped and imprisoned. We had no freedom of movement. Even in our own 'home,' we had to explain why we weren't at our desks or if we got up to go to the loo – and even then, we were told to 'be quick.' Our time was never free.

For 24 hours a day, we were accountable to someone, but we were also left utterly unprepared and unprotected. It was an odd juxtaposition.

So, we experimented with alcohol, sex, Ouija boards, spirit calling, hitting each other, kissing each other in bed after lights out, and dares – such as sneaking around. Before my imagination was squashed out of me, we had many adventures, and the most fun ones happened after lights out. The stakes were high, but that just fuelled the adrenaline and fun.

The split between home and school carried over into my sleep. It was not uncommon for me to wake up and not remember where I was. The sinking feeling when I realised I was at school always left me distraught and my heart aching for most of the day. On the flip side, when I was at home, realising I had days or weeks left of a holiday was a blissful feeling.

In my GCSE years, I had a history teacher who terrified me. He picked on me a lot, making me give answers out loud to the rest of the class. More often than not, I had no clue what the answer was, and – to make matters worse – my class of about 15 had at least five scholars in it.

I would feel the prickle of sweat under my armpits, and sometimes, I would cry quietly as I just felt so stupid and useless. I was so ashamed of being so thick!

He would always comment, "You'll be lucky to scrape a D in your exams!"

When I announced to him, after the fact, that I'd received a C, in my GCSE he replied, "I knew you would."

In that moment, all the torture he'd put me through for the past two years flashed before my eyes!

The drive back to school after half terms or long holidays sitting in the taxi from the airport, was always so tense for me. There was always a certain point when I knew we were close that the dread would creep in. When I saw Leeds Castle, the start of the grassy verges, and the Ten Bells pub, my heart would leap into my throat and I would start to feel sick and swirly in my head. There was nothing I could do to stop the inevitable. I was being dragged back there and that was that.

The familiar sight and smell of my boarding house, the 30 pairs of school shoes lined up by the front door, the brown carpet tiles, the yellow/orange lights, the mundane noises of so many mentally battered school girls… it never changed.

The experts call this back and forth 'multiple traumas' – the split between home and school. Not belonging in either and not being able to be yourself in either. It gives a homelessness tinge to your life. You start to disassociate and live in a bubble, far away from everything and everyone else.

The high expectations for our behaviour both at home and at school were exhausting and unfair. The idea that children must always behave… I guess it stems from the 'children must be seen and not heard' adage. Follow the rules – no matter how ridiculous and unfair – and never, ever make a scene.

It was all so isolating. The divide of the more important, older year groups. How they were used to keep us in line as there most likely wasn't enough staff. The sixth formers being allowed to walk on the 'prefects' lawn' and having the 'top' tables in the refectory. Being allowed to walk to the front of the queue to get food. They, like the men in authority, were so much more special and important.

We had to be kept in line, with punishments being dished out if we left our allocated slots.

I have carried with me this feeling – for the whole of my life – that I've been left behind, that everyone around me has figured out how to 'adult' and that I'm just play-acting.

I believe I have spent so long trying to survive, being in survival mode, that only now am I starting to flourish. Now, at 44 years old, I am finally starting to feel the stirrings of being a real adult. I do not conform. I do things my way. My life feels more real and I am much more able to feel present in it.

I am covered in tattoos, I allow my older children to swear in front of me, and I choose to only allow the good into my life – and shun the 'should' and 'supposed to.' I believe I'm seen as a rather 'controversial' person. I now live my life how I see fit rather than worrying about how it should be or how it looks to others.

I no longer care about my image or what people think.

My mother's emphasis on image and what others think has rubbed off on me – but in reverse. Her dislike of my tattoos and her opinion that they were 'disgusting' doesn't bother me. I am still working hard on getting her damaging view on 'bodies' out of my system. Bigger was bad. Any evidence of nipples was 'disgusting.' She looked down on pretty much everyone, I think.

I want my children – especially my girls – to know that their worth does not come from the size of their clothes. That a tummy roll or some cellulite does not take away from the amazing beauty within them.

Trying to heed my own teachings, however, is proving to be a very challenging task.

I don't believe my parents knew what they were sending me and Jeffrey off to, and I don't believe there was anything malicious in it, but I do blame them for not seeing the signs that I was unhappy. They were never curious about my life at school. Never queried what it was like. They simply shipped me off and were glad to not have to deal with me for nine months of the year – that is what I truly believe. To not care what your child is experiencing when they are away from you… that is neglect. It is certainly not love.

I was taught, implicitly, to, "Put up and shut up." I felt unimportant and unloved.

Another side effect of attending boarding school is that, even today, I worry about running out of things. I have worked hard on this over the years, and the anxiety surrounding it has waned, but it's always still there on some level.

I would hoard things – especially shampoo, conditioner, and the like. At school, one of my under-bed drawers was full of body hygiene products and, until recently, my cupboards at home would be stacked at least three deep.

It was like doomsday prepping!

Chapter 41
Dickhead and Mum, Revisited

The people-pleasing persisted after leaving school, and it caused real issues for me, especially in terms of my marriage to Dickhead.

He would wake up for work and immediately expect me to roll over and give him a massage.

When we were selling our house, he expected me to take two kids and two dogs out while also having the house looking immaculate, to the point where he said I was to "leave nothing in the dishwasher, even; it all has to look unlived in." The work and stress of trying to achieve such perfection, on top of my own perfection standards, was beyond exhausting.

He had coercive control* over me from the start, and he still tries to exert it to this day.

> **What is Coercive Control?**
>
> https://www.womensaid.org.uk
>
> Domestic abuse isn't always physical. Coercive control is an act or a pattern of acts of assault, threats, humiliation and intimidation or other abuse that is used to harm, punish, or frighten their victim.

> Coercive and controlling behaviour is at the heart of domestic abuse.
>
> This controlling behaviour is designed to make a person dependent by isolating them from support, exploiting them, depriving them of independence and regulating their everyday behaviour.
>
> Coercive control creates invisible chains and a sense of fear that pervades all elements of a survivor's life. It works to limit their human rights by depriving them of their liberty and reducing their ability for action. Experts like Evan Stark liken coercive control to being taken hostage. As he says: "the victim becomes captive in an unreal world created by the abuser, entrapped in a world of confusion, contradiction and fear." (Stark, 2007).

The only time he would ever lift a finger would be if he knew he'd pushed me too far, at which point I'd leave the house with the kids to go somewhere; when I returned, he would have done the hoovering 'for me' as a way to ingratiate himself. I was supposed to see this as a peace offering and as him doing something nice to help me out. It just made me angry!

It was a ludicrous, weak, and pathetic way to apologise.

Dickhead didn't allow me to grow or be my own person.

There were times when I thought of some training I could attend or jobs I would like to pursue, but when I talked to him about it, I was always met with, "What about the kids?"

It was made clear that they were 100% my responsibility and that he was the breadwinner; his job was the most important thing, and nothing should get in the way of that.

Not even a five-day course I wanted to go on.

I was well and truly stuck. I was financially reliant on him.

I think this is why I saw my inheritance from my father as a way out. I wouldn't need Dickhead to financially provide for me anymore. And what else was he providing for me? He had literally no other purpose.

I thought I was dead inside. I thought I was going to have to live this unhappy, unfulfilled, miserable life forever. So, of course, I deduced that there must have been something wrong with me!

When my parents visited, Dickhead would say, "What can I do to look good to your dad? I want to impress him."

It would end with him trying to suck up by pumping up the rental car types or similar. While I don't think this worked on my dad at all, my mum was easily impressed by him.

All through our marriage, he would say that things were going to get better, that they were going to get easier… that he was going to make a million pounds. He was obsessed with this 'making a million.'

He refused to believe my opinion that someone couldn't be an attentive, present father and make a million at the same time. This was my experience; it was all I'd ever seen.

He was 'future faking,'* promising that life would improve just over the horizon. Yet that horizon never seemed to draw any nearer. It had been the same story since the moment we met: hollow promises, always followed by 'when this happens, then things will improve.'

'If I lose weight, I will have more confidence and then I can make more money.'

'When I get 10 clients, then we will have the money to do X, Y, and Z.'

Of course, none of his future plans ever became reality.

There is only so much a person can take!

> *** What is future faking?**
>
> Future faking is a manipulation tactic employed when a narcissist or toxic person promises to fulfill your desires in the future to get something they want in the present — which is often simply to get off scot-free, delay a commitment, obtain resources, or avoid a conflict.

From the outside, it must have looked like we had it all. Like we were happy. I recall some people being so shocked when I told them about the divorce. To them, we looked like the 'perfect couple.' Oh, how looks can be deceiving!

He would often say, "Their love is for sale and I'm buying." 'Their' refers to the children. This awful epitome of conditional love and materialism continued after the divorce – I think this is illustrated by the number of gaming consoles and 'stuff' the children have at his house.

Of course, he tried to deny this when I brought it up, saying it had just been a joke.

His house is full to the brim with stuff, in every nook and cranny. It's a mess. Things are constantly getting 'lost' there and, on occasion, his mother and sister have to go and tidy and clean for him. I imagine that when my mum was alive – and going to his house regularly – he made more of an effort, but I'm sure she also helped him keep things in order. That is a woman's role, after all, and I was wicked enough to leave him in such a mess!

A few years after the divorce, I asked Dickhead to meet me for coffee. I wanted to discuss with him the mess of the divorce and the horrible situation we were currently in.

Over the two-hour conversation, the only 'bad things' he could come up with to say about me were that I had 'forced him' to get one of our dogs – who later had to be rehomed – and that I had 'punished him' for my past boyfriends' actions. He declared me and Mark to be 'reckless,' but gave no evidence or reasoning for this. It is probably because we both show our emotions and do not adhere to societal norms. Kim thought it was funny and ridiculous that he would use such language – it was just his way of trying to belittle us and assert his superiority.

Dickhead accused me of abusing him, he even said his therapist (!) said I was abusive.

This is called Reactive Abuse *

*REACTIVE ABUSE

If someone is being physically or verbally abused, their fight-or-flight response<https://www.verywellmind.com/what-is-the-fight-or-flight-response-2795194> might kick in, to help them protect themselves. If they are unable to flee, they might fight back against their abuser by attacking them physically or verbally. They may resort to yelling, screaming, insulting, or even assaulting their abuser.

Self-Defense Is a More Accurate Term

It's important to understand that someone who has to resort to reactive abuse is not the instigator. Rather, they are a victim who is reacting to being abused.

> The term "reactive abuse" can therefore be problematic, because it labels the victim as an abuser. A more accurate term to describe this behavior is "self-defense."
>
> Unfortunately, reactive abuse often works against the victim<https://www.verywellmind.com/why-do-people-blame-the-victim-2795911> of abuse, because their abuser may use it as leverage against them.
>
> Once the victim of abuse responds this way, the perpetrator often claims that the abuse is mutual, says Connors. In some cases, the abuser might even claim to be the wounded party and try to use these instances as proof that they have been abused, instead of the other way around.
>
> Perpetrators may use these manipulation tactics as a way to justify their abuse, control their victims, and keep them from leaving or speaking about the abuse, Connors explains.
>
> They may even try to record the person's reaction, or provoke a response in public so that they have witnesses who can say they saw them being "abused."

Of course, these 'reasons' did not explain or excuse his abhorrent behaviour towards me during the marriage or the divorce.

For some reason, he believed he knew the costs of the holidays I took with Mark and, consequently, he told Mum and Jeff that I was spending frivolously. He tried to use this against me during our divorce.

Although we did go away for travel, we used an app called 'Secret Escapes,' which offers remarkably affordable holidays at beautiful resorts. We both wanted to explore and experience life; after all, we had both been denied this in our respective bad marriages. This is not a crime – and it certainly doesn't make us bad or reckless people.

We have swum with nurse sharks in the Maldives, hand-fed hummingbirds in Jamaica, walked with lions in Mauritius, and ziplined through the rainforest in Saint Lucia. We've felt the crashing water on our heads from magnificent waterfalls, explored little alleyways in Venice, and learned to scuba dive together. Our travels are always exciting and full of adventures; we are making wonderful memories together.

During COVID, when the kids were having online lessons, Dickhead slagged me off to my mum as I'd decided it would be best if they just stuck to English, maths, and science during the first lockdown. He agreed that this was a good idea... but that doesn't make for a good story to use against me, does it?!

Mark then did some practical things with them – such as making bird feeders and teaching them how to wire a plug – while I taught them cooking, baking, and art. I wanted them to not be overly stressed and to also enjoy the summer a bit.

As it turned out, Dickhead didn't have all the info, as when I spoke to Mum about it, she had no clue about everything Mark and I did with them. I suppose it's easier to slag people off when you make up the facts.

Over the years, when staying at Dickhead's house, the girls have missed out on going to a fair few parties. When I asked them why they couldn't go, their response was always, "Don't know."

This makes me really angry, because – despite my own discomfort with social situations – I've always made sure they had the chance to attend every event they were invited to.

As much as Dickhead tried to declare me an unfit and useless mother, he's always come to me with any child illnesses or injuries, asking my advice. I'm always the one who has to decide if they need medicine or a doctor's appointment.

I am more than happy to do this, as they are my children, but he can't put all this on me and then go around telling people – and me – that I need to 'up my game' and that I'm a no-good mother.

In fact, it is only from my observations and motherly knowledge that any of them have been seen by therapists, had their ADHD diagnosed, and had 'extras' put in place at schools – not to mention the fact that my middle child is now homeschooled. I've had to fight long and hard to ensure they all got what they needed, when they needed it, even though it's been exhausting and the backlash has, at times, been soul-destroying.

To have to fight the children's own father, for their best interests, boggles the mind!

I even have to double-check with him that PE kits and uniforms have been washed when he brings them over whenever there's a switchover during holiday time. I also have to check that their homework has been done. For instance, I know he doesn't do reading with my youngest. I can't trust him to get anything done, so I constantly need to double-check. It's so tiring!

He didn't even give my son any cash to spend at the airport recently when he went on a school trip!

I've learnt the hard way that, often, whatever accusations these types of people level against you are actually projections of their own actions or behaviour. If I look back over the last five years, I see that every mean and nasty accusation Dickhead made about my parenting, about my behaviour towards him… anything… they were all things he was doing himself.

This is called Projection*, and it's scary when you realise this is what's happening.

PROJECTION

www.choosingtherapy.com

*Narcissistic projection is a defense tactic narcissists use to pivot the blame of their actions onto others. This is often done unconsciously to protect their low self-esteem, as any mistake on their part could rupture the idealized image they create of themselves. Narcissistic projection can be subtle and easy to overlook, but its long-lasting impact on victims is substantial.

Narcissistic projection can be hurtful for the person on the receiving end. A narcissist may use this alongside typical narcissistic manipulation tactics, making it more challenging to deal with. Regardless, a narcissist will do whatever they can to protect their fragile self-esteem and prevent others from uncovering their insecurities. Because of this, those in relationships with a narcissist often find themselves endlessly falling victim to narcissistic projection.

Projecting aspects of ourselves we are uncomfortable with, such as aggression or jealousy, is a defense we all engage in from time to time, particularly in childhood and adolescence. For the narcissistic personality, which suffers from a fundamental lack of ego integration in early childhood, projection is an ongoing compulsion in which repressed and split-off parts of the divided self (all "good" or all "bad") are attributed to others.

When Dickhead moved out, one of the interesting things he shared with me was something his mother said to him: "You won't be able to have fancy things anymore." Yet more evidence of what they all thought my purpose was!

Once he was diagnosed with ADHD – after recognising many of his own symptoms in the children's diagnoses – I did consider the possibility that now he was medicated, things might improve. But, by that time, I was just so disillusioned with him and so deeply wounded by his treatment of me. I was also certain that even if he began to tidy up around the house, to be more helpful and less chaotic, it wouldn't alter his perception of me or his behaviour towards me. Those things were him; they were not his ADHD. I was simply too tired of him to try to put any more 'systems' in place to get my needs met. Though now I am not sure he truly has ADHD but it is actually just very lazy, entitled and narcissistic.

Thank goodness I followed my heart and gut, and left when I did.

On April 12th, after fighting for Jeff to release some money to pay for school fees, I asked Dickhead for just over £13,000 for his children's education.

This would have been the first time since they started private education that he'd been asked to pay anything, and he would receive every penny back once Jeff paid the children their inheritance.

His reply was, "No, ask the bursar for an extension."

So he couldn't even be arsed, or care enough, to use his stolen money to pay, temporarily, for his kid's schooling. He loved the prestige of them going private, but he didn't want to part with his ill-gotten riches for them.

That behaviour says more than words ever could.

There are many examples over the years of Jeffrey's and my mum's bad treatment of me.

When we were kids, Jeffrey and I would race around holiday hotels together and, in lifts, he would always push the emergency alarm to stop the lift. He knew this scared me and, often, he struggled to get the lift to start up again. He enjoyed the feeling of having that power and control over me. This is still evidenced today in his power moves to control the situation with my mother's Will.

Later on, after I'd had my kids, if I ever told my mother I was tired or that it was hard, her reply would always be, "Well, you chose to have children."

This was neither helpful nor empathetic. She had no compassion for anyone or anything – not even herself, I believe.

I often felt like I was the parent and she the child, though I'm not clear on what event or incident in her childhood led her to behave this way… maybe she married too young? I have no idea.

Either way, she wasn't strong enough to have her own views and thoughts on how to parent, so she simply carried on with the generational abuse and trauma.

I never shared that, when I was around seven years old, when we were on a very crowded bus together, the man behind me started to rub himself up my back and down to my buttocks. I could feel something hard, and it was only when I became an adult that I realised this would have been his erect penis.

I knew that something wrong was happening, but I was too scared to turn around and look – or to call out in case I was mistaken. I was scared of being rude.

Unfortunately, there was no room on this bus to move in any direction, so I was just stuck in that position.

Growing up, if I did ever say anything about what my mother said or did, she would reply with, "Well, I just won't say anything then." I know now that this is a victim-blaming, passive-aggressive response, and that it shuts down any line of communication. It turns the tables on the person trying to voice their concerns and improve the relationship; it silences and shames them into submission.

I would go out of my way to ensure, whenever she came to stay with me, in any house, that it was always freshly deep cleaned, with fresh sheets and fresh flowers ready for her. She never acknowledged my efforts.

I assumed it was because she didn't notice, but perhaps it was also because she felt she deserved such treatment. As my mother, I felt she deserved it too, but as a child and as an adult – trying to please her and show her care – it would have been nice to have had my efforts praised and thanked.

One day, in town, she tried to pretend she hadn't seen me and Mark. She was walking towards us and would have just walked past if I hadn't waved her down. This was the first time they'd met, and after I'd introduced them, Mark shook her hand and was very pleasant to her. Her coldness and rudeness were overtly evident to me. I had to apologise to him for her demeanour.

When she was dying, Mark offered to come and mow her lawn, or do anything else that would be of use to her. Obviously he was not allowed in the house so he offered to do stuff outside. " I have a gardener." Was her response.

At my father's wake, there was no room for me on the table with my mum and brother. Once again, I'd been forgotten about –

not considered and not thought of. I had to go and sit with Dickhead on a table by ourselves.

I remember being so anxious and nervous throughout the wake that, any time anyone spoke to me, I would nervously take the clip out of my hair and then put it back in, over and over. It must have looked odd to whoever was talking to me.

Where we lived in Madrid, we had to drive to the tube station. Along the way, through the woods, was where all the prostitutes gathered, waiting for customers. Mum would always point out the 'fatties' and laugh.

On one occasion, I was late calling her to come and collect me after a trip to town. It was summer and I was wearing shorts. When the train pulled in, she wasn't there to meet me, so I waited anxiously by the steps.

I quickly realised that, being a single female hanging around, I was potentially in danger of being mistaken for a prostitute.

I moved as close to the train area as possible, sat on the steps, and tried to make myself as small as possible. It didn't work; it didn't take long for two men to approach me and a car to stop in front of me.

The men started asking me how much, and to get in their car. Even when I explained that I was waiting for my mother, they kept insisting I get in the car – and kept asking, "How much?"

I was getting quite scared when, finally, my parents' car pulled up and I ran over to them.

They asked if the men had touched me and I told them they hadn't. In their eyes, that was the end of it. But I was quite distressed; it had been very scary!

As soon as I got home I asked if I could call Tom, my boyfriend. They said yes; I think they were pleased to not have to deal with the emotion!

I cried to him and told him how scared I'd been.

After my miscarriage in 2014 I lost about three friends; I guess what they say about true friends sticking around in times of need and distress is correct. These were ladies I'd confided in about my pregnancy, and had then shared my sad news with. They just started avoiding me and not talking to me.

It hurt and left me feeling even more alone.

When I did my Soul Midwife course, the teacher told me she saw a white light surrounding me, and that I must be careful as people with bad intentions would try to take it from me. I had also been told in the past about this light that I carry, and while I'm not sure I 100% believe it, I would love to.

My deep, inner belief is still that I am not good enough.

In his book, *Child Abuse and Neglect: Attachment, Development and Intervention*, David Howe states that the most severe psychological abuse arises from neglect. He also goes on to say that child neglect has a more severe adverse effect on children's development than abuse.

Children need a carer who is emotionally intelligent, who recognises the links between thoughts, feelings, and behaviour, and who is interested in these things within the child. Children cannot make sense of themselves if no one else makes time for them.

I take from this that being seen and heard leads to a child feeling safe and comforted. I never felt these things – not at home nor at school.

I've been conditioned to believe I am in the wrong, always, and have consequently grown up with no inner confidence or self-esteem.

I spent the majority of my life trying to learn to survive and then trying to make connections with anyone who would show me any ounce of attention or kindness.

'Where do I belong?' has been a lifelong question of mine.

Being abandoned, betrayed, and lied to has had a deep effect on me – one that I'm sure will last my entire life, though I'm slowly learning to find my place within myself.

Even to this day, I wake from nightmares, not knowing where I am or who is supposed to be in my house. I have to walk around the house figuring out where my children are, where my mother is (dead), and what stage of life I'm currently in.

It leaves me exhausted, anxious, and having flashbacks. I don't know why I still live in this anxious state – this place between worlds – but I imagine that not having my children with me 100% of the time is a big cause.

If I have to deal with Evil Lawyer or Dickhead, my nights are usually disturbed and nightmarish.

Dickhead was always so stingy with the time he would spend with me when we were married. On several occasions, he said, "I've just spent time with you. What more do you want?"

I was an inconvenience, a bother, and spending time with me was simply a chore to get through. This was what I took from these interactions.

For much of my life, I have spoken very fast. I do this unconsciously, as I've been made to believe I'm not worth talking to, not worth listening to. This has been shown to me time and time again. Recently, even. I was chatting to a school mum at a hockey game and, every time I tried to say something, she would interrupt me. I tried five times to say the same sentence and, every time, she spoke over me. She never once asked me what I was going to say.

I have found this a lot over the years. I have always been left with the impression that either I'm not interesting enough or I'm just not worth listening to.

I think, therefore, that if I talk fast to make my point, maybe I'll get it all out and some value may be given to my words.

Now, with Mark, I can talk at a proper pace – and I know I'm being heard.

My migraines and nightmares return every time I have to deal with Evil Lawyer or Dickhead.

Recently, there has been some movement on the estate; they may be ready to make a distribution. Confusion, however, has been colossal – as you would expect, I suppose, with her level of incompetence.

Further texts between me and dickhead.

> You are too funny. That money has gone!! 9 years of private school!! And since you stole a £75000 of it... it went quicker than it should have. The money from kids is tied up and inaccessible! ill Why don't u use some of your gotten gains from my self, my dad and my mother to put Ure hand in Ure pocket for your own children... just for once!! I have been using my savings for the past few years to pay for everything! About time u stepped up.

> Ha! Ur really shameless and the only thief here. Managed to get yourself a nice chunk of the kids money diverted to yourself didnt you? I guess all those holidays are expensive. Ive been covering for you for too long.

> Have a think about how things would have been if you had left the school fund alone and it had been allowed to grow as it should have. If it is so critical maybe you can dive in to your hoard of 'school money' and pay for something!

> Dont threaten me, I have proof of your indiscretions as well. All you have been paying should have come from their accounts and should be repaid when the new fund is set up, so dont plead poverty to me! You got everthing and still it wasnt enough What hoard? You mean the one I had to use to repay the loan that I needed to buy a home after you took mine?? When you encouraged the estate to sue me and take my new home?!? Twice in ann lifatima ah HALL at havin

I have never lied, hidden anything, or manipulated the truth throughout the divorce or the Will process. I was always the first to offer information and to seek resolutions.

I have no indiscretions.

I have not taken a penny from the children and I never tried to sue him.

The crap that comes out of his mouth is astonishing to me; it's truly mind-boggling, and it leaves me laughing yet speechless at the same time.

> He it at a critical time in his education and now is not the time for you to start playing your games, grow up and get over it, it been 5 years already

> Your delusion is incredible!! I have no idea where you get these ideas from. It is astonishing. I have no time for your projections. I have proof of every penny of where it is, where it's gone. I have proof of your indiscretions too. + I have no issue with *** having lessons. I am telling that with. ***'s therapy, lessons and all the other stuff I have been. paying for out of my money for the last few years I have very little money left. It is about tim paid for something. Don't worry thoigh... it will be

> What hoard? You mean the one I had to use to repay the loan that I needed to buy a home after you took mine?? When you encouraged the estate to sue me and take my new home?!? Twice in one lifetime eh, you must have felt lucky.

> I have no idea what on earth you are talking about. You do make me laugh!! Just put your hand in your pocket and pay for something for once.

> *** told she needs to wear the uniform next week.

> I need her waist and chest measurements

This was because I was paying for extra lessons for my daughter that I had arranged. He then went and arranged lessons for my son without discussing it with me then expected me to pay for it. When I questioned where the money was coming from this happened!

CHAPTER 42
NARCISSISTIC PERSONALITY DISORDER & MORE

I have recently bought the book, *It's Not You* by a clinical psychologist named Dr Ramani Durvasula. It is about narcissistic abuse from the perspective of the victim. I have learnt so much.

I wasn't just the scapegoat; I was mobbed as the scapegoat. It seemed my entire family assigned me this role and colluded in maintaining it. I was also the 'Invisible child,' which is exactly what it sounds like – left to figure out life alone.

On top of this, I was also the 'Truth seer,' so I was vilified for seeing and speaking the truth of the dysfunction.

I also assumed the 'Helper' role. I was the one relied upon to organise family gatherings and sort things out for others. I had to 'do' things to feel loved. I learnt very early on that love is conditional and that I had to perform to receive it.

There are a few different types of narcissists; here, I'm going to describe the ones I feel I've had to deal with. Kim, my therapist, confirmed my belief that these people were narcissists.

Jeffrey – malignant narcissist

www.choosingtherapy.com describes this type as:

Someone who shows traits of both narcissistic personality disorder and antisocial personality disorder. These include:

* Being extremely arrogant and self-centred

* Disregarding the feelings and needs of others

* Manipulating, using, or exploiting others for personal gain or pleasure

* Having an extreme need for power

* Acts of revenge against those who criticised them

* Fantasising about ways to obtain more power or dominance over others

* Lacking conscience, regret, or remorse for their actions

* Being cruel and taking pleasure in the pain of others

* High levels of aggression towards other people

* Paranoia or mistrust of others

* They use, abuse, and discard people

* Everything is personal to them; there's no such thing as an innocent mistake or joke

* They hold grudges and take revenge

* Nothing is ever their fault

* They are ruthless in the pursuit of what they want

* They lack empathy and a conscience

* They are defensive when they feel insecure.

Possible causes include:

* Experiencing abuse or neglect

* Being held to unrealistically high expectations as a child

* Being excessively praised or criticised as a child (or both)

* Possessing irritable, neurotic, or aggressive personality traits

* Having a low stress or frustration tolerance

* Being overly sensitive and unable to regulate emotions

* Being bullied or rejected in childhood

* Being told one is special or has extraordinary talents

* Witnessing entitled, grandiose, or narcissistic traits in a caregiver

* Seeking external validation or praise to compensate for low self-esteem

* Learning that vulnerability is a sign of weakness

* Learning that failure and mistakes are intolerable or unacceptable

* Excessive focus on status, recognition, power, and success

* Lack of self-awareness and trouble recognising emotions in self and others

* Disrupted identity development.

Mother and Dickhead – covert narcissists

Checklist taken from www.psychologytoday.com

* Passive aggressive

* Criticises and judges from the sidelines

* Is condescending and superior

* Is threatened by honesty and directness

* Swings between idolising and devaluing themselves and others

* Denies and dismisses others' feelings

* Cultivates a public image sharply different from their private behaviour

* Identifies as a victim

* Is cynical and sarcastic

* Makes unreasonable demands

* Turns your problems into their dramas

* Belittles and blames

* Exploits and attacks others' vulnerability

* Is reactive to questioning or criticism

* Plays on sympathies

* Fakes or exaggerates illness/injury for attention

* Withholds and stonewalls

* Gaslights

* Avoids introspection and lacks self-awareness

* Uses platitudes in place of genuine insight

* Denies own anger

* Focuses on unfairness

* Is envious and vengeful

* Prefers to remain behind the scenes

* Gossips

* Triangulates

* Holds a grudge

* Needs reassurance

* Is inattentive or annoyed when others talk

* Has double standards

* Hates to lose

* Fixates on others' problems and misfortunes

* Flatters and fawns to win favour

* Displays rage and contempt in private

* Resists decision making

* Does not sincerely apologise

* Avoids direct responsibility

* Has an exaggerated sense of entitlement

* Is impressed by the overt narcissist's appearance of confidence

* Lacks emotional empathy

* Focuses on appearance over substance

* Rushes to (false) intimacy

* Is anxious and hypervigilant

* Displays false humility and humblebrags

* Is prone to paranoia and conspiracy theories

* Crosses normative boundaries and codes of conduct

* Pokes, prods and pries

* Feels special through association

* Feels above the rules

* Uses guilt and shame to control and punish

* Expects caretaking

* Conducts smear campaigns.

I see most of these traits in my mother and Dickhead – the way they controlled me, how they used me to take care of them, how appearance was more important to them than reality, how they gaslighted me and wouldn't let me be myself or talk about what they'd done that had wounded me… it all adds up.

I was the scapegoated child, described here by www.psychologytoday.com:

> "Scapegoating is a common yet widely unacknowledged reality in family systems dominated by narcissistic parents. A scapegoated child is targeted with negative projections from one or both parents, often in a lifelong pattern of devastating character assassination."

Smear Campaign

Compounding the situation for the scapegoated child, the parents typically also induce other members of the family and the family's social circle to accept their narratives about that child, which amounts to an ongoing smear campaign. Other children in the family, particularly younger ones, may accept without question the scapegoated child's role as the recipient of anger and blame. Ones who recognize the injustice of the scapegoat's position are often too intimidated to challenge the parents for fear they will be targeted. Depending on their level of mental health and awareness, extended family members and friends may have some insight into the scapegoating and reach out to that child with forms of support, but more often, they accept the parents' narratives about their "problem child" and may even participate in further pathologizing and ostracizing that child.

Dickhead launched a full-on smear campaign against me.

Long-Term Impacts of Family Scapegoating

As devalued and bullied members of hierarchical narcissistic family systems, scapegoated children struggle with a traumatized nervous system, self-esteem deficits, and eroded personal boundaries that make them vulnerable to health problems and further abuse dynamics in their adult relationships. They typically enter adulthood with anxiety, anger, depression, and other symptoms of complex trauma with only a vague sense of the roots of their suffering.

You can see so many of these traits in the text messages sent between them, and they have projected all of their own traits onto me.

I did not act in the way they described; they made up a delusional story amongst themselves, a story that portrays me as this evil, reckless, uncaring villain. Someone who never considers anyone else and who is the worst kind of person imaginable.

What did I actually do?

Kick my mum out of my house and get divorced?

Yeah, I took the kids to his house after bedtime, but I was having a mental breakdown. At the time, I was not in control of my emotions. I regret what happened and wish I could take it back, but I don't think that can be held against me as evidence of being a terrible, uncaring, unloving mother who never puts her children first.

The lies they whipped up are astounding to me, and I still struggle to understand where they even got the ideas for them.

Kim said I should stop trying to figure it all out, as I never will. And, in a way, it's a good thing I never will – it shows that I'm nothing like them.

They've taken their personal actions and attributed them to me!

Why is it that when an adult child decides to cut off contact with a parent, all anyone /says is, "But that is your mum – you only have one mum!"? It's never, "Oh wow, what could she have done to make you want to cut her off?" Or even, "How could you treat your child that way?"

The onus is always on the child to maintain and heal the relationship, never the parent.

Why is that? What kind of fucked-up world do we live in where it's deemed acceptable to lay blame on the child for the mistreatment they suffered at the hands of their own parent?

Despite Dickhead and I supposedly sharing 50/50 custody, it is still 100% my responsibility to sort out everything for the children. I know I can't trust him to do things, but it's also the fact that he doesn't recognise their needs.

He doesn't notice when they need a doctor, or if their ADHD needs treating, or even that they have ADHD! When it came to my middle daughter, I had to fight him for years to make him see how unhappy she was at school and that she needed to be homeschooled.

It is so tiring having to navigate parenting with him.

CYCLE BREAKER

Taken from

https://www.holisticchildandfamily.org/blog/power-of-cycle-breakers

"A cycle breaker is someone who recognizes harmful or dysfunctional traits that exist in the culture of their family and decides to discard these traits and trade them in for something different. This can be life-changing and liberating work that, unfortunately, may trigger a negative response in other family members. For many, doing the hard work of dismantling the structures of these cycles is often ridiculed by the family of origin. In these cases, the cycle breaker of the family is scapegoated for trying to discard family traits that do not serve them anymore. Families with a cycle breaker often develop the defensive belief that everything was fine until this one person decided to point out areas for growth and refused to carry the weight of generational curses any further.

Deemed an unwelcome whistleblower for calling out toxic behaviours or dysfunctional family norms, these individuals put a spotlight on the problems that have most likely existed for decades. This can make the rest of the family feel like their illusion of the perfect family, or their deep denial to face any imperfections, is shattered. Watching the cycle breaker make changes can bring up feelings of judgement, shame, or guilt for the rest of the family as they see them doing work they have not been able to do yet. It can also trigger fear regarding having to do their own work because they are now grappling with the fact that they have been suffering for a long time as well and could possibly feel grief that they didn't address it earlier before they passed it on. A common response from family members towards a cycle breaker is gaslighting, making them believe that they are making up the traits they are dismantling, exaggerating how bad they are, or convincing them that they, instead of the dysfunctional traits, are the problem.

Generational cycles are like stones being dropped in a lake, with the impact rippling out over generations to come. The ripples of abuse, neglect, and trauma flow through generations unconsciously due to parents not being critically aware that they internalized dysfunctional and harmful patterns from their own parents and now lack the insight to see that they are replicating these same patterns in a different language to their own children. Disrupting these patterns is like stepping out of a river you've been floating down your entire life. The path of least resistance is to continue floating as you have been. Brains are attracted to familiarity. They crave taking the same paths again and again regardless of if the path is healthy and good for us. For cycle breakers, the river has turned into violent rapids, making it worth considering doing the work to steer to shore in order to escape the chaos, dry off, and step into a new landscape of healthy communication, boundaries, empathy, and collective compassion. By stepping out of the river and committing to creating positive changes for your bloodline, you liberate not only yourself from these cycles, but all who come after you as well."

Gaslighting

www.newportinstitute.com

Gaslighting is a form of psychological abuse or manipulation in which the abuser attempts to sow self-doubt and confusion in their victim's mind. Typically, gaslighters are seeking to gain power and control over the other person, by distorting reality and forcing them to question their own judgment and intuition.

I was abandoned, betrayed, and lied to. My own family treated me abysmally and then turned it around and blamed me for their horrendous behaviour.

My life is now my own and I regret none of what I did.

I've never been happier or more confident than I am now, and I feel validated by the confirmation of my lifelong suspicions about my so-called family.

My family is my children now, and I will do everything in my power to ensure that they never feel even a tiny bit of what I felt growing up. My sole aim in life is to show them love, compassion, and empathy and to teach them the wonders of the world, allowing them to see that they can be anything – and that I will support them in anything they choose. They are the masters of their own destiny and I will provide them with guidance and any assistance they may need.

Neither of my parents talked about their childhoods, their parents, their pasts… anything. Consequently, I know very little about my family history. They also didn't share stories of my birth or my childhood.

All I know of my birth was that it was in a London Hospital just before the maternity wing closed (it was all a mess due to its closing). She said she was the last woman to give birth there, and she had to give birth not on a bed but on a gurney, so it was all hard and uncomfortable.

For one of our births, she was given a pethidine injection – which she didn't ask for nor wanted – and it made her feel woozy and nauseous.

I only ever heard the negative stories, though the births did sound awful and I felt bad for her that her experiences weren't better. I suspect that, with my brother, she may have had postnatal depression, as she told me he barely slept for the first five years.

Apparently, I was a 'good' baby for my first two years.

And there ends the extent of my knowledge of my birth and early years.

After mother's funeral, my uncle (Dad's brother) asked me if we'd been told things about my grandma and grandad. It hit home then just how little I knew and how it was not 'normal' to not know anything.

It is so sad that more stories weren't shared. My parents were such a closed-off pair.

My kids love to hear about their babyhood and times when they were little. I constantly tell them how cute they were and all the little things they said and did.

They always have big smiles on their faces as they listen.

I will be a hands-on grandmother – as much as they will allow – and I'll do my best to ensure they have a good new parent experience… the exact opposite of what I was given.

I want them to never question if they are loved or cared for, and to know their worth and value in this world – to never settle for anything short of exactly what they deserve.

I hope they know how proud I am of the kind, intelligent, and thoughtful young people they have grown into. That who they are is so much more important than what grade they get, and that the way they treat others says more about them than any academic achievements they can boast about.

I know in my heart that I am a cycle breaker. My efforts and hardship have paved the way for my children to have a better life and future than I ever did and, in turn, my grandchildren – and even my great-grandchildren – will have happier, more loved lives than I could ever have dreamt of.

This keeps me going and helps me make peace with everything I've been through.

I know, for sure, that what happened to me will never happen to them.

And that makes it all worth it.

I have been grieving not only all that was done to me, but also all that was NOT!

I have missed out on so much, and so many things that should be beautiful memories… are not.

A happy and safe childhood. Memories of a loving wedding day. The births of my children, where I felt safe and taken care of. Being able to enjoy the moments where my babies were growing. Being able to be the parent I always wanted to be instead of being in survival mode – I grieve this one a lot.

A loving and supportive husband who had my back and wanted the best for me.

I often still see her.

I catch sight of an older lady with a stupid old lady haircut and an M&S-style coat.

My heart leaps and I get a shock of fear.

Once I settle, I realise she can't hurt me anymore, but it still brings all the memories flooding back.

It is a struggle to even try to wrap your head around how your own mother – the one person in the world who is supposed to love you unconditionally – didn't.

Although we have our ups and downs – it would be weird if we didn't – Mark and I are continuing a cycle of healing and nurturing rather than a vicious cycle of destruction. We work hard to show each other love and tenderness and we strive to help each other heal. We are each trying to change what upsets the other and have been on a few couples retreats to learn healthy ways to communicate. We both want this love to flourish even more and be ever-lasting. I think we have gone through more together in our 6 years than many do in lifetimes.

I can't change the past, but I can commit to living authentically – and creating lasting, joyful, and loving memories from this moment forward.

Now, I have a supportive husband who encourages me and loves me, and I am truly thankful for this.

I am now not just surviving but thriving. I am working hard to heal and quieten my thoughts. I see Susie still once a month, I now also see a lovely energy healer lady called Jade and have recently started somatic yoga with Uyen. All of these ladies don't know the profound impact they are having on my mental health. Just their care and kindness is refreshing and very welcome.

I will need to work on my mental health for years to come, possibly a lifetime, but I now know who I am, I know I am a good person and I have someone supporting me and showing me love every day – the very things I have spent my life looking for.

Epilogue

Despite my best efforts, intentions and my desire to make sure my children never experienced what I did growing up; in May 2024 my world came crashing down in the worst way imaginable.

The dramatic change in the children's attitude towards me and the subsequent behaviour took me to a new low.

As the months went on and they refused to see me or live with me it became obvious what had happened.

Parental alienation.

An insidious, toxic, abusive, destructive, and destroying consequence of having a bitter, narcissistic father who would go to any lengths to destroy their mother – even if that meant in the process; destroying them.

After having spent my childhood, and then my adulthood being made to believe I was nothing, worth nothing and deserved nothing, you can only imagine the heartbreak at having my eldest two children treat me the same way.

To be told to my face that I deserved no respect and that I had destroyed their childhoods.

To have my daughter tell me I was not a mother, that she did not feel like my daughter and that she never wanted anything to do with me was worse than a knife to the heart.

It is now February 2025 and we are still on a rollercoaster of emotions and their fabricated disdain and hatred of me. Not one of them can give me a reason for their verbal abuse yet it continues never the less.

I have found a fabulous new therapist called Kate who specialises in trauma, narcissistic abuse and neurodiversity. She and I are making massive leaps into my understanding of what is happening and making peace with my past and a future that will look so different to what I ever imagined.

I have worked so hard to heal and be the best mother I could be, only for the dickhead to cause the children all the hurt I tried to make sure they never experienced.

I can see the pain and confusion he has caused and the distress to everyone.

I know he will never stop.

I will probably need to wait till they have their own children for them to realise how manipulated, gaslit and deceived they are being.

The lies that are being subtly conveyed to them are scary.

The last 7 months have changed me as a person, I have been to hell and back but am slowly getting stronger and putting in tough boundaries and learning my worth.

My healing journey continues and although I suffer setbacks often, I am committed to becoming the best version of myself I can be so that when they do finally return, I will have the healthiest me to offer them.

Who knows – maybe this will be the subject of my next book?

Thank you so much for reading to the end.

I hope you have learnt something of import to improve your own life and your own healing journey.

I am bringing out a book of quotes that I saw all through my healing journey that helped me feel less alone. I hope it can help you too.

Useful Contacts And Books

- **Kate** - https://www.brightmindstherapy.co.uk
- **Jade** - https://www.jadegaia.co.uk
- **Susie** - https://www.intuitivebreathwork.co.uk

Books

1. The Making of Them – Nick Duffell
2. Boarding School Syndrome – Joy Schaverien
3. Stiff Upper Lip – Alex Renton
4. Almost Boys – Isobel Ross
5. It's Not You – Ramani Durvasula
6. The Body Keeps the Score – Bessel Van Der Kolk
7. The Betrayal Bond – Patrick J. Carnes
8. Waking the Tiger – Peter Levine

Podcasts

1. Piers Cross
2. Dr Ramani Durvasula
3. Mel Robbins
4. The holistic psychologist
5. The workout witch
6. Steve Bartlett
7. Jefferson Speaks
8. SpeechProf
9. Jimmy Knowles
10. Mind Positive
11. Lewis Howes
12. Manjit Kaur Ruprai
13. Dr Sarah Hensley
14. Dr Julie Smith
15. Josh_ffw

www.ingramcontent.com/pod-product-compliance
Lightning Source LLC
Chambersburg PA
CBHW061204070526
44583CB00025B/3116